P9-CKE-326

The Undivided Past

ALSO BY DAVID CANNADINE

Lords and Landlords

The Pleasures of the Past

The Decline and Fall of the British Aristocracy

G. M. Trevelyan

Aspects of Aristocracy

Class in Britain

History in Our Time

Ornamentalism

In Churchill's Shadow

Mellon

National Portrait Gallery

Making History Now and Then

The Right Kind of History

The Undivided Past

HUMANITY BEYOND OUR DIFFERENCES

DAVID CANNADINE

ALFRED A. KNOPF · NEW YORK

THIS IS A BORZOI BOOK
PUBLISHED BY ALFRED A. KNOPF

Copyright © 2013 by David Cannadine
All rights reserved. Published in the United States by Alfred A. Knopf,
a division of Random House, Inc., New York and in Canada
by Random House of Canada Limited, Toronto.
www.aaknopf.com

Knopf, Borzoi Books, and the colophon are
registered trademarks of Random House, Inc.

Grateful acknowledgment is made to the following for permission
to reprint previously published material: Doubleday and Cambridge
University Press: Excerpt from "We and They" from *Debits and Credits*
by Rudyard Kipling, copyright © 1926 by Rudyard Kipling, copyright
renewed © 1953 by Elise Bambridge and from *The Cambridge Edition
of the Poems of Rudyard Kipling*, edited by Thomas Pinney. Used by
permission of Doubleday, a division of Random House, Inc., on behalf
of U.S. print rights and by permission of Cambridge University Press,
on behalf of Canadian print rights and World electronic rights.

Random House, Inc.: Excerpt from "Human Family" from *I Shall Not
Be Moved* by Maya Angelou. Copyright © 1990 by Maya Angelou.
Used by permission of Random House, Inc.

ISBN 978-0-307-26907-2

Jacket image: Commerce Brings Peoples Together (Eastern Merchants
on a Western Shore) *by Theodore Chasseriau. Louvre, Paris, France
© RMN-Grand Palais / Art Resource, New York*

Jacket design by Jason Booher

Manufactured in the United States of America

Book Club Edition

For Nomi and Rick

If we would indicate an idea which throughout the whole course of history has ever more and more widely extended its empire . . . it is that of establishing our common humanity—of striving to remove the barriers which prejudice and limited views of every kind have erected amongst men, and to treat all mankind, without reference to religion, nation or colour, as one fraternity, one great community.

—Wilhelm von Humboldt, quoted in Ashley Montagu,
Man's Most Dangerous Myth: The Fallacy of Race

Human groupings have one main purpose: to assert everyone's right to be different, to be special, to think, feel and live in his or her own way. People join together in order to win or defend this right. But this is where a terrible, fatal error is born: the belief that these groupings in the name of a race, a God, a party or a state are the very purpose of life and not simply a means to an end. No!

—Vasily Grossman, *Life and Fate*

Are we so sure of ourselves and of our age as to divide the company of our forefathers into the just and the damned . . . ? When the passions of the past blend with the prejudices of the present, human reality is reduced to a picture in black and white.

—Marc Bloch, *The Historian's Craft*

Where previously our history has been characterised by a plundering of the past to separate and differentiate us, our future now holds the optimistic possibility that . . . we will re-visit the past more comfortably and find . . . elements of kinship long neglected, of connections deliberately overlooked.

—President Mary MacAleese of Ireland, "Changing History,"
Longford Lecture, November 23, 2007, quoted in Margaret
MacMillan, *Dangerous Games: The Uses and Abuses of History*

CONTENTS

Introduction 3

ONE Religion 11

TWO Nation 53

THREE Class 93

FOUR Gender 133

FIVE Race 174

SIX Civilization 219

Conclusion 258

Acknowledgments 265

Notes 267

Index 325

The Undivided Past

Introduction

*When I was coming up, it was a dangerous world, and you
knew exactly who they were. It was "us versus them," and
it was clear who them [sic] was. Today, we're not so sure
who they are, but we know they're there.*

—President George W. Bush,
quoted in the *New York Times*,
April 16, 2006

*The world is awash in divisions rooted in the human compul-
sion to believe our differences are more important than our
common humanity . . . .[But] our common humanity is more
important than our interesting and inevitable differences.*

—President Bill Clinton,
*Giving: How Each of Us
Can Change the World*

This book sets out to explore and investigate the most resonant
forms of human solidarity as they have been invented and created, established and sustained, questioned and denied, fissured
and broken across the centuries and around the world, and as
they have defined the lives, engaged the emotions, and influenced the fates of countless millions of individuals. It does so by
looking at the six most commonplace and compelling forms of
such identities, namely religion, nation, class, gender, race, and
civilization. Sometimes regional, sometimes national, and sometimes more global in their compass and in the claims made on
their behalf, these groupings have commanded widespread allegiance and commitment, on occasions for good, but often not,
since every collective solidarity simultaneously creates an actual
or potential antagonist out of the group or groups it excludes.
Even if we confine ourselves to the twentieth century, there have
been many such confrontations and conflicts variously described
as religious wars, or national wars, or class wars, or gender wars,
or race wars, or wars for civilization. And whatever the solidari-

ties specific to our own time, analogous groupings and analogous conflicts have existed across the millennia and around the world, from Christians versus pagans during the later Roman Empire to the white supremacists versus anti-apartheid campaigners until 1994; and there is no reason to suppose that the twenty-first century will be free of such confrontations. As a consequence, it has come to seem almost axiomatic that the best way to understand past worlds, as well as present circumstances and our future prospects, is in the workings and outcomes of latent or actual conflicts between antagonistic identities, or of how things go in the great game of "us versus them," exemplified in the words of President George W. Bush quoted above.[1]

What is perhaps most remarkable is how well the appeal of "us versus them" works over a range of categories, aggregations, and identities that are scarcely comparable. For much of recorded history the two most prominent have been (initially) religious affiliation and (subsequently) national allegiance. It is only in relatively recent times that they have been augmented, and in some measure superseded, by the secular, international trinity of class consciousness, gender awareness, and racial solidarity. And since the events of September 11, 2001, the even larger identity and more capacious category of civilization, earlier invoked by historians from Edward Gibbon to Arnold Toynbee, has made a comeback, embodied in the writings of Samuel P. Huntington, which were subsequently invoked by his neoconservative followers in the United States and by his New Labour admirers in the United Kingdom. But the fact remains that each of these solidarities is constituted around a distinctive axis of interest and awareness: religious cohesion is an expression of faith and belief (or, depending on one's sympathies, of superstition and irrationality), and can be as much concerned with the next world as with this; national identity relies on a shared narrated memory and sense of geographical belonging, reinforced by a common language and culture and state power; class consciousness is seen as the outcome of the different relations of people to the modes of production, leading to the hostile solidarities of workers and employers; gender and race identities are partly the result of biology, but also of the meanings and antagonisms constructed and projected onto anatomical features shared by some human beings but not by others; while civilization is perhaps the most flexible form of human grouping, which can be defined according to any number of criteria.

Yet however disparate and incommensurable, these collective identities have all been defined and reinforced through confrontation, struggle, and conflict—against an alternative religion, an enemy nation, a hostile class, the other gender, a different race, or an alien civilization. The result has been the serial reiteration of the Manichean view that the world is divided into conflicting groups, with a monolithic "good" on one side (those with "us"), and a no less monolithic "evil" on the other (those against "us"). This ultimately apocalyptic perspective has resonated on many terrible occasions throughout history, and it was vigorously and unapologetically reiterated by President George W. Bush in his final address from the Oval Office: "I have spoken to you often," he told his fellow Americans, "about good and evil, and this has made some people uncomfortable. But good and evil are present in this world, and between the two there can be no compromise."[2] The trouble is, whether good and evil exist as such, the absolutes they imply have been ascribed with various degrees of literalism to every manner of perceived difference. And so a battle of cosmic significance might be claimed between Protestant and Catholic, America and Russia, employee and employer, women and men, black and white, or "the West" and Islam, confrontations in which each side seeks to galvanize its supporters by exaggerating their solidarity and virtue, and by imputing to the other side a no less exaggerated solidarity and wickedness.[3] This impulse thus to sunder all the peoples of the world into belligerent collectivities has existed as long as humanity itself, and in our own day the easy recourse to such polarized thinking by many political leaders and public figures, and by pundits and commentators, is further exaggerated by an increasingly strident media. It has also been underscored by some historians who have been more concerned to legitimate the claims and urge the merits of one collective identity over and against any (or all) others than to take a broader view of the human past.[4]

During the last half century or so, the conventional wisdom

that "the history of humanity is based upon the immemorial divisions of its peoples" has been reinforced by a growing academic insistence on the importance of recognizing the "difference" between collective groups.[5] According to the anthropologist Clifford Geertz, "difference is what makes the world go round, especially the political world"; many of his colleagues as well as literary scholars and cultural critics would agree, and so do those historians who have focused their attention on the creation, perception, working, meaning, and significance of what they varyingly describe as "difference," or "otherness," or "alterity," or "unlikeness," or "dissimilarity."[6] Beyond doubt, such historical approaches have yielded significant work of enduring value, illuminating dimensions of human experience once unexamined; but as William H. McNeill, one of the pioneers of global history, has pointed out, the academic preoccupation with the binary simplicities of difference, and with the antagonisms based on them, results in a version of "the past as we want it to be, safely simplified into a contest between good guys and bad guys, 'us and them,' " which disconcertingly resembles the polarized, apocalyptic perspective of President George W. Bush—or, indeed, of the late Osama bin Laden.[7]

But the fact that humanity *is still here*, that no one has vanquished "us" or "them" on either side of any of these divides, despite such "ultimate" confrontations and conflicts, suggests that there is a case for taking a broader, more ecumenical, and even more optimistic view of human identities and relations— a view that not only accepts difference and conflict based on clashing sectional identities, but also recognizes affinities and discerns conversations *across* these allegedly impermeable boundaries of identity, which embody and express a broader sense of humanity that goes beyond our dis-similarities.[8] This alternative perspective is well put by the poet and civil rights activist Maya Angelou:

> *I note the obvious differences*
> *Between each sort and type,*
> *But we are more alike, my friends,*
> *Than we are unalike.*[9]

In the same vein, if more prosaically, the historian Timothy Garton Ash has deplored the "Manichean cultural dichotomies" that are peddled by a partisan media, at the expense of the alternative conversation "about what all human beings have in common"; and Neil MacGregor, the director of the British Museum, has lamented the "brutally over-simplified notions of identity" that "sustain entrenched conflicts," when in reality, cultures constantly "overlap, borrow from each other and live together" in "a conversation with the whole of humanity."[10] Hence the second epigraph to this introduction, in which President Clinton urges us to see humanity in less paranoid and more imaginative ways than the exaggerated polarities embraced by his successor in the White House.[11]

In his recent book, appropriately entitled *The Fear of Barbarians*, the Franco-Bulgarian philosopher Tzvetan Todorov puts this point emphatically: "the facile dichotomies between Light and Darkness, free world and obscurantism, sweet tolerance and blind violence, tell us more about the overweening pride of their authors than the complexity of the contemporary world." "No merit," he goes on, in words that might be an explicit riposte to President George W. Bush, "lies in preferring good to evil when we ourselves define the meaning of these two words."[12] But most of the academic writing that is skeptical of these Manichean ways of seeing the world, and which urges the broader claims of our common humanity, has been produced by scholars whose interests are philosophical rather than historical, and who are concerned with the present and the recent past rather than with more distant epochs.[13] This book, by contrast, seeks to address these issues from a longer-term historical perspective: by examining each of these six collective identities over substantial periods of time; by drawing attention to the excessive and inaccurate claims that have invariably been made for them in terms of their unity, homogeneity, and shared consciousness; and by investigating the conversations and interactions that have gone on across the boundaries of these allegedly impermeable identities, in the sustained and successful pursuit of a more sympathetic vision of a shared humanity. Like Todorov, I argue that the unrelenting insistence on seeing the world in Manichean terms is at best partial and divisive, at worst reductive and misleading: for these very categories of "us" and "them," whatever their particular articulation, and though proclaimed to be irreducible and absolute, frequently reveal themselves to be unstable and ambiguous; they often prove to be incoherent even in the thick of their confrontations with the implacable foe; and they are held together not so much by shared self-awareness as by the exhortations of leaders, journalists, activists—and by some historians, too.

This book addresses these issues, by investigating each of those six divisive collective identities with which we seem most preoccupied, even while acknowledging and demonstrating that they are in some ways very different sorts of solidarities. For they are sufficiently similar to one another in their polarizing propensities to merit an urgently needed comparative analysis that is evenhandedly skeptical of each and of all their claims to priority and supremacy. Accordingly, the following chapters examine how theologians and priests, politicians and pundits, commentators and historians have each asserted the incomparable importance of one particular form of collective human identity over any other, and how in so doing they have encouraged among those on one side of any divide a sense of the ultimate righteousness of their cause and collectivity. I go on to describe how, on occasion, people have indeed behaved in accordance with these Manichean analyses and prescriptions, in terms of religious fervor, national patriotism, class consciousness, gender awareness, racial solidarity, and civilizational identity. And I note how historians frequently contributed to this identity-obsessed way of seeing the world, most fully in the chapter on class. But I also look at the many conversations that have gone on in denial and defiance of these allegedly impermeable boundaries and antagonistic solidarities, which are too often presented, either mistakenly or mischievously, as if they are the only version of the human condition that has any salience or plausibility. For as individuals, we often recognize the common humanity that we lose sight of when called upon to act in groups.

To tackle such a large, important, and controversial subject over such a long-term and broad range is, nevertheless, to run serious risks. For one thing, the collectivities and confrontations based on religion, nation, class, gender, race, and civilization stir powerful passions on the part of politicians, pundits, and the public—and also of many engaged academics. They want to believe the world is simple in form and easily understood, readily divided between a virtuous "us" and an evil "them," and in their determined part in helping construct such adversarial identities, they have provided much of the intellectual underpinning for seeing the world in antagonistic, binary ways.[14] Another difficulty is the scale and scope of this enterprise. Of each of these chapters it is reasonable to say that a lifetime's reading and research is insufficient to acquire even a halfway competent understanding of the subject matter involved; and the same may be said of many of the subsections, too. To this charge, I can but reply that the attempt to open up the subject, if only to encourage (or provoke) others to do it better, is worth incurring the accusation of overreach.[15] A further objection might be that in this search for common humanity amid the ruins of what has mostly been portrayed as its divided past, more of the examples are taken from European history than from any other part of the world. But there are limits to any author's knowledge and range, and in any case, many (though not all) of the identities explored here did originate and have been most manifest in Europe, or in the nearby Middle East.

It has rightly been observed that one of the prime justifications for studying and writing history is to free ourselves from the tyranny of present-day opinion, and these pages seek to contribute to that liberating endeavor by questioning the conventional wisdom of single-identity politics, the alleged uniformity of antagonistic groups, the widespread liking for polarized modes of thought, and the scholarly preoccupations with difference. Most academics are trained to look for divergences and disparities rather than for similarities and affinities, but this relentless urge to draw distinctions often results in important connections and resemblances being overlooked.[16] Despite constant urgings to the contrary, humanity has not been, is not now, and should not be best or solely understood in terms of simple, unified homogeneous collectivities locked in perpetual confrontation and conflict across a great chasm of hatred and an unbridgeable gulf of fear. The real world is not binary—except insofar as it is divided into those who insist that it is and those who know that it is not. For it is in the very range, complexity, and diversity of our multifarious and manifold identities, and in the many connections we make through them and across them, and in the varied conversations we sustain as a result of them, that we each affirm and should all celebrate the common humanity which is the most precious thing we share.[17]

ONE

Religion

The Christian and Muslim worlds have been religious, geographical and economic rivals and competitors since their point of first contact, and it is no wonder that words of hate rather than words of love have predominated . . . to define communal differences between "them" and "us."

—Andrew Wheatcroft,
*Infidels: The Conflict Between
Christendom and Islam, 638–2002*

If one thing should come out of what follows, it is that there was (and is) nothing quintessential, ineluctable or necessary about conflict and misunderstanding between Crescent and Cross, East and West, Muslim and Christian.

—James Mather,
*Pashas: Traders and Travellers
in the Islamic World*

IN THE TWENTY-FIFTH CHAPTER of the Gospel according to Matthew, Christ sets out his vision—and his division—of humanity, proposing two very different and seemingly irreconcilable collective categories: those in this world who are believers in the one true religion and the one true God, and those who lack such a faith and reject such a single omnipotent deity. And this earthly cleavage in turn anticipates and explains the eternal distinction that will be drawn in the next world, between those who will be saved and comforted, and those who will be lost and damned. On the final day of judgment, Jesus tells his listeners, when "the son of man shall come in his glory, and all the holy angels with him," he will sit upon his throne, and from there he will sort out all humanity, "as a shepherd divideth his sheep from the goats." Those he will place on his right hand, the blessed and the elect, will inherit the kingdom of heaven prepared for them since the creation of the world; but those positioned on his left will be condemned to endure the everlasting fire and perpetual punishment that have been "prepared for the devil and his angels."[1] Here is exemplified what some have seen as the most fateful legacy of Zoroastrian Persia to the Christian religion, namely "a belief in the absolute division of the spiritual world" between good and evil powers, between angels and demons: a permanent schism in the hereafter already prefigured in this life on earth, where humanity is split and sundered between the true believers who are destined for heaven, and the unrighteous and the ungodly who are equally certain to be headed for hell.[2]

The Persian prophet Zoroaster, from whom Zoroastrianism, an ancient Near Eastern religion, takes its name, is believed to have flourished during the late fifth and the early fourth centuries BCE. He is often credited with having first proclaimed that the universe is divided between the principles of light and of darkness, the cosmic struggle between their respective forces continuing to the end of time, and he believed it was the duty of all human beings to join the angels in the battle against the devil. This prototypical fissure between the righteous and the unrighteous has since proved extraordinarily and continually appealing, finding expression not only in Christianity but in other creeds, too.[3] Nearly three-quarters of a millennium after Zoroaster, in the middle of the third century CE, another Persian prophet, named Mani, whose followers were scattered across both the Persian and the Roman empires, and all the way from South Asia to Spain, would once again partition the populated universe, this time between the children of the "Father of Greatness" and those of the "Father of Darkness." He bolstered his claims with stories and evidence derived from both the Old and the New Testaments, though this was not enough to keep the early church from dismissing Mani as a heretic. His most enduring legacy is the term "Manichean," which is often used to describe the views of those of whatever religious conviction who insist on seeing human circumstances in such stark and simplistic terms, with the respective partisans of good and evil slugging it out for supremacy in this world and sometimes in the next as well.[4]

For at least two millennia, from the time to which the origins of the major religious belief systems can be traced, there has been division and difference with (literally) a vengeance, as humanity has often seemed irreconcilably polarized by competing and conflicting faiths—whether pagans versus Christians, Islam versus Christianity, or Catholics versus Protestants. The leaders of most of these faiths (all of them, with the exception of paganism, being monotheistic) have claimed exclusive monopolies on both human wisdom and divine revelation, and at certain stages in their histories they have condemned, scorned, denounced, ridiculed, humiliated, assailed, oppressed, imprisoned, maimed, tortured, and killed their religious opponents and competitors for being, by contrast, the very embodiment of sin, error, wrongdoing, folly, wickedness, depravity, and iniquity. In such ways have religious groupings defined themselves against each other and gone to war, with each faith convinced of the supremacy of its own unique deity and thus of its own unique cosmic superiority. From this perspective, and as the American religious scholar Martin E. Marty notes, in a book aptly titled *When Faiths Collide*, "the history of religions often appears to be little more than the history of conflict among those who are strange to each other." Or as his fellow countryman Walter Lippmann put it more than seventy years earlier, "every church in the heyday of its power proclaims itself to be catholic and intolerant." Or as Jesus Christ himself observed, elsewhere in Matthew's Gospel, in fighting words that may also stand proxy for other religious militancies, "he that is not with me is against me."[5]

Yet, as so often in the history of collective identities (and of the antagonisms and animosity that they express and engender), open war has never been the whole picture in the history of religion, for alongside (and even during) periods of wrenching disagreements and searing spiritual conflicts, there have also been times of toleration and episodes of peaceful interaction, even accommodation—certainly among individuals, but among groups, too. Indeed, the virtue of such amity across religious lines is implied, even in the passage from Matthew's Gospel already mentioned, for while it proposes an unbridgeable gulf between the saved and the damned, it also plainly distinguishes those destined for paradise from those doomed to perdition by the former's kindness to "strangers": their willingness to take them in, and to befriend, feed, and clothe them.[6] It may be no surprise that the identity of such outsiders is unspecified, in terms (as we would now say) of their age, gender, race, or sexual orientation—but religion isn't mentioned either. It is because of their *humanity*, not their faith, that "strangers" should be cared for. Whatever his churches would later do in his name, Christ's injunction to love one's enemies and to turn the other cheek suggests that even religious difference was no grounds for mistreating one's fellow human beings. Unfortunately, and too often, it has been the imperative to make war in his name that has seemed easier to heed literally. But not always, for though less well attested than the violence resulting from religious difference, toleration and cooperation have a history all their own.[7]

This point has been well made by the historian John Wolffe, when he observes that in addition to deeply rooted, widely held, and frequently publicized religious animosities, based on antagonistic collective identities, "there is another equally important side to the coin." To be sure, he goes on, "religious conflict has always been what catches the headlines, both in history books and in newspapers," but it has also been the case that

> [n]umerous states and societies, from the Roman Empire to the contemporary United States, have for long periods experienced considerable religious diversity without significant overt conflict. Even in eras seemingly characterized by religious conflict, such as the Crusades and the Reformation, for many at the grassroots, daily life involved peaceful, if sometimes uneasy, co-existence with people of other faiths and traditions.[8]

The conversations and encounters that have often taken place (and that still do) in various forms across the supposedly impregnable boundaries of religious identity provide the essential counterpoint to the dangerously oversimplified master narrative of inevitable and perpetual faith-based animosity—a story that has been revisited and reinforced in certain quarters in the aftermath of the events of 9/11 and the subsequent Iraq War (which will be taken up in the final chapter). But this latest attempt to depict the world in terms of Manichean religious conflict merely remind us that, as with all master narratives, the reality of religious encounters and identities is never so tidy or simple.

PAGANS AND CHRISTIANS

For many in the West, the prototypical case of two religious communities locked in inexorable conflict, from which it was thought only one could emerge victorious, is still the one that preoccupied the first half millennium of the Common Era, when the pagan Roman Empire was undermined and overwhelmed by the rise of what has been termed "Christian Europe."[9] Within three hundred years of the crucifixion of Jesus, a small and localized religious sect in the eastern Mediterranean, having survived relentless and murderous imperial persecution, came to be recognized as an official religion by the emperor Constantine in 313 CE under the so-called Edict of Milan, and went on to vanquish paganism across the whole of Rome's realms. This extraordinary story, of one religious collectivity defeating and conquering another, was recounted in heroic terms by the earliest chroniclers of the Christian church, such as Eusebius, bishop of Caesarea in Palestine, and was only much later to receive an exhaustive (and much more skeptical) treatment by Edward Gibbon in his *The Decline and Fall of the Roman Empire*.[10] Gibbon would describe and explain Rome's collapse as "the triumph of barbarism and religion." What barbarism meant to Gibbon will be treated in a later chapter. For now, suffice it to say that by religion, Gibbon meant Christianity, a vigorously assertive new belief system that would prove fatal not only to paganism but to the Roman Empire as well.[11]

Gibbon was much influenced by the Enlightenment ideas of his time, which helps explain why *The Decline and Fall* is shot through with so many contrasts, polarities, dichotomies, and antitheses, of which that between paganism and Christianity is one of the two most prominent (along with that of barbarism and civilization). Having been attracted at different times to Protestantism and to Catholicism, Gibbon in his mature attitude to the Christian religion was by turns cool, ironic, skeptical, and detached. He disliked priests, monks, and ecclesiastical hierarchy;

he was suspicious of saints and scornful of miracles; he deplored religious asceticism and the "superstition" on which it was based; and he thought the historic role of the church had been more destructive than creative. But Gibbon was also an ardent follower of theological disputes, and he recognized that religion was a major force in history, albeit one that needed to be understood in human terms rather than just accepted uncritically and credulously as the preordained working out of the divine will and providential purpose.[12] As he once observed, "For the man who can raise himself above the prejudices of party and sect, the history of religions is the most interesting part of the history of the human spirit." More than half a century after Gibbon's death, Cardinal Newman grudgingly admitted that he was the most incisive historian of religion that Britain had ever produced, and Gladstone (who was no less alert to religion's importance in human motivation and identity) regarded Gibbon as one of the three greatest historians of all time.[13]

According to *The Decline and Fall,* paganism was one of the two principal reasons why the Roman Empire managed to expand and endure long enough to reach such heady heights of achievement by the time of the death of the emperor Marcus Aurelius in 180 CE. The Roman belief system was capaciously and inclusively polytheistic, while also effectively reinforcing the imperial virtues of civic duty and public commitment.[14] Across the empire, a great variety of gods were worshipped and venerated, many of them carried over from indigenous cults that had long thrived before the arrival of the conquering legions. These diverse deities provided Rome's many peoples with the comfort of local loyalties, while an overlay of official Roman idols and cults ensured that the fortunes of the empire actively engaged the hopes and concerns of its citizens and subjects. As Gibbon described and acclaimed it, this "mild," eclectic, flexible, nonproselytizing civic religion, devoid of any separate priesthood or church hierarchy, and without any agreed scriptural authorities, was a great source of strength, and the resulting imperial culture of tolerance and forbearance, enforced by local magistrates, effectively prevented religious discord or doctrinal conflict.[15] In an oft-quoted summation, he writes, "The various modes of worship which prevailed in the Roman world were all considered by the people as equally true; by the philosopher as equally false; and by the magistrate as equally useful." However cynical Gibbon's admiration, he recognized in paganism's practice a tolerant spirit that engendered among the subjects and citizens of the empire not only a disinclination toward religious strife, but also actual social concord.[16]

Christianity, by contrast, was a very different kind of religion: it was monotheistic, it was dogmatic, it was all-consuming, it was proselytizing, it was exclusive, it was well organized, and it had its own priesthood and hierarchy.[17] Gibbon outlined five reasons why, from its unpromising beginnings in the eastern Mediterranean, it eventually triumphed over paganism to become the state religion of the Roman Empire.[18] To begin with, the early Christians were "obstinate" in their faith: once converted, they felt zealously that they were on the right side of an absolute, Manichean divide between the godly and the unrighteous. Moreover, in a world where life was hard for most, Christianity benefited from its doctrine of the immortality of the soul and its promise of future glory in heaven, which boosted conversions and stiffened the morale of the faithful. In the third place, the many early claims of miracles and visions established Christianity's truth and efficacy, appealing especially to what Gibbon lamented as the "dark enthusiasm of the vulgar" (although it was hardly a faith restricted to the lower echelons of society). Fourth, it was difficult not to respect the Christians for their superior conduct and rigid rectitude; in aspiring to holiness and salvation, they were highly moral, sometimes extraordinarily ascetic, and often exemplary in their fortitude in the face of persecution. Finally, Christianity was remarkably well organized, with its cellular network of churches and its hierarchy of priests and bishops. So it was scarcely surprising that in the aftermath of the emperor Constantine's conversion, and with unprecedented official support, Christianity "was received throughout the whole empire" in "the space of a few years."[19]

Yet Gibbon saw a great irony in Christianity's triumph as the official religion of Rome, in the faith's subsequent destruction of the empire itself. In stark contrast to paganism's reinforcement of the quintessential Roman virtues of imperial patriotism and public duty, Christianity undermined them from within. Being so preoccupied with the life in the hereafter, Christians were far less interested in fruitful engagement with the affairs of this world; indeed, many of them repudiated and disdained the political and cultural and technological achievements of the Roman Empire. The result, according to Gibbon, was a corruption of the civic and martial values of Rome: "the active virtues of society were discouraged, and the last remains of military spirit were buried in the cloister."[20] This preoccupation with otherworldliness was especially true of Christian ascetics, whom Gibbon scorned and ridiculed not only for their self-indulgent self-denial, but also for their lack of civic commitment and neglect of public duties: "the lives of the primitive monks were consumed in penance and solitude, undisturbed by various occupations which fill the time and exercise the faculties of reasonable, active social beings." There was also the fanatical dogmatism of Christian theology, unleashed in the aftermath of Constantine's conversion, which further destabilized the empire. "Tolerance" disappeared and "concord" vanished, the persecution of pagans by Christians was more savage and bloody than the persecution of Christians by pagans had been, and "the attention of the emperors was diverted from camps to synods [and] the Roman world was oppressed by a new species of tyranny."[21]

Such, as Gibbon saw it, were "the human causes of the progress and establishment of Christianity," and this in turn explained "by what means the Christian faith obtained so remarkable a victory over the established religions of the earth."[22] The narrative that would later be celebrated as "the rise of Christian Europe" was far from being a happy story or a triumphant outcome in Gibbon's eyes, for "on the ruins of the [Roman] Capitol," Christianity had "erected the triumphant banner of the Cross," an ironic gesture of an empire's self-conquest in which he took no pleasure.[23] As he explained in a letter to his friend Lord Suffield, "The primitive Church, which I have treated with some freedom, was itself, at that time, an innovation, and *I* was attached to the old Pagan establishment."[24] Indeed, Gibbon would later claim that it was a sudden realization that Christianity had ruined a once-great empire that inspired him to undertake his great historical work—an awakening that occurred on his only visit to Rome, in 1764, as he had "sat musing amidst the ruins of the Capitol while barefooted friars were singing vespers in the temple of Jupiter."[25]

Yet in chronicling the divisive and decisive conflict between paganism and Christianity, and its destructive impact on the Roman Empire in the West, Gibbon was well aware that he was describing two very different religious constituencies, and he also recognized that neither of them was anything like as united or homogeneous as his generalized accounts sometimes suggested to the inattentive reader. It bears repeating that paganism had no priesthood, no canonical texts or ethical codes, no single, all-encompassing belief system, and no concept of orthodoxy, heresy, or unbelief; nor did it embrace a Manichean view of humanity. Pagan practices in the Roman Empire took myriad forms and comprised varied modes of relating to the divine world, and such "mild" requirements and definitions meant that paganism's diverse and geographically dispersed adherents could have possessed only a loose collective sense of themselves.[26] Worshipping different gods in different places in different ways, pagan cults were generally tolerant of one another, and felt no imperative to convert those following an alternative set of practices or beliefs. Accordingly, it was not they but their Christian antagonists who in the fourth century CE first referred to them as "pagans" (or "gentiles"), as a disparaging way of imputing to non-Christians a collective identity that they themselves had no consciousness of possessing.[27]

Between the death of Christ and the Edict of Milan, Christians, by contrast, came to feel a powerful sense of identity and community, which, as Gibbon recognized, was only reinforced by their escalating persecution at the hands of the imperial authorities.[28] Yet as he also took pains to point out, as soon as it had triumphed to become the established faith of the Roman Empire, Christianity split and sundered into warring sects and disputatious factions, typically characterized by mutual accusations of heresy and by more hostility to one another than to their pagan opponents.[29] In keeping with his fascination with theological disputes, Gibbon devoted a great deal of attention to explaining (and often ridiculing) doctrinal schisms among different Christian groups, on such matters as the nature of the Eucharist and of Christ himself, and he traced with great skill the splintering and subsequent anathematization by the church of various sects adhering to Arianism, Nestorianism, and Monophysitism.[30] Between the loose affiliation of the pagan world and the factious disputations of the Christians, the epic drama of a pitched battle between two warring monolithic religious collectivities, with one "winner" and one "loser," dissolved in Gibbon's telling into a more varied, localized, ambiguous, and complex series of encounters, interactions, relationships, and outcomes.

To be sure, there were significant episodes of conflict between pagans and Christians during the late third and early fourth centuries, and again during the late fourth end early fifth centuries. But the massive imbalance which existed between the empire's pagan majority and the Christian minority made any sort of large-scale armed confrontation both unfeasible and unlikely. As late as 313 CE, when Christianity was declared an official religion, it seems probable that only 4 or 5 percent of the citizens of the empire actually espoused the faith.[31] And so, despite the triumphalist tone of the early church historians (there are, incidentally, hardly any comparable pagan sources to provide a balanced perspective), the emperor Constantine's decree can scarcely have transformed the whole of the Roman Empire overnight into a unified and monolithic Christian community according to some preordained divine purpose. Moreover, Constantine's belated baptism may not have been wholehearted; he remained in some significant ways wedded to the traditional belief systems; when he created his new imperial capital at Constantinople, he adorned it with statues of pagan gods and deities; the Roman army and administration were still overwhelmingly pagan in their beliefs and practices; and in the aftermath of the promulgation of the Edict of Milan, most people prudently said that they were Christian, but many of them went on living and believing much as they had done before.[32]

So it is hardly surprising that it is Gibbon's more nuanced sense of the relations and divisions between faltering paganism and assertive Christianity that has found widespread support among scholars of this period, one indication of which is that since the 1970s they have preferred to describe it in religiously neutral terms as the epoch of "late antiquity."[33] Despite the triumphalism of early church historians, and even the gloomy pagan nostalgia of Gibbon, it has become clear that paganism and Christianity coexisted as the joint heirs and successors of Rome, in what has been described as a "patchwork of religious communities" representing a wide variety of arrangements and interactions, the scene bearing little resemblance to the empire-wide clashes of earlier accounts.[34] To be sure, these localized encounters were sometimes confrontational, but whether the violence was rhetorical (polemical writings or speeches) or actual (riots and protests, persecution and martyrdom), it stopped short of religious war or outright armed conflict. Sometimes it was resolved by conversion from paganism to Christianity, a change that might be imposed and coercive, or persuasively negotiated, or the result of the converts' free and voluntary choice. But the encounter might also take the form of peaceful coexistence, sometimes achieved by social and residential segregation, but sometimes also possible in more integrated circumstances, implying a genuine acceptance of religious diversity. Accordingly, relations among pagans and Christians in the world of late antiquity were much more fluid and interactive than any simplistic dichotomy between them would suggest.[35]

Let us briefly consider three examples of this encounter, beginning with North Africa (especially the region corresponding to present-day Libya and Tunisia) during the early fourth century CE, the period immediately before the promulgation of the Edict of Milan. North Africa was a prosperous, prominent, and cosmopolitan region of the Roman Empire, where Christianity had gained an early hold, perhaps explaining why the new faith was espoused there with particular passion and conviction, and why the region produced many important writers, apologists, and clerics. These, in turn, wrote narratives of persecution and martyrdom, some of which were apparently based on court records, others on alleged eyewitness reports of martyrs' imprisonment and death, and yet others on the writings of the martyrs themselves.[36] These contemporary accounts vividly depict a classic Manichean confrontation between two competing and conflicting religions, in which the Christian martyrs were hounded and hunted and compelled to die for their faith. Yet it is far from clear that this is what always happened, for while these Christian narratives cast the local pagan magistrates in the role of religious persecutors, they also show that the authorities were often patient and forbearing, and in many cases were reluctant to send Christians to their deaths. In those cases where this was the final outcome, it would seem the magistrates had no choice, for it was the Christians themselves who, keen to suffer a passion worthy of Jesus himself, seemed determined to invite martyrdom by refusing to recant their faith.[37]

As a second example, consider the city of Rome itself, during the later third and early fourth centuries, when Christians were experiencing their last period of persecution and their first phase of imperial favor. At the time, the imperial capital was declining in influence and prosperity, which meant that few new public buildings or monuments were being constructed. But the Christian residents began to create their own distinctive works of art, by introducing their own religious subject matter into conventional decorative schemes, initially in paintings in underground burial chambers, and subsequently on the carved marble sarcophagi used by the wealthier among them in accordance with general fashion. Yet in so doing they often adopted and adapted familiar pagan images, as when they intruded the Gospel likeness of the Good Shepherd into recognizably classical rural landscapes. Once the Edict of Milan was put into effect, Rome's Christians became more confident and assertive, but even in the new churches they were now free to build, much of their artwork continued to merge the new Christian iconography with earlier classical models.[38] Nor was this the only religious syncretion during the years immediately after 313 CE, for while every emperor except Julian "the Apostate" was Christian, the Roman Senate remained strongly pagan, and a long and heated debate took place about the continued use of the Altar of Victory in Rome, at which senators traditionally performed official rites and sacrifices. The altar would not be removed until 382 CE at the behest of the emperor Gratian, and even at that relatively late date pagan art was still being commissioned for domestic decoration by families who could afford it and who had not converted.[39]

On the eastern shore of the Mediterranean, the city of Antioch offers a third version of the varied encounters between pagans and Christians in late antiquity, this time toward the end of the fourth century CE, when it was among the most prosperous and influential urban centers of the Greek-speaking world.[40] Antioch was also a Roman administrative and military headquarters, it commanded a large Syrian hinterland, and it contained a significant Jewish community. The city's cultural traditions were strongly Greek, and fundamental to its civic life were the public observances of its long-established religious cults. But as related in the Acts of the Apostles, Christianity had come to Antioch early, through the ministries of Paul and Barnabas, and it flourished there peacefully alongside paganism, as well as other religious and ethnic groups. In the aftermath of the Edict of Milan, pagans and Christians were brought together on Antioch's city council as representatives of the imperial government, and debates ensued about coexistence between pagan and Christian, Christian and Jew, religion and secularism. The ensuing tensions and compromises are vividly described in the writings of three very different men who happened to be in the city in the second half of the fourth century: the emperor Julian "the Apostate," the pagan orator and teacher Libanius, and John Chrysostom, then the local bishop. Together, their testimonies chart the many varied and different levels of interaction between paganism and Christianity, and they also show that neither constituted a monolithic self-enclosed religious system.[41]

Many ancient Christian writers, following Eusebius, described the period from the third to the fifth centuries CE as witnessing the inevitable progress of Christianity from its persecution to its total victory over paganism, and insisted that within such a master narrative, conflict, conversion, and coexistence all worked to Christian ends in a providential and preordained way.[42] Yet as these three examples suggest, the encounters between paganism and Christianity were often more complex, nuanced, and open-ended, with adherents of both religions often living together, and on a more equal and tolerant footing than the triumphalist accounts recognized. In many large cities of late antiquity, it is clear that pagans and Christians got along well enough; in smaller towns, they formed their own separate enclaves; in the countryside, Christianity was generally slower to take hold. The result was not an open war between good and evil, saved and sinners, the light and the dark, but rather what has been described as "a high degree of un-enforced co-existence."[43] Pagans and Christians alike often seem to have been generally indifferent to the organized expression of their religion, with elements of paganism and Christianity coexisting in individuals' lives, as the religiously inclined worked out their own faith in a sort of compromise with the norms and demands and conventions of the society to which they belonged. And despite their religious differences, Christians and pagans (and Jews) were held together by the bonds of a common culture, which derived from what were, after all, their shared experiences of life in the Roman Empire.[44]

Recent writing on the world of late antiquity has emphasized the diversity of both Roman and Christian traditions, rather than the deep and divisive differences between them. From this perspective, of endlessly shifting frontiers and constantly blurred boundaries, where generalizations about religious identities and confessional antagonisms distort more than they reveal, it is just too simplistic to suggest that two separate, competing religious collectivities did battle to the death, as a result of which pagan Rome "fell" while Christian Europe "rose." The grand narrative of "the Christianization of the Roman world," which a cursory reading of *The Decline and Fall* seems to confirm, has been superseded by a pluralistic picture, rejecting a single final, definitive outcome—a complexity with which Gibbon himself became in some ways more comfortable as his own great work progressed, developed, and matured.[45] After all, the "Fathers of the Church" had been educated in the rhetoric and philosophy of the Roman Empire. Many aspects of their ostensibly triumphant new faith were derived from or were adaptations of earlier religious forms and festivals, which proved to be remarkably tenacious and persistent.[46] Far from having caused the "fall" of the Roman Empire by vanquishing paganism, it seems more appropriate to suggest that "Christianity was part of the Roman legacy to medieval Europe." There may be a Manichean battle taking place between the forces of divine light and demonic darkness in the next world, but here on earth, in the endlessly varied places and cultures of late antiquity, there was no such clear-cut sheep-and-goats conflict between pagans and Christians.[47]

CHRISTIANITY AND ISLAM

As with the allegedly collective and apparently clashing identities of pagans and Christians, so too with those of Christianity and Islam, Gibbon is by turns a vivid, influential, flawed, and suggestive place to start. He began *The Decline and Fall* with the Roman Empire at its majestic height, during "the second century of the Christian era," and in the first three volumes he traced and sought to explain its destruction in the West. Then, in an artful reprise that is almost a mirror image of what he had already written, he opened the fourth volume with the eastern empire of Byzantium (now Christianized, and with its capital, Constantinople, portentously regarded as the "second Rome") at its own equivalent apogee during the reign of the emperor Justinian in the early sixth century. But as Gibbon made plain in a famously disparaging chapter, Justinian's successors were not up to the job of safeguarding their realms from the external danger that would be presented by the new and militant religion of Islam, which would turn out to be a less insidious but no less mortal threat to the eastern empire than Christianity had earlier been to the first Rome. Riven with internal religious disputes, and cut off from the Catholic Church of western Europe, the Byzantine Empire was no match for the predatory Arab invaders of the seventh century CE, who overran the eastern Mediterranean and North Africa; and still less could it later withstand the even more formidable forces of their Muslim successors, the Ottoman Turks, who besieged and eventually captured Constantinople itself in 1453. Thus was the Roman Empire finally vanquished, overwhelmed by the soldiers of an alien and all-conquering religion, as "Mahomet, with the sword in one hand, and the Koran in the other, erected his throne on the ruins of Christianity and of Rome."[48]

This fanciful description of the fall of Constantinople to the Turks unmistakably echoes Gibbon's earlier remarks in *The Decline and Fall*, about the banner of the Cross being unfurled triumphantly on the ruins of the Roman Capitol. Once again, he depicts a deeply rooted and seemingly diametrical conflict between two religious collectivities as the determinative and implacably destructive agent of history. But whereas in the West, Christianity had (to Gibbon's regret) undermined paganism from within, in the East, by contrast, militant Islam had (this time to Gibbon's delight) vanquished Christianity from without. Incorrigibly hostile to the Byzantine Empire, as well as to its emperors, he dismissed its entire history as "a tedious tale of weakness and misery."[49] Islam, by contrast, Gibbon viewed more sympathetically, as a tolerant, unmystical, undogmatic religion, which was preferable to Christianity. Although it revered its sages, who were learned in sacred writings, Islam had stopped short of developing a rich, privileged, and powerful priesthood; this meant that, in contrast to the tortuous elaborations and schismatic tendencies of Christian thought, it retained a primordial doctrinal simplicity, which did not compete with and deter human aspirations. Nor did Islam weaken the sinews of the state by preaching disengagement and otherworldliness; instead, it actively encouraged such civil and civic values as hospitality, honor, and justice. In short, and like many of his contemporaries who were influenced by Enlightenment thinking, Gibbon found in Islam a less clerically and theologically oppressive religion much preferable to Christianity (and especially to Roman Catholicism).[50]

In retrospect, it is clear that Gibbon's views of Byzantium were excessively and exaggeratedly hostile, for no empire could have lasted for more than a millennium being as corrupt, degenerate, and sclerotic, as infirm of purpose, or as wholly devoid of redeeming characteristics as the one he described in the second half of *The Decline and Fall*.[51] Moreover, the fact that this Christian imperium had lasted for so long after the demise of the Western Empire casts serious doubt on the notion that the rival religion of Islam was a direct cause of its demise (can an empire be plausibly described as "declining" for over a thousand years?). By the same token, much that Gibbon wrote in praise of Islam was just plain wrong: it did in practice possess a sort of professional priesthood, its theology was neither static nor monolithic but evolving and disputed, and there was fierce internal strife and schism. To a greater extent than Gibbon was prepared to recognize (and it was an error of perception that many since have also made and, regrettably, still do), Christianity and Islam were in many ways mirror images of each other: both were monotheistic, both had spread thanks to charismatic early leadership, expanding rapidly after the deaths of their founding figures, and both were inclined to internal schism.[52] As a result, the interrelations between an ostensibly monolithic "Christianity" and a no less putatively homogeneous "Islam" were more complex and equivocal than Gibbon's Manichean depiction of that sustained and belligerent encounter suggests.

To be sure, when he came to write *The Decline and Fall*, violent clashes between Christianity and Islam had been taking place for more than a thousand years, as the death of the Prophet Muhammad in 632 CE was immediately followed by the initial Arab conquests of Antioch, Jerusalem, Alexandria, Tripoli, and Carthage between 637 and 698, and by two sieges of Constantinople itself in 674–78 and 716–18. Nor was it just the Byzantine Empire that was thus threatened; at the other end of the Mediterranean, the entire Iberian Peninsula was in Arab hands by the early eighth century. Charles Martel's subsequent victory at the Battle of Poitiers in 732 and Constantinople's stubborn and successful resistance blunted these Arab attacks for a time, but in the ninth century, Sicily was conquered, Rome itself was raided, and for the next hundred years or so, Christianity was on the defensive throughout the Mediterranean.[53] From the eleventh to the thirteenth centuries, there was a Christian counterattack: five brutal and bloody Crusades for a time won back the holy places in the eastern Mediterranean, Sicily was reconquered by the Normans, and the Arabs were pushed back on the Iberian Peninsula. But the holy places were soon lost again, and from the fourteenth to the seventeenth centuries a revived and reinvigorated Islam, espoused by the Ottoman Turks, not only captured Constantinople (the point in time at which Gibbon had ended *The Decline and Fall*), but subsequently took Belgrade, conquered Crete, and twice besieged Vienna, in 1529 and again in 1683.[54] Nor was that the end: the Ottomans' last major westerly conquest was of Oran in North Africa in 1709, less than thirty years before Gibbon was born; anxieties about the "Islamic threat" to "Christian" Europe thus remained real and vivid, albeit diminishingly so, throughout his lifetime; and the Ottoman Empire would survive long after his death until its defeat and dismemberment at the end of the First World War.

This confrontation between the collectivities of "Christianity" and "Islam" was more protracted and more warlike than that between pagans and Christians had been, and it also took place across a much greater geographical area. From the seventh to the seventeenth centuries and beyond, and from one end of the Mediterranean to the other, Christians and Muslims (mainly Arabs) were aggressively yet also anxiously made aware of the "other" as the infidel—a wicked, rapacious, and virtually subhuman being, by turns a terrible threat and an inferior creature, to be both feared and loathed.[55] Hence the summons of Pope Urban II for Crusader knights to take part in a "holy war" in 1095; hence the many atrocities and acts of aggression that followed, as the Crusaders established their small Latin kingdoms collectively known as Outremer; and hence the Islamic response to such "infidel" encroachment: the proclamation of a "jihad," justified by the Koranic injunction to "kill the idolators wherever you find them."[56] As contemporary and competing monotheisms, Christianity and Islam were alike intolerant, their respective followers equally convinced that anyone espousing an alternative belief system was evil in this world and damned in the next. There were countless polemics produced on both sides, full of vitriol, hatred, and negative stereotyping, and on the Christian side, which had no injunction against representational art, there were many lurid visual images—paintings, engravings, or caricatures—depicting the hideousness of the irredeemable horde on the other side of the unbridgeable chasm.[57] Even after the Ottoman Empire was dismantled, the reciprocal sense (and the fear) of a great, threatening, and unresolved Christian-Muslim divide remained throughout the twentieth century—and still remains in our own time.

One twentieth-century version of this confrontation, and of an unbridgeable gulf, was vividly outlined by the great Belgian historian Henri Pirenne in *Muhammad and Charlemagne*, in which he described (and lamented) the shattering of the "Mediterranean unity" of the Roman Empire as a result of the seventh-century

Arab conquests. The sea "which had hitherto been the centre of Christianity became its frontier," as two "different and hostile" faiths now faced and fought each other "on the shores of Mare Nostrum."[58] It cannot be coincidence that Pirenne wrote his essentially Manichean account when the western European powers were again fighting the Turks during the First World War, and in the aftermath of 9/11 this interpretation of the long-term relations between Christianity and Islam as eternally prolonged has been reinvigorated by pundits and historians. Here are two examples that must stand proxy for many more. According to Andrew Wheatcroft, in a book entitled *Infidels: The Conflict Between Christendom and Islam, 638–2002*, there was a "single thread" of sustained and cumulative "antagonism between the western Christian and the Mediterranean Islamic worlds," characterized by "atavistic" hatred, fear, loathing, disgust, enmity, antipathy, abomination, and abuse on both sides, which makes it "permanent, natural, inevitable and pre-ordained."[59] In the same way, Anthony Pagden's *Worlds at War: The 2,500-Year Struggle Between East and West* has recently given extended attention to what he describes as the "perpetual enmity" and the "perpetual hostility" between Christianity and Islam, focusing on such antagonistic and confrontational episodes as the early Arab conquests, the Christian Crusades, and the subsequent expansion of the Ottoman Empire.[60]

Both Wheatcroft and Pagden repeatedly insist that "the Christian and Muslim worlds have been religious, geographical, political and economic rivals and competitors since their point of first contact," and their accounts of successive battles, sieges, massacres, pillaging, and violation add up to a vivid and horrifying story of religious war and confessional vengeance between collective identities in what seems to be preordained and unavoidable conflict.[61] But as the two authors coyly concede, in qualifying passages buried deep in their texts, animus was far from being the whole of the picture, for the chasm they depict was often "illusory" or merely "metaphorical." In practice there was "endless" "ambivalence" and "ambiguity" in the relationships between these ostensibly monolithic and antithetical faiths, so that "statements of enmity may not represent the reality of everyday life." Indeed, conflict between the two supposedly ever-warring sides "has been neither continuous nor uninterrupted," as in certain places "Christianity and Islam existed side by side over a long period" when, pace Pirenne, there was a "skein of mutual economic and political interests that dominated the Mediterranean and the Balkans."[62] Such significant qualifications to these faux-Gibbonian depictions of clashing creeds and battling beliefs deserve examination in more detail.

To begin with, there is as much evidence characterizing both Christianity and Islam as religions of peace and mutual accommodation as there is supporting the view of them both as creeds of confrontation and conquest. It may be, as one historian has argued, that "western Christianity before 1500 must rank as one of the most intolerant religions in world history," but against this must be set Christ's exhortations to take in strangers, to love one's enemies, to turn the other cheek, and to "do unto others as you would wish to be done to you," and also the views of such Christian critics of the Crusades as Isaac de Étoile, who was against "forcing infidels to accept the faith at the point of the sword."[63] In the same way, the teachings of the Koran had been more pacifically interpreted, based on its injunction that "there is no compulsion in religion." Indeed, Muhammad had explicitly set himself and his followers against religious wars and forced conversions, and he did not see himself as the founder of a new religion, but as bringing the fullness of divine revelation, granted partially to such earlier prophets as Abraham, Moses, and Jesus, to the Arabs. As a result, Muslim teaching regarded Christians and Jews as slightly errant relatives, who were worshipping the same God, in receipt of similar revelations, and even reading some of the same scriptures. They were categorized and respected as "people of the book," with whom Muslims were urged to live in some form of tolerant amity. As for the doctrine of "jihad," this too could be interpreted in varying ways, not just (and not even primarily) as an exhortation to wage collective holy war against the Christian infidel, but rather (and more importantly) as an injunction to strive for individual self-improvement in finding and following the demanding path of God.[64]

Since neither the Bible nor the Koran existed as a single

coherent text with a single uncontested religious message, it follows that neither "Christianity" nor "Islam" embodied a uniform, monolithic, collective religious identity.[65] As Gibbon wryly and repeatedly notes, Christians had been prone to schism and division from almost the very beginning, and this remained the case after the fall of Rome. Let three of the most conspicuous examples suffice. In 1054, papal legates entered the basilica of Hagia Sophia and on behalf of the pope excommunicated the patriarch of Constantinople—an interdict that would remain in force until 1965. In 1204, the Latin knights of the fourth Crusade, ostensibly on their way to the Holy Land to reinforce their Christian brethren there, got no farther than the Byzantine capital, which they sacked and pillaged and plundered. And in 1453, the Ottoman Turks were poised to take Constantinople, but the Christian West sent no help to the embattled capital of the Christian East.[66] In the same way, and this time pace Gibbon, the greater Muslim world was also rent and divided, between Sunni and Shiite factions, between the Umayyad and Abbasid caliphates, between those who looked to Baghdad and those who looked to Cairo, between Arab and Berber, Turk and Persian. So while by the fourteenth century Islam had spread from modern-day Morocco as far as Indonesia, it assumed so many varied, particular, and localized forms that there was no real sense of collective consciousness or unitary religious identity among the millions who espoused it across three continents. As with Christianity, Islam's initial cohesion soon evaporated, it subsequently splintered into hundreds of rival sects, and it has not been reunified since.[67]

So lacking, indeed, was such cohesion that on many occasions when the forces of "Christianity" and "Islam" confronted each other in what was alleged to be another head-on conflict, the reality was often of Christian and Muslim leaders (and followers) allied on one side, against Christian and Muslim leaders (and followers) taking up arms together on the other.[68] In eleventh-century Spain, the legendary warrior known as El Cid not only fought alongside the Christian king Alfonso VI of Castile against the Arabs, but also, when circumstances warranted, joined with the Muslim king of Zaragoza against the Spanish; and early in the twelfth century, in Outremer, the Frankish count of Edessa allied with the emir of Mosul to fight the Latin prince of Antioch and the Muslim king of Aleppo.[69] Three centuries later, the Turkish sultan Suleyman the Magnificent was willing to join in a military alliance with the Catholic French against the equally Catholic Habsburg emperor, and sometime after, Queen Elizabeth of England was equally prepared to contemplate a similar arrangement with the ruler of Morocco and his Ottoman overlords against Catholic Spain. As the traveler and historian Barnaby Rogerson notes, having surveyed relations between Christendom and Islam during the fifteenth and sixteenth centuries, the notion that the two leading empires, the (Christian) Habsburg and the (Muslim) Ottoman, were "locked in an obsessive war of attrition" that was "real, destructive and bloody" was far from being the whole truth, since this conflict "often took second place to obsessive rivalry with neighbours of their own religious faith": the Shiite empire of Persia in the case of the (Sunni) Ottomans, and the French monarchy in the case of the Habsburgs.[70]

There is also ample evidence of peaceful coexistence between Christians and Muslims extending far beyond the official business of diplomatic alliances and international statecraft. In the immediate aftermath of the first phase of Arab conquests following the death of Muhammad, cooperation with the "people of the book" was both essential and widespread, for otherwise such vast and recently acquired dominions could never have been effectively taxed, governed, and administered. Many centuries later, the Ottoman emperors were also famously accommodating to people of different religions: once Constantinople had been taken, the Orthodox Christian patriarch was restored; professionals, military leaders, and civil servants were recruited from among Christians and Jews; and later Ottoman emperors were often themselves the result of mixed marriages between Muslims and Christian princesses.[71] These interconnections in bureaucracy and government reflected the wider contacts that Muslims and Christians (and Jews) forged in business, commerce, and trade across and around the Mediterranean. Pace Pirenne, such activities never died out after the fall of the Western Empire, and the half millennium from 1000 CE witnessed an unprecedented mercantile flowering, as luxury products from the East such as silk and spices were exchanged for raw materials from the West such as skins and wood. Such interactions were also more localized, in places often mistakenly seen as being solely areas of conflict: in the twelfth-century Levant, the inhabitants of the Crusader states and the neighboring Muslim emirates energetically traded and not infrequently intermarried. Thus were people on both sides of the confessional divide "more than willing to consort with their opposite numbers, their religious allegiance less important than the business of life."[72]

The result, according to the French historian Fernand Braudel (with whom we shall be engaging at greater length in the next chapter), was a common experience shared by those many people who lived, traded, did business, and prospered across and around the Mediterranean, their myriad day-to-day contacts and encounters proclaiming a broader human community, rather than the fundamental religious division, of that increasingly interconnected maritime world.[73] Moreover, this burgeoning commerce in material goods was paralleled by a growing exchange of culture and ideas, which was equally indifferent to religious barriers, and which further contradicted and undermined the negative stereotypes of each other that Christians and Muslims created, namely of infidel enemies as being scarcely human and thus incapable of any sophisticated interest in the higher concerns of life. During the eighth and ninth centuries, most of the greatest authors of ancient Greece, including Aristotle, Plato, Euclid, Galen, and Hippocrates, were translated into Arabic. But it was not until the eleventh century that these Arab texts were in turn translated into Latin, in which form medieval European scholars first encountered many of the greatest works on medicine, astronomy, chemistry, mathematics, and philosophy that had been produced by their classical forebears. Here was cultural borrowing and intermingling across the boundaries of religion on a spectacular scale, for it transformed Europe's intellectual landscape and made possible its twelfth-century Renaissance.[74]

Even at times of heightened confrontation between Christians and Muslims, these transreligious encounters and cultural interactions continued as a feature of life in many parts of Europe, North Africa, and the Near East. They were often associated with particular places or regimes, characterized by what William Dalrymple has called "a kind of pluralist equilibrium," which espoused a "culture of tolerance" whereby people of different faiths coexisted and commingled, and to which the epithet "convivencia" has been attached.[75] During the ninth century, the Abbasid rulers of Baghdad tolerated Christians and Jews, and presided over a golden age of learning, which drew on the mathematics, philosophy, medicine, theology, and literature of ancient Greece, Persia, and India. At the other end of the Mediterranean, the Umayyad caliphate of Córdoba witnessed an equally remarkable cultural flowering, which found its most significant expression in the city's libraries, then the greatest in Europe, housing many of the recent Arab translations of ancient Greek texts.[76] In twelfth-century Sicily, under the Norman rulers who had recently conquered the island, Muslim scholars were retained at court, and in the city of Palermo Arabs lived in relative amity and harmony with Christians and Jews. It was an arrangement mirrored and even exceeded, from the fifteenth to the nineteenth centuries, in cosmopolitan cities and multifaith communities of the Ottoman Empire, such as Alexandria, Aleppo, Jaffa, Beirut, Smyrna, and Salonika.[77]

In the same way, many medieval and early modern Italian cities maintained and expanded a profitable commerce with Muslim traders and merchants, which resulted in (for instance) a profound Islamic influence on Venetian architecture, painting, town planning, jewelry, and speech; this helps explain how and why across the whole of Italy there was a serious regard for and knowledge of many aspects of Arabic learning.[78] After the Ottoman Turks captured Constantinople in 1453, these contacts widened and deepened far beyond Italy. In 1536, King Francis I of France negotiated a mercantile and military treaty with the sultan Suleyman the Magnificent, giving the French direct access to trade with Ottoman ports, and half a century later Queen Elizabeth of England would sign similar agreements with Suleyman's successor. And the enthusiasm went both ways: from the late fifteenth century onward, Ottoman sultans were eager to establish links with the great courts of western Europe, concerning such matters as artistic patronage and trade agreements (in addition to political alliances). In 1479 the sultan Mehmed II was painted by the Venetian artist Gentile Bellini, and Suleyman would later welcome to his court printmakers, artists, and jewelers from across Europe. The result was that Ottoman sultans were increasingly portrayed in the "Western" style, and at the same time, highborn Muslim travelers visited Europe in increasing numbers, where they were fascinated by Western science, literature, music, politics, and opera.[79]

Across the centuries, and across the Mediterranean, what have been termed the "practices of Christian-Muslim complicity" took place at many levels and in many modes, encompassing rulers and aristocrats, clerics and men of affairs, scholars and translators, merchants and traders, many of whom journeyed far and wide making connections and doing business.[80] One such sixteenth-century wanderer was Leo Africanus, who moved easily across the regions and the religions of the Christian-Islamic Mediterranean. Born in Granada of Muslim parents during the late 1480s or early 1490s, he fled to Morocco when the last Islamic outpost in Spain fell to the Christians; he subsequently journeyed across North Africa to the Middle East; he was later captured by pirates before escaping and settling in Rome, where he converted to Christianity and translated the Koran into Latin; and he may thereafter have returned to Africa and to Islam.[81] There is much concerning Leo's life that is unknown (including even his full name), but he moved across the supposedly impermeable boundaries of religious identity with remarkable ease and frequency: from Spain to Morocco, from Europe to Africa, and from Christianity to Islam—and back again. And he was not alone: as it was before and would continue being, the early-sixteenth-century Mediterranean was continually being navigated by merchants, embassies, pirate ships, travelers, scholars, and refugees, to whom it was more a highway than a barrier. In certain quarters and at specific times, there may have been intensified consciousness of religious and cultural differences, but it was balanced by increasing migration, trade, travel, and contact.[82]

None of this is to deny that the Battle of Poitiers, or the Crusades, or the sieges of Vienna took place, or that hatred and intolerance, demonization and negative stereotyping, violence and conflict were among the ways in which Christians and Muslims interacted across the length and breadth of the Mediterranean from the seventh to the seventeenth centuries, or that convivencia was often "fraught and fragile," and that cultures of intolerance often lay just below the surface of "cultures of tolerance." But focusing only on such conflicts is rather like ignoring every other page while reading a book: the resulting account isn't just incomplete, but is misleading to the point of incoherence.[83] For while Christianity and Islam often clashed and collided, they also coexisted, conversed, and collaborated across these supposedly impermeable barriers and impenetrable boundaries of confessional identity, and they did so in many places, in many forms, and in a long sequence of interaction and fusion.[84] According to the historian Richard Fletcher, having observed the full range and complexity of the Christian-Islam interconnection and interaction during this period, "wherever and whenever we direct our gaze, we find a diversity in the type or the temperature of the encounter."[85] And it was such diversity of behavior on the part of Christians and Muslims, as they encountered and engaged with each other at levels that were more usually individual (and accommodating) than collective (and conflictual), and on many matters that often had little if anything to do with faith, that constantly counsels against depicting their relations as a perpetual Manichean confrontation, in which religious identities trump and transcend all others.

Such, at least, are the measured and evenhanded conclusions reached by the most careful scholars and thoughtful historians who in the aftermath of the events of September 11, 2001, have studied the many and varied encounters between Christianity and Islam, for they have roundly rejected the historical claim of unbroken animosity and perpetual conflict between these two religious faiths extending all the way back to the Crusades (and before) and all the way up to the present (and beyond).[86] On the contrary, the evidence is clear that Christians and Muslims have often lived together constructively and amicably, that they have taught one another much about how to live, and that they have learned a great deal from each other. When looked at as a whole, the "Islamo-Christian world" has much more in common and binding it together than it has forcing it apart.[87] Throughout history, its inhabitants have traded, studied, negotiated, and eaten, imbibed, and loved across what have often been the porous frontiers of their religious differences. According to the global historian Felipe Fernández-Armesto, "a true history of Muslim-Christian relations would encourage tolerance and convince us that collaboration is normal. . . . For most of history, in most places, Muslims and Christians have been at peace and have lived in mutual respect."[88] That may be overstating the case, but not by much, and it remains a case that needs making (and a perspective that deserves expression) ever more insistently and repeatedly in our post-9/11 world.

CATHOLICS AND PROTESTANTS

One of the prime reasons why these interfaith relations between paganism and Christianity, and Christianity and Islam, were so complex, ambiguous, localized, nuanced, and individualized was the invariable tendency of these ostensibly monolithic religious beliefs and confessional identities to fracture and fragment, and this was something of which Gibbon was very well aware. *The Decline and Fall* is full of discussion (and on occasion derision) of the fissures and the schisms that characterized the Christian church almost from the very beginning, and although Gibbon was less well informed about this matter in the case of Islam, one of his original and lasting insights was to suggest that conflicts within the *same* religious identity were in practice more bitter and more divisive than confrontations between *different* creeds: "all that history has recorded," he noted, was "that the Christians, in the course of their intestine dissentions, have inflicted far greater severities on each other, than they have experienced from the zeal of infidels."[89] Using a rather different mode of approach and analysis, Sigmund Freud would subsequently make the same point, when he explored what he termed "the narcissism of minor differences": "it is precisely communities with adjoining territories, and related to each other in other ways as well," he argued, "who are engaged in constant feuds and in ridiculing each other."[90]

The major consequences of such "minor differences" generating "constant feuds" within ostensibly unified communities were devastatingly displayed between the mid-sixteenth and the mid-seventeenth centuries, even as the encounters between "Christianity" and "Islam" continued. Across this hundred-year span, the Protestant Reformation and its rejoinder, the Catholic or Counter-Reformation, led religious persecution and conflict on a scale Europe had not witnessed before and would not since. Switzerland was the site of the first such faith confrontations, between 1529 and 1531. The next occurred in the Holy Roman Empire, where the Schmalkaldic War erupted in 1546, to be followed by the so-called Princes' War, which would not end definitively until 1555 with the Peace of Augsburg. But these were mere skirmishes compared to the French Wars of Religion and the Dutch Revolt against Catholic Spain, which took place during the second half of the sixteenth century, and these would be followed by the British Civil Wars, the Polish Deluge, and the Thirty Years War during the first half of the seventeenth.[91] The result was widespread material devastation, economic ruin, and a terrible loss of life. From the time of Martin Luther's first protests in 1517 until the negotiation of the Peace of Westphalia in 1648, Europe was increasingly a divided continent: torn between those who espoused Catholic Christianity and those who embraced the Protestant alternative, the two sides seemingly locked in what Thomas Hobbes would call "the war of every man against every man."[92]

This in turn meant that many God-fearing Europeans came to view what had once been their shared confessional world according to a grotesque earthly interpretation of the Manichean division between the (saved) sheep and the (damned) goats that Christ had outlined in Matthew's Gospel.[93] For during these continental "wars of religion," the battle between good and evil, or between truth and falsehood, or between the light and darkness, or *between* the forces of Christ and those of the devil was no longer between Christians and those believers in other deities or in none; instead the conflict was *among* those who subscribed to one version of Christianity and those who subscribed to another. From this perspective, "heretics," whose beliefs were by definition perverted and debased, and who espoused an erroneous interpretation of the Gospels, were much more reprehensible than "infidels," who did not recognize the Gospels at all.[94] In such a confrontation between those who differed about how to worship the very same God, there appeared to be no scope for compromise or conversation or coexistence. As (the Protestant) King Gustavus Adolphus of Sweden put it in an unyielding letter to his brother-in-law, the elector of Brandenburg, written in 1630, at a crucial stage in the Thirty Years War, "I don't want to hear about neutrality. His grace must be my friend or foe. . . . This is a fight between God and the Devil. If his grace is with God, he must join me, if he is for the Devil, he must fight me. There is no third way."[95]

These belligerent remarks were not unusual, and they help explain why the Reformation era came to be regarded as one of irreconcilable creedal extremism and confessional polarization. For in such a world of opinion and belief, the very idea of toleration seemed tantamount to condoning theological error, and the slope leading from doctrinal disagreements down through judicial persecution to full-scale war between Catholic and Protestant communities would prove both slippery and seductive. The biblical injunction "he that is not with me is against me" now became a clarion call—for princes and armies to confront each other on battlefields across Europe; for popes to excommunicate wayward rulers and their erring subjects; for assassins to murder sovereigns in the name of the one true religion; for scholars and theologians and polemicists to scorn, mock, deride, and denounce their opponents; for lynch mobs and bloodbaths such as the "massacre" of French Protestants on St. Bartholomew's Day 1572; and for individuals to be imprisoned, tortured, and burned at the stake for having accepted (and refusing to renounce) the "wrong" version of the Christian faith. As the historian Sir Keith Thomas has observed, with an eye also turned to the confrontations of our own day, the Reformation's rupture of Christianity "offers a salutary warning of the tragic consequences which follow when the world is envisaged as a cosmic battleground on which opposing forces of good and evil contend for supremacy."[96]

Many of Europe's rulers and priests, generals and polemicists fanned the flames in the manner of King Gustavus Adolphus of

Sweden, habitually saluting their supporters and denouncing their opponents in stark, adversarial terms, and their intransigent utterances, irreconcilable attitudes, and belligerent deeds informed the no less partisan narrative histories of both the Reformation and the Counter-Reformation, the earliest of them produced in the midst of the very events they sought to chronicle.[97] Hence, on the one hand, the lengthy tradition of anti-Catholic writers, beginning with such figures as Johannes Pappus and Lucas Osiander the Elder in Germany, who sought to establish precedents in the early church for later Protestant practices—a tradition eventually encompassing such authors as W. E. H. Lecky, Lord Macaulay, and John Lothrop Motley, who traced and celebrated "the rise of toleration," a barely disguised proxy for "the rise of Protestantism" and its triumph over the iniquities of "popery"—and on the other, an equally august lineage of Catholic historians from Cesare Baronio to Hilaire Belloc acclaiming the survival and revival of the one true church and denouncing schismatic and heretical Protestant "reformers" from Martin Luther onward. In the pages of these competing confessional histories, the battles of the Reformation and Counter-Reformation would continue to be fought again and again across subsequent centuries, thereby reasserting, reaffirming, and reinforcing these long-standing adversarial religious identities.[98]

Yet while it may be true that "on every level, from the local to the international, co-religionists felt an impulse to make common cause with one another," this picture of entrenched religious communities at war was by no means universally valid, even in the undeniably polarized Europe of the Reformation and Counter-Reformation.[99] As with the former divide between "paganism" and "Christianity," or with the continuing confrontations between "Christianity" and "Islam," neither the "Catholic" nor the "Protestant" side was as united, coherent, or monolithic as their prelates and princes repeatedly claimed at the time, and as partisan historians have regularly described since. By the end of the sixteenth century, Protestantism was no longer a single oppositional creed, in thrall to the commanding personality of Martin Luther, but had split and subdivided into many local and national variants: Calvinist in Geneva, Lutheran in North Germany and Scandinavia, Reformed in the Netherlands, Anglican in England, and Presbyterian in Scotland. There were also many deep divergences and disagreements among Roman Catholics, about reform, about doctrine, and about relations with the Protestant churches, which were lengthily (and sometimes acrimoniously) displayed and debated at the many meetings of the Council of Trent held between 1545 and 1563. Moreover, by the end of the sixteenth century virtually every European kingdom and principality was home to significant religious minorities, with the result that in many parts of the countryside, and in most major cities, from Paris to Augsburg, Basel to Amsterdam, Cologne to Vienna, Protestants and Catholics of whatever particular persuasion often lived close together and sometimes side by side, in intricate and irregular patterns that were impossible to map or control.[100]

With the practical boundaries of collective religious identity far from clear or agreed, it is scarcely surprising that conversations did take place across them, in some instances sponsored and supported by religious and political leaders. During the half century after Martin Luther's initial protests, there remained hopes that the recent religious divide might be temporary, with some prelates and scholars making determined efforts to bridge the emerging doctrinal gaps and to promote engaged dialogue and negotiation. Such figures included the Italian cardinal Gasparo Contarini, Archbishop Hermann von Wied of Cologne, and Charles de Guise, the cardinal of Lorraine, on the Catholic side, and Martin Bucer and Philipp Melanchthon, both of them renowned Protestant scholars.[101] The most significant of such gatherings, known as the Colloquy of Poissy, was held in 1561 in a small town on the Seine north of Paris. It was summoned by the French queen regent, Catherine de' Medici, on behalf of her young son, King Charles IX, and by the cardinal of Lorraine, with both Protestants and Catholics invited in an attempt to accomplish a general reunion of the churches. Here, and at the Colloquy of Nantes held in the following year, were serious people engaged in serious conversations, and making serious attempts to avert a permanent split in western Christendom, by seeking a "third way" of conciliation and accommodation rather than proclaiming and entrenching a Manichean division between Catholics and Protestants.[102]

There were also some lay writers who tried to outline a middle position between the ostensibly irreconcilable "confessional totalities" of Catholicism and Protestantism.[103] One such figure was the poet and philologist Sebastian Castellio, who in 1554 published a work entitled *Concerning Heretics: Whether They Are to Be Persecuted and How They Are to Be Treated* in response to the execution of a Spanish physician named Michael Servetus. Heretics, he insisted, should never be executed, by Catholics or Protestants, and certainly not (as in this case) at the behest of John Calvin.[104] Another such writer was Jean Bodin, who in *The Six Books of the Republic*, published in 1576, expounded the "political" and "prudential" case for religious moderation. Public disputes about faith, he urged, brought all matters concerning belief into disrepute, and if they took on a belligerent character, they might bring ruin to the state. Accordingly, Bodin argued that where a new branch of the Christian faith found firm support in society at large, it was a matter of common sense for the authorities to tolerate it rather than persecute it. Over a decade later, he returned to these subjects in *The Sevenfold Colloquium*, a sequence of six dialogues among seven wise men, each representing a different point of view: Lutheran, Calvinist, Catholic, Jew, Arab, Skeptic, and Natural Rationalist. At the close, they part, never to converse on such subjects again. Their harmonious discourse on religious differences was over, and the reader is left to decide whether this transfaith conversation was a dead end—or perhaps the promise of a way forward.[105]

With cogent arguments for religious moderation and dialogue being made, even as divisions were hardening and intensifying elsewhere on the continent, some European rulers sought to promote accommodation and conversation between Catholics and Protestants. Hence in Transylvania the Declaration of Torda, passed by the Diet in 1568, which set down that ministers should everywhere be free to preach and proclaim the Gospel "according to their understanding of it," and that "no one is permitted to threaten to imprison or banish anyone because of their teaching, because faith is a gift from God." Likewise, in Poland-Lithuania, the nobility approved the Confederation of Warsaw of 1573, in which it was agreed that "we who differ with regard to religion will keep the peace with one another, and will not for a different faith or change of churches shed blood nor punish one another by confiscation of property, infamy, imprisonment or banishment."[106] Similarly, in France, the Edict of Nantes, promulgated by King Henri IV in 1598, established the sort of religious compromise that successive monarchs had been seeking since the time of the Colloquy of Poissy, allowing freedom of worship in perpetuity for Catholic and Protestants alike, in return for acknowledgments of loyalty to the crown. Thus did France reject the Manichean divisions that had previously damaged and disfigured it during its Wars of Religion, and for most of the seventeenth century it stood, alongside Transylvania and Poland-Lithuania, for compromise and toleration in matters of belief.[107]

Although often regarded as the ultimate European conflict over faith and God, the Thirty Years War was a further indication that monolithic religious identities, and their attendant antagonisms and confrontations, were in practice increasingly difficult to justify or sustain. In his conduct of French foreign policy, Cardinal Richelieu held the view that "the interests of a state and the interests of religion are two entirely different things." He thus not only respected the provisions of the Edict of Nantes, but even entered into an alliance with Protestant powers in his country's battles against the Catholic Habsburgs.[108] Likewise, Pope Urban VIII, who was Richelieu's contemporary, was no friend of Catholic Spain or the Spanish Habsburgs, and on occasion he even gave thanks for the victories of Protestant "heretics." In the same way, the Protestant prince Gábor Bethlen of Transylvania was prepared to negotiate with the Catholic Holy Roman emperor, with a view to gaining territories in Hungary. Differences of religion were thus no impediment to cooperation, and confessional commonality was no guarantee of collaboration: no Protestant rulers came to the aid of their coreligionist, the king of Bohemia, when his lands were invaded by a Catholic army at the behest of the Holy Roman emperor.[109] Among Catholic and Protestant rulers alike, practicality and considerations of statecraft increasingly won out over religious commitment, as was made plain in the Peace of Westphalia, which brought the Thirty Years War to an end. According to the principle of *cuius regio, cuius religio*, each ruler would have the right to determine the religion of his own state, but Christians living in principalities where their denomination was not the established church were also guaranteed the right to practice their faith in public during allotted hours and in private at their will.[110]

Notwithstanding the powerful urgings of conciliatory writers such as Castellio and Bodin, and the contrary examples of Transylvania, Poland-Lithuania, and France, it took most rulers of early modern Europe a long time to learn the simple lesson that wars waged against fellow Christians were decidedly ill-advised. But away from the theological disputations and the body-strewn battlefields, many of their humble subjects, who were also confronted with the challenges of living, coping, and surviving in an era of unprecedented religious turmoil and animosity, had already reached these more measured conclusions. For in the wake of the Protestant and Catholic Reformations, as historian Benjamin J. Kaplan notes, "millions of Europeans" were compelled to struggle with an elemental question: "can people whose basic beliefs are irreconcilably opposed live together peacefully?" "More often than usually recognized," the author concludes, "the answer in that earlier era was yes." Despite so much evidence to the contrary, many "viable alternatives to bloodshed" were developed and practiced, which proved both compelling and appealing. Unlike many of their temporal and spiritual superiors, the ordinary men and women of Europe "did not have to love each other in order not to kill each other," and even in the darkest periods of religious persecution and interfaith conflict, they worked out many successful "arrangements for peaceful co-existence."[111]

The result was that there developed during the Reformation and the Counter-Reformation a widespread, pragmatic, and accommodating "indifference to certain kinds of difference." Such attitudes, modes of behavior, and resulting interactions, reminiscent of those in late antiquity between pagans and Christians, and in the medieval and early modern periods between Christians and Muslims, were again found in the unofficial spaces of private life, where the practical necessity for day-to-day negotiation could successfully override political imperatives or military demands or theological exhortations.[112] Arcane scholastic disputes, about issues such as the role of the priesthood, or the metaphysics of the eucharist, or the status of scriptural authority, might be deeply contentious matters between elite and educated Catholics and Protestants, yet they were not only impossible to resolve or reconcile, but they also meant less to most people, whose knowledge of religious doctrine was rudimentary and unlettered. From this perspective, confessional enmities, talked up and exaggerated by princes and prelates, were less important than the abiding realities of a shared humanity and a common Christian faith. As the Catholic author of a Dutch pamphlet put it in 1579, "we have been told that these [Protestant] people are monsters. We have been sent after them as after dogs. [Yet] if we consider them, they are men of the same nature and condition as ourselves . . . worshipping the same God as us, seeking salvation in the same Christ, believing in the same Bible, children of the same Father, asking a share of the same heritage by virtue of the same Testament."[113]

Put another way, this meant that within the increasingly fissured territories of European Christendom, the venerable principles and hallowed practices of charity, generosity, friendliness, loving-kindness, and good-neighborliness, which long antedated the Catholic and Protestant split, were alive and well; indeed, they were much more prevalent, tenacious, and important than has until relatively recently been recognized by historians working on this period. This general sentiment was expressed by the Polish Jesuit Peter Skarga, who remarked of Protestants in 1592, "their heresy is bad, but they are good neighbours and brethren, to whom we are linked by bonds of love in the common fatherland."[114] So while official records and the Catholic and Protestant histories subsequently fashioned from them suggest deep and complete polarization, a broader and more nuanced investigation (including an appreciation of those many significant social spaces from which little or no evidence survives) suggests that ordinary lives were often lived in more peaceful ways and on less sectarian terms. If there was a persistent and unbridgeable gulf, it was between "the rhetoric of intolerance" and the "generally benign and conciliatory character of inter-confessional relations." Most ordinary people, left to their own devices and decisions, were eager to continue living with their neighbors, whatever their unresolved religious differences, and despite what prelates and princes urged, they were not minded to denounce or to kill those of other faiths.[115]

To this end, a whole range of stratagems were successfully devised for coping with the demands of officialdom and for getting on with one's life and one's neighbors beyond the confessional boundary.[116] During the closing decades of the sixteenth century, Protestant burghers living in Catholic Vienna left the city on Sundays to worship on neighboring estates and in village churches where they were free to practice their own religion. In the same way, at the Jacobskerk in Utrecht, the pastor Hubert Duifhuis welcomed all Christians to Communion, Catholic and Calvinist alike, and he was supported in this ecumenical work by the city magistrates. In many parts of Europe, "clandestine churches" ("schuilkerk") were constructed, allowing Catholic majorities to tolerate Protestant minorities and vice versa, and the existence of such buildings and services was an open secret.[117] Alternatively, and much more publicly, Catholics and Protestants might agree to share the same church ("simultankirche"), or at least the same city, and many such "bi-confessional arrangements" were to be found in the urban centers of Switzerland, Transylvania, the Holy Roman Empire, and France (after the Edict of Nantes). In some cities, and especially in the Dutch Republic, diverse creeds were jumbled up together in what has rightly been termed a "religious melting pot"; in others, such as Augsburg, religious freedom depended not so much on integration as segregation, as different religious groups were sharply separated. By such varied means were those of divergent religious faiths able to cohabit on amicable terms.[118]

So while Protestants and Catholics might be urged by their spiritual and political leaders to disapprove of each other en masse, on the grounds that "he that is not with me is against me," most ordinary people preferred to obey Christ's alternative command, to "love thy neighbor as thyself," and sought to live accordingly.[119] As a result, interpersonal relations were much informed by the inclination to accommodate and to cooperate across religious divides. Although, for example, all churches harshly condemned intermarriages between those of different Christian denominations, none denied that such unions were an "honorable state of matrimony," and mixed unions were regularly presided over by Calvinist, Catholic, Lutheran, and Anglican clergy. In diverse religious communities, families habitually hired domestics of other faiths, and this practice was especially widespread in Dutch, French, and German cities, where Protestants often employed Catholic servants. During the late sixteenth and early seventeenth centuries, the reputation of Jesuit colleges in France and in Poland was so high that they attracted many Protestant students who wanted the best education available, regardless of its alien religious doctrines. And Protestants and Catholics often participated in common recreations—so much so that in France, Calvinist clergy vainly reprimanded Huguenots who habitually joined Catholics in dances, hunting parties, fairs, carnival celebrations, and saints' day festivals.[120]

As with relations between pagans and Christians, and between Christians and Muslims, most encounters between Catholics and Protestants were generally conducted individually rather than collectively, and amicably rather than adversarially. Recent work on villages, towns, and cities in early modern England, France, the Netherlands, and the Holy Roman Empire strongly supports the view that "co-existence and inter-confessional co-operation" more aptly described the encounters than "ubiquitous conflict and fratricidal strife," at least in the lived experiences of ordinary people.[121] Even in Habsburg Spain, which since the establishment of the Inquisition in 1478 and the conquest of the last Muslim kingdom of Granada in 1492, had become the most intolerant of the Catholic nations, there is evidence that in practice later relations between those of different faiths were more relaxed and harmonious at the local and the individual level; and the same may also have been true across the Atlantic in the Spanish Empire in Mexico and Peru, whose native inhabitants and (later) African slaves were in thrall to very different systems of belief. It was even occasionally suggested that there might be alternative roads to salvation in addition to the strictly Catholic one: in the words of Francisco de Amores, defending himself against the Inquisition, "each person can be saved in his own law, the Moor in his, the Jew in his, the Christian in his, and the Lutheran in his."[122] The Reformation and the Counter-Reformation may in many ways have been very dark times, but humanity and decency, cooperation and conciliation kept making their voices heard.[123]

RELIGIOUS WAR, RELIGIOUS PEACE

It cannot be denied that during the last two millennia, across Europe, North Africa, and the Middle East, Manichean modes of thinking about confessional identities and interactions have often been pervasively seductive and tenaciously appealing. Time and again, temptations and exhortations to hatred and rage, to demonization and negative stereotyping, and to torture and murder and war, all in the name of one true faith rather than of another, have proved to be irresistible; incitements by secular leaders and religious fanatics have regularly proclaimed that "he that is not with me is against me." So it is scarcely surprising that in turn, historians have often taken a highly partisan view of these matters, and have been more interested in replicating and justifying these creedal confrontations than in explaining them or setting them in the broader context of critical perspective. Yet these simplistic and fractious identifications have never exhaustively described the historic experience of men and women, even as people of faith. Some leaders, both religious and secular, have urged the importance of moderation, dialogue, and conciliation, while at the day-to-day level of personal encounters, those of different creeds have often sought to get along, and have found many ways of successfully doing so. Whatever the claims of political or scriptural authorities to the contrary, the intuitive apprehension of a common humanity, transcending religious differences, has always moderated the extravagant and invariably overstated claims of faith on individuals.

Similar arguments about the ambiguities and limitations of religious identities may also be made for other places and other times, although only two further examples can be given here. It is, for instance, both possible and (for some) tempting to present South Asian history as a perpetual confessional conflict between Hindus and Muslims, as exemplified by the protests and massacres during India's independence and partition in 1947, and by the more recent displays of Hindu assertiveness following from the rise of the Bharatiya Janata Party.[124] But against this tableau of religious antagonism may be set an alternative history of interfaith encounters and conversations, vividly exemplified by the reign of the Muslim Indian emperor Akbar, who in the 1590s, in support of dialogues between the adherents of different faiths (including Hindus, Muslims, Christians, Parsees, Jains, Jews, and even atheists), adumbrated principles of confessional freedom very much like those that had recently been adopted in Transylvania and Poland-Lithuania, proposing that "no man should be interfered with on account of religion, and anyone is to be allowed to go over to a religion that pleases him."[125] In the same way, the history of relations between Israelis and Palestinians since 1948 has sometimes been presented as one of irreconcilable conflict and perpetual confrontation between different and hostile religious communities. Yet there have also been, and still are, voices in that region calling for "understanding, peaceful co-existence and acceptance of common humanity," while many Palestinians and Israelis try to share their lives together despite their different faiths.[126] In the present as in the past, humanity and decency keep making their voices heard, and compromises and accommodations are made: and humanity and decency and compromises and accommodations have their own histories.

While acknowledging that religious identities have often been (and still are) individual as well as collective, and that modes of religious practice behavior have often been (and still are) adaptive rather than confrontational, it is also important to avoid what the economist and philosopher Amartya Sen has rightly called an "exaggerated focus on religiosity," by recognizing that for relatively few people of any faith is religion the be-all and end-all of existence. There are many facets of lives, activities, and identity, among both elites and common folk, not significantly informed or significantly explained by religious sentiment.[127] On many occasions in the past (and in the present?), rulers and other political leaders have invoked the imperatives of a shared religious identity, largely as a proxy for alternative and more compelling considerations such as dynastic ambition, national rivalry, economic competition, territorial acquisitiveness, and so on, while life for ordinary people has never been organized, undertaken, carried on, and ended on the basis of religious beliefs and injunctions alone.[128] To see, describe, and explain the conduct of men and women, either individually or collectively, exclusively in terms of their religious identity is thus to deny the obvious: that one's sense of self is always constituted by many identities at the same time. As the historian, economist, and political analyst Zachary Karabell rightly puts it, in words that may apply equally well to relations between pagans and Christians, Protestants and Catholics, Hindus and Muslims, and Jews and Muslims, "in both 'Christendom' and the 'house of Islam' (as Muslims have called their world), religion was one identity among many. And what that identity meant to the political, social or cultural life of any particular village, town, state or society is beyond generalization."[129]

As a contrasting example, the recent tragic history of Northern Ireland affords a cautionary case study of what happens when collective religious identity is exaggerated to define and divide people, and is also institutionalized in order to entrench and perpetuate such communal antagonism. When Ireland was partitioned in 1921, the educational system established in the north was completely bifurcated, between relatively well-funded state schools, which were Protestant, and less well-funded independent schools, which were Catholic. Protestants sent their children to state (that is, Protestant) schools, while Catholic parents educated their children in independent (that is, Catholic) schools, in both cases to protect and preserve their separate faiths, which also had the intended effect of perpetuating antagonisms in the next generation. Indeed, from the 1960s until the 1990s, surveys reveal percentages "in the high nineties" of pupils attending schools wholly segregated between Protestants and Catholics. Moreover, these institutions taught irreconcilable accounts of Irish history: one of a strong, stern, fortified resolve on the part of the Protestants, with such iconic events as the Battle of the Boyne and the Ulster Covenant of 1912; the other a narrative of grievance and victimhood on the part of Catholics, stressing the Cromwell massacres of 1649 and the famine of the 1840s. As a result, hostile negative stereotyping prevailed on both sides, and a scheme of inimical collective identities was inculcated in all Ulster schoolchildren, expressing and embodying "entirely incompatible social cosmologies and grossly inaccurate views of each other."[130]

To be sure, there has been an integrated schooling movement in Ulster since the early 1970s, entitled All Children Together—a valiant but largely vain attempt to open up a conversation across the hitherto mostly impermeable boundaries of educationally conditioned religious identity.[131] It draws its membership from across the spectrum of religious and nonreligious groupings, though they are (perhaps unsurprisingly) generally liberal, middle-class, and committed (but tolerant) Christians. In 1978, All Children Together helped bring about the passage of the Education (Northern Ireland) Act, permitting the establishment of multidenominational schools where desired by sufficient numbers of parents. But the legislation did not affect the existing segregated system, and alternative schools had to be self-funding until they had signed up enough pupils—a serious challenge since Northern Ireland opinion generally supports denominational education.[132] So while many Catholic and Protestant politicians and clergy increasingly urge interfaith dialogue and cooperation, and although the integrated schools movement grows steadily, these institutions serve at present less than 5 percent of the attending population, which means that even in the more placid and prosperous Ulster of the early twenty-first century, these conversations are still pitifully few among young people across these still powerfully institutionalized sectarian identities.[133]

As the unhappy experience of Northern Ireland suggests, this is what happens, and this is what can go wrong, when a religious identity is officially imposed and promoted as the only one that matters. For obviously these Ulster schoolchildren cannot possibly be described wholly and exclusively in terms of their religious beliefs and identities: they are also boys and girls, working-class and middle-class, straight and gay, and so on. As the historian Marianne Elliott rightly notes, having investigated both Protestant Ireland and Catholic Ireland, it is "absurd to think that religious . . . identities take primacy over others in deciding human behaviour," be that behavior individual or collective.[134] But instead of encouraging young people to think about their many and varied identities, faith-based schools ghettoize them, so that the only contemporaries they are likely to encounter are also their coreligionists, the purpose of their education being in significant part to reinforce their sense not only of collective religious identity, but also of collective religious superiority. Thus can schooling fail at what must surely count as one of its essential purposes in a pluralistic world, namely to foster an understanding of who other people are, and of what one might oneself become. For as has often been recognized, it is better to be kind to strangers than to embrace the bigotry and intolerance of militant Manicheanism, and this in turn means that the twenty-fifth chapter of the Gospel according to Matthew needs to be read with considerable care.[135]

TWO

Nation

Love your country. Your country is the land where your parents sleep, where is spoken that language in which the chosen of your heart, blushing, whispered the first word of love; it is the home that God has given you that by striving to perfect yourselves therein you may prepare to ascent to Him.

—Giuseppe Mazzini, quoted in W. V. Byars, ed.,
*The Handbook of Oratory: A Cyclopedia of
Authorities on Oratory as an Art*

Our country is not the only thing to which we owe our allegiance. It is also owed to justice and humanity.

—James Bryce,
*University and Historical Addresses:
Delivered During a Residence in the United
States as Ambassador to Great Britain*

THE FIRST VOLUME OF General Charles de Gaulle's peacetime memoirs begins with his return to power in France in 1958, and offers an eloquent and emotional evocation of national history, geography, "genius," and identity. "France," de Gaulle writes, "has emerged from the depths of the past. She is a living entity. She responds to the call of the centuries. Yet she remains herself through time." Accordingly, although somewhat paradoxically, "her boundaries may alter, but not the contours, the climate, the rivers and seas that are her eternal imprint." For, he insists, "her land is inhabited by people who, in the course of history, have undergone the most diverse experiences, but whom destiny and circumstance, exploited by politics, have unceasingly moulded into a single nation," which "comprises a past, a present and a future that are indissoluble." As a result, "the state, which is answerable for France, is in charge at one and the same time of yesterday's heritage, today's interests and tomorrow's hopes." Across a millennium and a half, de Gaulle believed, these obligations had been discharged in the name of the French people by the

Merovingians, the Carolingians, the Capetians, the Bonapartes, and the Third Republic, whereupon he himself was twice invested with "supreme authority" as he sought to "lead the country to salvation" by offering his compatriots "no other goal" but that of the summit and "no other road but that of endeavour." Such, for de Gaulle, was the uniquely "enduring character" of the French nation, embracing "countless generations" of the dead, the living, and the as yet unborn: the ultimate embodiment of the most significant and long-lasting form of collective human solidarity.[1]

Charles de Gaulle was born in 1890 and died in 1970, and his life virtually coincided with what has often been described (and sometimes deplored) as "the apotheosis of the nation state."[2] From the signing of the Peace of Westphalia of 1648, so this argument runs, the religious identities (and antagonisms) of faith were gradually superseded by the secular identities (and antagonisms) of "the nation." Hence the Great Powers that dominated Europe during the eighteenth and nineteenth centuries; hence the creation of the United States as "a new nation," soon followed by the Latin American republics to the south; hence the Revolutionary and Napoleonic Wars that unleashed across Europe the pent-up forces of romantic nationalism; hence the "nation-making" that characterized the continent across the nineteenth century, culminating in the First World War; hence the Treaty of Versailles, which reorganized Europe according to the principle of "national self-determination"; hence the Second World War, when nations in Europe, Asia, and North America went into battle with each other all over again; hence postwar decolonization, when new, independent countries were created across the globe as the European empires were dismantled; and hence, two decades after de Gaulle's death, the collapse of the Soviet Union and the emergence (or reemergence) of many old-new nations in eastern Europe and in Asia.[3] From this perspective, it seems clear that initially across Europe and subsequently around the world, people have increasingly thought of themselves as, and organized themselves in, "nationalities." The result, according to the Australian transnational historian Ian Tyrrell, is that in modern times collective human identities, "though multiple," have become "primarily national ones."[4]

During the years between the death of Charles de Gaulle and the breakup of the Soviet Empire, his compatriot Fernand Braudel began a multivolume work, *The Identity of France*, that aimed to uncover, explore, and celebrate a nation whose "entire history" was that of "the process of creating or recreating itself." Combining mysticism, exceptionalism, and nationalism in an elegiac, epic narrative, Braudel's last work, left incomplete, was a Gaullist account of the French national past, beginning in "the mists of time" and ending with a disparagement of the Vichy regime and homage to the wartime Resistance.[5] "I have never ceased," the author wrote in his introduction, "to think of a France buried deep inside itself, a France flowing along the contours of its own age-long history, destined to continue, come what may." Inspired by a sense of civic duty and a long-pent-up patriotism, this enterprise was Braudel's belated declaration of his love for France, which he admitted was "a demanding and complicated passion." And in writing this "age-long history" of the nation he understood "almost instinctively," Braudel defined his subject in the familiar appositional terms essential to the formation and articulation of any collective identity: it was France against the world, "*nous vis-à-vis* the others, a bit like the sportscaster of an international match unable to conceal in myriad small ways his predilection for his nation's team." Here was a history of France's national identity that was also intended to reinforce its present and future sense of itself, for "to define France's past," Braudel explained, "is to place the French people within their own existence."[6]

Yet Braudel's extended, unfinished love letter to the identity and exceptionalism of France represented the late-life endeavor and declaration (or, alternatively, the misguided recantation and apostasy) of a scholar who had made his reputation by denouncing and transcending what he once disparaged as "the usual framework of national histories, in which every historian worthy of the name has long ceased to believe."[7] Inspired by such innovative *Annaliste* scholars as Marc Bloch and Lucien Febvre, Braudel had spent most of his career proclaiming that history should no longer be written along exclusively national lines, and in his most famous book, *The Mediterranean and the Mediterranean World in the Age of Philip II*, he furnished a pioneering and bravura example of how to approach the past in a very different way, in deliberate opposition to the "frankly traditional historiography" of nationalist historians such as Leopold von Ranke. For Braudel was convinced that the bounded territorialities, parochial differences, and petty quarrels of nation-states were too narrow a field and too constrained a subject; he dismissed them as "l'histoire événementielle," the flotsam and jetsam of superficial happenings and transient episodes, insignificant compared to the more deep-rooted patterns, trends, and developments concerning the environment, climate, demography, production, and consumption, which formed "the essentials of man's past."[8] From this very different viewpoint, history was not the pious handmaid of national identity, but its implacable enemy, for "nations per se were abstractions if not accidents, radically disjointed and epitomized versions of an infinitely more complex whole."[9]

The zeal, energy, commitment, and self-contradiction of Fernand Braudel's move from one position to its polar opposite suggests both the strengths and the weaknesses, the attractions and the limitations of regarding "the nation" as the most significant focus and resonant form of collective identity (and hostility) in the secular, Great Power world that allegedly came into being in the aftermath of the Peace of Westphalia. In his earlier, iconoclastic days, Braudel was not only reacting against the prevailing belief in the nation as the ultimate unit of historical action and group awareness, but was also signaling his hostility to the role of historians, past and present, in the deliberate creation of these often adversarial national identities.[10] Indeed, by refusing to analyze the past in what he regarded as such parochial and chauvinistic terms, Braudel was suggesting that national identity was not the only form of collective human solidarity that mattered, nor even was it necessarily the most significant. Yet in his later and more traditional phases, Braudel *did* argue that national identity was a more important and long-lived phenomenon than had been claimed by those who argued it had only begun in 1648 (or in 1789 or even later); by then, he seemed to imply that the nation-state, and national identities, were the most important form of collective association, indeed the culmination of all human history. The late-life conversion of so strong and unconventional an historian as Braudel to this commonplace and highly sentimentalized perspective on "the nation" well attests to the seductive power of its claim to being the preeminent category of human identity; but it also opens the way to seeing the contradictions, limitations, and ambiguities of that claim.

THE BEGINNINGS OF NATIONAL IDENTITIES

As in the case of Charles de Gaulle, most recent attempts to define national identities focus on the history, geography, territoriality, and language of collective allegiances and antagonisms, and on the alignment of a national culture and the nation-state; but they have also been conceived to fit and describe what is believed to be the rise of nation-building (and national confrontation) that took place in Europe from the eighteenth century onward, and that since then has spread across the world.[11] In the last twenty years or so, this "modernist" interpretation of national identity has received new impetus following the collapse of the Soviet Empire into many separate nations, and it has been persuasively and influentially advanced by such scholars as Benedict Anderson, John Breuilly, Ernst Gellner, and Eric Hobsbawm.[12] All of them sought to treat the subject in historical terms, but they have done so over a relatively circumscribed time span, and as none of them were friendly to the idea of national identity, they all treated it as though it were a recent and ephemeral phenomenon already on the wane.[13] Yet such a view of the nation as an upstart and transient focus of human identity and conflict is not necessarily correct, and in recent years, historians of the medieval and early modern periods have insisted that it is mistaken to associate "national identity" only with "modernity." Indeed, one scholar has gone so far as to urge that it is "the similarities between medieval and modern expressions of national identity that are fundamental, and the differences that are peripheral."[14] That may be overstating it, but the "fundamental similarities" between the solidarities of national identity, and also as regards the limitations to those solidarities, are well worth investigating.

While de Gaulle and Braudel believed the French nation first began to take shape in the nebulous "depths of the past," historians have been unwilling to accept that such collective identities can be discerned so vaguely, or so far away in time. Egypt under the pharaohs may have resembled a nation, with a shared sense of history and a precise territorial attachment, but there was no accompanying sense of public culture or collective identity. As for the ancient Greeks, their limited pan-Hellenic aspirations, embodied in their shared language, Homeric epics, and Olympic games, foundered on the disputatious reality of their fiercely independent city-states. Similar objections have been made to claims that the Sumerians, the Persians, the Phoenicians, the Aramaeans, the Philistines, the Hittites, and the Elamites were ancient nations, or that the Sinhalese, the Japanese, or the Koreans might be so described during the first millennium of the Common Era.[15] Only in the case of Israel does it seem plausible to discern a recognizably ancient nation, with its precise (though disputed) territoriality, its creation and ancestry myths, its shared historical memories of the Exodus, the Conquest, and wars with the Philistines, its strong sense of exceptionalism and providential destiny, its self-definition against a hostile "other," and its common laws and public culture. These were, and are, essential themes in the unfinished history of the Jews, but this example has also furnished ever since "a developed model of what it means to be a nation." From this perspective, the Bible was not just concerned (in the New Testament) with the collective religious identities (and confrontations) of the saved and the damned; it also provided (in the Old Testament) the prototype for the self-imaginings and collective identities (and confrontations) that were essential to becoming and being a nation.[16]

Notwithstanding Israel's subsequent defeats, the destruction of the Temple in Jerusalem, and the resulting dispersals and diaspora of the Jewish people, their vivid and compelling narrative of the making and maintenance of "the original nation" furnished a powerful biblical precedent for what would become, after the fall of the Roman Empire, the peoples and polities of medieval Christian Europe.[17] As strains of national consciousness emerged from new communities forming across the continent, the example of Israel was constantly invoked, and by the thirteenth century different groups of people were being referred to in terms of their specific national identities.[18] When the emperor Frederick II wrote to his fellow rulers in 1241 warning of the Mongol threat, he enumerated the qualities of the varied continental peoples—or nations—as follows: Germany was "fervent in arms"; France was "the mother and nurse of chivalry"; Spain was "warlike and bold"; and England was "fertile and protected by its fleet." He also distinguished the lands at the extremes of what was then the known world, describing "bloodstained Ireland, active Wales, watery Scotland and glacial Norway." These stereotypes may have exaggerated the autonomy and territoriality of these nascent nations, but they suffice to suggest that such identities were already in the thirteenth century an important element in a ruler's relation to his subjects, and in the assertion of power over his neighbors.[19] Nor was this sense of secular solidarity exclusively confined to those who governed; it was also a collective sentiment, with medieval peoples expressing the belief that they belonged to nations and using the words "people" and "nation" in their Latin forms ("gens" and "natio") interchangeably.[20]

Such was "the medieval construction of the world," of which the chronicler Regino of Prüm had claimed as early as 900 CE that "the various nations differ in descent, custom, language and law."[21] Distinctiveness may not have been everywhere so pronounced, but it was certainly present in England by the reign of Alfred the Great when the joining of the kingdoms of Wessex and Mercia meant that one collective identity of Englishness first came recognizably into being. Promoted by the monarch, who drew on the precedents of ancient Israel, as well as a shared sense of the past, a common religion and language, and opposition to the pagan and predatory Danes, this English national solidarity was readily and widely shared.[22] And despite the traumas of the Norman invasion of 1066, it would reassert itself soon after, being fully reestablished by the fourteenth century. Just as Alfred the Great had drawn on the Venerable Bede's revealingly entitled *Ecclesiastical History of the English People* (or *Nation*), as well as the

Anglo-Saxon Chronicle, in promoting a shared sense of English national identity, so twelfth century writers lent historical validation to the same development, among them William of Malmesbury, Henry of Huntingdon, William of Newburgh, and Geffrei Gaimar, who created an interpretation of the past that was "triumphantly English and almost teleologically English-centred." They would be followed by Geoffrey Chaucer, who was "the first writer in English explicitly to claim status as a national poet," and by growing declarations that English was the natural national language. The result was that by the early fourteenth century more Englishmen than ever before felt themselves to be part of a national community.[23]

By then, the continental analog to this revived English sense of "collective solidarity" and "national feeling" existed in many of the medieval realms.[24] In France, Kings Louis VI and Louis IX were able to draw on a growing sense of national consciousness, reinforced by the historical claim that all the Franks traced a common descent from the Trojans, which was also expressed in their great national epic *Chanson de Roland*. The same was true among the Germans, many of whom shared a common kingdom (as well as their own Trojan ancestors) and also took pride in their superior national cultural achievements. As the poet Walther von der Vogelweide put it around 1200, "I have seen many countries, and I liked to observe the best of them," but Germany was "above all of them. From the Elbe to the Rhine and from there to the frontier of Hungary certainly the best people live whom I have been acquainted with in all the world."[25] The "collective character" known as the nation, often reinforced by mythical accounts of common origins, could likewise be found in medieval Poland and Denmark, and by the late thirteenth century the word "patria" had acquired a recognizably modern meaning, denoting not only a delineated national territory but also a loyalty to it as one's fatherland.[26]

As with King Alfred's battles against the Danes, these burgeoning national identities were often forged, defined, and strengthened as the result of conflict with an aggressive enemy or "other." In the case of England, it was the wars against the Welsh and the Scots that produced the most strident, abusive, and self-congratulatory writings in praise of Englishness. "The English," remarked one contemporary author, "like angels are always conquerors. . . . As though a swine should resist the valour of the lion, the filthy Scots attack England." "The two nations," commented Archbishop FitzRalph of Armagh, "are always opposed to one another from traditional hatred, the Irish and Scots being always enemies of the English."[27] Demonizing the enemy has always worked wonders at galvanizing self-identity, and during the twelfth century this solidarity morphed into what later became a characteristic mixture of "superiority and xenophobia" on the part of the English nation.[28] And it was in response to such arrogance and hostility that in 1290 the Treaty of Birgham insisted that Scotland was "separate and divided from England," and that in 1320 the Scots proclaimed their collective identity against the English in the Declaration of Arbroath. Made on behalf of the whole *Scottorum nacio*, it was an eloquent affirmation of the Scots' solidarity and distinctiveness, as one people under their own king.[29]

But no national animosity in Europe during an age of growing rivalries could rival that between the English and the French. In his chronicle of the reign of Louis VI, the abbot Suger of Saint-Denis recorded that in 1214 the king had appealed to "tota Francia" to protect the nation against the English (and the German) invaders, and celebrated his subsequent victory at Bouvines as follows: "neither in our days, nor in far-gone ancient times, has France achieved anything more illustrious than this, nor has she with the united forces of her members proclaimed more gloriously the honour of her power than she at one and the same time triumphed over the [Holy] Roman Emperor and the English king." The Hundred Years War between England and France further cemented these solidarities, as victories (especially Crécy, Poitiers, and Agincourt for the English, and Orléans and Castillon for the French) became defining moments in the developing national narratives, from which each side anointed its emblematic heroes and heroines (respectively the Black Prince and Henry V, and Joan of Arc and King Charles V). But this was merely a violently intensified version of a now familiar pattern: national identity defined not only intrinsically, in terms of one nation's special virtues, but also relationally, in opposition to the negative characteristics and stereotypes ascribed to "the other," which must be confronted and fought and vanquished, as in earlier times.[30]

As royal authority was solidified across large parts of western Europe during the sixteenth, seventeenth, and early eighteenth centuries, collective national feelings and awarenesses seemed correspondingly to strengthen.[31] "All nations," wrote the German theologian and astrologer Heinrich Cornelius Agrippa von Nettesheim in 1526, "have their own special customs and habits that distinguish them from one another, and can be recognized by their discourse, manner of speaking, conversation, favourite food and drink, the way they go about things, the way they love and hate or show anger and malice, and in other ways besides," and he went on to enumerate natural characteristics in a manner reminiscent of the emperor Frederick II nearly three hundred years before. Unusually, Agrippa von Nettesheim tended to be least charitable toward his own nation, but it was more common to sing the praises of one's own homeland, as did the Englishman Richard Mulcaster in 1582: "I love Rome, but London better," he wrote. "I favour Italy but England more, I honour the Latin, but I worship the English. . . . I do not think that any language, be it whatsoever, is better able to utter all arguments, whether with more pith or greater pleasure, than our English tongue is."[32] This cultural sense of competing national superiority was complemented by growing notions of separateness and uniqueness, as well as by feelings of providential approval. The result, as the Frenchman Claude Seyssel remarked in the early sixteenth century, was that "all nations and reasonable men prefer to be governed by men of their own country and nation—who know their habits, laws and customs, and share the same language and life-style as them—rather than by strangers."[33]

As in medieval times, war was a major means of firing national consciousness and its shared sense of identity, by demonizing a belligerent and predatory "other." During the reign of Queen Elizabeth I, the enemy of England ceased to be the French and became the Spanish, and Gloriana identified herself personally with the English nation in battle, as in her stirring "Armada speech" at Tilbury, when she poured "foul scorn" on any for-

eigner who would dare to try to invade her borders, and in what
became known as her "Ditchley" portrait, which depicts the monarch standing over a map of her realm. At the same time, Shakespeare's history plays promoted an enhanced sense of English
national identity: John of Gaunt in *Richard II*, acclaiming "this
royal throne of kings, this sceptred isle, . . . this blessed plot, this
earth, this realm this England"; and in *Henry V*, the eponymous
monarch, looking back on the earlier wars with France, urging
"cry God for Harry, England and St George!"[34] *Henry V* was also
full of the anti-Celtic stereotypes in existence since the twelfth
century: traitorous and opportunistic Scots, garrulous Welshmen,
and drunken, brutal Irishmen.[35] In the same way, and in response,
the Spanish came to feel their own intensified sense of collective
identity, well expressed in these words spoken at the time of the
Armada: "if the honour of Spain is at stake, what Spaniard would
fail to seek the fame and glory of his nation?" By the reign of
Philip II, such feelings were widely shared among Spaniards.[36]

Under the secular Great Power system ushered in by the Peace
of Westphalia of 1648, this sense of nations in conflict became
both more geographically widespread and emotionally charged.
Beginning in 1688, and following the Glorious Revolution, there
had been a "Second Hundred Years War" between England and
France, a succession of increasingly far-flung conflicts fed by the
bitter personal animosity between King William III and King
Louis XIV, and culminating in the Revolutionary and Napoleonic
Wars, which pitted the venerable Hanoverian George III against
the upstart emperor. Military aggression fed mutual stereotyping, with the French depicting the British as vulgar, uncultured,
perfidious, and anarchic, and the English (and increasingly the
British) regarding the French as the cringing, overtaxed, frogs-
legs-eating subjects of a diminutive despot. The result was that
for every virtue a nationalist might claim for his own side, a corresponding vice was ascribed to the other.[37] But these Franco-
British antagonisms were only the most intense and protracted
instances of a development overspreading the continent, as Prussia, Russia, and Spain were caught up in conflicts during the
eighteenth century, with the result, in each case, of a heightened
sense of national identity, focused on the person of the sovereign,

whether Frederick the Great, Catherine the Great, or the Spanish Bourbons.[38]

Beyond any doubt, some degree of collective national identity had periodically existed here and there across medieval and early modern Europe.[39] But these national solidarities and antagonisms were often complicated by alternative claims upon people's loyalties and identities.[40] The universal church under the pontificates of Gregory VII or Innocent III, and the universal monarchy of such Holy Roman emperors as Charlemagne, Otto the Great, and Frederick Barbarossa, forcefully countered the competing claims of nascent nationhood, while the presence of the church in every town and village and in the fabric of individual lives surpassed the pull of any secular power or national attachment.[41] And even if they did not engender a strong collective sense of religious identity, they may have occluded the development of an alternative secular solidarity. By the early modern period, these universalist claims had in practice (though not in theory) been given up, but the continued presence of the Holy Roman emperor in Germany and the pope in Italy were powerful restraints on the development of any strong sense of national identity in those parts of Europe. Moreover, while different versions and variants of the Christian religion may on occasion have helped to unify some nations and give them a sense of providential greatness and global destiny, as in the case of Catholic Spain under Philip II or Protestant Britain under the Hanoverians, Christianity also divided and undermined other nations from within, as in France during the second half of the sixteenth century, or in the Habsburg lands of Hungary and Bohemia during the first half of the seventeenth.[42]

In medieval and early modern Europe, then, religious identities and national identities were elaborately and intricately interconnected, and while they were sometimes mutually reinforcing, they could also militate against each other. Moreover, and as the example of the Holy Roman Empire suggests, secular power was not so much national as dynastic in its geographical grounding and articulation. At one extreme, the greatest sovereigns held their many lands as personal fiefdoms, in extended and elaborate territorial agglomerations. The emperor Charles V was the classic exemplar of such a "composite monarchy," holding dominions in what would become Austria, Hungary, Spain, Italy, Belgium, and the Netherlands, as well as acquiring rapidly expanding possessions in the Americas, each with its own laws, languages, cultures, and traditions. The same was later true of the kings of Spain, the emperors of Russia and Austria, and even the king of Great Britain, none of whom were sovereigns of a single or unitary nation.[43] In the "composite states" over which these monarchs ruled, and which had often been cobbled together by the accidents of succession or the imperatives of arranged marriages, or had been expanded thanks to victory in war, regional loyalties (and animosities) were stronger than national solidarities, as in the continuing division of ostensibly united Spain between the kingdoms of Aragon and Castile.[44] At the other end of the territorial scale, in Italy and Germany there were many great cities and minor principalities that retained their independence down to the nineteenth century, as in Florence and Milan, or in Hamburg and Cologne.[45]

At the beginning of the sixteenth century, five hundred such "political units" existed in Europe, and two hundred years later there were still enough of them to suggest that across much of the continent national identity was never more than feebly and unevenly developed.[46] And while many of these "units" clashed across the centuries, they usually did so because of the dynastic rivalries and conflicting ambitions among their ruling houses rather than because of antagonistic national feelings. The Hundred Years War may have been between "France" and "England," but the mainspring of these "national" confrontations was the royal claim made by the English monarch to the French throne. Most of the conflicts during the first half of the sixteenth century, especially those between King Francis I of France and the emperor Charles V, were fought to assert or to defend personal rights of property and succession.[47] Even by the eighteenth century, "national" confrontations were still in practice between monarchs, furthering their dynastic claims and ambitions, as in the Wars of the Spanish Succession (1701–14) and of the Austrian Succession (1740–48). These conflicts were essentially the kings' wars, and the armed forces involved were regarded as part of the royal household rather than as the embodiment of the nation. This in turn explains why lands and territories were so readily traded back and forth when peace treaties were negotiated, for they were primarily seen as bargaining counters and trophies, rather than as constituent and integral parts of a broader and more inclusive national solidarity that must be maintained at all cost.[48]

Even the undoubted horrors of the Thirty Years War only involved a relatively small proportion of the continental population in military service and fighting battles. Moreover, from medieval times to the mid-eighteenth century, most Europeans were preoccupied either with the unrelenting imperative of mere survival or, at a higher level, with "commerce, travel, and cultural and learned intercourse." Thus understood, life was (as Braudel had insisted in *The Mediterranean World*) either so localized and particular, or alternatively at such a remove, that the vague jurisdictions and often shifting boundaries of any nation rarely constrained or impinged on it.[49] During the Middle Ages (and for centuries thereafter), most people lived and died in or near the locality of their birth, and acquired little if any notion of a distant if ultimate "national" authority. At the same time, Italian and German Hanseatic merchants established far-flung trading networks in the Mediterranean and the Baltic; most of them inhabited city-states, they were happy to trade wherever markets could be found; and they were essentially cosmopolitan in their outlook and activities. Thus the medieval West was united by trade as well as by religion, both undermining and transcending any claims to territorially grounded nationhood, and this continued across much of the continent for most of the early modern period.[50]

In the same way, the majority of people across most of Europe spoke local and regional dialects rather than a "national" language. Yet whether in universities or in monasteries, the intellectual life of the continent was being conducted largely in the lingua franca of Latin, while the social and diplomatic life that took place in royal courts or castles or in country houses was routinely carried on in French.[51] Likewise, while vernacular architecture may have differed from place to place and region to region, the Gothic, the classical, and the baroque styles transcended political boundaries, whether local or national, and much the same was true in music, painting, and literature.[52] Even monarchs and princes fighting one another for dynastic advantage and territorial gain also shared a sense of belonging to a cosmopolitan, continental cousinhood of royalty, beyond particular identities or national interests. Moreover, by the eighteenth century, Britain, France, the Netherlands, Portugal, and Spain had each acquired extensive transoceanic dominions, and for those who settled or worked overseas, the focus of their abiding metropolitan loyalty was the composite monarchy and the person of the sovereign, or an extended version of a "greater" nation encompassing the whole empire.[53] So while national identities and antagonisms did develop in medieval and early modern Europe, they were nothing like as solid or as significant as they would later become.

MODERN NATIONAL IDENTITIES

The last two decades of the eighteenth century and the first two decades of the nineteenth witnessed a marked intensification of such national feelings and identities, as exemplified by the creation of the United States of America, by the renaming of the French Estates-General as the "National Assembly" in June 1789, and by the overthrow of Spanish imperial dominion in Latin America by the early 1820s.[54] The United States defined itself against the British nation (and the British king); Revolutionary and Napoleonic France did the same; and the Latin American republics defined themselves against the Spanish nation (and the Spanish king). Thus did the "age of revolutions" usher in the "age of nationalism" (the word itself was first coined in the 1790s), an epoch of nation-building and the nation-state, as new countries were created in North and South America, as "old" nations consolidated (France, Spain, Russia) or evolved and emerged as new versions of themselves (England-Britain and Austria-Hungary), as two new nations were "belatedly" unified (Italy and Germany), and as the Balkan nations won their independence from the Ottoman Empire (Greece, Albania, Bulgaria, Romania). With the exception of Spain and the Latin American republics, all these countries would be caught up in the First World War, when for the first time millions volunteered to fight out of a shared sense of national loyalty and identity, as wars of whole populations superseded the traditionally limited conflicts of armies, and when to die in battle for their country became the highest calling: *dulce et decorum est pro patria mori.*[55]

The Harvard historian Charles Maier identifies the heyday of the nation-state as beginning during the 1860s; it arose out of the notion of "territoriality," by which he means the control of "bordered political space," which created the essential framework for exploiting material resources, for wielding temporal power, and for nurturing common notions of national consciousness.[56] This, he argues, was not just a European but a global development, taking place in the United States in the aftermath of the Civil War, in Japan following the Meiji Restoration of 1868, in Germany with unification and in Italy with the Risorgimento, in the Austrian and Hungarian halves of the Habsburg Empire, and also in countries such as Canada, Mexico, Australia, and Argentina. All across the globe, Maier contends, national societies were forged and reforged during the second half of the nineteenth century, often in a sudden and violent stroke. The result was the strengthening of central government at the expense of local or regional authority; the continued mobilization of internally and externally quartered military capacity; the official co-opting of new leaders of finance and industry, science and the professions into a ruling cartel alongside the still powerful, but no longer supreme, members of the landed elite; and the development of an infrastructure based on the technologies of coal and iron as applied to long-distance transport of goods and people and on the mass production of finished products assembled by a large and increasingly unionized labor force.[57]

Hence the creation of the modern nation, as a coincidence and convergence of geographical specificity and human solidarity.[58] One indication of this convergence was an unprecedented concern with delineating borders and securing boundaries: as Lord Curzon put it in 1907, in words more portentous than he could then have known, "frontiers are indeed the razor's edge on which are suspended the modern issues of war and peace, of life and death to nations."[59] A second indication was that the lands within carefully defined and policed national borders were increasingly "pervaded" with prefectures and post offices, newspapers and telegraph networks, and, eventually, electrical power, all of which served political authority as well as everyday life. There was thus no area inside its frontiers that was beyond the state's control, and this resulted in a correspondingly enhanced consciousness of national territoriality. Of particular importance were the railroads, not only in tying nations together, as in the United States, Canada, Russia, and Australia, but also in connecting national capitals more closely with the provinces that were integrated into the "national domain," as in Germany, France, Spain, and Britain; and where the railways led, the personnel and bureaucracy of an increasingly intrusive state soon followed. Here were the acts and facts of that unprecedented process of "nation-building" to which Walter Bagehot, the journalist, commentator, and editor of *The Economist*, rightly drew attention.[60]

From this perspective, the nation as a unit of collective loyalty overwhelmed and subsumed all other shared forms of human identity, as regional, linguistic, ethnic, class, and religious solidarities were subordinated to what has been called the "nationalization of the masses." Accordingly, the years from 1870 to 1914 have been described as witnessing the transformation not only of peasants into Frenchmen (or into Germans, or Italians, or Spaniards, or Russians), but also of workers, the middle classes, and even aristocracies and monarchies into national loyalists, too.[61] There were many mechanisms and processes by which this national assimilation was accomplished: the growth in universal, state-sponsored education; the gradual expansion of the franchise to include unpropertied men and even, in some cases, women; the rise of mass political parties and charismatic political leaders such as Gladstone, Cavour, and Lincoln; the provision of state welfare programs beginning in Bismarck's Germany; the imposition by many nations of protective tariffs from the 1870s onward; the militarization of society, whereby the armed forces were no longer part of the royal household but had become the embodiment of the nation; and the invention or reinvention of a whole host of pageants, ceremonials, and festivals, centered on an hereditary or an elected head of state and providing the spectacular focus for an enhanced national consciousness and loyalty. As a result, monarchs such as the German and Russian emperors not only belonged to a pan-national, cosmopolitan, continental caste, but increasingly became the embodiment of particular nationalities.[62]

The result of these developments was that people were more than ever, as G. M. Trevelyan put it, "thinking in nationalities," and to this unprecedented mode of thinking (and feeling) historians contributed substantially, with best-selling books that appealed to the new mass reading public. Hence the rise to prominence of Macaulay and J. R. Green (and Trevelyan) in Britain, Michelet and Guizot in France, Parkman and Bancroft in the United States, and Ranke and Mommsen in Germany: each wrote narrative history tracing the rise of his respective nation and insisting on its exceptionalism and providential blessing and thus its superiority to the rivals against whom it had often made war, its military triumph having set the seal on its national consciousness and its distinct, long-lived unity as one people.[63] Such writers provided the carefully selected collective memory that became an essential prop to this new and widely shared sense of national identity, and this creation of a common national past in print was accompanied by the proliferation and cultivation of national images, myths, anniversaries, monuments, and heroes, from the German chieftain Arminius to England's King Alfred to Joan of Arc of France to America's George Washington.[64]

The nations thus created were widely regarded as the final stage of human history and as the ultimate form of human identity, and the phrase "secular religion" has been used to describe the veneration they seemed to inspire in the decades that culminated in the First World War—a religion and an identity that to many seemed far more appealing than the traditional sacred alternative, and also significantly more widespread and intense than any national feeling that had gone before.[65] For while national sentiments and identities had existed in medieval and early modern times, especially on the part of monarchs, aristocrats, warriors, writers, and priests, they were rarely if ever shared by the population as a whole. As the historian of France David Bell has observed, in words more generally applicable, "neither . . . Richelieu nor Mazarin envisioned taking entire populations . . . and forging them all, in their millions, into a single nation, transforming everything from language to manners to the most intimate ideas." They did not "imagine programmes of national education . . . , or massive political action to reduce regional differences, or laws demarcating national citizens from foreigners."[66] Yet despite its undeniable plausibility, this argument cannot be pushed too far, for just as there were significant limits to national identities during medieval and early modern times, the same was true during this later period, even as such solidarities were more developed and encompassing than before.

To begin with, the idea that the belligerents of 1914 were unified, homogeneous nations does not survive detailed examination. Consider, for example, the matter of common language, often regarded as essential to any shared sense of national identity. It certainly did not exist in the nation created by the Risorgimento. "We have made Italy," Massimo d'Azeglio observed at the time, "now we have to make Italians." With less than 5 percent of the population using Italian for everyday purposes, they had a long way to go. In France, almost half the schoolchildren engaged with French as a *foreign* language, speaking another tongue at home: dialect and patois were widespread, and in departments bordering other nations, it was often Flemish, Catalan, or German that was spoken.[67] A similar picture could be found in Germany, where in the east many spoke Polish as their first language, whereas in Alsace and Lorraine many spoke French; and in Russia, educated people conversed in French, while workers and peasants used a wide variety of Slavic languages and dialects. In Austria-Hungary, the array of different tongues was even more varied, including German, Czech, Italian, Hungarian, Polish, Croatian, and Greek, and many of the Habsburg emperor's subjects were multilingual, speaking one language at school or at work and another at home. Insofar as a common tongue could be considered an essential criterion, none of the major powers that went to war in 1914 qualified as a "nation." Apart from Portugal or Sweden, there were few linguistically homogeneous European countries.[68]

The reach of the late-nineteenth-century European state, and its capacity to exhort solidarity among its population, has often been exaggerated, for many people in these ostensibly unitary nation-states felt excluded from the allegedly shared practices and customs of national life.[69] Universal male suffrage was limited to France and Switzerland, and in Britain only 60 percent of adult males possessed the vote in 1914, while all women were disenfranchised, which meant less than one-third of the population played any part in the process of electing the government that ruled over them: so much for those "common rights and duties" that have been described as an essential attribute of nationhood and national identity.[70] Moreover, the unity of some of these "nations" was far from consensual. In the United Kingdom, there were growing demands during the late nineteenth century for independence for Scotland, Wales, and (especially) Ireland. There were similar rejections of the notion of a unified Spanish nation by the Basques and the Catalans, and of a unified Russian nation by (among others) the Finns, Armenians, Georgians, and Lithuanians. Although they owed allegiance to the same Habsburg monarch, Austria and Hungary were in many ways separate nations, and elsewhere in that empire there was growing nationalist agitation on the part of the Czechs, Ruthenians, and Croats. In reality, most countries in late-nineteenth- and early-twentieth-century Europe were polyglot and multiethnic—veritable stews of competing identities that constantly undermined the calls for national solidarity.[71]

Indeed, many of the so-called European nations that existed on the eve of the First World War still bore a significant resemblance to the composite states and multiple monarchies of the early modern period from which they had only partially evolved. The United Kingdom was a nominally unitary polity, but Scotland and Ireland retained their respective religions and educational systems, and British sovereigns crossing the border dividing England and Scotland were obliged to change their faith from Anglican to Presbyterian. The German Reich was at one level a federation of distinct princely states, with their separate royalties and legislatures, and it was further divided by religion, with the north generally Protestant and the south generally Catholic. But in addition, an unwieldy (and dysfunctional) imperial constitution, imposed in 1870, provided that the ruling Hohenzollern family were not only kings of Prussia but also emperors of Germany, thereby creating with this greater Reich conflicting loyalties even among its crowned heads. As for the Habsburgs, the Romanovs, and the Ottoman sultans, their dominions were so vast and varied that it was only the person of the sovereign that held them together. Indeed, as the full titles of their rulers suggest, Germany, Austria-Hungary, Russia, and the Ottoman realms were not single-identity nations at all: they were land-based empires where many nationalities coexisted, with varying degrees of amity and success.[72]

Farther afield, this description was equally valid in the case of China, another monstrosity of territorial agglomeration encompassing many languages, ethnicities, and religions. The same was true of the United States, which had created an empire by conquering and settling a continent, and which was becoming an increasingly diverse "melting pot," as black slaves were freed in the aftermath of the Civil War, and as immigrants poured in by the millions from southern, central, and eastern Europe in the decades before 1914. Moreover, nineteenth-century empires were not only land-based but also maritime, which further modified and undermined any clear-cut national identities. The French regarded their imperium as an integral part of their nation, be it in Indochina, Saharan or equatorial Africa, or the Caribbean, but such possessions increased the diversity and diminished the identity of de Gaulle's or Braudel's "France" a hundredfold. The British Empire spawned four great dominions, but those who settled in them could not decide whether they were British, or Canadians, or Australians, or New Zealanders, or South Africans.[73] Indeed, the very existence and expansion of so many imperial agglomerations encouraged some politicians to suppose that the nation was becoming obsolete: as Joseph Chamberlain put it in 1904, "the day of small nations has passed away; the day of empires has come."[74] The idea of the fatherland may have been sold persuasively enough to compel millions to volunteer ten years later, but in reality the First World War was a global conflict among empires that both transcended and subverted the particular claims of national identities.[75]

Empire was not the only force militating against national coherence and identity in the nineteenth century; indeed, some of the very innovations and developments that served the purposes of national integration and territorial consolidation also produced powerful countervailing effects. Consider the railways. To be sure, they helped tie nations together, but as such they were not only instruments of peace but also agents of belligerence. The First World War was famously described by the historian A. J. P. Taylor as a "war by timetable": it was the trains that transported the men and carried the matériel to the battlefronts; the Germans surrendered to the French in 1918 in a railway carriage in the Forest of Compiègne outside Paris; and the French capitulated to the Germans in the same piece of rolling stock twenty-two years later. Railways were also the agents of a new internationalism and cosmopolitanism, crossing and transcending national borders and moving people and goods between countries and across continents on a scale and with a frequency that had never been seen before. It was the railway that enabled Thomas Cook to take British tourists around Europe in their hundreds of thousands. It was the Orient Express that linked Paris directly with Constantinople. Even Queen Victoria took to the rails, often visiting the capitals, spas, and resorts of the continent under the preposterously implausible incognito of the Countess of Balmoral.[76]

Like most late-nineteenth-century European royalty, Victoria became a uniquely venerated symbol of national identity and imperial greatness; but like them again, she was also very much aware of herself as a member of the continental royal cousinhood.[77] They might now be national icons and imperial cynosures, but European royalty still intermarried, and continued to regard itself as a pan-continental caste, with interests and connections that transcended national boundaries. Queen Victoria herself was almost entirely of German ancestry, and her husband was a minor German prince; she married off her own children internationally rather than domestically, including her eldest daughter to the crown prince of Prussia. By the end of her reign there was scarcely a royal house in Europe unconnected with the British monarchy, the ties with Germany and Russia being especially close.[78] This transnational perspective was also shared by many European aristocrats: they were brought up to speak French as the language of diplomacy and high society; they were equally at ease in London or Paris or Rome or Vienna or St. Petersburg; and many of them shared a love for Italy or Greece engendered by a youthful grand tour. No less cosmopolitan were plutocratic dynasties like the Rothschilds, with their finance houses in Austria, Germany, Italy, France, and Britain, all closely linked by different branches of the family, giving their critics to believe their first loyalty was more likely to be to their fortune and their dynasty than to any mere nation-state.[79]

Transnational character and internationalist attitudes were not limited to the uppermost parts of society.[80] An essential element of the nineteenth-century bourgeois ideology was a commitment to free trade, peace, and global amity that transcended the parochial limitations of any particular nation. The Great Exhibition of 1851 may have been the symbol of Britain's economic preeminence, but it was also a celebration of common humanity, internationalism, and harmony.[81] Sons of European manufacturers and merchants traveled the world in search of markets, and this global diaspora embraced Catalans, Basques, Germans, Danes, Chinese, Parsees, Jews, Armenians, Portuguese, Greeks, Dutch, North Americans, Scots, and English. The outcome was a cosmopolitan trading community, in which nationality was often very blurred. Nor was it confined to the distant reaches of the globe: there was a German-speaking community in Manchester and also in Liverpool, where one merchant, Alfred Horn, remembered how in the course of his education at St. Edward's College he had rubbed shoulders with young men from Venezuela, Colombia, Haiti, Brazil, and Spain. "I believe," he recalled, "the old idea in mixing the young Britisher with his brothers of every climate was to make him cosmopolitan, and naturally enough we soon learned each other's language."[82] A generation earlier, Marx and Engels had made the same point in *The Communist Manifesto:* "The bourgeoisie has through its exploitation of the world market given a cosmopolitan character to production and consumption in every country," and the result was a new world order characterized by the "universal interdependence of nations."[83]

In different ways, then, nineteenth-century internationalism and imperialism both limited and undermined the nation-state and the particular national identities constructed on the basis of such territorial delineations, and it became increasingly difficult for national boundaries to impede the flow of anything during what has rightly been called an age of globalization prior to our own.[84] Consider in this regard the North Atlantic world where people, goods, capital, production techniques, and ideas all "slipped across national borders" with what has been described as "the fluidity of quicksilver." In the case of people, this initially meant immigration by Irish Catholics to the United States in the aftermath of the Potato Famine in the 1840s, followed by southern and eastern Europeans, who crossed the Atlantic in record time thanks to the advent of the steamship and the liner. Many of these millions who settled in the United States retained close family connections with their country of origin, often sending money, sometimes visiting back home, and welcoming distant relatives to join them. The result was the creation of elaborate and long-lasting transatlantic kinship networks extending far beyond the confines of any European nation, and this in turn meant the newly arrived immigrants themselves rarely assimilated as fully into the United States as the common notion of the melting pot would imply.[85]

These transnational flows of people were accompanied by equally unprecedented transnational flows of capital and commodities, resulting in a global order of industrial interdependence extending from Birmingham to Toronto, from San Francisco to Berlin, in which national boundaries and national differences often seemed to dissolve and disappear. By the late nineteenth century, visitors to the advanced industrial regions of the Old and the New World were not so much impressed by their differences, but rather by their marked similarities. They were generally to be found astride coal-bearing seams, extending from the Ruhr to Belgium and northern France, across the English Channel to the "Black Country," Manchester, and the Clyde, and thence across the Atlantic to western Pennsylvania, Ohio, and Illinois.[86] They spawned a new breed of monster city or urban agglomeration, increasingly populated in both Europe and North America by recently arrived immigrants: in the German Ruhr, for instance, over a quarter of the miners spoke Polish in 1890, and in Andrew Mellon's Pittsburgh twenty years later, the same proportion of the city's population was foreign (i.e., European) born.[87] With an attendant growth in trade unionism, engaging in ever more bitter disputes between employers and workers, organized labor also assumed an unprecedentedly international perspective. During the 1880s, the organizers of the American Knights of Labor canvassed for recruits in the English Midlands, and in the decades that followed, British and American fraternal delegates traded places at their respective annual labor union gatherings.

Likewise, when politicians, professors, policymakers, and pundits addressed the social problems of industrialization and urbanization, they did so as part of an international rather than a nationally specific conversation. Factory legislation pioneered by the British in the 1840s was replicated in France and Germany in the 1870s; Danish old-age pensions were imported (via New Zealand) to Britain: these are but two examples of a widespread pattern of national legislative borrowing that formed "a crazy quilt of transnational influences and appropriations."[88] Many individuals with particular interests and expertise in contemporary social issues moved from nation to nation and from continent to continent. Among them was William Pember Reeves, the architect of the late-nineteenth-century New Zealand labor reforms. Forced out of government in 1896, he gravitated to London, where, absorbed into Fabian circles, he lectured widely on New Zealand welfare policy. Another was William Dawson. A British economic journalist, he was dispatched to Germany in the 1880s and wrote a series of books explaining German welfare reforms to a British audience. Ties between American progressives and policymakers in England and Germany were equally close. None of these figures would have considered the nation to be the best unit of collective existence or identity in which to treat, analyze, or assess contemporary social issues: they thought about them in transnational and global terms.[89]

As Frederick Jackson Turner put it in 1891, "ideas, commodities even, refuse the bounds of a nation. . . . This is true especially in the modern world, with its complex commerce and means of intellectual connection."[90] Twenty years later, in words reminiscent of Joseph Chamberlain's, Franklin Jameson made the same point: "the nation is ceasing to be the leading form of the world's structure; organizations transcending national boundaries are becoming more and more numerous and effective."[91] He was aptly articulating the spirit of an era that saw the establishment of a host of new international bodies, among them the first European common market in 1860, comprising Britain, France, Belgium, Italy, Prussia, and Austria; the International Red Cross, which was set up three years later and based in Switzerland from the 1880s; and the Latin Monetary Union of 1865, involving France, Belgium, Italy, Greece, and Switzerland.[92] To be sure, these transnational initiatives and organizations were unable to prevent the outbreak of the First World War. But they do serve to remind us that there was a great deal more to the history (and to the habits of thought) of the nineteenth-century world than the fact of the nation-state—and the attendant national identities and national enmities.[93]

TOWARD POSTMODERN NATIONAL IDENTITIES?

This interconnected world, characterized by multinational empires and composite monarchies, and underpinned by the relatively unhindered movements of people, money, goods, and ideas across the oceans and around the globe, crashed and burned in 1914–18, with the defeat and disintegration of four great transnational, land-based, polyglot, multiethnic empires: the Russian, the German, the Austro-Hungarian, and the Ottoman. And it was Woodrow Wilson, president of the United States—one of the surviving land-based empires, with an increasingly diverse population—who insisted that the problem of pre-1914 Europe had been too many empires but too few nations.[94] Hence the task of the peacemakers was to reconstruct Europe (and the Middle East) according to "historically established lines of allegiance and nationality," by creating nation-states out of the wreckage of the former empires, as the most compelling units of collective human loyalty and identity, in which all citizens would speak the same language and come from the same stock. By better aligning nation-states with national identities, on the basis of rational principles and democratic ideals, Wilson believed that he would bring into being a new, better, and more stable world.[95] Hence the appearance (and in some cases the reappearance) in central and eastern Europe of Finland, Estonia, Latvia, Lithuania, Poland, Austria, Hungary, Czechoslovakia, and Yugoslavia (to which, farther west, would soon be added the Irish Free State), and the creation in the Middle East of a Turkish nation, and also of the League of Nations Mandates of Syria, Lebanon, Transjordan, Iraq, and Palestine.

Never before had so many names so suddenly appeared (or reappeared) on the maps of Europe and the Middle East, but in truth the peoples of these regions were still so mixed up that it was impossible to create such coherent nations (and with them identities) as envisioned by Wilson's doctrine of self-determination in all its simplistic grandeur. In 1919, the American secretary of state, Robert Lansing, asked himself, "When the President talks of 'self-determination' what unit has he in mind? Does he mean a race, a territorial area, or a community?"[96] These were good questions, which were never adequately addressed or satisfactorily answered. Sometimes strategic and diplomatic considerations were too urgent to yield to the claims of nationality: as when Germany lost lands to France and Poland, Austria to Poland, Czechoslovakia, and Italy, and Hungary to Romania, Czechoslovakia, and Yugoslavia; and as when any union between Germany and Austria was explicitly forbidden, in defiance of the principle of self-determination. For such reasons did France and Italy obtain large German-speaking populations (in Alsace-Lorraine and South Tyrol), while in Romania the acquisition of Transylvania and large swaths of Hungarian territory meant the number of native inhabitants declined from 92 percent of the population in 1914 to 70 percent in 1920.[97] But by far the greater obstacle was that the nations that were reestablished or newly created were themselves unavoidably multiethnic and multilingual. Poland, as reconstituted, contained more than two million Germans and three million Ukrainians and Belorussians; Czechoslovakia, according to Lloyd George, was a "polyglot and incoherent" amalgam of Czechs, Slovaks, Magyars, Ruthenes, and Germans;

while Yugoslavia was populated by Serbs, Croats, Slovenes, Albanians, and Hungarians. So much in practice for Woodrow Wilson's much-vaunted principle of "national self-determination": as a basis for redrawing the boundaries of postwar Europe, it was utterly impracticable and did not work.[98]

Matters were no better when the victorious powers turned to creating new nations in the Middle East, as the Ottoman Empire was partitioned with little cognizance of existing tribal solidarities or ethnic identities. When Turkey became independent, straddling Europe and Asia across the Dardanelles, it still included substantial minorities of Kurds and Armenians, who in 1920 briefly but unsuccessfully set up their own autonomous states.[99] The new nations of Lebanon, Syria, Iraq, Palestine, and Jordan were administered by France and Britain as League of Nations Mandates, but they were effectively colonies, all of them artificial constructs, devoid of any shared sense of national unity or historic or collective identity. King Faisal, the first ruler of Iraq, a nation in which Arabs and Kurds, Sunni and Shia had been summarily bundled together, was well aware of the problem:

> There is still—and I say this with a heart full of sorrow—no Iraqi people, but unimaginable masses of human beings devoid of any patriotic idea, imbued with religious traditions and absurdities, connected by no common tie, giving ear to evil, prone to anarchy, and perpetually ready to rise against any government whatsoever.[100]

It would be even worse in Palestine, where in accordance with the Balfour Declaration of 1917, the British resolved to establish "a national home for the Jewish people," while at the same time doing nothing to prejudice the civil and religious rights of the existing inhabitants, 90 percent of whom were Muslim Arabs.[101]

The result of this meddlesome mapping was that much had changed—yet very little had changed. Before 1914, the land-based polities of Europe and the Middle East were not so much nations as imperial agglomerations, with many ethnicities, languages, and religions; after 1919, the new nations of Europe and the Middle East were smaller political units, but each contained many ethnicities, languages, and religions, making it difficult to achieve any viable identity or collective sense of solidarity. At the same time, the creation by Lenin of the Union of (fifteen) Soviet Socialist Republics successfully perpetuated most of the tsarist multinational and multiethnic empire under a new Communist despotism.[102] Nor was it believed that nation-building, to the extent it was accomplished, would suffice to keep the peace that had proved so fragile in a simpler world of a few empires related by royal blood and terrifyingly inflexible alliances of mutual defense. Even Woodrow Wilson, for all his (flawed) faith in the principle of national self-determination, recognized in national autonomy a danger of national aggression that needed to be checked, and he fought to establish the League of Nations, in the hope of providing some structure of global governance.[103] The Republican administrations that succeeded Wilson were in their own way no less internationalist, as they sought to restore the global system of finance and trade, based on the gold standard, by which money and goods and people moved easily across national boundaries, as they had done before 1914. And in a very different idiom, when Eglantyne Jebb established the Save the Children Fund in 1919, she did so specifically to help alleviate the widespread postwar famine that had broken out in central and eastern Europe as a result of the Allied blockade, but more generally as "an effective assertion of the oneness of mankind [and] . . . our common humanity."[104]

The inadequacy of the nation as a redemptive form of human solidarity was thus doubted virtually as soon as it was revived; but in the aftermath of the Wall Street crash and the ensuing Great Depression, these transnational endeavors were effectively given up, and it is often argued that the 1930s suffered from the vigorous reassertion of national interests—diplomatically, militarily, and economically—amid the fatigue and fecklessness of global efforts at harmonizing the world's political and economic aspirations. The League of Nations failed to restrain national aggressors, especially Germany, Italy, and Japan, while the international financial system that had been so laboriously reconstructed during the 1920s collapsed into ruins, as autarky and national self-sufficiency became the new economic doctrines. In reality, though, it was not so much national as *imperial* interests that again reasserted themselves, the ensuing hostilities of the Second World War amounting to another global battle waged by and for empires, rather than a struggle of nations. However intense their galvanizing nationalistic rhetoric, Germany, Italy, and Japan sought to enlarge their territorial dominions in, respectively, eastern Europe, North Africa, and the Far East. Meanwhile, Britain and France sought to defend their empires in Africa from Mussolini and Hitler, and to win back the colonies they had lost to Japan in the Far East.[105] And in victory the United States and Soviet Russia greatly expanded their empires, not only as maritime powers, with their mighty fleets dominating the oceans, but also as land-based hegemons, as the ostensibly free nations of western Europe became increasingly dependent on American financial aid and military protection, and as the new nations of eastern Europe were annexed into the Communist sphere. The First World War had been a conflict of empires disguised as a conflict of nations, and the same was true of the Second.

Just as the years after 1919 had witnessed the flawed creation of nations and national identities in Europe and the Middle East, the three decades after 1945 saw similar developments, over a longer time span and a greater area of the globe, this time in Asia, Africa, and elsewhere in the Third World. The British Raj in South Asia was given its independence and divided up between India and Pakistan; the Far Eastern dominions of Britain, France, and the Netherlands were dismantled; the African empires of the European powers were brought to an end; and most of the islands in the Caribbean and the few colonies in Latin America became independent. In virtually every case, following what would become a familiar pattern, the indigenous leaders of the fight for freedom and liberation would seek to define their new nation and unify their followers by exploiting and fomenting resistance to the imperial metropolis and its local proconsular agents. And in most cases, the former colonies were launched on their way to independence with the familiar and essential accoutrements of national autonomy and identity: not just a state structure and government bureaucracy, but also flags, anthems, stamps, currency, and ceremonials, as well as foundation myths and founding fathers, all in due course to be celebrated in new statues and new national histories.[106] The singular irony is that these new nations and postcolonial identities were modeled on those very same European nations and identities as had allegedly evolved in the decades before 1914, and whose domination they had struggled to overthrow.

Yet in the Third World after 1945, as in Europe and the Middle East after 1919, these instant contrivances of overnight nationality rarely achieved the hoped-for reality of coherent unity or collective identity. Britain's Indian empire was brutally partitioned, and this was done largely (and hurriedly) on the basis of religious differences (which seemed clear) rather than of distinct national solidarities (which were far less apparent). In Africa, the colonial boundaries that subsequently became national borders had been set by the European powers when they divided up most of the continent during the late nineteenth century. Many of these boundaries were arbitrary and artificial, as they took no heed of historic precedents, local circumstances, or tribal or ethnic or religious groupings. In the case of the British colony of Kenya, for example, the mix of Lwo, Masai, Kikuyu, and Turkana tribes had no ethnic, linguistic, or historical reason to be regarded as one nation. Nor was this an atypical example. As Chief Awolowo, one of Nigeria's leading nationalists, observed in 1945, in words reminiscent of King Faisal of Iraq a generation earlier, "Nigeria is not a nation. It is a mere geographical expression." (Indeed, it contained more than two hundred ethnolinguistic groups.) Accordingly, when African colonies became African nations, they typically lacked any shared sense of history, language, or identity beyond that which had been briefly superimposed by the departing colonial power, and then been taken up by the nationalists themselves as they agitated for independence, which was often the only issue on which they could agree.[107]

Not surprisingly, it has often proved exceptionally difficult for those in charge of these new postcolonial countries to establish a common sense of national unity or collective solidarity. Attempts to create instant federations out of former British colonies that were themselves often artificial constructs met with scarcely any success: in Central Africa (Northern and Southern Rhodesia and Nyasaland), in East Africa (Kenya, Uganda, and Tanganyika), in Malaysia (Malaya, Singapore, Borneo, and Sarawak), and among the islands of the Caribbean. In three cases, they failed completely, and even in the partially successful instance of Malaysia, Singapore later withdrew.[108] Religion has failed to keep some nations together, when it might have been expected to do so, and it has also divided others, when it was clearly expected not to do so. Even while sharing the same Muslim faith, and thus an antipathy to the predominantly Hindu India, West and East Pakistan shared little else (not even a common language apart from English), and they eventually fell out, the latter becoming the separate nation of Bangladesh in 1971. Nigeria and Sudan have both sundered into a Muslim north and a Christian south: in Nigeria, the original federal structure quickly disintegrated, with Biafra seceding for a time, while in Sudan, civil war has been rife for decades, and recently the country has formally split in two.[109] Meanwhile, tribal and ethnic divisions have on occasions resulted in protracted civil wars, sometimes culminating in secession and genocide, as in Zaire, Sri Lanka, Cambodia, and Uganda.

The most recent phase of nation-founding also followed the consequence of the collapse of an empire, this time the implosion of the Union of Soviet Socialist Republics, which ended the Warsaw Pact and saw the demise of Communism. Coming into being since the fall of the Berlin Wall in 1989, these postimperial successor nations fall into six distinct categories. First are those in eastern Europe already in existence, but under the thumb of Moscow since the end of the Second World War, and now free and independent again, namely Poland, Hungary, Romania, and Bulgaria. Second are those born of some significant adjustments and dissolutions: the reconfiguration of East Germany (reunified with West Germany); the division of Czechoslovakia (peacefully sundered into the Czech Republic and Slovakia); and the breakup of Yugoslavia (brutally shattered into Bosnia and Herzegovina, Serbia and Montenegro, Slovenia, Croatia, and Macedonia). Third are the former Baltic nations, created in 1918–19 and forcibly annexed by the USSR in 1940, and now independent again, namely Estonia, Latvia, and Lithuania. Fourth are the emancipated Soviet republics bordering eastern Europe and on the Black and the Caspian Seas, namely Moldova, Ukraine, Belarus, Armenia, Georgia, and Azerbaijan. Fifth are the former Soviet republics of Central Asia, which now became independent, namely Kazakh-stan, Kyrgyzstan, Tajikistan, Turkmenistan, and Uzbekistan. And finally there is the keystone, and now the residuary legatee of the old Soviet Empire, namely Russia itself.

This was an extraordinarily sudden and rapid transforma-tion, as a new generation of European and Asian leaders sought to mobilize their peoples in mass opposition to the Commu-nist imperium. Yet it would again be a gross oversimplification to describe the motivations, trajectory, and outcomes of these revolutionary movements as the successful realization of national aspirations and identities, let alone functioning national polities. In fact, the cataclysmic events that began in 1989 were in many ways not so much national but transnational, particularly in terms of the complex interactions and coordination of the revolution-ary leaders and participants, as in the case of the links between activists in Poland and Ukraine.[110] It is also clear that the causal link between the rise of nationalism and the fall of Communism did not operate in just one direction: the breakdown of Soviet power and will (largely unanticipated by Western analysts) did at least as much to stoke the sudden upsurge of national feeling, solidarity, and identity in subject countries as nationalist senti-ment did to topple Soviet Communism. This was certainly the case in the former Central Asian Soviet republics, which had been a construct of Soviet intellectuals in the early 1920s rather than a primordial aspiration of any of those Central Asian peoples, and where nationalist sentiment was the fruit rather than the cause of Soviet collapse.[111]

To be sure, there were discernible feelings of national soli-darity in parts of eastern Europe: this was (and remains) true in Estonia, Latvia, and Lithuania, where these identities persisted during the decades of Soviet occupation, and where hostility to the USSR was strongest in 1989.[112] In the same way, the failed uprisings in Hungary (1956) and Czechoslovakia (1968) offered a unifying narrative of national suffering and striving in the minds of those peoples. But few of the countries that regained their independence in 1989 did so within the same borders as had existed in, say, 1938, and such national aspirations and solidarities as did develop were, as so often, rarely simple or straightforward.

In Poland, they relied heavily on the patronage of the Catholic Church and on the support of the native-born pope, John Paul II. In the former Soviet republics of Central Asia, Islam was a more unifying force during the initial stages of disengagement from the USSR than nationalist sentiment, which only developed later—if at all.[113] And among other new countries such as Belarus and Moldova, national identity was notional at best, while the independence of Georgia and Ukraine "was not so much about self-determination as self-preservation."[114] As for the further division of Czechoslovakia in 1992, and the brutal fragmentation of Yugoslavia between 1991 and 1999, even the smaller shards of allegedly national communities remained multiethnic, multilingual, and multireligious—characteristics they shared with most of the new nations in Europe and Asia.[115]

The contradictions, limitations, and uncertainties lingering around these new countries may also be explained in broader geopolitical terms, for they all came into being at the very moment when the nation-state as the primary unit of sovereign authority, and as a prime focus of collective identity, seemed to be increasingly in doubt and under siege. Charles Maier identifies such a trend as being discernible from the 1960s onward, and one that has become increasingly pronounced in recent decades as traditional notions of bounded and autonomous territoriality have been significantly eroded.[116] The historical and geographical coincidence of political power and popular consciousness of affiliation—the conjuncture he believed to have been so fundamental during the heyday of the nation-state and national identities—have been seriously undermined as national sovereignty has been ceded to ever-proliferating supranational agencies and global organizations, ranging from the United Nations and the European Union to the IMF and the World Bank; as immigrants move back and forth across national boundaries in ever greater numbers, from Mexico to the United States and from eastern to western Europe; as media moguls and multinational banks and corporations have put themselves beyond the reach of national jurisdictions or regulation; as worldwide threats such as climate change and international terrorism demand transnational solutions; as heavy industry has been superseded by the new technologies of semiconductors and a global economy based on digital data transmission; and as information can cross the world immediately and instantaneously.[117]

From this perspective, and despite the recent and unprecedented increase in their number to almost two hundred, nation-states and national identities are widely regarded as being among the most threatened species of the still-emerging post-Communist, postcolonial, and globalizing world. As Benedict Anderson has famously (and provocatively) argued, nations should not be seen as eternal and precisely defined units of territorial sovereignty and collective solidarity, but rather as "imagined communities": as transient, provisional, ephemeral, made-up associations, encompassing a multitude of shifting boundaries and subjective identities—but never for long. By these lights, there was (and is) nothing absolute, uniform, or immutable about the late-nineteenth- or early-twentieth-century European nation-state, or about those countries that have cropped up across and around the globe in the hundred years since. On the contrary, "the nation" was (and is) merely one temporary and contingent way of organizing, governing, and identifying large numbers of peoples, which rested (and rests) on the uncertain foundations of manufactured myths and invented traditions, and which was (and is) never as homogeneous or as unified as those earlier national historians (or later scholars such as Charles Maier) had been inclined to insist.[118] From the 1970s onward, many historians, no longer concerned to reinforce national identity in the way that their predecessors had done, have gone about exploding these myths and undermining these traditions. Far from celebrating them as eternal verities, historians are now more likely to describe nations and the identities and loyalties they claim as contested, disaggregated, and disputed phenomena, and by approaching these once-hallowed subjects so skeptically, they are in their own way intensifying the crises of legitimacy and identity through which many countries, nations, and states are passing.[119]

Taking the long view and a cosmopolitan perspective, it is clear that in recent times, nation-states and national identities have for the most part appeared, vanished, and reemerged so frequently and so variously as to cast serious doubt on nationality's past and present claims to being some sort of platonic ideal of human affiliation or even the preeminent and most enduring form of human solidarity.[120] There are multiethnic agglomerations, such as the United States, China, and post-Communist Russia, that are territorial empires presenting themselves as unitary nations.[121] There are "old" and more recent European nations, such as Britain, France, Spain, Germany, and Italy, but all of them face serious challenges to their identities from separatists or religious minorities or otherwise unassimilated groups or incomplete reunification (problems sometimes acknowledged bureaucratically, as with the establishment by President Sarkozy of France of the clumsily but revealingly entitled Ministry of Immigration, Integration, National Identity, and Codevelopment).[122] There are the new—or re-created—nations in central and eastern Europe, and in Asia on the borders of Russia, whose cohesiveness and sustainability are far from certain. There are the artificial constructs of the Middle East, where in one symptomatic case, namely Iraq, identity "remains contested between Islamists, secularists and the military, and between ethnic Turks and Kurds."[123] There are the no less artificial constructs of Africa, where some nations scarcely hold together at all, and the former colonies in Asia and the older republics in Latin America, which are still struggling to find any shared sense of collective solidarity.[124] There are former imperial dominions such as Canada, Australia, and New Zealand, which have abandoned the traditional paradigm of "from colony to nation" and are now trying to include their native peoples in a new and more inclusive national narrative—with varying degrees of awareness and success. And so on . . .

As Eric Hobsbawm noted in 1992, in words even more valid today, we live in "a world in which probably not much more than a dozen states out of some 180 can plausibly claim their citizens coincide in any real sense with a single ethnic or linguistic group."[125] Two conclusions follow. One is that few nations have ever aligned "in any real sense with a single ethnic or linguistic group": it is too easy to exaggerate the homogeneity of nations and the solidarity of national identities in the decades before 1914, and it is even more mistaken to do so since. One must acknowledge there has never been a golden age of nation-states and national identities, even—indeed especially—today when there are more of them than ever before and when more of them are "failing" then ever before.[126] A second conclusion is that the appearance of so many new nations and identities in the Middle East, Africa, Asia, and eastern Europe has not been a belated "catching up" by the rest of the globe according to the pattern initially established in northern and western Europe before the First World War. The early twentieth century was not characterized by homologous nation-states and homogeneous national identities across the globe, nor is the early twenty-first century either. As the late Clifford Geertz rightly noted, "the illusion of a world paved from end to end with repeating units that is produced by the pictorial conventions of our political atlases . . . is just that—an illusion."[127] Can it, then, be seriously maintained that "the nation" is now (or has ever been?) the preeminent form of collective human identity?

WHAT IS A NATION?

In 1882, just over a decade after France's humiliating defeat in the Franco-Prussian War, and less than ten years before the birth of Charles de Gaulle, another Frenchman, the theologian Ernest Renan, delivered a celebrated address at the Sorbonne entitled "Qu'est-ce qu'une nation?" in which he took up several familiar definitions of nineteenth-century nationhood and national identity, and subjected all of them—except one—to a devastating critique. To begin with, he insisted, a nation was not the same thing as a race, since all modern nations were ethnically mixed: Germany was Germanic, Celtic, and Slavic, and even France was peopled by those of Celtic, Iberian, and Germanic ancestry. Nor, Renan went on, was a nation the same as its language: otherwise how could the separation of the United States from the United Kingdom, or the South American colonies from Spain, be accounted for—or, conversely, the unity of Switzerland despite its linguistic variety? Nor could a common religion be considered an essential, unifying national basis, since confessional boundaries and national boundaries rarely coincided or aligned. As for "common interests," a customs union or Zollverein was scarcely the same thing as a "patria" or fatherland. And as for "geography," the "living space" of nations, as embodied in their allegedly "natural frontiers," had always been subject to change. Having demolished these inadequate definitions of nationhood, Renan advanced his own, and it bears a striking similarity to that which de Gaulle would later espouse and evoke. A nation, Renan insisted, was above all a state of mind and an expression of the collective will: drawing from the past a shared "store of memories," especially of "the sacrifices that have been made"; displaying in the present "the agreement, the desire to continue a life in common"; and in looking to the future, accepting and recognizing "the sacrifices the nation is prepared to make" again, as it has done before.[128]

Before discussing the five faulty definitions of nationhood that he would debunk prior to advancing his own, Renan had bravely observed that "forgetting, and I would even say historical error, are an essential factor in the creation of a nation, and thus the advances in historical study are often threatening to a nationality." (Eric Hobsbawm's translation of the first part of this observation is more tellingly abrupt: "getting its history wrong is part of being a nation.")[129] Renan was—rightly—of the view that most of the criteria by which nations could be defined were historically unconvincing or unsustainable, but he erred in supposing that his own alternative definition was somehow immune from the same problems. Shared memories, an agreed life in common, and a willingness to make future sacrifices: all these deemed by Renan to be more plausibly constitutive of the nation and of national identity can also be shown to be partial, limited, selective, and timebound, and they have been as much undermined by "advances in historical study" as the definitions Renan himself demolished. For if in one guise, history has often been the willing and complicit handmaid to the creation of national identities and the celebration of national consciousnesses, in another, more skeptical guise, it is the implacable enemy of the selective myths, the sanitized memories, and the carefully edited narratives that galvanize collective resolve and sustain national solidarities over time. As Sir Michael Howard has noted, history that challenges the comfortable assumptions and providential narratives of a shared group identity may be painful, but it is also a sign of maturity and wisdom, and this is as true for the solidarities of nations as for those of religions.[130]

Yet like all the aggregations discussed here, religion and nation also differ markedly in their nature and their essence.[131] Religious identities derive much of their appeal from their claims to universal rather than to particular truths, which are (at least in theory) applicable to everyone willing to convert and believe. Here, for example, is Saint Paul, asserting the claim of Christianity to encompass and override all lesser and alternative identities: "There is neither Jew nor Greek," he observed, "there is neither slave nor free, there is neither male nor female, for you are all one in Christ Jesus." Indeed, Christ's final commission to the apostles was to "go forth and teach all nations."[132] By contrast, and indeed by definition, a nation sets out deliberately to exclude from its collective embrace all those who do not live within its boundaries (and on occasions also some of those who do), and since that means the vast majority of people, the result is that no nation, however large or rich or powerful or imperial, can ever comprise more than a minority of the human population. So while religious collectivities claim transnational, continental, or indeed global reach, and have done so across more than one millennium, national identities are much more local, particular, and temporally circumscribed. As such they are in many ways very different forms of collective human solidarity.[133]

Such variety helps explain why identities are not like hats, which can only be worn one at a time, to the exclusion of any or all others. Most people in the past, like most people in the present, maintain several loyalties, attachments, and solidarities (of which religion and nation are but two) simultaneously, and any one of which might at any one time be foremost in their minds, as occasion suggested and circumstances required.[134] Pace Ian Tyrrell, this means it is not at all self-evident that collective identities are now or have ever been "primarily national ones." Only in those relatively recent and rare periods of total war have the claims of the nation (or at least the claims of something presented by its leaders as "the nation") become paramount and overriding. Whatever politicians or magistrates may declare the demands and imperatives of the nation to be, day-to-day life for most people in most times is not dominated by these concerns. Indeed, in every "mature national community," there is a "crisscrossing of loyalties" that make up the fabric of people's individual and collective lives.[135] In times of peace, national identity recedes, and other solidarities of loyalty, awareness, and calls to action may seem more compelling and more convincing. Among these are the alternative collectivities of class, gender, and race, which, unlike religion, are secular in their concerns, and unlike the nation, are (at least in principle) global in their reach. It is to these alternative identities that we now turn.[136]

THREE

Class

Classes struggle, some classes triumph, others are elimi-
nated. Such is history.

—Mao Zedong,
"Cast Away Illusions: Prepare for Struggle"
(August 14, 1949), in *Selected Works*
of Mao Tse-tung, vol. 4

"Class" was perhaps overworked in the 1960s and 1970s,
and it had become merely boring. It is a concept long past
its sell-by date.

—E. P. Thompson,
"The Making of a Ruling Class,"
Dissent (Summer 1993)

ON AUGUST 28, 1844, two young intellectuals joined each other
for drinks at the Café de la Régence on the Place du Palais-Royal
in Paris. Their names were Friedrich Engels and Karl Marx, and
they had first met in Germany two years previously, but that "distinctly chilly" encounter had given no indication that one of the
most portentous collaborations and influential literary friendships
of modern times had just begun.[1] Despite the hostile view they
shared of the middle classes, both men came from quintessen-
tially bourgeois backgrounds. Engels, born in 1820 in the Rhineland town of Barmen, was the son of a successful cotton-spinning
entrepreneur who owned factories in Germany and Manchester,
while Marx, who was two years older and another Rhinelander,
was the son of a Jewish attorney who was also a vineyard owner.
But by the time they joined each other at the café, both men had
rebelled against their comfortable upbringings. Engels had been
initiated into the cotton business, and had reluctantly undertaken
compulsory Prussian military service, but he soon gravitated, via
studies at Berlin University and his first prolonged period of residence in Manchester, overseeing family interests, toward radical politics, dissenting journalism, and Hegelian thought. Marx,

meanwhile, having turned his back on the study of the law, completed a doctorate in philosophy, his thinking likewise influenced by Hegel, and had also taken up subversive newspaper writing, briefly editing the Cologne-based *Rheinische Zeitung*, until it was closed down by the Prussian authorities.[2]

This second meeting between Marx and Engels was more agreeable than the chilly standoff their first had been, and in a mood of "cheerfulness and goodwill" they began a clutch of literary projects.[3] The first, of which Engels was sole author, would be *The Condition of the Working Class in England*, published in 1845. Drawing on his experiences in the family business in Manchester, he depicted the "shock city" of that decade as bitterly polarized between rapacious mill owners and exploited industrial workers. Engels believed this cleavage into "two great camps" was so deep that the bourgeoisie and the proletariat existed in a state of intransigent antagonism and perpetual conflict, and this description persuaded Marx that the alienated, impoverished industrial working class would become the instrument of a final transformative historical revolution.[4] The second work, which Marx and Engels wrote together between 1845 and 1847, was *The German Ideology*, in which they developed the idea that social structures were the products of economic and technological forces, and that history should be understood as an unending struggle between different groups of people in different economic circumstances.[5] Their third effort, also jointly authored, appeared early in the revolutionary year of 1848, when for a time it seemed as though traditional authority was collapsing across much of Europe, and was entitled the *Manifesto of the Communist Party*. "The history of all hitherto existing society," Marx and Engels confidently proclaimed, "is the history of class struggles," and it was a history leading inexorably toward a revolutionary future in which the reviled bourgeoisie would be overthrown and cast aside: "The proletarians have nothing to lose but their chains," the authors concluded. "They have a world to win. Working men of all countries unite!"[6]

This rousing, bravura, fortissimo exhortation was written by Marx and Engels at the end of a remarkable period of collaboration, drawing upon a wide range of legal, historical, philosophical, sociological, theological, and political works in French, German, and English, from Hegel to Saint-Simon, Adam Smith to Feuerbach, Proudhon to Fourier.[7] Of all those writings, *The Communist Manifesto* would most significantly influence the course of twentieth-century history, not just within Europe but also around the world. For in that crusading and coruscating polemic, Marx and Engels sought to provide the most complete and comprehensive analysis of past human identities, both on their own terms and as they related to those of the present, thereby also foretelling how the inherent conflict in these existing solidarities might—indeed, must—define the future. In predicting that all current bourgeois societies must eventually be vanquished by an energized, mobilized, and self-consciously revolutionary proletariat, Marx and Engels would eventually inspire legions of political activists in Europe, Asia, Africa, and both North and South America who dreamed of helping move history ahead toward the fulfillment that Marx and Engels had envisioned for it, by overthrowing the much-reviled bourgeoisie and ushering in the socialist utopia of a classless society. Marx and Engels would also influence two generations of Western scholars and academics, many of whom would espouse their view that the history of all human societies should indeed be understood and explained in terms of class identity and class struggle.

Their claims for the importance of class as the preeminent form of collective solidarity were breathtaking in their historical scope, and they were no less audacious in their insistence that it would be the working class that would eventually bring into being a new future that had to be struggled for and won, yet that was also, paradoxically, predestined and foreordained. But as many would-be revolutionaries would later discover, this analysis and these predictions raised more questions than they answered. Why did Marx and Engels believe class was the most potent and portentous of all forms of collective identity? What did they mean by class, how had it fulfilled, and how would it fulfill, the momentous historic tasks that the authors had assigned to it? Why and how did later leaders take up their call to bring about a revolution against the bourgeoisie and in the name of the proletariat? Did their triumphs, beginning in Russia in 1917, conform to the

Marxist model of revolutionary working-class solidarity, ushering in the proletarian millennium and the classless society? In what ways did the subsequent global spread of Communism also come to influence how history was written, or rather rewritten, as the story of class identities? What has happened to these class-based solidarities, and to these class-cased accounts, since the fall of the Berlin Wall in 1989? And when all is said and done, has class ever been the most important and influential form of collective human identity and consciousness in the ways that Marx and Engels and their disciples, both practical and academic, repeatedly insisted that it was?

CLASS AS IDENTITY

By the time they had been put forward so forcefully and influentially in *The Communist Manifesto*, claims that class was the preeminent form of human aggregation and awareness were scarcely novel. Albeit less stridently and polemically, similar views had been anticipated and advanced by British political economists such as Adam Smith and David Ricardo, by German philosophers such as Hegel and Feuerbach, and by French historians and social theorists such as Thierry, Guizot, and Saint-Simon.[8] But Marx and Engels were the first to assert the much larger claim that class identity and class conflict were the keys to understanding *everything* significant that had happened in the past, that was going on in the present, and that would occur in the future. In so doing, they offered a wholly new perspective on collective solidarities, for by asserting the primacy of class, they directly challenged the conventional—albeit competing—wisdoms which held that religion, or the nation, were of paramount importance. Instead, Marx and Engels maintained that class was of much greater salience and significance, in part because it was a secular rather than a faith-based identity, which recognized the primacy of material interests and circumstances, and also because it was potentially a global solidarity, transcending the petty parochialisms of national loyalties and national boundaries.

In prioritizing the conflicts of classes over the confrontations of creeds, Marx and Engels were also rejecting the assumptions and practices of their own families and their faiths. Both had been brought up in the North German Protestant tradition, Engels because his forebears subscribed to the aggressive form of Pietism characteristic of Barmen and its neighborhood, and Marx because his parents had converted from Judaism to Christianity. He himself had been baptized at the age of six, and his senior thesis at his gymnasium had been entitled "Religion: The Glue That Binds Society Together."[9] But from the mid-1830s to the mid-1840s, both men were caught up in the heated debates among German intellectuals as to whether Hegel had successfully reconciled philosophy and religion; independently, Marx and Engels concluded that he had not. By now self-confessed atheists, they came to despise religion as irrational and as an illusion and, even worse, as a hypocritical justification for the prevailing economic, social, and political inequality.[10] Thus understood, Christianity was no more than a "bourgeois prejudice": Engels deemed it "as full of holes as a sponge," while Marx dismissed it as "the sigh of the oppressed creature, the heart of a heartless world, and the soul of soulless conditions." In short, it was "the opium of the people"—a regrettable narcotic engendering superstition and delusion, rather than a significant basis for human belonging, aggregation, and identity.[11]

Likewise, by insisting that the solidarities and conflicts of class were more significant than the unity and struggles of nations, Marx and Engels rejected such contemporary theorists of nationalism as Mazzini in Italy, and Fichte and Treitschke in Germany, and with them the evolving political culture (and political cult) of the nineteenth-century nation-state.[12] They were prepared to concede that the bourgeoisie had helped to bring it into being, but as rootless, exiled, itinerant intellectuals, Marx (who would die a stateless person) and Engels (who spent more of his life in Britain than in Germany) were no more sympathetic to nations and nationalism than they were to the middle classes. They thought it more significant, and more hopeful, that in addition to creating the nation-state, the bourgeoisie had brought into being a more extensive and cosmopolitan capitalism, which had called forth what was—or what must eventually become—a more extensive and cosmopolitan proletariat. This was what Marx and Engels meant when they claimed, in *The Communist Manifesto*, that workers "had no country" and that their natural concerns were "the common interests of the entire proletariat, independent of all nationality." "National differences," they went on, "are daily vanishing, owing to the development of the bourgeoisie. . . . The supremacy of the proletariat will cause them to vanish still faster."[13] Or, as Marx would put it in a later *Manifesto Addressed to the Working People of Austria*, "the age of division into nationalities is past, the principle of nationality survives only on the agenda of reactionaries . . . . The labour market knows no national frontiers, world trade crosses all language barriers."[14]

In trying to understand, explain, and predict the evolution of past, present, and future solidarities and societies, Marx and Engels accordingly believed that it was essential to deal with the lives and consciousnesses of entire populations, not just with those of their religious or political or military leaders. But how were the deeds and identities of whole peoples to be comprehensively described and convincingly understood? Following the interpretation earlier advanced by Adam Smith and developed by David Ricardo, Marx and Engels began by classifying individuals into distinct collective categories, according to neither their religious faith nor their nationality, but as determined by their relations to the "means of production." On this basis, they derived three such groupings: feudal landowners, who drew their unearned income from their estates as rents; bourgeois capitalists, who obtained their earned income from their businesses in the form of profits; and proletarian workers, who made their money by selling their labor to their employers in exchange for their weekly wages. According to Marx and Engels, these three classes and the conflicts and battles among them, which ultimately derived from their divergent relations to the means of production, and which had raged unabated across the centuries, had been the essential dynamo of the historical process.[15]

These primordial classes, as Marx and Engels discerned them, and as delineated in *The German Ideology*, could be understood in two distinct but complementary ways: as what they termed class "in itself," and also as what they called class "for itself."[16] Class "in itself" was no more than an objective social category, which grouped individuals together on the basis of their shared economic characteristics: the source of their income, the extent of their wealth, and the nature of their occupation. Thus regarded, these classes had no collective identity or shared sense of their own solidarity, history, prospects, or objectives. On the contrary, they were merely inert social and inanimate statistical aggregations; they did not do, feel, desire, or achieve anything together; they were not locked in perpetual struggle with other classes; and so they neither made history nor changed its course. As such, these classes anticipated and resembled the groupings in the national census. They also lie behind the work of sociologists who continue to refine and debate the number and nature of the classes to be found in modern societies, and the degree of social mobility between them. Such classes will always be with us, as long as there remain inequalities in income, differences in occupation, and variations in wealth, which can be objectively observed and precisely measured.[17]

But Marx and Engels were less interested in class as objective social description than as a subjective social formation; thus they sought to explore and explain how, why, and when class "in itself" became energized and vivified into class "for itself." By what processes, on what occasions, and with what results, they asked, did these supine social categories become enlivened and transformed into a community of historical actors, who became aware of their common circumstances, shared identity, collective history, group trajectory, and mutual objectives? According to Marx and Engels, the answer lay in the perpetual tussle among landowners, capitalists, and laborers over rents, profits, and wages. Sooner or later, they believed, this economic contest for the spoils and the gains of production was bound to result in social conflict, which would in turn lead to political confrontation.[18] Thus regarded, these struggles were both caused by and helped to consolidate that active, adversarial sense of collective solidarity known as class "for itself" (Marx's original formulation), or as "class consciousness" (the fashionable phrase of the 1960s, earlier popularized by Georg Lukács), or as "class identity" (as we would most likely put it today).[19] Class formation, or the making of a class, was the shorthand term employed to describe this shared process of self-discovery and self-actualization. Thus transformed, energized, and brought into being, classes ceased to be lifeless and inert sociological categories: over time, they became active forces and historical agents, as they acquired a sense of shared identity, discovered where their rational self-interests lay, and did battle with each other in order to promote them and realize them.

According to Marx and Engels, the climax of these class conflicts was the sudden, dramatic upheaval of revolution, when the structure of society was completely transformed, when a ruling class was vanquished and overthrown, and when the balance of economic, social, and political power shifted irrevocably from the defeated class on the way down and toward the triumphant class on the way up. Moreover, these revolutions would happen in an ordered and preordained sequence, with bourgeois revolutions (which had already taken place in some countries, and would soon occur elsewhere) followed by proletarian revolutions (which had not yet happened anywhere, but would eventually take place everywhere). Bourgeois revolutions had previously occurred when the new, rising capitalist middle class had overthrown the traditional, declining landed aristocracy, thereby ending "all feudal, patriarchal, idyllic relations" between people. This had first happened in England during the 1640s, then in North America in the aftermath of 1776, and most recently in France following the events of 1789. The modern bourgeois world, of which Marx and Engels were themselves both privileged products but also fierce critics, and which they grudgingly recognized as an extraordinary accomplishment and unprecedented achievement, was essentially the creation of these earlier upheavals. Hence their hostile yet admiring observation that in transforming the modern world, "the bourgeoisie, historically, has played a most revolutionary part," and their certainty that in 1848 another bourgeois revolution would take place, this time in Germany.[20]

Marx and Engels believed that another stage in this class-based process of revolutionary historical change was still to come, for in creating the modern world of industrial capitalism, the bourgeoisie had unwittingly "called into existence" those very people that would turn out to be its own nemesis, namely "the modern working class, the proletariat." For the result, as was daily made plain to Engels in contemporary Manchester, was that "society is more and more splitting into two great hostile camps, into two great classes directly facing each other."[21] As relations between capitalists and laborers became more antagonistic and confrontational, and as wages were driven inexorably downward so as to increase profits, Marx and Engels believed the new, expanding, factory-based working class would eventually rise up and overthrow the hated and hostile bourgeoisie in a second sequence of revolutions that next time would be proletarian—and universal. Just as the bourgeoisie had been predestined to vanquish the aristocracy, so too the industrial working class was predestined to overthrow the bourgeoisie: "its fall and the victory of the proletariat are inevitable." Judging the time to be ripe in early 1848, once the bourgeois revolution had taken place in Germany, it was to this portentous task of remaking society for a second and final time that Marx and Engels now exhorted the "workers of the world." And when the proletariat succeeded in this final, global revolution, the result would be a socialist utopia, in which the state structure and class identities would become redundant and wither away, to be replaced by "an association in which the free development of each is the condition for the free development of all."[22]

Despite the passion and force of their rhetoric, Marx and Engels never fully worked out their ideas about class as the preeminent form of collective identity and as the prime mover of change over time. Nor could they have done so, for their attempts to explain, and to predict, all of human history on the basis of the three distinct classes they believed to be in perpetual, sequential, and revolutionary conflict were deeply flawed.[23] One of their underlying suppositions was that economic activity and economic growth proceeded in an essentially linear way, driving social change in one direction only, namely toward class formation, class identity, and class conflict; yet the patterns of economic development, and of transformations in the mode of production, have never been that neat or coherent. The growth of the medieval economy, the advent of capitalism, the coming of the Industrial Revolution, the rise of new technologies during the late nineteenth and early twentieth centuries, the subsequent expansion of consumer-oriented industries, the decline of traditional heavy industry since 1945, and the IT revolution of recent decades: all these phases of economic change were complex, varied, localized, and often gradual developments. "Even if," as the sociologist W. G. Runciman puts it, "the story is a story about the success of Europe only, to tell it as a unilinear progression from 'ancient' slavery to 'medieval feudalism' to 'modern' capitalism is to oversimplify it far beyond what the evidence can bear."[24] And this, in turn, meant that changes in the economy were never so momentous, straightforward, or pervasive as to bring about those homogeneous, collective consciousnesses among landowners, or capitalists, or laborers, much less the perpetual conflict that Marx and Engels and their heirs said made history go.[25]

A further problem was their lack of precision concerning these three classes and the relations among them. Was the aristocracy exclusively supported by rental income from their estates, or did its members also enjoy the profits from capitalistic enterprises? Had they been vanquished by the bourgeois revolutions, or were they still in the nineteenth century a force to be reckoned with? As for the bourgeoisie, was it primarily national or cosmopolitan in its geographical salience? Were those who belonged to it so distinct from the aristocracy, even as they bought their way into land and married their children off to patricians? Were they financiers or industrialists or professionals? How had they become, or did they ever become, revolutionary? Were self-styled intellectuals members of the bourgeoisie (despite the fact that they did not control the means of production), or might they decide to join the proletariat (even though they were not industrial laborers)?[26] As for the proletariat, the vagueness of this concept and categorization is well exemplified in the concluding sentences of *The Communist Manifesto*, which have been described as "a transparent falsehood in the interests of rhetoric."[27] Who were these "workers," did they all share the same relationship to the means of production, and what were their connections to their economic and social superiors? In which parts of "the world" were they to be found, and how might it be possible to "unite" and unify such disparate and disconnected groups? Would their leaders be proletarian, or would they come from another class? What were the "chains" with which the workers of the world were imprisoned, and how would they be broken? The answers to these important questions were more varied and complex than Marx or Engels would ever allow.

This in turn meant they failed to understand that most societies comprised a complex hierarchy of ranks, levels, and gradations, which melded and merged imperceptibly one into another across the boundaries of what Marx and Engels believed were these three impermeable and antagonistic class identities. As the complex residential patterns of cities, towns, and villages made plain, people were rarely cut off from each other in homogeneous, hermetically sealed suburbs or settlements, which meant there were many internal divisions within their three ostensibly uniform and united classes that Marx and Engels ignored: between aristocrats and landed gentry, between bankers and businessmen, between industrialists competing for the same market, and between the many different layers of skilled and unskilled labor. Nor could the aristocracy, bourgeoisie, and proletariat be directly elided into partisan political activists or organizations, and there would never be one single historical example of "all" the bourgeoisie or "all" the proletariat embracing revolutionary doctrines. Finally, Marx and Engels were mistaken in asserting that their three classes, based on specific relationships to the means of production, were more important than individual identities more usually expressed in patterns of consumption. For most people, work has only ever been part of their life (especially when it is seasonal, casual, or intermittent), and has never been the sole determinant of how they see themselves, or themselves in relation to others.[28]

The reality of these more complex and varied patterns of economic development also meant the existence of other anomalous classes and groups whose existence Marx and Engels were grudgingly compelled to recognize, yet whose relations to the means of production did not fit into their simple tripartite scheme. There were the agrarian peasantry, rural laborers and farm workers, who were compelled to endure what Marx and Engels dismissed as "the idiocy of rural life": they were neither urbanized nor industrialized proletarians, yet they formed the largest single occupational group in the mid-nineteenth century, not just in Europe, but around the world, and they would continue to do so well into the twentieth century.[29] There were the petty bourgeoisie, who were urbanized but not industrialized, and who were neither wholly proletarian (though some worked with their hands) nor fully bourgeois (though others, on a small scale, did own means of production), and whose numbers greatly expanded during the closing decades of the nineteenth century. And at the very bottom of society was the "lumpenproletariat," who had given up on finding employment altogether, and whom Marx and Engels wrote off as "that passively rotting mass."[30] None of these classes, they concluded, had any serious revolutionary potential, but this would not matter, since Marx and Engels predicted they would all disappear as industrial capitalism inexorably advanced. It was a view of the future that would prove completely mistaken.[31]

The efforts of Marx and Engels to endow their three chosen classes with collective identities and clear trajectories as the drivers of past, present, and future change owed more to their powerful but reductive imaginations and to their engaged and impassioned rhetoric than to the refractory and complex nature of historical reality; and for the same reasons, their understanding of the recent past was equally flawed. They interpreted the French Revolution of 1789 as a major historical discontinuity, by arguing that a rising and increasingly unified middle class had overthrown a declining and enfeebled nobility, and had "abolished feudal property in favour of bourgeois property."[32] Yet in reality there was no such stark division between the middle and upper classes, and there was no such burgeoning capitalist class, eager to pioneer industrial progress, while those few who were formally described as bourgeois were "a legally defined social category which granted the non-noble elites of many towns privileges similar to the aristocracy." In 1789 and across the ensuing decade, none of the major players in the Revolution and its aftermath claimed to be bourgeois or to be acting on behalf of a social grouping to which that name was applied. As late as the 1830s, industry had made little progress, and France remained a predominantly agrarian nation, governed by—and in—the interests of a largely traditional elite of landed notables. Only during a brief period, from the 1820s to the 1840s, did a body of literature emerge, produced by liberal politicians and writers such as Thierry and Guizot, implausibly casting the French bourgeoisie as the anti-aristocratic heroes of

1789.[33] Yet it was this flawed and polemical interpretation, written with immediate political objectives in mind, that Marx and Engels mistakenly accepted and exaggerated and wrote into their own work.[34]

In the same way, their hopeful predictions that 1848 might witness a continent-wide proletarian revolution, in the aftermath of the German bourgeois revolution, were based on Engels's serious misreading of the situation in Manchester, which Marx had uncritically accepted. Following his initial sojourn in the city, Engels had taken away an exaggerated picture of proletarian and bourgeois class solidarity and of the conflict between them. Beyond doubt, Manchester was the largest industrial metropolis devoted to the manufacture of cotton, and it had grown with unprecedented rapidity since the 1800s. But the economic and occupational structures were more varied than Engels appreciated, for there were also many retail, service, construction, and distribution businesses.[35] Moreover, the social cleavages were less marked than he claimed, and they would lessen still further when the economic downturns of the 1840s were past and the workers became (contrary to his hopes and expectations) better off. Relations between employers and their men were also more nuanced and less distant, thanks to common religion, shared political loyalties, and the local celebration of civic milestones or great national events.[36] The two separate, sundered collective aggregations Engels claimed to discern in Manchester were in reality neither wholly homogeneous nor invariably antagonistic, for as was also the case with the assumed solidarities and antagonisms of religions and nations, there were many connections and conversations across these allegedly all-encompassing identities and impermeable boundaries of class.

Engels also confused the broader implications of developments in Manchester with the process of industrialization that was already taking place in Britain, and was now starting to happen elsewhere in Europe. To begin with, he failed to appreciate that Manchester was unusual among large British industrial cities, for in many of them, such as Birmingham, the units of production were small workshops rather than factories, which meant relations between men and their masters were correspondingly closer. In addition, Engels did not realize that industrial cities (and industrial production) were not typical of mid-nineteenth-century Britain. Scarcely 10 percent of the nation's working population was factory-employed, and since Britain boasted the most advanced economy in the world, this meant the percentage was even lower across the continent. Despite the hopes of Marx and Engels to the contrary, neither the whole of Britain nor the whole of Europe was in the process of becoming like Manchester, and it was a serious mistake to inflate the unique history of this small part of the British working class into a universal template of global proletarian development. Yet it was only on the basis of such an unrealistic view that they could ever have entertained the implausible hope that in 1848 vast numbers of industrial workers across the whole of the continent would emerge from their factories to stage a unified proletarian revolution against the bourgeoisie, and thereby usher in the socialist utopia.[37]

The arguments that Marx and Engels advanced for the primacy of class identities over those of religion or nation, and for the unique importance of class conflict in driving the historical process, were thus highly tendentious. As the (formerly Marxist) historian Gareth Stedman Jones has written, "much of what was first put forward in the *Manifesto* and later accepted as a commonsense understanding of the making of the modern world belongs more to the realm of mythology than fact."[38] By the end of 1848, the year when it was predicted with quasi-millenarian anticipation that everything would change in Europe as a bourgeois revolution in Germany would be followed by its proletarian successor, the traditional forces of authority successfully reasserted themselves across the continent, and Marx grudgingly admitted that it had been premature to claim in the *Manifesto* that the "formation of the proletariat into a class, [the] overthrow of the bourgeois supremacy, [and the] conquest of political power by the proletariat" had been imminent.[39] Pace *The Communist Manifesto*, even bourgeois revolution was not inevitable, and nor did the proletariat of 1848, such as it was, evince much enthusiasm for giving history a helping hand in the direction of the ultimate classless society.

Marx and Engels were not only mistaken in their predictions of an imminent revolutionary future, initially bourgeois and subsequently proletarian; they were also suspiciously light on detail when they described the nature, the working, and the institutions of the postbourgeois world—and of the postbourgeois identities—that the triumphant revolutionary proletariat was expected eventually to bring into being.[40] They offered no considered guidance as to how private property would be abolished, how the state would wither away, or how class would disappear—their vague imaginations carrying them no further than an unspecified "association" in which "the free development of each is the condition for the free development of all."[41] But this was naïve verbiage, for if all capital, property, and productive resources were initially centralized in the hands of the state, then they would have to be administered and allocated by those in authority (in which case both the state and a ruling class, far from withering away, would still exist), or they would have to be given over to the workers (in which case private property, albeit redistributed among new owners, would continue in being).[42] Either way, there would still be economic (and political) inequality, and according to the criteria devised and deployed by Marx and Engels, this would mean that the class differences and class identities they believed they had discerned would survive and endure rather than vanish and disappear.

CLASS AS POLITICS

Given its manifold limitations, blind spots, exceptions, and outright errors, it is not surprising that the view of class-based identity and conflict developed by Marx and Engels during the late 1840s made little immediate impact. *The Condition of the Working Class* originally appeared in German, but was not translated into English until 1885 (in the United States) and 1892 (in the United Kingdom). *The German Ideology* was never completed, and only appeared in print in 1932. A limited edition of *The Communist Manifesto* was initially published in German in 1847, but plans to translate it into English, French, Italian, Flemish, and Danish were postponed indefinitely.[43] After the failed revolutions of 1848, the Communist League, which had commissioned the *Manifesto*, was disbanded, and although Marx later tried to make the First International (which he helped found in London in 1864) into a vehicle of global working-class solidarity, it was for most of its existence little more than a "paper organization," riven by doctrinal disputes, and disbanded in 1876.[44] By then new socialist parties were coming into being, but they were more concerned to further the participation of organized labor within the existing political system than to bring about a continent-wide proletarian revolution. On Marx's death in 1883, Engels claimed that "just as Darwin discovered the law of development of organic nature, so Marx discovered the law of development of human history"; but he had done no such thing, and few besides Engels believed he had. In an era of growing (albeit still limited) national consciousness and solidarities, class as an alternative form of collective identity possessed very limited appeal, while the idea that it was the most important aggregation of all had gained little traction.[45]

During the twenty years after Marx's death, Europe urbanized rapidly, industry and factory employment proliferated, the Second International was founded in 1889, socialist parties spread across the continent, and *The Communist Manifesto* belatedly achieved a global readership in translation (Engels died in 1895, his deeds as Marx's friend and funder, collaborator and champion soon forgotten). But of what new relevance were the teachings and predictions of the *Manifesto* under the changed conditions of the fin de siècle? The philosopher Karl Kautsky, who would be referred to by some as the pope of Marxism, insisted that Marx's doctrines of class identity, social polarization, and proletarian revolution retained their value and urgency. But the German politician Eduard Bernstein argued that such "orthodoxy" needed significant "revising," since relations between the bourgeoisie and workers had significantly improved since 1848, which meant the prospects for a proletarian revolution were dwindling, and that "evolutionary" socialism was the more likely path forward.[46] Contemporary social developments would largely vindicate Bernstein's revisionist view: the new, factory-based proletariat was still a minority of the working class, while the growth of reformist trade unions, which preferred to get a better deal for their members than overthrow the capitalist system, cast doubt on the likelihood of a workers' revolution anywhere or anytime soon. Moreover, Europe's socialist parties were nationally rather than internationally constituted, and for all their claims to have espoused the revolutionary doctrines of Marxism, they accommodated themselves to "bourgeois" parliamentary politics and the significance they attached to the *Manifesto* was "mainly emblematic."[47]

These acrimonious and arcane controversies within the dwindling ranks of Marxist believers about whether, when, and how the proletarian revolution might occur were rendered abruptly irrelevant by the outbreak of the First World War, when it became apparent that they had mistaken the identities and misjudged the aspirations of the European working class, in whose name and interests they had presumptuously claimed to speak. As the international crisis ran its course during the summer of 1914, Marx's die-hard followers expected that the proletariat would rise up against their bourgeois leaders who were hell-bent on war and, refusing the nationalist ardor and patriotism that had been foisted upon them, would choose instead continent-wide revolution. Yet the very opposite occurred, as the overwhelming majority of workers volunteered in their hundreds of thousands, as the leaders of the socialist parties declared their support for war, and as the Second International collapsed.[48] In direct refutation of the claims and predictions of Marx and Engels, it turned out that the early-twentieth-century workers of Europe *were* very strongly attached to their respective countries and fatherlands, and that the belligerent patriotic identities ascribed to them, however oversimplified and misleading, were more important to them than any shared, transnational solidarities as members of the working class. "Seen from the perspective of August 1914," Eric Hobsbawm notes, "one might have concluded that nation and nation-state had triumphed over all rival social and political loyalties."[49] Indeed one might, and many certainly did at the time.

In one of his last prefaces to *The Communist Manifesto*, written in 1890, Engels had claimed that "the eternal union of the proletarians of all countries . . . is still alive, and lives stronger than ever."[50] But the immediate future did not bear him out: in

1914, as in 1848, the revolutionary politics built around proletarian class identity and visceral hostility to the bourgeoisie, which were meant to have ushered in the socialist utopia, failed to materialize. Yet despite this missed opportunity, and notwithstanding the flaws in the writings of Marx and Engels about the collective identities, political significance, and historical trajectories of class, the subsequent years from 1917 to 1989 *would* be dominated by attempts to remake the world on the basis of *The Communist Manifesto*. In the end, most of these experiments, which amounted to totalitarian repression and a denial of basic liberties rather than "the free development of all" that had been promised, would fail, collapsing under the weight of their internal contradictions, as well as the assaults of competing identities and ideologies, and as they were ultimately rejected by the very people in whose name they were supposedly instituted. Nevertheless, during the period from the Bolshevik Revolution to the fall of the Berlin Wall, the most significant theme in the history of Europe, and of many other parts of the world, was the effort to construct a new form of politics and a new form of society based on the ideas derived (albeit in developed and distorted form) from Marx and Engels concerning the collective identities of class and the revolutionary potential of the urban, factory-based proletariat.[51]

Dismayed in 1914 by the failure of the European working class to assume its putative historic role and carry out the proletarian revolution, Marx and Engels's remaining followers faced some seriously challenging questions: if the workers of the world showed no inclination to unite and revolt in circumstances as propitious as those that had briefly obtained when war broke out, then how should they be helped, by whom could they be persuaded, and by whom must they be commanded to take up this essential and momentous task? The most portentous answers were offered by a self-styled revolutionary named Vladimir Ilyich Lenin, who argued that the prediction of a decisive class war between a monolithic capitalist bourgeoisie and a monolithic industrial proletariat, leading inevitably to revolution in France, Germany, and Britain, needed significant modification, especially farther east in his tsarist Russian homeland. (Marx and Engels had themselves briefly entertained such a modification of their arguments in their preface to the second Russian edition of *The Communist Manifesto*, published in 1882, in which they hinted that Russia might undergo a revolution led by the agricultural rather than the industrial workers, and that this might become a "signal" for the proletarian revolution in the West; but after Marx's death, Engels reverted to the original story, casting the industrial proletariat in the vanguard of revolutionary transformation.)[52]

As Lenin recognized, in such a vast, backward, and preponderantly agricultural country as early-twentieth-century Russia, whose peasantry constituted more than 80 percent of the population, even a bourgeois revolution had not yet taken place, while the industrial proletariat that had recently grown in cities such as St. Petersburg and Moscow formed a smaller minority of the working class than anywhere else in Europe. Marx and Engels had believed that the bourgeois revolution must come first, and that a subsequent proletarian revolution must be patiently (if confidently) awaited. Lenin, by contrast, concluded that in Russia there must soon be a single revolution, which at one audacious stroke would propel the country almost overnight from backward feudalism to futuristic socialism.[53] In such an endeavor, Lenin reasoned, the participation of the urban-industrial proletariat would be essential, but they would also need the sort of vigorous, ruthless, secretive, and conspiratorial leadership that could only be provided by members of the very class that was the proletariat's sworn enemy, namely the bourgeoisie. Instead of revolution resulting from a struggle between two massive, homogeneous classes, as Marx and Engels had insistently predicted, Lenin's Bolshevik model proposed a very different vision: a high-level coup, led by an elite vanguard of committed, disciplined bourgeois professionals, willing to resort to violence and terror if circumstances required, and ready to persuade as many as possible of the (still relatively small) factory-based proletariat to follow them.[54]

In November 1917, Lenin and the Bolsheviks accomplished just that, as they stormed the Winter Palace and with the support of the industrial working class of Petrograd replaced the Russian provisional government. Although they claimed to have carried out their coup in the name of the proletarian revolution, and as the culmination of the historical processes that Marx and Engels had discerned and predicted, the sudden seizure of power by Lenin and the Bolsheviks was scarcely the result of a class war in which the industrial workers had duly and deservedly triumphed by vanquishing the bourgeoisie.[55] Nor could it have been, because (as Lenin had recognized) the collective categories of class, with their attendant identities, did not exist in early-twentieth-century Russia in the way Marx and Engels had thought they must if an authentic and broadly based proletarian revolution was to occur. Instead, the "top-down" Bolshevik Revolution was a combination of bourgeois leadership and proletarian support, along with the backing of what would soon become the Red Army, but as Kautsky noted, the revolution was in essence elitist and dictatorial, rather than a popular expression of aroused and belligerent collective identities. The majority of Russians, namely the peasantry, were far from enthused by the Bolsheviks, and between 1917 and 1921 Lenin and his followers had to fight fiercely to assert and maintain their domestic authority. This was not the classless utopia that Marx and Engels believed the proletarian revolution must eventually bring about.[56]

Far from eliminating the class-based Russian state, Lenin was compelled to expand it, and because there were no other options, it was run by those despised "bourgeois experts" who had survived the tsarist regime. Instead of ushering in the "dictatorship of the proletariat," the Communist Party now exercised dictatorial powers, allegedly on behalf of the workers, but in practice on behalf of itself. And rather than abolish class, the Bolshevik Revolution perpetuated it, and even expanded it: "the reactionary clergy and the reactionary bourgeoisie" were not eliminated, and neither was the peasantry, but all were joined by a new hierarchy of party managers and officials. "How," a Soviet worker inquired in 1934, "can we liquidate classes, if new classes have developed here, with the only difference being that they are not called classes?"[57] As these words suggest, it was the same under Stalin, who by the late 1930s had made peace with the peasants, the priests, and the bourgeoisie, and who urged that national unity mattered more than the global solidarities of class. "Socialism in one country" was more important than world revolution, and this view became the conventional wisdom during the years of the "Great Patriotic War," from 1941 to 1945, during which Stalin blatantly and successfully appealed to Russian nationalist sentiment, persuading his countrymen to endure unspeakable hardship and deprivation. Yet this was more sleight of hand with respect to identity, since many in the USSR were not Russian by nationality—among them Stalin himself, who had been born in Georgia, and served as commissar for nationalities under Lenin.[58]

The Bolshevik Revolution also failed in that it did not become the expected "signal for proletarian revolution in the west," because as in 1914, the "workers of the world" refused to unite around a class-based identity in preference to their sense of nation-based solidarity. In 1919, Lenin had established the Third International (known as the Comintern) to support Communist parties abroad in their quest for revolution, and at its first meeting Trotsky had delivered his "Manifesto to the Proletariat of the Entire World," proclaiming global revolution to be imminent.[59] But with the exception of Mongolia, no other nation would officially espouse Communism during the next twenty years. At the end of the First World War, there were some initially promising signs: a Communist-supported uprising in Berlin of January 1919, and later in the year the establishment of Soviet republics in Hungary, Bavaria, and Slovakia, followed by renewed Communist agitations in Germany during 1921 and 1923.[60] But they were all successfully suppressed, as the forces of "bourgeois" authority reasserted themselves, and by the end of the 1930s no significant or lasting Communist advances had been made, in Europe or anywhere else, despite (for example) the Republican efforts in the Spanish Civil War and the creation of the Popular Front in France. Once again, the great global revolution that Marx and Engels had urged and foreseen had failed to materialize.[61]

Neither domestically nor internationally did Lenin's original revolution conform to Marx and Engels's formula. Yet from the late 1940s to the early 1980s, it often seemed that the "specter" of Communism was "haunting" Europe more dangerously than in 1848 or 1918, and was also insinuating itself in many regions for beyond.[62] In the aftermath of the Second World War, Soviet

Russia extended its formal borders, gobbling up Estonia, Latvia, and Lithuania and parts of Poland, while it further enlarged its European sphere of influence via the satellite states of Albania, Bulgaria, Czechoslovakia, East Germany, Poland, Romania, and Yugoslavia. At the same time in China, Mao Zedong and his followers overwhelmed the nationalist forces of Chiang Kai-shek, thereby establishing the most populous Communist regime in the world. In Indochina, Marxist-inspired insurgents, most famously Ho Chi Minh, expelled the French imperialists from the whole region, and would eventually drive the United States from Vietnam. In Africa, the writings of Marx and Engels appealed to many anticolonial agitators, and in 1980 Angola, Benin, the Congo, Ethiopia, Madagascar, Mozambique, and Somaliland all claimed to be Marxist-Leninist states. In Latin America, Fidel Castro established a Communist regime in Cuba, and Che Guevara would inspire freedom fighters everywhere, battling against American imperialism. Even in the United States, the combination of civil rights agitation, protest against the Vietnam War, and unprecedented student unrest suggested that at least among the college-educated younger generation "almost everyone was, or wanted to be thought, some sort of Marxist."[63]

Hence the era of the Cold War, when from either side the world looked deeply divided, in a stark and Manichean way, between the antagonistic identities and ideologies of Communism and capitalism, the USSR and the USA, "the East" and "the West." According to Winston Churchill, the divisions "between the creeds of Communist discipline and individual freedom" were "spread over the whole world."[64] Harry S. Truman believed his presidency had been "dominated by this all-embracing struggle between those who love freedom and those who would lead the world back into slavery and darkness." His successor, Dwight D. Eisenhower, made the same point in his first inaugural address, when he declared that "the forces of good and evil are massed and armed and opposed as rarely before in history.[65] It was to help "the West" in this struggle that MIT professor Walt Rostow wrote his famous and influential book *The Stages of Economic Growth*, which was revealingly subtitled *A Non-Communist Manifesto*, and which offered advice as to how the West might (and must) win the adherence of the newly independent and nonaligned nations of the Third World, who were constantly being courted by Moscow. Rostow later served in the White House as a hawkish advisor to President Lyndon Johnson during the Vietnam War—a conflict that both men believed was a vital part of the global struggle against Communism. China and North Korea had already been "lost": Indochina must not be allowed to go the same way.[66] Thus were the supposedly irreconcilable identities of class transposed onto the world stage and transmuted into the supposedly no less irreconcilable identities of social, economic, and political systems.

But while the rhetoric was that of a global Communist revolution, and of confrontation between two antithetical but internally homogeneous and ideologically coherent blocs, the reality was very different and more nuanced. The newly established Communist regimes took many forms, but despite repeated claims to the contrary, none of them achieved power by the means, or were wielding it for the ends, that Marx and Engels had set out in *The Communist Manifesto*.[67] In the Soviet satellites of eastern Europe, Communism was externally imposed, and depended on a hierarchy of party collaborators and apparatchiks—a far cry from proletarian revolution vanquishing the bourgeoisie. In China, Mao's brand of Communism depended above all on the peasantry (of whom there were many millions) rather than on the factory proletariat (of whom there were very few), but this was in deliberate (and necessary) defiance of the stress Marx and Engels (and Lenin) had placed on the industrial working class as the agents of the proletarian revolutionaries, and it was not easy to reconcile with their disparaging remarks about "the idiocy of rural life."[68] In Indochina, parts of Africa, and Latin America, Marxist-inspired movements of colonial liberation were a conceptually dubious amalgam of Communist internationalism and anti-imperial nationalism, usually with the latter preponderant. And on the campuses of universities in the West, many self-styled Marxist students were more interested in individual liberties, sexual emancipation, and freedom of expression than in espousing or leading proletarian revolution.[69]

This may have seemed monolithic Communism to those on the outside looking in, but it was not the reality on the inside looking out. As the novelist and pundit C. P. Snow lamented in 1966, "we have tried to divide the world into two—just sharp black and white, like that. Nothing is more an over-simplification in terms of the real world." He was right. In Soviet Russia, Khrushchev repudiated Stalin in the late 1950s, for (among other things) having perverted the doctrines of Marxism, and from the late 1940s to the late 1960s there were displays of dissent in East Germany, Poland, Hungary, and Czechoslovakia, while Tito's Yugoslavia successfully asserted its independence from Moscow.[70] For much of the postwar period, relations between Soviet Russia and Communist China were deeply strained, so that by 1961 "the Communist bloc was irrevocably split," and neither country wielded the power over Ho Chi Minh in Vietnam that some Americans claimed. Elsewhere in Asia, and in Africa, few of the newly independent nations became lastingly Marxist or Communist: most were determined to be "nonaligned," as their leaders had no wish to become the clients of Washington, D.C., Moscow, or Beijing. Despite the worldwide fame and glamour of Che Guevara, there were few successful Marxist revolutionaries in Latin America, and the students who wore Che T-shirts in the United States did so to express a general defiance of authority rather than an inclination to take Marxist teachings seriously.[71] As the American political scientist John H. Kautsky (grandson of Karl Kautsky) put it in the late 1960s, "Communism has come to mean quite different things in different minds, and quite different policies can hence be pursued in its name. As a descriptive category, 'Communism' has become useless."[72]

Moreover, just as the "internal struggles between classes" had constantly been modified by conversation and interaction, so too when recast as "conflicts between geo-political blocs," relations were in fact often characterized by dialogue and exchange. Throughout the Cold War period, such encounters across this allegedly impermeable divide often went on, even though the Communist authorities officially deplored them: there was a growing amount of trade and tourism and cultural diplomacy (such as the visits of the Bolshoi and the Kirov ballets to "the West"); despite his tough talk, Churchill's last great initiative as peacetime prime minister was to try to broker a meeting "at the summit" between the Americans and the Russians; the Cuban Missile Crisis was successfully resolved by negotiation between Kennedy and Khrushchev, and soon afterward, the "hotline" telephone was established to connect the leaders in Washington and Moscow directly; and both Ronald Reagan and Margaret Thatcher would later see in Mikhail Gorbachev a Russian leader with whom they could (and did) "do business."[73] By the time the Berlin Wall was demolished in 1989, attempts to prevent contact between the inhabitants of the Communist bloc and those living beyond its borders had clearly failed. In an increasingly globalized world of information technology, it had proved impossible for the Soviet authorities to prohibit conversations across, above, and underneath what became the increasingly ineffectual and eroded "iron curtain."

In the light of its global collapse, the verdict has to be that the once-bright Communist future had not worked, and since 1989 it has increasingly become the Communist past, relegated to that very dustbin of history that Trotsky hubristically believed awaited all other systems, except that which the Bolsheviks themselves had created. But even when abetted and assisted by self-styled and self-appointed revolutionaries, history did not unfold as Marx and Engels had insisted it would and predicted it must. Those Communist regimes that did come into being abolished neither class nor inequality nor property, and to the extent that class persisted, it was never the preeminent, all-encompassing identity that Marx and Engels claimed. Elsewhere, in the non-Communist world, their predictions have been even more thoroughly confounded: indeed, from the perspective of the early twenty-first century, they have been "invalidated beyond the possibility of recovery." Capitalism has survived, and with it the lumpenproletariat, the peasantry, and the petite bourgeoisie, and so (most disconcertingly) have the bourgeoisie themselves. While greed and exploitation persist, relations between the "proletariat" and the "bourgeoisie" have been characterized more in the long run by conversation, collaboration, and cooperation than by anger, antagonism, and animosity. The manual, industrial, factory-based working class, which Marx and Engels believed would be the instigator, the bearer, and the avatar of global proletarian revolution, has largely disappeared, except in emerging countries where the opportunity to participate in such production, even on harsh terms, is welcome relief from abject rural poverty. And since the 1980s, collective identities built around religious fundamentalism and ethnic nationalism have reasserted themselves with noteworthy virulence and ferocity, to the relative occlusion of class consciousness.[74] The faiths that Marx and Engels dismissed as mere "bourgeois prejudice" are very much still in existence, while the claim that "the age of division into nationalities is past" now seems utterly mistaken.

Since their underlying analysis of the past and present was incorrect, it is scarcely surprising that the predictions made by Marx and Engels have been falsified rather than borne out by subsequent events. Although they promised and urged the liberation of humanity, and although the *Manifesto* was later invoked as the inspiration by Communist leaders in many lands, the result in every case where they obtained power was ruthless single-party dictatorship, and the denial, not enhancement, of individual human freedom.[75] Perhaps this was what Margaret Thatcher was getting at when she once declared that class was "a Communist concept," which "groups people as bundles, and sets them against each other." But not for long, and not in the end successfully, since the twentieth century makes plain that class is an insufficient basis and an inadequately convincing or compelling identity from which, and with which, to set out to bring history to what Marx and Engels mistakenly believed was its culminating conclusion and predestined utopia. Small wonder that belief in the possibility or even the desirability of a future Communist society has become very largely extinct, and so has the belief in the collective categories and social identities on which the deluded Communist experiment was based.[76]

CLASS AS HISTORY

Yet while in retrospect Communism seems to have been doomed, because of error and failure that were built into it from the beginning, there was a period from the 1930s to the 1980s when the collective identities of class and the inevitability of class conflict seemed widely appealing, and the classless society was among the most alluring prospects imaginable: as Eric Hobsbawm recalls, it represented for people like him "the hope of the world."[77] Moreover, these Marxist doctrines were not only applied to practical politics with revolutionary aspirations for changing the imperfect present into the utopian future; they were also appropriated in academic endeavors with no less revolutionary aims of reinterpreting the past to help change the politics of the present. Since Communism claimed to be an historically validated ideology, and with class historically validated as the most important collective solidarity, it was scarcely surprising that during its heyday many scholars embraced a Marxist view of the past and insistently proclaimed that history should not be primarily concerned with investigating (and thereby helping to perpetuate) the trivialities of religious affiliations and disputes, or the superficialities of national identity and conflicts, but that it must itself be radicalized, reoriented, and redirected to investigate (and help realize?) those deeper truths of the past embodied in class formation, class consciousness, and class struggle.

This view of history was embraced by a generation of British-born or British-based scholars, for whom the defining decade of their lives was the 1930s, and who included Rodney Hilton, Christopher Hill, George Rude, E. P. Thompson, and Eric Hobsbawm.[78] They were among the first children of the Bolshevik Revolution; they believed Marxism offered the best way of understanding their stricken world; they wishfully viewed capitalism as being in terminal crisis in the aftermath of the Great Depression; and they embraced Communism by way of protesting against the Fascism of Hitler, Mussolini, and Franco and the infirm democracies of Baldwin's Britain and France's Third Republic.[79] They were also influenced by the pioneering writings of two older Marxist scholars, A. L. Morton and Maurice Dobb, who had begun to outline a new historical vision built around class identity and class struggle.[80] In 1938, Morton published his *People's History of England*, which sought to explain the national past not as a cavalcade of constitutional Whiggish progress but as the outcome of a continued (and unfinished) battle between the classes, initially between the feudal aristocracy and the peasantry, then between the feudal aristocracy and the bourgeoisie, and finally between the bourgeoisie and the industrial proletariat. And in 1946, Dobb published *Studies in the Development of Capitalism*, which proclaimed the special importance of the transition from feudalism to capitalism in the early modern period as the "main and central problem" for Marxist historians.[81]

After the Second World War, Rodney Hilton and his fellow Marxists organized the Communist Party Historians' Group, many of whom were involved in setting up the journal *Past and Present* in 1952. Following the Soviet invasion of Hungary in 1956, most members resigned from the Communist Party, but they remained loyal to Marx's teachings, and helped establish the *New Left Review* four years later. They shared A. L. Morton's view that English history must be understood as a history of class identity and class struggle, in relation to which certain eras and episodes were of particular significance. They agreed with Maurice Dobb that the central, defining problematic was the nature and timing of the transition from feudalism to capitalism, and the role of class conflict in bringing it about. They also believed that class "eventuated" as "men and women live their productive relations," for it was out of conflicts at the workplace that an awareness of class antagonism, and thus also a shared sense of class solidarity, developed and evolved.[82] By the 1960s, their works were widely read and exceptionally influential, for they not only set out to reinterpret the past by studying it from a class-based perspective, but also sought to support and reinforce contemporary working-class identities and to offer historical validation to the aspirations and policies of the parties of the left. As Eric Hobsbawm recalled, "Most intellectuals who became Marxists, . . . including Marxist historians, did so because they wanted to change the world in association with labour and socialist movements which, largely under Marxist inspiration, became mass political forces."[83]

Between the late 1930s and the mid-1960s, these Marxist scholars evolved a new version of English history, which filled out the major episodes in the class-based account first sketched by A. L. Morton. Rodney Hilton interpreted the uprising of 1381 as the first major eruption of class consciousness and class conflict, when an active and united peasantry, with a strong sense of its shared collective interests, rebelled against a feudal aristocracy.[84] Christopher Hill argued that the English Civil War of the mid-seventeenth century was neither a conflict over religion nor a fight for political freedom, but in fact the first bourgeois revolution, when a rising middle class vanquished the declining order of aristocracy and gentry, thereby bringing about the transition from feudalism to capitalism.[85] E. P. Thompson insisted that the years from the 1780s to the 1830s represented not only the transformation of the English economy as a result of the Industrial Revolution, but also the making of the English working class as the first self-conscious, and potentially revolutionary, proletariat, sharing "an identity of interest as between themselves and as against their rulers and employers."[86] And Eric Hobsbawm traced the later reinvigoration of this working-class self-consciousness, through the trade union movement and the ascent of the Labour Party, from the end of the nineteenth century to the 1960s and 1970s, by which time organized labor in Britain seemed more unified and powerful than ever—truly a "mass political force."[87]

All these scholars concurred that the collective identities driving the historical process forward were those neither of religion nor of nation, but of class. Although they focused on England rather than Britain or the British Isles, they also stressed the transnational connections and the transcontinental reach of the class identities they believed they had discerned. Rodney Hilton insisted that the English peasant rising of 1381 was part of a broader European class upheaval, including the revolt in maritime Flanders, the Tuchin movement in central France, and the wars of the *remensas* in Catalonia.[88] In the same way, the English Civil War was merely one aspect of a more pervasive European "crisis" of the mid-seventeenth century, one that extended from Sweden and the Ukraine, via Naples and Bohemia, and the Netherlands and France, to Catalonia and Portugal, which registered a decisive shift from feudal toward capitalist organization, as the landowning and bourgeois classes battled it out across much of the continent.[89] According to George Rude, it was this long-running conflict between the aristocracy and the bourgeoisie across the whole of eighteenth-century Europe that culminated in the French Revolution of 1789.[90] And Eric Hobsbawm argued that the near-miss proletarian uprisings in England during the 1830s and 1840s were also part of a wider European pattern of dissent, alienation, and insurgency, which could be traced back to the political revolution in France and the Industrial Revolution in Britain, and which reached its climax in the continent-wide revolutions of 1848.[91]

These Marxist reworkings of the English past were paralleled in France by interpretations of the Revolution of 1789 that were also based on class solidarities and antagonisms. In *The Communist Manifesto*, Marx and Engels had followed such recent writers as Thierry and Guizot in depicting the French Revolution as a bourgeois revolution, and although at the time highly tendentious, this view of 1789 subsequently carried all before it in the French academy, as the primacy of the struggle between a declining aristocracy and a rising middle class became enshrined in successive generations of French history books and accorded the status of self-evident truth. From Jean Jaurès's multivolume *Socialist History of the French Revolution*, published in the 1900s, to the works of Georges Lefebvre and Albert Soboul, which appeared from the 1940s to the 1970s, the prevailing interpretation of the French Revolution remained essentially unchanged: it was the outcome of predetermined conflict between two very different collective identities, and it not only changed France forever but also the world for the better. [92] Jaurès, Lefebvre, and Soboul all held the chair of the history of the French Revolution at the Sorbonne, all of them were members of the French Communist Party, and their views were summarized at the beginning of a book by one of Soboul's students: "1789: The bourgeoisie brought about the revolution," followed by a footnote dismissing all alternative interpretations with contempt.[93]

The work of these English and French Marxist historians seemed especially resonant during the 1960s. With many people viewing "revolution" as the mood and the mantra of the times, there was now an added incentive to discover how classes had come into being in earlier eras, and how they had struggled and fought to change the world. This interconnected model of historical change—which assumed that economic transformation led to social transformation, and eventually to political revolution—was extremely appealing, even to non-Marxists: it could be traced back to James Harrington and also to Aristotle; it underlay the work of Fernand Braudel and the *Annales* school in France (with whom the Marxist historians enjoyed a close and mutually admiring relationship); and it was also taken up by many social scientists during the 1960s.[94] In such a febrile political and scholarly environment, the interpretation of the past built around class formation, class consciousness, and class conflict was eagerly espoused by a new generation—indeed, a "New Left"—of radical historians inspired by the older cohort of Hilton, Hill, Thompson, and Hobsbawm. They were involved in the student politics of the time, they regarded 1968 as the most exciting year of their lives, when revolution did seem possible, they would obtain university appointments in England and across western Europe and North America, and they would create their own journals, of which the *History Workshop Journal* (United Kingdom, 1976) and the *Radical History Review* (United States, 1978) were the most important.[95]

The outcome was a widespread proliferation of history written in a Marxist mode around the collective identities and antagonisms of class. Following the lead given in *The Communist Manifesto*, some scholars rewrote the histories of ancient Greece and Rome as a succession of class struggles between those who owned property (including slaves) and those who did not (especially slaves), all these divisions and confrontations supposedly arising out of the "slave mode of production."[96] A new cohort of Marxist medieval historians, often inspired by Rodney Hilton, elaborated and extended his argument that there was a deep chasm separating feudal landowners and peasants, and that their relations were so vexed and antagonistic as to lead to class war.[97] Meanwhile, the earlier debates concerning the transition from feudalism to capitalism, and on the general European "crisis" that took place during the mid-seventeenth century, were revived by the American historian Robert Brenner, who insisted that "the issue of class exploitation and class struggle" was "essential" in understanding how the medieval economy and society had developed into the early modern economy and society.[98] The result was that the collective identities of class across many centuries of European history were declared to be much more important than those of religion or nation, and in the early 1970s Perry Anderson put all these newly fashioned pieces of the past puzzle together in a "Marxist grand narrative of world history" tracing social classes and social conflicts from the ancient world to feudalism, and then on to the early modern era of absolute monarchy.[99]

This new prioritizing of class made an even greater impact on interpretations of the relatively recent past, as historians sought and discovered bourgeois revolutions in America's Revolutionary and Civil Wars, in the Italian Risorgimento, in the unification of Germany by Bismarck, and in the Meiji Restoration in Japan; in each case they insisted that the old feudal order of landowners had been overthrown by a new, modernizing regime of capitalists.[100] And although proletarian revolutions had not yet followed these bourgeois upheavals, in the way that Marx and Engels had predicted they would and must, many historians were eager to follow E. P. Thompson and Eric Hobsbawm in discerning and describing the working-class identities that they were convinced had come into being. In the United States, the new generation of radical labor historians explored how the workers, in their heroic struggles against brutal managers and rapacious capitalists, had forged their own collective identity and class consciousness.[101] In Mexico, the political upheaval of 1910–11 was depicted in similarly Marxist terms, as Emiliano Zapata was credited with successfully mobilizing a popular, progressive, anticlerical, class-based revolution against the repressive regime of Porfirio Díaz.[102] In Russia the events of 1917 were still celebrated as the first ever triumph of a self-consciously revolutionary proletariat—albeit one under the decidedly nonproletarian leadership of Lenin and Trotsky.[103] And from China to Egypt, historians traced the making of the twentieth-century working classes coming to full collective self-awareness.[104]

This was a very different way to understand the past, to apprehend the present, and to predict the future than those underlying earlier histories centered mostly on the identities of religion or nation: whereas G. M. Trevelyan had written *Garibaldi and the Making of Italy*, E. P. Thompson wrote *The Making of the English Working Class*. Whereas Trevelyan had celebrated the creation of the Italian nation as the embodiment of liberty and

freedom, Thompson exalted the formation of the English proletariat as the superior and preferred embodiment of very much
the same things. While Whig history had been insular, patriotic,
and constitutional, Marxist history was cosmopolitan, subversive,
and class-based: "concentrated charges of intellectual explosive,"
according to Eric Hobsbawm, "designed to blow up crucial parts
of the fortifications of traditional history." Indeed, by the end of
the 1960s that seemed to be exactly the incendiary effect Marxist
history was having. "In recent years," Hobsbawm explained, "the
most direct approach to the history of society has come through
the study of classes." It was an exhilarating prospect:

> In no field has the advance been more dramatic and—given
> the neglect of historians in the past—more necessary.
> Classes . . . are today being systematically considered on the
> scale of a society, or in inter-societal comparison, or as gen-
> eral types of social relation. They are also now considered
> in depth, that is in all aspects of their social existence, rela-
> tions and behaviour. This is new, and the achievements are
> already striking, though the work has barely begun.

And this was not only of academic importance, for many of those
scholars writing about class were also offering historical validation and support for the "human collective projects of the
twentieth century" that were now being advanced in the name
of Communism.[105]

Yet even in its heyday, from the early 1960s to the early 1980s,
this claim that class-based solidarities were the most important
collective identities failed to carry all before it.[106] Many "traditional" historians disapproved of their Marxist colleagues, preferring to write about religion or the nation rather than about class,
and insisting that these remained more important forms of human
solidarity; meanwhile, some social historians continued to believe
that hierarchy, consensus, deference, and subordination were
more important forces than class solidarity and class conflict.[107]
While Marxist historians had captured the commanding heights
of French academe, their British and American counterparts were
less successful, especially in the universities of Oxford and Cam-

bridge, or in the Ivy League, where class-based approaches to the past remained essentially marginal, and where Marxism was never mainstream. And despite their close friendships and their in-house journals, the Marxist historians conspicuously failed to agree among themselves as to what these class groups were doing or achieving. Had feudalism disappeared by the mid-seventeenth century, or was the transition to capitalism further delayed by the advent of absolutism? If the bourgeoisie had triumphed so completely across the West, why was it that in Britain and elsewhere in Europe the traditional landed classes were still dominant during the nineteenth century? And why had the industrial working class, apparently so radical and so subversive during the 1830s and 1840s, subsequently shown such a lack of interest in the sort of revolutionary endeavor that Marx and Engels had been certain they would espouse?[108]

With the Marxist historians unable to agree about the trajectory and accomplishments of the classes they believed had existed in the past, it was scarcely surprising that scholars who did not share their faith were strongly critical of their overall approach, and since the 1980s, the flow of criticism has swollen to a flood. Nowadays it is very rare for historians of the ancient world to call themselves Marxists, and few believe that class identity and class conflict are the most applicable concepts: the economy and social structure were never completely divided between slave owners and slaves; there were significant regional variations across greater Greece and the Roman Empire; and political conflicts within the ruling elites were at least as important as their conflicts with other classes.[109] Similarly, the depiction of the medieval world as a two-class society, riven by pan-continental revolutionary peasant movements, has also largely been abandoned. (In the opening pages of The Communist Manifesto, Marx and Engels had admitted that the ancient and medieval worlds had been characterized by a complex gradation of ranks, and about this, at least, it seems they were right.)[110] As for the "bourgeois revolutions" or the "general crisis" of the seventeenth century, this no longer seems valid for England, where there was no neat division between the decline of the aristocracy and the rise of the middle class, and where change was gradual rather than cataclysmic; nor

does it fit for Europe as whole, where the revolts were too localized to form a cross-continental pattern, where the vertical bonds
of hierarchy were more significant than the horizontal solidarities
of class, and where the explanations for unrest and rebellion were
political and courtly rather than economic or social.[111]

There has been a similar overturning of Marxist categories
and concepts that had been used to explain the more recent past.
During the 1950s and 1960s, Alfred Cobban assailed the view that
the French Revolution was a bourgeois revolution, insisting that
the middle class and the aristocracy were not separate, monolithic, antagonistic entities—a skeptical interpretation that subsequent research has done much to affirm. Thus Simon Schama
wrote his bicentennial account of 1789 in opposition to the "dia-
lectical dance routine" of social classes, and insisted that "the
'bourgeoisie' said in the Marxist accounts to have been the author
and beneficiaries of the [Revolution] have become social zombies,
the product of historiographical obsessions rather than historical
realities."[112] The claim by E. P. Thompson that he had discerned a
single radical, self-conscious English working class, united by common experiences, was early on dismissed as "a myth, a construct
of determined imagination and theoretical presuppositions," and
subsequent work on the varieties of working-class experience, in
the context of what was an elaborately layered and interconnected
social hierarchy, has borne out this hostile verdict.[113] As for the
European revolutions of the 1830s and the 1840s, they were no
more a class-driven, continental phenomenon than those alleged
to have taken place during the 1640s and 1650s, having been set
in train by various forces in many different locations, and not by a
unified bourgeoisie or proletariat.[114]

The Marxist historians have also failed to establish their
class-based interpretations of twentieth-century history. In
Mexico, the old regime of Porfirio Díaz has been rehabilitated
by recent scholarship, and the revolution of 1910–11 has been
reinterpreted as a political rather than a social phenomenon,
in which unified and conflicting classes played no discernible
part.[115] Recent accounts of the Russian Revolution of 1917 have
downplayed the once-central class dimension, and the latest
studies of the industrial proletariat suggest that far from being

monolithic, it was deeply divided by the competing identities of social and geographical origin, gender, and nationality.[116] In both cases, once-seductive transhistorical forces have been disregarded, collective class identities have been denied and set aside, and the upheavals are no longer celebrated as the triumphs of cohesively virtuous and progressive social groups, but lamented as the destructive and illegitimate machinations of rootless, unprincipled, manipulative, and amoral conspirators. Likewise, in the United States, the attempt to consolidate the history of labor into one coherent, uplifting, heroic, and unifying narrative of working-class formation turned out to be unrealizable and unsustainable, for it soon became clear that it was a class that had always been "historically at odds with its own self," exhibiting "an eclectic pattern of behaviour and belief that defined any attempt to identify a coherent vision or purpose among working people." Meanwhile, new research has revealed that across the Pacific, the Chinese working class was similarly fissured and fractured along the lines of social origin, gender, and nationality. [117]

It is, then, no longer convincing to maintain that "the history of all hitherto existing society" is best understood and approached as "the history of class struggle." To be sure, the pioneering Marxist historians opened up huge swaths of past human experience to serious scholarly investigation, and that will remain their abiding achievement. And there are some historians, mostly of the 1960s generation, who alternatively fear, lament, and deny "the death of Marxism," continuing to insist that there was a bourgeois revolution in England in the seventeenth century and in France in 1789; that the "making" of the English working class did take place, albeit rather later than Thompson claimed; and that Marxist history-writing still has a future in the twenty-first century. But the credibility and conviction have long since gone out of such outmoded enterprises and nostalgic claims.[118] The heroic narratives and broad generalizations that Marxist historians constructed have been overturned by the unprecedented research onslaught of the last twenty-five years, which means it is no longer possible to view the past as a succession of gigantic Manichean encounters between rising, struggling, and falling classes, which have always been the preeminent forms of collective human identity, driving the historical process inexorably forward. As long as the Soviet Union survived, Communism endured and some historians remained loyal to Marxism, but the demise of the Soviet Empire during the late 1980s effectively finished it off as a way of interpreting the past, and with its exhaustion also went the claims that class was the most important form of collective solidarity.[119]

That, at least, has been the more realistic and resigned verdict of the older generation of Marxist historians. Christopher Hill gradually redefined his notion of the bourgeois revolution as being an intellectual rather than a class-based upheaval, and during the Thatcherite 1980s he shifted his attention from exploring successful progressives to describing "the experience of defeat."[120] Perry Anderson abandoned his multivolume Marxist history of the world before even reaching the era of so-called bourgeois or proletarian revolutions, and Gareth Stedman Jones gave up on Marxism altogether. Even Eric Hobsbawm, who had remained a member of the British Communist Party after 1956, admitted that times had changed. "Much of my life," he has observed, "probably most of my conscious life, was devoted to a hope which has been plainly disappointed, and to a cause which has plainly failed: the Communism initiated by the October Revolution." The best that could now be said for Marxist historians, he believed, was that they had "some practical experience of understanding the unintended and unwanted consequences of human collective projects in the twentieth century"; but that was hardly saying very much.[121] As the preeminent form of human identity and the most significant category of historical explanation, class has had a great fall and, like Humpty Dumpty, it seems unlikely that the pieces will be put back together anytime soon.[122]

CLASS IN HISTORY

The most measured conclusion is that the political activists and academic historians who followed the doctrines of Marx and Engels, and who sought to apply them to understanding the future and the past, were as much in error as the two founding figures themselves had been, not only in overstating the importance of class as the most significant collective identity, but also in underestimating the abiding importance of other forms of human solidarity, some quite ancient, others still emergent. This was certainly so in the case of religion, about which Victor Kiernan regularly (though without many allies) berated his Marxist colleagues, on the grounds that they did not take the subject, or the identities to which it gave rise, seriously enough. "To this day," he lamented, in a review of Eric Hobsbawm's *Age of Revolution*, "Marxism has scarcely corrected this underestimation, or made sufficient allowance in its general theory, for the energy and tenacity of religion," which he at least was willing to recognize was "one of the defining forces in human history."[123] It was a telling observation, yet this was an underestimation that went uncorrected, by both Marxist historians and Communist politicians, until it was too late. Stalin may famously (or notoriously) have asserted that the pope "had no legions," and that he, his faith, and his followers could be regarded with scornful indifference; but this was not the case in the late 1980s, when John Paul II commanded a Catholic population in Poland that had retained its identity as Communism had triumphed and subsequently crumbled, and that had refused to abandon its religious faith for this competing structure and system of belief.

This indifference on the part of Marxists and Communists toward the power and appeal of religion in human identity was particularly ironic, since as Engels had come to recognize toward the end of his life, there were strong and suggestive resemblances between Christianity and Marxism, even as the followers of each saw those of the other as irreconcilably antagonistic.[124] Both, after all, were built around a teleological narrative of history, which proposed collective solidarities in conflict, and led from an imperfect past and a sinful present to a glorious, redemptive, and transcendent future, in which good would triumph over evil. Both depended for their authority on sacred texts, written by the early prophets and about the early leaders, as sources of inspiration for the struggles, the sacrifices, and even the martyrdom expected of the faithful followers. Both suffered occasionally bitter internal schisms, caused by differences of doctrine and practice, which often seemed insignificant and incomprehensible to outsiders but led to accusations of heresy and acts of excommunication. And both held a Manichean view of the world, articulated in militantly denunciatory and apocalyptic language, in which antagonistic solidarities, based on a faith that subsumed and transcended all others, battled it out for supremacy. It is indeed a suggestive irony that Marxism and Communism appealed to successive generations of self-styled secular progressives, while being no less a religion than Christianity in relying more on the appeal of faith and hope than on fact.[125]

Their preoccupation with economic forces and material interests also helps explain why Marxists and Communists failed to recognize the attraction of nationalism or the allure of national identities, not just to ruling elites but also to ordinary people, and to what the historian Geoffrey Best memorably described as the "flag-saluting, foreigner-hating, peer-respecting" side of the plebeian mind. They persistently underestimated the extent to which industrialization and economic growth, far from creating transnational classes, led instead to the intensification of national rivalries and solidarities. But they also underestimated nationalism because they did not like it and did not empathize with it.[126] Isaac Deutscher claimed that Marx and Engels were great revolutionaries precisely because they were unfettered by the claims of nationality and had "seen the ultimate solution to the problems of their and our times, not in nation-states but in international society." Members of the British New Left agreed: following *The Communist Manifesto*, they rejected the "narrow categories of 'the national interest' " and dismissed nationhood and national identity as an instance of "the false identification of the group."[127] And in treating the history of nations and nationalism since 1870, Eric Hobsbawm not only made plain his lack of sympathy with the subject, but also insisted that the power of national identity had always been overstated and that the belief that it was "an irresistibly rising force ready for the third millennium" was no more than an "illusion." On the contrary, he saw national solidarities as merely one more instance of the "politics of identity" that, by reason of "anachronism, omission, decontextualization and, in extreme cases, lies," isolate one part of humanity from its wider setting. To all such solidarities and divisions Hobsbawm was deeply hostile—except in the case of class.[128]

Notwithstanding their contradictions and limitations, the collective identities of religion and nation had existed long before Marx and Engels discerned the existence of classes and proclaimed their unique importance, and they may continue to exist long after efforts to establish the politics of class identities and attempts to write class-based histories have been discredited and abandoned. But there is a third collective identity to which Marx and Engels, preoccupied by class, paid short shrift (although Engels did briefly address it toward the end of his life). For when, as they drew *The Communist Manifesto* to a close, the two collaborators urged that "working *men* of all countries" should "unite," they showed no interest in the subject of female employment or indeed in the existence of any collective form of female identity.[129] The Marxist activists who followed the founders were equally remiss: with the exception of Rosa Luxemburg, no woman was a major Communist politician in the fifty years after the Bolshevik Revolution. And later Marxist scholars were no less guilty. E. P. Thompson may have claimed, in *The Making of the English Working Class*, that "class eventuates as *men and women* live their productive relations" (my italics), but scarcely any females appear in the ample pages of his very long book. And looking back on his essay "From Social History to the History of Society," Eric Hobsbawm could only note in "embarrassed astonishment" that it "contained no reference at all to women's history."[130] In recent decades, class as identity has been undermined in many ways, and the claims advanced for the alternative solidarity of gender have been among its most powerful solvents. Yet like religion, nation, and class, gender has its own limitations as a category of human solidarity, and it is time to examine those strengths and weaknesses.

FOUR

Gender

Before you are of any race, nationality, region, party or
family, you are a woman.

—Germaine Greer,
The Whole Woman

Feminism constitutes the political expression of the con-
cerns and interests of women from different regions, classes,
nationalities, and ethnic backgrounds. . . . There is and
must be a diversity of feminisms, responsive to the different
needs and concerns of different women. . . . Contrary to the
best intentions of "sisterhood," not all women share identical
interests.

—Quoted in Margaret Walters,
Feminism: A Very Short Introduction

IN 1825, almost a quarter of a century before the authors of *The
Communist Manifesto* announced that class was the preeminent
form of human solidarity, a wellborn and well-educated Irish-
man named William Thompson had published a very different
polemic, urging the primacy of an alternative collective identity,
entitled *Appeal of One-Half of the Human Race, Women, Against the
Pretensions of the Other Half, Men, to Retain them in Political, and
Thence in Civil and Domestic Slavery.* Like Marx and (up to a point)
Engels, Thompson had rejected his privileged upbringing, but
his evolving radical ideas had also been influenced by a woman
named Anna Wheeler, to whom he addressed his *Appeal,* and
whose inspiration he acknowledged. "To separate your thoughts
from mine," Thompson wrote, "were now to me impossible, so
amalgamated are they with my own."[1] Anna Wheeler had been
married when she was fifteen, but having borne six children, she
left her drunken husband and went to France, where she joined
a group of Saint-Simonian socialists. In 1820, her husband died,
and Anna returned to England, where she embraced radical poli-

tics and met William Thompson. In the same year, James Mill published his *Essay on Government*, in which he argued for universal male suffrage but against enfranchising women, because they were all inescapably dependent on men, which meant they were incapable of forming considered views and so did not deserve to vote; nor, since their interests were already represented by their fathers or their husbands, did they need to do so.[2]

Early in 1825, the republication of Mill's *Essay* provoked Thompson into replying with his *Appeal*.[3] In response to Mill's assertion that there was no justification or need for women to be given the vote, he laid bare their systematic subjugation by men, which he believed was founded on the unjustifiable exclusion of women from all activities and institutions that were intellectual or political. "Business, professions, political concerns, local affairs, the whole field of sciences and arts, are open to the united and mutually sympathizing efforts of the males," Thompson wrote, but by "shutting [women] out from all means of intellectual culture, and from the view of and participation in the real incidents of active life," they were "confined, like other domestic animals, to the house and its little details." While married women were "imprisoned at home ... playing with bird, kitten, needle, or novel, the husband is enjoying abroad the manly pleasures of conviviality," and this was true whether they were "the wife of the richest as well as of the poorest in the country."[4] Thompson went on to expose the exclusively male world of the political realm, showing how notions of "independence" and "intelligence" were defined and appropriated by men and enlisted for the oppression of women, and he directed his particular wrath at the fashionable concept of "public opinion." Far from embodying the wise, disinterested judgment of all the people, it was a "male-created and male-supported" lobby, "the public opinion of the oppressors, of the males of the human race in their own favour."[5]

As Thompson's title reminds us, the division of humankind into two distinct "halves" of men and women has been a near-universal phenomenon around the world since the beginning of time. Accordingly, it has often been asserted that men and women are innately different on biological grounds, which means they constitute two separate sexes, rather than embody any shared

identity or common humanity. It is further argued that these anatomical dissimilarities are given their power and meaning by the
laws, rules, values, customs, conventions, and cultures of gender,
and that the combined effect of these physiological distinctions
and social constructions has brought about the domination by
(superior) men of (inferior) women.[6] But it has also been claimed
that the biological differences between men and women, and the
relations they are alleged literally to *embody*, are minor compared
with their overwhelming anatomical correspondences and the
natural complementarity of the sexes, and the fact that humankind could not exist without both argues for a moral equality that
should rightly inform social considerations. From this very different premise, it follows that if and when the artificial constructions
of gender difference, hierarchy, and subordination are overcome
and set aside, then women *and* men will cease to be two absolutely
different and antagonistic identities, and each will thus be able to
realize their full potential in the greater whole of humankind.[7]

Yet paradoxically, the very universality of gender differentiation has made it a less cohesive and potent basis for collective
identification and mobilization than virtually any other. There are
so many men and women, they are so geographically scattered,
and their circumstances are so varied that their shared awareness of themselves *as men* and *as women* has been more attenuated
and taken for granted than other identities.[8] In the case of the
inferior "half" and "second sex," this was something Simone de
Beauvoir knew very well. "They live," she wrote of women everywhere, "dispersed among the males, attached through residence,
housework, economic condition, and social standing, to certain
men—fathers or husbands—more firmly than they are [attached]
to other women."[9] And the result is that the identity formation,
shared consciousness, and collective struggles that have been
invented, created, and fought out in certain places and particular
times in the case of religious, national, and class solidarities have
been less in evidence in the case of women, and all but nonexis-
tent in the case of men. To adapt the typology of class invented by
Marx and Engels, there has been a great deal of gender "in itself,"
as the inert categorization and passive characterization of humankind as men and as women; but there has been significantly less of

gender "for itself," since it has been very rare that some women have come to feel such a collective sense of identity as women, and men only rarely, if at all, seem to have done so as men.[10]

DIFFERENCE AND INFERIORITY

"Men and women," the New York Times columnist Maureen Dowd observed in her postmillennial polemic Are Men Necessary? When Sexes Collide, "are further apart than we ever knew," and in it she quoted three authorities, each of whom insisted that this defining difference between the two "halves" of humanity is primarily the result of biology. The first was her own mother: "Women can stand on the Empire State Building," she warned her daughter on the latter's thirty-first birthday, "and scream to the heavens that they are equal to men and liberated, but until they have the same anatomy, it's a lie." The second was Dr. Edgar F. Berman, who was personal physician to Vice President Hubert Humphrey and an official on a national policymaking committee of the Democratic Party. In 1970, Berman declared his "scientific position" that "women are different [from men], physically, physiologically and psychically." And the third is Pope Benedict XVI, who, as Cardinal Ratzinger, proclaimed in 2004 that a woman has "roles inscribed in her own biology," and according to the Catholic Church, virginity and motherhood were "the two loftiest values in which she realizes her profoundest vocation."[11] (To these might be added the economist Professor Larry Summers, who, while president of Harvard University, and soon after Ratzinger's remarks, wondered aloud whether women's brains might be less capable of scientific research than men's, after which impolitic speculation he was compelled to relinquish his job, which was subsequently filled, for the first time, by a woman.)[12]

Thus do family, medicine, religion (and academe) combine to lament, declare, or proclaim (or hypothesize) that the differences between men and women are the natural order of things, since men have penises, testicles, testosterone, strong upper bodies, and male brains, while women have wombs, ovaries, estrogen, weaker upper bodies, and female brains. This view insists or implies that women are intrinsically inferior to men, and thus denies females and males a shared identity, and it has been in existence since the beginnings of Western thought. Aristotle, who often urged that the crucial difference between men and women was biological, considered women to be mutilated, deficient, and incomplete versions of men. They were both physically and mentally weaker, and as a result their position in ancient Greek society was so lowly as to be little better than that of slaves. Aristotle also insisted that women had colder bodies than men, and because he associated heat with life and soul, he concluded that women had less of each than men—a further indication of their physical and intellectual inferiority. This meant it was the male rather than the female who created new human life, since it was the man who contributed the form or essence of the embryo, while women merely contributed the womb and the nutrition that were necessary to maintain it during pregnancy. Being inferior to men in body and brain, Greek women, Aristotle believed, were rightly less well educated than men, and forced into marriages based on arrangement not affection; it was also fitting that they be denied active participation in the public realm and confined to the home, where their lives were an endless round of domestic trivia, punctuated by those biologically determined activities of childbirth and child-rearing.[13]

In a very different tradition and idiom, the Bible also proclaimed the divinely sanctioned difference between the two sexes, and their relationships of superiority and subordination.[14] As related in the book of Genesis, God first created man in his own image, and only as an afterthought did he make woman (Eve) from one of man's (Adam's) spare ribs, establishing her both in time and anatomically as the second and lesser sex. This fundamental biological difference had significant behavioral consequences, for while Adam wisely eschewed wicked temptation, Eve foolishly succumbed to the serpent's sinful entreaties and beguiling enticements, consuming the fruit of the Tree of Knowledge of good and evil, and thus tainting all men and all women with original sin. In the New Testament, Saint Paul pointed out the moral: "Adam was formed first, then Eve; and Adam was not deceived, but the woman was deceived and became a transgressor. Yet woman will be saved though bearing children, if she continues in faith and love and holiness, with modesty." From these observations and injunctions, several conclusions followed about the essential differences between men and women, which became the bedrock of all Christian teaching: unlike man, woman was weak in mind and body; she was the agent and scapegoat of man's downfall, for which her travails in childbirth were her punishment; and as a necessary precaution against her lesser mind, unruly nature, and fickle character, she must be subordinate to man in all things.[15]

These classically adumbrated and divinely sanctioned doctrines about the nature and ranking of men and women were also upheld by later secular thinkers. In *Emile*, Jean-Jacques Rousseau insisted that female deference, submission, and domestic dutifulness was in accordance with the natural law that underlay the common good, since women were weaker than men, and less clever.[16] Toward the end of the eighteenth century, Tom Paine subversively proposed the abolition of all hereditary distinctions of rank, and urged a significant broadening of the electoral franchise, but he upheld traditional gender hierarchies, proclaiming in the pages of his *Common Sense* that "male and female are distinctions of nature." In 1871, Charles Darwin took the same view in *The Descent of Man*, arguing that man was "more courageous, pugnacious and energetic than woman [with] a more inventive genius," and that compared to the female of the species, the male brain was "absolutely larger."[17] Friedrich Nietzsche embraced a similar view: "everything about woman is a riddle," he wrote in *Also Sprach Zarathustra*, "and everything about women has one solution: its name is pregnancy." And it was Sigmund Freud who coined the phrase "anatomy is destiny," and who divided humanity into the opposed constituencies of "masculine-active" and "feminine-passive." For Freud, sexual biology determined everything, explaining how and why women were defined and characterized by what he called their "castration complex," as they "envied" men their penises.[18]

The belief in such "essential differences" between men and women, which have always been an amalgam of the anatomical, the mental, and the behavioral, has persisted across the twentieth century into our own day, in both popular and academic writing. In the first category is John Gray, whose best-selling book *Men Are from Mars, Women Are from Venus* appeared in 1992, mingling self-help with popular psychology, and (albeit without apparent awareness) effectively updating the Adam-and-Eve dichotomy for our modern, secular world. For Gray depicts a binary division of the sexes, founded on "biological difference," that he believes is eternal and immutable. "Men and women," he writes, "are supposed to be different," as if they came from separate planets, and as a result they "think, feel, perceive, react, respond, love, need and appreciate differently." "When you remember," he portentously concludes, "that men are from Mars and women are from Venus, everything can be explained."[19] At a more sophisticated level, in a book revealingly entitled *The Essential Difference*, the Cambridge developmental psychologist Simon Baron-Cohen argues that the brains of men and women are fundamentally unalike, because of "essential sex differences in the mind," so that while "the male brain is predominantly hard-wired for understanding and building systems," by contrast "the female brain is predominantly hard-wired for empathy."[20] Although buttressed with extensive experimental research, this conclusion scarcely differs from the story of Adam and Eve, the Garden of Eden, and the serpent (with whom Eve had clearly empathized too much).[21]

If these views are correct, the dividing line between men and women, by virtue of their different biologies, brains, and behaviors, has always been a more significant fault line than that which religious leaders have drawn between the saved and the infidel, or that political leaders have proclaimed between their nation and its enemies, or that Marx and Engels thought they had discerned between the (male) employers and their (male) employees in the cotton mills of mid-nineteenth-century Manchester. One way of describing this alternative and apparently more fundamental sexual division of humanity is that men (whatever their economic status) are designed primarily for the purpose of *production*, whereas women (whatever their social status) are programmed primarily for the purpose of *reproduction*, and therein lies the most insuperable divide between people, which even gender reassignment cannot completely bridge. (Hormones can be administered to alter body fat and hair, and breasts can be enlarged or reduced, but penises and wombs cannot—as yet—be fabricated, and the DNA in every cell of a transgendered person still "knows" what sex it was born into.)[22] But as this male-female, production-reproduction dichotomy suggests, and as even John Gray himself concedes, the "biological differences" that divide and rank male and female are not the only ones, and are not necessarily the most important ones, for to the bodily dissimilarities and anatomical distinctions of sex must be added the cultural differences and social constructions of gender.[23]

In the Western world, the forces affecting these constructions of gender have included religion, the law, politics, education, and employment, all of which have accorded men privileges and opportunities that women were deliberately and systematically denied, and to these should be added such social conventions as the double standard, whereby men enjoyed sexual freedom whereas women were expected to preserve their virginity before marriage (and still are by Pope Benedict XVI).[24] One indication of this gendered ordering of the world was the pervasiveness of the language of "false universalism," based on the premise that "man embraces woman," so that what we would now call "humanity," in a nongendered way, was customarily referred to by the word "mankind," in which women were indeed embraced and incorporated, but only so as to disappear completely (as in such phrases as "the seven ages of *man*," or "*man* the measure of all things," or "all *men* are created equal," or "the rights of *man*").[25] A second aspect of this relationship of systemic male superiority and female inferiority was well summarized in Edward Gibbon's observation that "in every age and country, the wiser, or at least the stronger, of the two sexes, has usurped the powers of the state, and confined the other to the cares and pleasures of domestic life."[26] Hence the doctrine and practice of "separate spheres" for men and women, partly as a function of their different biologies, but also because the difference between them was asserted, constructed, and institutionalized in many other ways.

Although Gibbon believed this separation of men and women into the respective spheres of public and private life existed in "every age and country," many historians have argued that this gendered polarization between work and home took place at a specific time (between the late eighteenth and the mid-nineteenth centuries) and in a particular part of the world (the rapidly industrializing West), and it is noteworthy that Gibbon's comments on this subject, and also those of William Thompson, date from just this period. Before then, so this argument goes, men and women lived and worked together in conditions of relative equality, and interacted easily both in private and in public. But as a result of the Industrial Revolution, these arrangements and relationships were disrupted, and this was a change by which women were greatly disadvantaged.[27] For as production ceased to be domestically based and moved to the factory floor, the physical separation of home and workplace became the new pattern; the result was that women were increasingly denied the political, professional, and business opportunities they had previously enjoyed, and were confined to the home, prisoners of the private sphere, while men still enjoyed unrestricted access to the public sphere of paid work, sociability, politics, and government.[28] This construction of separate spheres, on the basis of more strict gender differentiation, was especially pronounced in the United Kingdom and the United States, and it coincided with a reassertion of the view that men and women, with their different anatomies, were so unalike as to be separate and incommensurable.[29]

According to this interpretation, between 1780 and 1850 biology and culture combined to divide men from women and to subordinate the latter to the former to a greater extent than ever before. But these changes did not take place at all levels of British or American society; they were confined to the middle classes who were both the creators and the beneficiaries of the Industrial Revolution. Here was an attempt to incorporate women into the male and Marxist narrative of class formation and class consciousness, by arguing that the bourgeoisie made itself during this formative period by establishing precisely demarcated places and roles for men and women. The result was that while energetic, happy, and eager men went out into the great world, making money, inventing new technologies, transforming the economy, building the railroads, governing the country, and waging war, women reluctantly embraced the cult of domesticity that was increasingly being foisted upon them, and dutifully devoted themselves to being wives and mothers and homemakers: the angel in the house, but with her wings firmly clipped. As such, the sexually and culturally polarized sexes of the Anglo-American middle classes, inhabiting their "separate spheres" and behaving in appropriately differentiated ways, were the direct precursors to those Martian males and Venusian females that John Gray claimed to have discovered a century and a half later.

Like E. P. Thompson's heroic chronicle of the making of the English working class, these recent attempts to chart the formation of the industrial bourgeoisie are also stories of undeserved damnation followed by hard-won redemption achieved by collective action made possible by the creation of a shared identity and consciousness. In the case of workingmen, a prelapsarian agrarian idyll is said to have been ruined by the abrupt and degrading Industrial Revolution, and it was only as they came to understand their situation as exploited and proletarianized labor that they were able to organize and agitate to win back lost freedoms, improve their circumstances, and change the world. Likewise for middle-class females, their traditional idyll of equal gender relations was shattered by the divisive impact of the Industrial Revolution, and it was only as they came to understand their situations as passive, isolated, alienated, and imprisoned wives that they were able to nurture a sense of gender-group solidarity that was ultimately expressed in mid-Victorian feminism, as the attempt to right the wrongs and fight the constraints of "separate spheres."[30] Thus understood, feminism was a necessary and spirited reaction to the new regime of domestic frustration and incarceration, in which sex and biology, gender and culture were powerfully allied to subordinate women more fully to men and to exclude them from the public realm. Indeed, it was directly from those deplored categories of difference and circumstances of inferiority that there issued forth what has been called a grand, inspiring narrative of "gender oppression, the experience of sisterhood, and a feminist consciousness."[31] Perhaps so, but then again maybe not.

SAMENESS AND EQUALITY

In November 1967, the United Nations General Assembly proclaimed a Declaration on the Elimination of Discrimination Against Women, its preamble asserting that "all human beings are born free and equal in dignity," which meant there ought to be "equal rights for men and women."[32] Discrimination against women was "incompatible with human dignity," since it was "an obstacle to the full development of the potentialities of women in the service of their countries and humanity" and it prevented "their participation, on equal terms with men, in the political, social, economic and cultural life of their countries." Yet such involvement and such equality were indisputable, because "the full and complete development of a country, the welfare of the world, and the cause of peace" required "the maximum partici-pation of women as well as men in all fields." That being so, the preamble concluded by "considering that it is necessary to insure the universal recognition in law and in fact of the principle of equality of men and women," and the eleven articles that followed declared that discrimination against women was "fundamentally unjust and constitutes an offence against human dignity," calling (among other things) for the abolition of laws and customs that deliberately disadvantage women, for the equal right to educa-tion regardless of gender, and for women to enjoy full political and constitutional rights, complete equality in civil law, and equal treatment in the workplace. These principles and these proposals were reaffirmed and extended in 1979, when the UN adopted its Convention on the Elimination of All Forms of Discrimination Against Women.

Here is a very different view of women, and of their relations with men, from that to be found in the West's foundational writ-ings of Aristotle or Genesis, or in the works of Charles Darwin or Sigmund Freud—one built around the essential sameness of "all human beings" rather than their anatomical difference, and thus around their innate equality. From this perspective, the biological dissimilarities between men and women are deemed to be rela-tively insignificant, their affinities and their likeness counting for more than relative upper body strength, or penises and wombs, or testicles and ovaries, or testosterone and estrogen, or male and female brains.[33] Yet all too often, the common humanity that the two sexes share with each other, but with no other living creatures, does not translate into the equality that it seems to promise, and these undoubted inequalities and differences between men and women are more likely to be matters of gender that are culturally determined than matters of sex that are biologically determined. This means that unlike the anatomical differences of sex, the cultural differences of gender could be eliminated and outlawed, by the sort of measures enumerated in the articles of the UN Declaration. Moreover, the impulse to see relations between the sexes this way was not a twentieth-century leap of insight, but has roots that reach back into antiquity, and arguments to this effect were advanced and developed alongside the alternative view stressing the ultimate and essential differences between men and women.

Once again, ancient Greece is the place to begin. In Book V of *The Republic*, Plato contended that the inferior status of women was not the expression of an immutable otherness based on the innate differences of body and brain, but a perversion of the natural state of affairs in which men and women were created equal, each the other's complement. A woman's biology, as Plato saw it, should not settle the question of her destiny, and it was only the educational, legal, constitutional, and cultural arrangements put in place by male authorities to divide and rank the sexes that made it appear as though it did. Plato insisted there was nothing inherent in a woman's nature to prevent her from engaging in all the social and political functions of an active and engaged citizen, and he believed it was a waste of human resources that half of the population stayed at home discharging the private duties of wife and mother. Instead, Plato argued, women should be brought fully into public life for the general benefit of society, the nuclear family should be abolished so that women might be relieved of the domestic chores that held them back, and if in such a more equal world her education and her talents allowed, then a woman might even become a philosopher-ruler.[34]

This belief in the intrinsic equality of men and women, on the basis of their common humanity and personal potential, was largely eclipsed with the ascendancy of Judeo-Christian teaching in the West, but it was revived in the more secular climate of the Enlightenment and the French Revolution. During the 1670s, François Poullain de La Barre, influenced by the principles of René Descartes, proposed that the human mind had no sex, either male or female, which meant that, in corroboration of Plato, there was no good reason to presume that women's brains were intrinsically inferior to men's.[35] In 1791, the Marquis de Condorcet, a leading philosophe, published *A Plea for the Citizenship of Women*, which in opposition to Tom Paine made the case for full political rights for women as well as men on the basis that the capacity to reason was universal, not sex-specific: "Now the rights of men result only from this, that men are beings with sensibility, capable of acquiring moral ideas, and of reasoning on those ideas. So women, having these same qualities, have necessarily equal rights." Condorcet accordingly concluded that "either no individual of the human race has genuine rights, or else all have the same," and by "all" he clearly meant women as well as men.[36] In the same year, Olympe de Gouges published her *Declaration of the Rights of Women*, which, again as a retort to Paine, insisted on adding women to the exclusively masculine discourse of contemporary radical political polemic; she critically challenged the false universalism of the word "man" by suggesting the alternative formulation of "men and women," and urged that "woman is born free and lives equal to man in her rights."[37]

At almost the same time, the English writer Mary Wollstonecraft published *A Vindication of the Rights of Woman*, much of which was a point-by-point rebuttal of the views of Rousseau and Paine that female difference, inferiority, and dependency were the natural order of things. But Wollstonecraft also insisted it was not biology that made women different from men, let alone inferior to them, but the prevailing social arrangements that were the result of the exertion of male power: women were not born to be different and subordinate, but to be part of humanity as a whole, yet from birth girls were taught and conditioned to be different and subordinate, and thus to be a separate, distinct, and lesser half of humanity. All this, Wollstonecraft argued, could and should be changed, by giving women the same opportunities as men to be educated and cultivate their reason: "The only method of leading women to fulfill their peculiar duties," she insisted, "is to free them from all restraint by allowing them to participate in the inherent rights of mankind." And Wollstonecraft offered another insight that would later be taken up, namely that allowing *women* to achieve their full potential would also result in improved and better *men*. "Make them free," she urged of women, "and they will quickly become wise and virtuous, as men become more so; for the improvement must be mutual." "I do earnestly wish," Wollstonecraft wrote on another occasion, "to see the distinction of sex confounded in society," and she was sure, given appropriate conditioning and education, that it could be.[38]

In the antebellum United States, an additional case was made for the innate equality between men and women that, despite the teaching of Genesis, was based on religious rather than secular enlightenment. For while the Christian church taught that women were by their nature inferior, it also proclaimed that all souls, regardless of their sex, were spiritual equals in the sight of God. Although Saint Paul urged wives to "submit yourselves unto your own husbands, as it is fit in the Lord," he also insisted that "there is neither Jew nor Greek, there is neither slave nor free, there is neither male nor female, for you are all one in Christ Jesus."[39] This sense that human beings were "all one" in the sight of God could be taken as implying that they should enjoy a moral equality here on earth, and this belief in shared humanity justified both the campaign against slavery and the active participation of American women in it. Yet the argument against slavery on the basis of the moral equality of all human beings, whether white or black, could clearly be extended to claim that men and women were moral equals too, for just as equality trumped the biological difference of skin color on the outside, so too did it override the difference in reproductive mechanisms within. "This regulation of duty," the abolitionist and suffrage campaigner Angelina Grimké wrote, "by the mere circumstance of sex, rather than by the fundamental principle of moral being, has led to that multifarious train of evils flowing out of the anti-Christian doctrine of masculine and feminine virtues." Her sister Sarah took the same view: "men and women," she observed in her *Letters on the Equality of the Sexes*, dissenting from Genesis, "were created equal. They are both moral and accountable beings, and whatever is right for man to do, is right for a woman."[40]

In 1848, and partly inspired by the revolutionary events in Europe, the first women's rights convention ever held in the United States took place at Seneca Falls, New York, at which these two American traditions, the rationalist and the religious, were interwoven in a new Declaration of Independence, which began by overturning the "false universalism" that had characterized the original document of 1776, replacing it with more appropriately inclusive language that recognized the existence and equivalence of the other "half" of humanity: "we hold these truths to be self-evident: that all men and women were created equal; that they are endowed by their Creator with certain inalienable rights," and "that woman is man's equal—was intended to be so by the Creator, and the highest good of the race demands that she should be recognized as such."[41] But recognition of this innate equality had not yet come, and the Declaration continued with a list of grievances at the legal, educational, financial, professional, political, and customary constraints under which all women labored. It was men who were responsible for this state of affairs, usurping "the prerogative of Jehovah himself" in claiming the right to assign to women "a sphere of action, when that belongs to her conscience and to God." Here was a commitment to the moral equality, universal rights, and common humanity of men and women, and to their shared identity, anticipating the UN Declaration 120 years later.[42]

Such writing about the intrinsic equivalence between men and women was not confined to the United States. In 1869, John Stuart Mill, son of James Mill, took a very different line from his father in his essay *The Subjection of Women*, arguing for the equality of the sexes and deploring the fact that half of the population was held in a state of subjugation by a mixture of bribery, intimidation, and legal sanctions.[43] Ten years later, Henrik Ibsen addressed similar issues in his play *A Doll's House*, which ends as Nora walks out on her beloved children, and also on the husband who adores but infantilizes her. "I've been your doll-wife here," she tells him, "just as at home I was papa's doll-child." Facing her husband's entreaty to stay, on the grounds that she is indeed a wife and mother before all else, Nora refuses: "I don't believe that any longer," she tells him. "I believe that before everything else I'm a human being—just as much as you are. . . . At any rate I shall try to become one."[44] A few years later, in the aftermath of Marx's death, Friedrich Engels turned to an exploration of the relations between the sexes, and concluded that the differences and inequalities between men and women were neither biological nor perpetual. On the contrary, "the development of the antagonism between man and woman in monogamous marriage" was a specific phase in human history, resulting from the advent of private property, capitalism, and bourgeois society. In the modern family, the husband was the bourgeois and the wife the proletarian, which meant that "true equality between men and women," which Engels claimed had existed in precapitalist times, could be restored only "when the exploitation of both by capital has been abolished, and private work in the home been transformed into a public industry."[45]

Engels naturally believed that such "true equality between men and women" could only be brought about by a proletarian revolution, but during the late nineteenth and early twentieth centuries, more moderate arguments were advanced on both sides of the Atlantic that the essential sameness and equality of the sexes would be most effectively proclaimed by giving women the vote: women, like men, were fully human, and so it was intrinsically unjust to deny them the political and constitutional rights that had already been granted to men.[46] These arguments gathered strength during the First World War, as millions of men went off to fight and women successfully took over much of their work back home, thereby demonstrating their equality in more practical and often in physical ways. For President Woodrow Wilson, this was a compelling case, as he explained to Congress when advocating the extension of the franchise to women in 1918: "The least tribute we can pay them is to make them the equals of men in political rights as they have proved themselves their equals in every field of practical work they have entered."[47] By this time, there were feminists who were insisting that equal partnerships between men and women would achieve the one single, all-encompassing "human sex," which was only incidentally divided into male and female. In the land of the "human sex," the differences and inequalities between men and women would finally dissolve, and the result, according to the Russian-born anarchist Emma Goldman, would be a "true companionship and oneness."[48]

"True companionship and oneness" was what Simone de Beauvoir later believed she had found with Jean-Paul Sartre: a relationship of equality based on their shared sense of common humanity. But in *The Second Sex*, she argued that most women had been denied the achievement of their full humanity—meaning the right to create, to invent, to go beyond mere living to find a meaning for life in activities of ever-widening scope—by male-centered men, who treated women as the "other," and dominated them as the inferior sex. Man was the absolute human type, with reference to whom woman was defined and differentiated; she was merely the afterthought. Yet, Beauvoir insisted, and in opposition to the Bible as well as Western writers from Aristotle to Freud, anatomy did not have to be destiny: "one is not born," she famously observed, "but rather one becomes, a woman; no biological, psychological or economic fate determines the figure that the human female presents in society."[49] Anatomy was less important than social arrangements and cultural conditioning, and unlike biology, society and culture could be changed. This insight of Beauvoir's, which harked back via Wollstonecraft to Plato, that the biologically constituted sex of womanhood was less significant than the culturally constructed gender of being female, would be crucial for a later generation of feminists.[50]

Yet cultural arrangements and social conditioning have turned out to be vexed matters, as in the case of the sudden differentiation between men and women into separate spheres that allegedly took place during the late eighteenth and early nineteenth centuries.[51] To begin with, such a view exaggerates the extent to which the two sexes had lived together on terms of equality in some "lost egalitarian Eden": there had always been some degree of separation between the sexes, and it was not uniquely the product of capitalist and/or industrial societies. It also exaggerates the pace of economic and social transformation during the Industrial Revolution: then, as before, changes in the relations between men and women, and in patterns of male and female work, seem to have occurred at a very slow rate—across the centuries rather than the decades.[52] The "separate spheres" interpretation also attached itself to a Marxist narrative of class formation and class consciousness that has long since become outmoded.[53] More-over, the claims that domesticity was uniquely associated with the middle class ignores the fact that many workers and aristocrats embraced it too, while much of the material cited in support of the doctrine of "separate spheres" was essentially prescriptive and didactic, rather than descriptive and evidence-based. It also seems clear that the coincidental reassertion of the difference between male and female bodies was less sudden and less significant: once again, the argument for such a linear transformation rested on a narrow basis of published texts, which were an imperfect guide to the realities of human behavior.[54]

Far from being passive victims who were subdued, margin-alized, and trapped in their homes, many British and American women from many different backgrounds were assertive, spirited, and capable beings. During the late eighteenth and nineteenth centuries, they actively engaged with the gradually industrializing economy as property owners and as producers, and they were also involved in many public causes, of which the campaigns against the slave trade in the United Kingdom and slavery in the United States were merely the most conspicuous.[55] This makes it difficult to explain the first stirrings of female consciousness and feminist mobilization as the effort by women to break out from the isolation, frustration, and confinement embodied in the ideology and the practice of "separate spheres." On the contrary, it seems more likely that the reason some relatively well-off and well-educated women began to campaign for equal rights was partly because they came from an established tradition of female participation in the public realm, but also because their own circumstances were in many ways *already* improving, so that for the first time the ideal of equality between the two sexes seemed worth the struggle, and perhaps even within reach.[56] Thus regarded, equal-rights feminism in the Anglophone world was not because the Industrial Revolution had made things worse for women by confining their circumstances and diminishing their expectations; rather, it was because the Industrial Revolution gave women who already believed they were intrinsically the same as men the rising expectation and the plausible hope that they might soon be accepted as the equals of men.

COMPLICATIONS AND CONTRADICTIONS

Such have been the two versions of conventional wisdom regarding what William Thompson called the male and the female "halves" of the human population. The first prioritizes biological unlikeness, and recognizes the reinforcing importance of cultural dissimilarity, validating the superiority of one sex over the other. The second downplays biological difference, emphasizing inherent sameness, and urges equality of males and females, but it recognizes that the cultural construction of gender differences and hierarchies prevents true equality between the sexes. But both these views of men and women have always been deeply confused and contradictory.[57] Consider, in this regard, the issue of the biological determinants of maleness and femaleness. Are the anatomical differences between men and women seriously significant? John Gray claims they are, but it has alternatively been argued that these "small sex differences" are "matters of degree not dichotomy": men and women are not separate species from different parts of the universe, but come from the same planet, namely earth.[58] Does the human brain also come in distinct male and female versions? Simon Baron-Cohen has stressed the "fundamental biological differences," but others have argued that this is another facile dichotomy, because these "essential differences" are far less significant than the "essential similarities."[59] In terms of what has been thought, written, and said about male and female bodies and brains, and about their likeness and dissimilarity, there is not now and never has been any agreement on any of these questions.

These unsettling interrogatives lead on to other questions no less disconcerting. There is, for example, no consensus about the relative significance of sex (biology) and of culture (gender) in determining and defining what some insist are the deep differences between men and women, and these matters are still much debated across a wide variety of academic disciplines. How is the undeniable anatomical division between men and women based on "raw biological sex" either denied in the name of religious and/or moral equality or extended and elaborated into an even more significant cultural division and inequality between them based on "social gender"?[60] Even Simone de Beauvoir seemed confused about the relationship between biology and culture. To be sure, she insisted that "one is not born, but rather becomes, a woman," which meant that "no biological, psychological or economic fate determines the figure that the human female presents in society," because culture and conditioning were all. But elsewhere she stated that women "are women in virtue of their anatomy and physiology" and that "the division of the sexes is a biological fact," and she spent a great deal of time dwelling on the many unpleasant aspects of female anatomy and bodily function. In truth, it is exceptionally difficult to distinguish between "sex difference" and "gender difference" in explaining how and why men and women are unalike, and this has led the psychologist Melissa Hines to suggest that the "distinction between biological and social/cultural causes" is a "false" one.[61]

Anyone who has persevered with this book thus far should be aware at least of this: the claim that the male and female identities established by biology and culture are more important than any other collective identities is at best highly tendentious. For it is merely one more example, alongside those made on behalf of religion, nation, and class, of the misleading but widespread practice of what has been termed "totalizing": namely, the habit of describing and defining individuals by their membership in one single group, deemed to be more important and more all-encompassing than any other solidarity—and indeed than all others—to which they might simultaneously belong. As Julia T. Wood rightly notes, "when we think of people primarily or exclusively as women or men," then all other aspects of their humanity and their identity "except their sex are pushed into the background and virtually erased," as "they are cast indiscriminately into two discrete categories that recognize only one aspect of human identity," namely biology and gender. From the same perspective, the African American feminist Bernice Reagon offers this powerful retort to Germaine Greer, whose totalizing sentiment is one of this chapter's epigraphs: "Every time you see a woman you're looking at a human being who is like you in only one respect, but may be totally different from you in three or four others."[62]

Indeed, it has generally been recognized since ancient Greece that there has always been more to being human, and to human identity, than just being either a man or a woman. Although their views were in many ways very different, Plato and Aristotle both recognized that men and women possessed other identities than those determined by their sex and their gender. Plato's ideal society was not primarily divided between men and women, but into three layers, largely on the basis of their public function: the producers (economic), the auxiliaries (military), and the guardians (political), and all of them supported by an underclass of slaves.[63] So when he expressed the hope that if suitably educated, women might be able to fulfill whichever of these functions they were most fitted to undertake, as men already did, Plato was urging that distinctions between the sexes would (and should) become redundant and irrelevant. As for Aristotle: in addition to dividing humanity into the separate and unequal categories of male and female, he also sliced it into the separate and unequal categories of free and slave, which identities he regarded as fundamentally dissimilar, on the basis of differing social, economic, legal, and political circumstances. In short, both Plato and Aristotle recognized that the alternative ways in which Greek society was stratified and layered significantly undermined any single, simple homogenizing division of the population into men and women.[64]

As this suggests, the tendency to overstate the extent to which all men are alike (in contrast to women) and all women are alike (in contradistinction to men) also ignores the substantial variations that have always existed *within* each sex. For there have always been many different, simultaneous versions of femininity, ways of presenting and representing oneself as a woman, and they are often defined against those of other women rather than against those of men (as, for instance, in the case of sexual orientation); by the same token, there have always been many different variants of masculinity and ways of presenting and representing oneself as a man, which are likewise often defined against those of other men rather than against those of women (as, again, in the case of sexual orientation).[65] There are, in short, multiple femininities, as well as multiple masculinities, which means, as the historian Alexandra Shepard observes, that we need to appreciate "the multifaceted nature of gender identities," which go substantially "beyond the binary opposition of men and women. . . . To discern the full complexities of the workings of gender in any society, we need to be as aware of the gender differences *within* each sex as those *between* them." We need to understand that despite the Bible or Thomas Paine or John Gray, gender is not exclusively a male-female dichotomy.[66]

Such differences within each sex are well documented among the men and women of the Middle Ages. In a classic essay, Eileen Power argued that all medieval women were "Christian wives," but she also admitted that they were divided by class and geography into feudal ladies, townswomen, or countrywomen, and were also differentiated in many other ways. For example, their marital status varied over time: some passed their entire lives as single women, some married so young that they spent their adult lives as wives, some lost husbands so early that their lives were mostly shaped by widowhood, and some passed slowly through all three stages. Religious status also cut across many lines, not just in terms of Christian, Muslim, and Jewish identities, but also because there were laywomen, professed nuns, pious mystics, true believers, or heretics. Legal status incised deep divides too, differentiating free from serf, and serf from slave; so did ethnicity, locality, and sexual orientation.[67] The same was true regarding the varied gendered identities and plural masculinities of medieval men, and many of their distinctions revolve around the same axes as those of women, namely age, class, marital status, religion, legal status, ethnicity, locality, and sexual orientation. An elderly, peace-loving, celibate monk was a very different version of masculinity than a young, aggressive warrior who was also a sexual predator. All this made for a bewildering array of different forms of masculinity and femininity, a reality often in sharp contrast to single, divinely sanctioned polarity between the two sexes on which most medieval writers insisted.[68]

The same ambiguities hold in the early modern period, during which those distinct and monolithic categories of men and women were repeatedly broken down, disarranged, overlain, and undermined by the competing differentials of age, marital status, material resources, religious conviction, legal position, language, region, and sexual preference; and they were further complicated by differing modes of conduct and behavior, for there were many ways of fashioning and conducting oneself as an early modern man or woman. By the end of the eighteenth century, there were fewer nuns, mystics, and witches than at the beginning of the sixteenth, and there were more women teachers, writers, and governesses. There were also mistresses, harlots, and unmarried mothers, and there were pious evangelical women.[69] In the same way, there were many different archetypes of early modern masculinity, ranging from youthful misrule to aged dependency. Some men expressed their maleness by being self-consciously strong, courageous, prudent, and reasonable, and by embracing appropriate religions and employment and wives; others did so by being self-indulgent, profligate, spendthrift, drunk, disorderly, even violent. The social practices of manhood and womanhood were thus "enormously diverse," destabilizing the rigid male-female dichotomy by means of a multiplicity of early modern gender identities.[70]

By the nineteenth century, the alleged polarity between the sexes had been further broken down under the impact of urbanization and industrialization. It was, for example, not the case that all men were for production while all women were for reproduction. Many working-class men were frequently out of work during economic downturns, or were only casual laborers, or unfit to do a job owing to illness, injury, or old age. Most middle-class men, whether in business or as professionals, did not produce anything, while many gentry and aristocrats did not work with their hands. By contrast, many women not only bore children but also worked, even joining trade unions, while (as always) some women could not or did not have children. Nor did the nineteenth century witness an alleged hegemonic bourgeois masculinity that eventually embraced the whole male population. Some middle-class men were entrepreneurial, individualistic, and religious, but by no means all of them. On the other hand, the "strong sense of social responsibility, purpose and commitment to hard work" so often thought characteristic of Victorian middle-class men was also to be found among all classes—and in both sexes. This means it is surely right to question whether "gender trumped class as the basis of social identity."[71] In truth, neither identity was all that pervasive, which means that Engels's late-life attempt to link and conflate the two, by arguing that under capitalism all men were dominant bourgeois while all women were exploited proletarians, was unsustainable—although this would not prevent feminists such as Germaine Greer from later embracing this view.[72]

These many significant qualifications to humanity's essential division into the two distinct sexes cast serious doubt on the numerous accounts based on the assumption that this is how things have always been and still are.[73] The supposedly all-pervasive polarity of male and female often turns out on closer inspection to be nothing of the kind, and men and women have generally gone through life in ways at least as much dividing each sex as unifying them, and in ways at least as much uniting the two sexes as setting them in opposition to each other. It is thus scarcely surprising that the billions of men and women spread around the globe have for the most part existed inert and lifeless in their self-consciousness as males and females, embodying their sex and gender biologically and culturally "in itself," but not energizing and mobilizing it "for itself." [74] As Simone de Beauvoir noted, women lacked "concrete means for organizing themselves into a unit which can stand face to face with the correlative unit" (by which she meant men), because they had no "solidarity of work and interest" that might have provided the sort of common and shared experience that would help them acquire a sense of shared identity.[75] Only at "certain moments," as Joan Scott observes, "have 'women' become consolidated as an identity group." "The identity of women," she goes on, "was not so much a self-evident fact of history, as it was evidence—from particular and discrete moments in time—of someone's, some group's effort to identify and thereby mobilize a collectivity."[76]

A further barrier to the successful mobilization of women as such has been what is termed the "difference-versus-equality" dilemma.[77] For if the initial presumption is of women's essential *difference* from men, then what are their special needs, how should they be recognized, and how should they be met? But if the starting premise is of women's no less essential *sameness* as men, then how should they set about defining and achieving the equality that is their common right, and ought to be their shared possession, as morally equivalent human beings? Across the last century and a half, women's movements have oscillated uncertainly between what seem to be mutually exclusive approaches to their common history and identity, to their mobilizing strategies, and to their collective ambitions.[78] Meanwhile, other feminists have sought a way out of this dilemma by urging the need *both* to recognize the differences between men and women *and* to achieve equality between them, with the aim of realizing a new version of common humanity, which will include happier and more fulfilled women and might also include happier and more fulfilled men.[79]

The "difference-versus-equality" dilemma faced by feminists has also forced a choice between alternative strategies as to how to realize either of these ends. Should women, when organized and energized to self-awareness and self-consciousness, be reformist or revolutionary? Should they seek to achieve their goals by collaboration with men, or should they preserve their gender solidarity and act entirely on their own? Are women willing to make gradual but incremental gains, with the help of men, or should they seek to usher in the feminist utopia by getting rid of patriarchy in one single, heroic, self-reliant effort? Should they want a share in what men already do and have, or should they want the true liberation that can be achieved only by creating a new postgendered world? Should women want to make capitalism work better, by getting more involved with it, or should they prefer to overthrow it in the name of a feminism that is committed to socialism? Should they wish to join the male bourgeoisie, or should they see themselves as a revolutionary female proletariat bent on eradicating it? Are the collaborationist writings of Betty Friedan or the subversive polemics of Germaine Greer the better inspiration?[80] And one further question reveals the haziness of the feminist project even more forcibly: for how many women the world over, who do not belong to the well-educated and comfortably well-off Western middle class, are any of these matters of immediate and practical relevance? Who could plausibly claim to speak for them, or for women as a whole?[81]

CONSCIOUSNESS-RAISING AND MOBILIZATION

Movements of women mobilized to improve the position of their sex and articulate its collective identity are scarcely 150 years old. To be sure, there are occasional episodes from earlier times when some women took public affairs into their own hands and organized with demands that were specific to their sex and gender. In ancient Greece, according to Aristophanes's play *Lysistrata*, they mobilized by denying their husbands and lovers sex in an effort to force them to stop fighting in the Peloponnesian War; and in ancient Rome, according to Livy and Plutarch, the Sabine women tried to keep Roman and Sabine men from killing each other. Women subsequently participated in riots across early modern Europe, but they were mainly about food, they took place in collaboration with men, and they were not specifically concerned with women's issues or rights. Not until the French Revolution, and in part inspired by such authors as Olympe de Gouges, was there a visible flurry of political activity by groups of women with a discernible feminist agenda, who sought to advance the claims of women, or a segment of them, to greater political participation. Yet they were also divided among themselves; they spoke the language of equality but they mixed this with an awareness of biological difference; and their movement did not last long, and in the short run it achieved nothing.[82]

Since then, the collective mobilizations of women have been virtually confined to the Western world, generally emerging in industrialized, urbanized, and developed countries, where married and well-educated women already played a significant part in the labor force and sought to assert themselves further on the basis of rising rather than falling expectations.[83] The so-called first wave of feminism that crested during the late nineteenth and early twentieth centuries in the United States, Australia and New Zealand, and much of Protestant Europe was largely reformist, and it was mainly (but not exclusively) concerned with winning legal and political rights.[84] At a time when more men than ever were able to vote, extending the franchise to women was both important in itself and was also seen as the necessary precondition for further reforms. Many of the women who campaigned for the franchise were benefiting from the greater educational and career opportunities that were opening up by the final quarter of the nineteenth century, and they organized on an unprecedented scale. In 1897, more than fifty campaigning associations in England joined to form the National Union of Women's Suffrage Societies. In France, all women's groups united into a feminist council, which grew from twenty-one thousand members in 1901 to nearly one hundred thousand in 1914. The following year, the National American Woman Suffrage Association, which had been established in 1890 by merging two rival organizations, boasted two million members.[85]

These were large, national organizations, and the next step was to create an international women's suffrage association. The International Council of Women was established in America in 1888 on the fortieth anniversary of the Seneca Falls Declaration, and in 1904 the International Women's Suffrage Alliance was set up in Berlin to function as a coordinating and policymaking group, pushing national organizations toward effort and cooperation.[86] For just as the campaign for women's suffrage was both national in focus yet also international in scope, so the winning of votes for women required national legislation yet also contained an international pattern, beginning in late-nineteenth-century Australia and New Zealand, and ending on both sides of the Atlantic in the immediate aftermath of the First World War. Of all "Western" countries, New Zealand was the first to grant the vote to women in 1893, and the confederation of Australia did so from the time it was established in 1901 (though not to Aborigines). In Europe, Finland led the way by granting full female suffrage in 1909, and the rest of Scandinavia soon followed: Norway in 1913, Denmark and Iceland in 1915, and Sweden in 1921. By then, women had been given the vote in the United Kingdom and the United States, and also in many of the new nations of central Europe that were created from the ruins of the prewar German, Russian, and Austro-Hungarian empires.[87]

Here was a remarkable achievement, involving unprecedented numbers of women being mobilized into gender consciousness; but there were serious limitations and qualifications. Those who were campaigning for suffrage were a minority of all women, and they often disagreed on the arguments they should put forward, as they found themselves caught (for the first time, but not the last) on the horns of the "dilemma of difference." Some suffragists campaigned for the vote on the grounds that women were the same as men and in all ways equal to them, so the extension of the franchise was a matter of universal rights and natural justice. But others contended that while women were equal to men and in no way inferior to them, they were also different, and it was that very difference which would enable them to make a unique and necessary contribution to the political life of the nation. In the United States, the concept of equal rights for men and women had been active from the time of the Seneca Falls Convention, but by the 1900s the unique qualities of women were being increasingly emphasized: "womanly women, stamping the womanliness of our nature on the country," as one campaigner put it.[88] In the United Kingdom, the arguments in favor of difference carried more weight, and most supporters of suffrage stressed the specific contributions women would make to political culture: they were domestic, and would help soften the hard masculine world of Westminster; they were more moral than men, and would elevate the substance and the tone of politics; and they were anxious about the welfare of women, children, and the poor, whose concerns they would bring before Parliament.[89]

There were other ways in which campaigning women disagreed. Should the vote go to single, propertied women (primarily widows and spinsters), or to all women, whether married or unmarried, propertied or propertyless? Should the means of getting the vote be gradualist, reformist, peaceful, and in collaboration with men, or (as in the case of the suffragettes in England) radical, aggressive, noncollaborationist, publicity-seeking, disruptive, even violent?[90] There were other divisions concerning level of commitment, marital status, party affiliation, region, religion, employment, class, and race.[91] Married women with households to run and children to bring up had less time than single and childless women. Many campaigners were liberals, but there were more conservatively inclined feminists than has often been recognized, as well as radicals drawn to the socialist parties that were expanding across much of Europe at this time.[92] Moreover, many regional suffrage organizations were only loosely affiliated with their national headquarters, and were often exclusively organized around religious or professional affiliations. In Britain women campaigning for the vote tended to be more radical in large industrial cities like Manchester than they were in London, and a similar pattern was marked in the United States, where suffragists were more conservative in Henry James's Boston than Edith Wharton's New York. Cross-class alliances encompassing patrician and plutocratic ladies, middle-class graduates, and working women were always inherently unstable, while in the United States, Australia, and New Zealand there was also the vexed question of whether the vote should be extended to women of color.

But it was not just that the campaigners were divided among themselves, for while they often claimed to be advancing the cause of womankind as a whole, they could not plausibly speak on behalf of all women. Some committed feminists did not think that winning the vote was the most important matter, and they preferred to work on substantive rather than (as they saw it) symbolic issues, in particular with reforming the divorce laws (which in terms of property and procedure and child custody were strongly weighted in favor of men) or with repealing legislation concerning sexually transmitted diseases (because they made clear the connection between women's sexual and political subordination).[93] Some women were opposed to giving the vote to *any* members of their sex, among them Queen Victoria, who thought the whole cause of women's rights was "mad, wicked folly"; the novelist Mrs. Humphry Ward, whose essay "An Appeal Against Female Suffrage" was signed by many prominent women; and large numbers of Catholic women, which explains why feminist movements were weak in non-Protestant countries such as France, Spain, and Italy.[94] And working-class women, who often felt patronized by college-educated middle-class feminists, were more committed to the collective advancement of their class than of their gender— with getting the vote for working-class men (often still unenfranchised) than for comfortably well-off women, or in campaigning for improved pay and better working conditions.[95]

There were also the competing claims of international gender loyalty versus national solidarity comprising both sexes. As a global movement, "first wave" feminism was far from cohesive: it was divided between the moderate International Council and the more radical Suffrage Alliance; its congresses and meetings expressed only the vaguest of aims; and the competing claims of nation in the end proved more appealing. When the First World War broke out, the majority of feminists pledged their loyalty to their homelands: even the most determined British suffragettes abandoned their disruptive campaigns for the duration of the conflict. To be sure, a small minority preferred global pacifism to nationalist belligerence, and they met at the International Congress of Women at The Hague in April 1915 to persuade the bellicose male powers to end the war. They did not succeed.[96] By then, what remained of first-wave feminism was long past its peak, and the granting of the vote to women in many countries in the years 1918–20 effectively brought it to an end. There is little evidence that the massive extensions of the franchise to women during those years was the result of feminist lobbying; it had more to do with the need to reconstruct large parts of Europe in the aftermath of the First World War or to buttress the increasingly beleaguered position of white, middle-class, Anglo-Saxon Protestants in the United States. At that point, the issue of votes for women largely stalled, and it was not until after 1945 that the franchise was extended to them in most of Latin America, in France, Italy, and Portugal, in eastern Europe and Communist China, and in the newly independent states created out of the rapidly dismantling European empires.[97]

From the 1920s to the 1950s, little effort was made to address women's issues beyond the franchise, as the Western world was preoccupied with depression, war, and recovery.[98] But just as first-wave feminism had developed in the West in response to the unprecedented prosperity of the second half of the nineteenth century, so "second-wave" feminism was the offspring of the unprecedented affluence of the consumer society that came into being in the years of peace after 1945. Developing some of the arguments first advanced by Simone de Beauvoir in *The Second Sex*, Betty Friedan depicted the world of 1950s American suburbia as a terrible time and place of female enslavement to the separate, segregated sphere of domesticity: while their husbands

were at work, women were incarcerated in the "comfortable con-
centration camps" of home, suffering "a slow death of mind and
spirit" because of the limited opportunities for education and a
career. Yet in reality, second-wave feminism, for which *The Feminine Mystique* was such an inspirational book, was brought about
not so much by frustration at the diminishing opportunities and
circumscribed freedoms as by the hopes and challenges of rising
expectations. For in many ways, Friedan exaggerated the plight of
her housewives: during the 1950s, middle-class American women
had more money and more leisure than ever before, being a
homemaker consumed less time and less energy than it had in
earlier decades, and as life expectancy increased, women faced
many active years after child-rearing was over. What were they
to do with them?[99]

These issues and questions were beginning to surface by
the early 1960s, and they gained momentum from the popular
disturbances that erupted during that decade among blacks and
students. The resulting Civil Rights Act of 1964 banned discrimination not only on the grounds of race, but also on the grounds
of gender. It also generated its own feminism as black and white
women activists were radicalized by the received condescension
of male colleagues, for whom they were often mere cooks, sec-
retaries, and camp followers. The experience of what would be
termed "male chauvinism" in the student protests of the time
had a similar effect on many women undergraduates, who were
more engaged by Germaine Greer's radical *The Female Eunuch*
than by Friedan's reformist *Feminine Mystique*, and who also drew
inspiration from the teachings and the categories of Marx and
Engels. Some even came to believe they could make a revolution of their own in which bourgeois patriarchy would be overthrown by women who proudly proclaimed themselves to be both
feminists and socialists.[100] This in turn led to the creation of new
American organizations expressing female solidarity and promoting women's collective identity, including the National Organization for Women (NOW) in 1966, of which Betty Friedan was
the first president, and the National Women's Political Caucus
in 1971. The previous year, the Women's Equity Action League
began filing class-action suits against the discriminatory practices

of graduate and professional schools, and the impact was immediate: women entrants to medical school rose from 9 percent in
1969 to more than 20 percent in 1975.[101]

Here was the mobilization of women in America on an
unprecedented scale, as "consciousness-raising" sessions (a phrase
and a concept also derived from Marx and Engels) enabled them
to break out of the domestic isolation that Beauvoir and Friedan
had vividly depicted and deplored, to discover a shared sense of
collective identity and gender solidarity, and to join up with crusading and campaigning feminist organizations.[102] One result was
congressional passage of the Equal Rights Amendment in 1972
(although it would never be ratified by the states); another was
the Supreme Court decision the following year in *Roe v. Wade*
to legalize abortion on demand during the first three months of
pregnancy. By then, the contraceptive pill had also become widely
available to women and the last state laws banning either its use
or sale had been repealed or struck down. By the early 1970s, Ivy
League schools had opened their doors to women, which meant
their numbers in previously all-male professions soon grew, developments further assisted by the provision of daycare centers for
working mothers, and a gradual but growing awareness of issues
of sexual harassment in the workplace. "Sisterhood is powerful,"
proclaimed Robin Morgan in one of the most resonant slogans
and influential books ("conceived, written, edited, copy-edited,
proofread, designed and illustrated by women") of the time, and
by the end of the 1970s, women had organized themselves in
many western European nations, where they campaigned successfully for abortion and the pill, for greater access to higher education and the professions, for equal pay, and for improved rights
and facilities at work.[103]

The women's movement not only was influential in the
United States and Europe, but was also increasingly international
in scope, reaching out to women in the Third World. In recognition of these developments, the United Nations designated 1975
to be "International Women's Year," and in June a two-week conference was convened in Mexico City, attended by delegates from
133 countries, including Betty Friedan, Germaine Greer, Princess
Ashraf Pahlavi of Iran, and Sirimavo Bandaranaike of Sri Lanka,

the world's first female prime minister. There were also infor-
mal sessions, involving some six thousand women, mostly from
North and South America, who discussed such practical issues as
health, nutrition, and education; and they agreed on an action
plan for a UN Decade of Women, with conferences in Copenha-
gen (1980), Nairobi (1985), and Beijing (1995). This sequence of
meetings helped to spread information, raise consciousness, and
establish international women's networks; they also placed "wom-
en's issues" on the map and encouraged Western governments
and philanthropists to support women's organizations concerned
with Third World development.[104] The result was the creation
of "a cosmopolitan body of women whose loyalties to sex transcended their national identities," and this unprecedented sense
of a global women's identity was celebrated by Robin Morgan,
who, a decade and a half after declaring that sisterhood was powerful, proclaimed in 1984 that it was also global. Thus were the
women of the world exhorted to unite in "a consolidated feminist
network on the cross-national front."[105]

As a result of these developments, many women in many parts
of the world are better educated, are more in control of their own
bodies and lives, are enjoying more fulfilling sex, are freer from
the threat of male violence, are economically more independent,
and are occupying positions of greater power in both the private
and public sectors than ever before. Even if women will always
be biologically different from men, the cultural constructions
of gender hierarchy have been significantly dismantled in many
countries, where women are no longer now regarded as the "second sex."[106] Part cause, part consequence of these developments
has been the burgeoning study of the history of women and of
the history of gender, which has been one of the most marked
phenomena in academe during the last fifty years. These histories have (among other things) recovered from oblivion the lives
of the "other" half of the human population that hitherto were
largely unknown, and they have explored how notions of femininity and masculinity were constructed. In so doing, they have
helped to consolidate women's sense of collective identity and to
strengthen feminist campaigning agendas. These changes have
been so significant that Robin Morgan has recently concluded

that sisterhood is not only powerful and global, but is "for ever," that "feminism is the politics of the twenty first century," and that "new world women have just begun."[107]

Yet despite these undoubted successes, second-wave feminism has been riven and divided from the outset. Many women writers who have become canonical feminist authorities did not think much of the mass of ordinary women whose lot they nevertheless claimed they wanted to improve. This had earlier been true of Mary Wollstonecraft, and it was also true of Simone de Beauvoir and Betty Friedan: they held themselves apart from the female commonality about whom they presumed to write, and they often portrayed women as unsympathetically as men frequently did, both in terms of their unappealing anatomical attributes and their weaknesses of intellect and character.[108] The same held good for some exceptionally successful female professionals and politicians, such as the American historian Lucy Salmon, who recognized the disabilities under which women labored in her profession, but insisted that these "must be removed . . . by women individually rather than collectively," and Margaret Thatcher, who was not a feminist and did not think of people in collective categories, least of all women.[109] And most of the early feminist leaders were relatively well-off, college-educated, and middle-class, and their writings on women reflected these limitations of experience, empathy, and imagination. Betty Friedan's world of frustrated and alienated housewives was confined to the affluent suburbs of greater New York; Germaine Greer later admitted that "*The Female Eunuch* does not deal with poor women (for when I wrote it I did not know them) but with the women of the rich world"; and Maureen Dowd's recent book is confined to the men and women who inhabit the rarefied political cum journalistic world of Washington, D.C.[110]

As this suggests, the claim of some feminists to be speaking on behalf of all women, and to be mobilizing the newly self-aware sisterhood into a state of shared collective consciousness, has not been valid even in the West, where no more than a tiny percentage of women were ever enrolled in feminist organizations at their peak of membership during the 1970s and 1980s.[111] Most active feminists were in their twenties and thirties, and their agendas and priorities reflected their youth: they showed little interest in the particular concerns and preoccupations of their middle-aged and elderly sisters. They also tended to be secular liberals or radical campaigners, to whom the politics of right-wing parties and the patriarchal Catholic Church were alike anathema; but ever since women had been enfranchised, many had voted conservatively, attended church regularly as devout Catholics, and were in favor of "family values" and opposed abortion.[112] Even among well-educated, middle-class Western women, then, there were many who felt no solidarity with the younger and more radical members of the women's movement, while most black and working-class women, whose main concerns were with keeping body and soul together, were largely indifferent to the actions and aspirations of what they saw as a self-indulgent and privileged group pursuing an essentially self-interested agenda, occasionally acknowledging in a lofty manner those less fortunate than themselves. All of this helps explain why black feminists like bell hooks have accused white, well-educated, middle-class Western activists of being both condescending and racist.[113]

Meanwhile, second-wave feminists in the West fell out among themselves over how to campaign for the equal treatment of women in work and society: should the appeal be based on the argument that women were essentially the same as men, or essentially different from men? In the latter case, compensating accommodation in the private sphere would be needed to make justice in the public sphere possible.[114] In the United States, Betty Friedan and the members of the National Organization for Women were "genteel" liberal reformers, whose approach was integrationist and egalitarian: they wanted to campaign with the support of men (despite its acronym, NOW was by choice and design an organization *for* women, in which men were welcome, not *of* women, which would have kept them out), so that both sexes could enjoy equal rights in public life in the name of their common humanity. But to Friedan's dismay, they soon found themselves outflanked by younger radical activists, who were inspired by the "ungenteel" writings of Germaine Greer, and more concerned with the special issues of women's bodies and sexuality ("the personal is the political"); they saw men as the problem rather than as the solution, and inclined toward separatism rather than egalitarianism, demanding dedicated female institutions to avoid co-optation into the patriarchal order. Still more radical were those lesbian feminists whom Friedan scornfully dismissed as "man-haters," and who preferred to collaborate with homosexual men in pursuit of gay rights rather than with their heterosexual sisters in pursuit of women's rights. These cracks and fissures first appeared among American feminists, but they later opened up among European feminists too.[115]

Such have been the limitations of appeal, the deep divisions, and the competing agendas of women's movements in the West since their emergence in the early 1970s, and once sisterhood aspired and began to go global, these cracks and fissures became more pronounced. It was at the United Nations conference in Mexico in 1975 that transnational antagonisms first emerged; indeed, it would later be claimed that they crystallized in an angry confrontation between Betty Friedan and Domitila Barrios de Chungara, the militant trade union leader from Bolivia. This row was said to expose a gaping divide between First World women, who were liberal, middle-class and white, and primarily concerned with sex-specific issues such as reproductive freedom, wage equity, and women's educational and professional opportunities, and Third World, Marxist, working-class, and nonwhite women, who were more concerned with structural problems of economic inequality and poverty. In fact, no such showdown between the two women ever took place. But the deep divisions in the nascent international women's movement were real enough: between rich and poor, developed and underdeveloped, North and South, West and non-West, capitalist and Marxist, middle-class and working-class, reformist and radical, heterosexual and homosexual, white and nonwhite.[116]

These fissures have continued to undermine subsequent attempts to sustain and strengthen a transnational feminist consciousness. As the black American poet Audre Lorde argued in 1983, the notion of sisterhood as being powerful and global glosses too easily over "differences of race, sexuality, class and age."[117] Such competing claims, conflicting identities, and "diverse feminisms" also undermine the idea of the "universal woman" as a global, unifying symbol. But whereas the universal epithet of "man" was false because it claimed to embrace and subsume all women, the feminist universal epithet of "woman" is also misleading because it makes "wild, improbable leaps across chasms of class and race, poverty and affluence, leisured lives and lives of toil, to draw basic similarities that stem from the shared conditions of sex." In the nineteenth century, feminists filled in the outlines of universal woman with images of female slaves, prostitutes, and impoverished seamstresses; in our own times, "extravagant universals reach around the world, plucking out Third World sex workers, Cambodian entrepreneurs, and African female farmers, among others, to add to the imagined figure of woman."[118] Even if all women are biologically similar and also the victims of culturally constructed discrimination, this attempted universalism, expressed in the ostensibly all-encompassing sisterly pronoun of "we," has never quite rung true, and by the late 1990s the political philosopher Jodi Dean conceded that "no one really knew who 'we' were" anymore.[119]

Among those who do not know are historians of women, who have found it difficult to agree what this history looks like, whom it is about, how it should be written, and what it shows.[120] There are affirming, identity-creating narratives, celebrating the ascent of women to collective consciousness and public prominence; but other historians have questioned the construction of this "imagined lineage for defiant women," pointing out that women's organizations have been ephemeral and their successes limited.[121] Some scholars concentrate exclusively on the lives of women, ignoring men; others look at gender relations and at the interconnections between the two sexes. Some historians focus on the modern period of first- and second-wave feminism; others with earlier interests deplore such "presentism" and "modernist self-absorption."[122] Some feminists write only for each other, in highly technical language; others deplore the retreat of feminism from the pressing issues and messy circumstances of the real world into the rarefied halls of the academy, and into arcane jargon and inaccessible prose.[123] As Daniel T. Rodgers notes, having surveyed the recent battle-scarred landscape of feminist scholarship, "conceptions of womanhood" have become "more complex and fractured," and "visions of a common sisterhood," founded on shared experiences, have been given up as a result of a "cascade of disaggregation," deconstruction, and particularity. Even some committed feminists accept that being female is not their only identity, and that feminism is not necessarily a cause to be embraced for life, but something from which women might be well advised to take a break.[124]

CAVEATS AND QUALIFICATIONS

"To go for a walk with one's eyes open," opined Simone de Beauvoir, echoing William Thompson, "is enough to demonstrate that humanity is divided into two classes of individuals whose clothes, faces, bodies, smiles, gaits, interests and occupations are manifestly different." So, indeed, humanity is; and so, indeed, these individuals are.[125] Between them, the two sexes constitute the whole of humankind in a way that no two religions or nations or classes have ever done. But that fact has always hindered more than it has helped either sex's potential for solidarity and for forging a shared identity, and for most of human history the identities of men and women *as men and as women* have scarcely been galvanizing or politically significant. While today there are probably more variants of maleness and more versions of femaleness in existence than ever before, and in their diversity and fluidity they constantly undermine, destabilize, and complicate such a single, simple divide. In the words of Donna Haraway, "there is nothing about being 'female' that naturally binds women" (any more than there is anything about being male that naturally binds men).[126] Mobilizing all women on the basis of their shared gender has never been possible, while mobilizing even some women has hardly been easy, and mobilizing any men in this way has yet to happen. So it is scarcely surprising that there has never been for women *as women* a triumphantly revolutionary moment, their own version of 1917, when the forces of patriarchy and male dominance were suddenly shattered and irrevocably overthrown.

Nor indeed is it clear how such a revolution would happen, or what form it would actually take.

Over the long haul of history, and notwithstanding their many limitations, it has clearly been easier to mobilize people on the basis of their religious faith, national pride, or class identity than because of their gender, and even during the second half of the twentieth century only a tiny percentage of women were members of feminist organizations. To be sure, this makes the significant changes that have been achieved to the benefit of women all the more remarkable. As Germaine Greer concedes, "in the last thirty years, women have come a long, long way," one indication of which, she claims, is that "feminist consciousness now leavens every relationship, every single social and professional encounter."[127] Every relationship? Every encounter? This is surely an exaggeration: there are many women (and even more men) in large parts of the world as yet untouched by feminism, and even where feminism has made an impact, its "leavening consciousness" is more the awareness of women's individual or class-based concerns than their universal collective identity. Moreover, such limited mobilization may be only one of several reasons why the position of some women in some parts of the world has recently improved. Essential alterations to the law required the consent of predominantly male legislators and predominantly male judges. Changes in work patterns have been greatly facilitated by the decline of male-dominated heavy industry and the rise of the service sector and the knowledge economy, in which men and women work on a more equal footing. The contraceptive pill was another technological innovation enlarging women's freedom, whether their consciousnesses had been raised or not. None of this is to deny that organizing, mobilizing, campaigning, and writing have played a significant part in improving women's circumstances; but as with first-wave feminism and the extension of the franchise, the limited collective action of the second wave is certainly not the only, and may not turn out to have been the major, explanation.[128]

Yet it is still repeatedly maintained that mobilizing women for feminist ends "has contributed more to the world's store of human happiness than it has taken away; and has undone some of its most banal and many of its most insufferable oppressions with-out significantly increasing others."[129] No Western secular liberal would be likely to deny that; but this is not the only view. To the Catholic Church, that most conservative and patriarchal of insti-tutions (as exemplified in the views of Pope Benedict), modern secularism, liberalism, and feminism are anathema, undermining biblical teaching and subverting the natural order of things, of which the submission of women to men, and their providentially ordained roles as virgin, wife, and mother, are among the most important.[130] Moreover, mainstream Islam is no less conservative and patriarchal, while its more radical expressions, such as Wah-habism, forbid women to drive or appear in public with more than their hands and eyes exposed. From these very different perspec-tives, the limited but misguided mobilization of women in the West, and the export of their feminism to other parts of the world, has *not* increased the sum total of human happiness. Far from bringing them fulfillment and satisfaction, freedom and emanci-pation, so this argument goes, it has led too many women to deny their essential nature and to undertake mistaken journeys along the unrighteous paths of sin, selfishness, and self-indulgence.[131]

There is one further and final qualification. Many feminists claim that although women have come a long way, there is still much more work to do, and that the task of safeguarding the bodies, educating the minds, and enhancing the opportunities of women is far from complete. In this they are surely correct. But others insist that the whole journey thus far has been misdirected, and that the wrong sort of feminism has triumphed, because making women more the equal of men has not brought them the full and fulfilled humanity that they crave, which can only be attained when patriarchy is finally overthrown.[132] Although they are significantly different in their aims and objectives, both interpretations assume that women will continue to organize, to campaign, and to assert their collective identity. But it is far from clear that they will do so. The generation of active feminists who were the children of the 1960s are reluctantly moving on, and as they do so, they increasingly lament that those women coming after them, who enjoy greater opportunities in part thanks to their predecessors' efforts, are uneager to carry on fighting, organizing, and mobilizing, either because they cannot see the point of it or because they cannot see the need for it. Having enjoyed no 1917-style triumph, feminism is unlikely to suffer a 1989-style defeat; but Robin Morgan's latest claim that mobilized and collective sisterhood is the pre-eminent collective identity that will last "for ever" seems more than a touch overstated.[133]

FIVE

Race

Segregation today! Segregation tomorrow! Segregation forever!

—Governor George Wallace, 1963

We're all God's children. All God's children are equal.

—Governor George Wallace, 1973

DURING THE LATE 1840S, a disgraced Scottish doctor named Robert Knox went on a lecture tour of the north of England, speaking on "the races of men," and he subsequently published a book of that title.[1] His career as a successful medical researcher and anatomical teacher was behind him, his reputation having been irretrievably damaged by his association with two grave robbers who had supplied him with the cadavers of men they had recently murdered.[2] Rejected by the Scottish medical establishment, Knox turned to study human history from a medical and anatomical perspective, also drawing on his earlier experiences as an army surgeon at the Cape of Good Hope, where he had encountered dark-skinned people in significant numbers. The conclusions he reached about the past content, present nature, and future trajectories of human identities were as all-encompassing as those drawn at the same time by Marx and Engels, but they were so different as to be incommensurable with them. For according to Knox, the history of all hitherto existing societies had not been built around the struggling collectivities of class, but around the antagonistic groupings of race. "That race is in human affairs everything," he began his book, in a grandiose opening rivaling *The Communist Manifesto* in its all-embracing claims, "is simply a fact, the most remarkable, the most comprehensive, which philosophy has announced." "Race," Knox reaffirmed, was "everything."[3]

Although he accepted that humanity had initially known

some primeval unity at the dawn of creation, Knox insisted that the various races existing throughout history were separate species living in distant habitats, different from one another biologically and behaviorally; they were also unequal in their attainments and destined to be in conflict as they always had been. In Europe, he believed there were four major races, which he ranked in descending order of sophistication: the Saxons, concentrated in Britain, northern Germany, and Scandinavia; the Celts, inhabiting France, Spain, parts of Italy, most of Ireland, and the western extremities of Great Britain; the Slavonian, found in much of middle Europe and the Balkans; and the Sarmatian or Russ, who lived farther east. To these Knox added other, lesser races, such as the Goths, the Latins, and the (especially disliked) Jews; lower still down the scale, separated from the others by a vast gulf, came the mongoloid and negroid races. The black was the inferior of the white, not only with respect to color but in everything else as well: "He is," Knox insisted, "no more a white man than an ass is a horse or a zebra." These races were also immutable in their separateness, for just as "nature produces no mules," so there could be "no hybrids" in people. Thus understood, race and its natural hierarchy would, Knox believed, be the "overweening determinant" of collective identities.[4]

Though Knox was little read in his day, his views on race consciousness, rankings, and conflict were more widely subscribed to than those of Marx and Engels concerning class. For obvious reasons, Benjamin Disraeli did not accept Knox's disparaging opinion of Jews, but he did agree with his general outlook. In 1847, he made one character observe in his novel *Tancred*, "All is race; there is no other truth," and two years later he elaborated the point in the House of Commons: "Race implies difference, difference implies superiority, and superiority leads to predominance."[5] Even closer to Knox's were the opinions of the Frenchman Comte Joseph Arthur de Gobineau, who constructed "a fully furnished intellectual edifice where race explained everything in the past, present and future" in his *Essay on the Inequality of Human Races*, published between 1853 and 1855. Its dedication to King George V of Hanover proclaims that "the racial question overshadows all other problems of history, that it holds the key to them all," and that "the inequality of the races" was part of the immutable order of things.[6] At the same time, the American writer Ralph Waldo Emerson, who shared Knox's veneration for the Anglo-Saxons, devoted a chapter in his *English Traits* (1856) to the subject, arguing that race determined history and trumped all other identities, because "in the deep traits of race . . . the fortunes of nations are written."[7]

Drawing upon this recently developing body of literature on race, Knox's writings offered validation to the continuation of slaveholding societies in the Caribbean and the Americas, and for the next century and more, belief in the preeminence of racial categories and identities as a "total explanatory system" of human behavior would remain a powerful—and pernicious—force in apprehending the world and in governing large parts of it.[8] Yet this morphological view of human identities, built around skin color and other external features, never went uncontested, even in its heyday. In part this was because there were always the competing collectivities of religion, nation, class, and gender to challenge and undermine the primacy of race. But it may also be said that race, appealing as it did to the most visceral sense of human difference, also inspired the most visceral refusal of its claims, for it was in answer to the divisive and value-laden hierarchies of race in particular that the universalist claims of a common humanity were first articulated and invoked in modern times. In one guise, these counterarguments were religious, drawing on the biblical teaching that God had made all human beings equal in his own image. But in another, they were scientific, as the findings of anthropologists and geneticists accumulated to reveal that apart from certain superficial differences, the so-called races were more nearly the same than they were different from each other.

THE RISE OF RACE

Unlike religious or class identities, which derived from and depend on a limited number of sacred texts, namely the Bible and the writings of Marx and Engels, racial identities have been underpinned (or undermined) by a more varied corpus of (often contradictory) writings. This helps explain why historians cannot agree when race became an important form of collective perception, identity, ranking, and antagonism.[9] But it seems generally accepted that no such way of conceptualizing and contrasting human aggregations was widespread in the ancient world. To be sure, ancient Greece and the Roman Empire were societies built on slavery, but there were no clear-cut physical differences, such as skin color, distinguishing slaves from masters: servitude was a matter of individual personal history rather than collective racial identity.[10] The Greeks may have believed they were better than all other peoples, but they made no attempt to rank non-Hellenes in a hierarchy of superior or inferior types. And while black Africans, usually referred to as Ethiopians, were well known in ancient times, they were not regarded as lesser beings by virtue of their skin color. Neither the Greeks nor the Romans thought that way about the many peoples living in the Mediterranean, in Asia Minor, and in North Africa, and later attempts to impute to Plato and Aristotle a nineteenth-century view of racial identities and rankings, anticipating the opinions of Robert Knox and his contemporaries, were ahistorical and anachronistic.[11]

The Bible was also largely color-blind and "oblivious of the fact of racial difference": Old Testament descriptions of encounters between different tribes and peoples were generally devoid of racial connotations, and a fundamental tenet of Christian teaching was the essential unity of humankind, for as was made plain in the Book of Genesis, everyone was descended from the two originally created parents, Adam and Eve. This doctrine of a common humanity was frequently and brutally set aside during religious wars and persecutions, but the injunction that "God hath made of one blood all nations of men for to dwell on all the face of the earth" remained deeply embedded.[12] This was certainly the view of Saint Augustine:

> Whoever is anywhere born a man, that is, a rational, mortal animal, no matter what unusual appearance he presents in colour, movement, sound, nor how peculiar he is in some

part, or quality of his nature, no Christian can doubt that he springs from that one protoplast . . . if they are human, they are descended from Adam.[13]

Such anatomical differences as skin pigmentation were merely superficial, and since all human beings originated from the same stock, they were all equal in the sight of God. The fourth-century Christian author Lucius Lactantius put this well:

> All men are begotten alike, with a capacity and ability of reasoning and feeling, without preference of age, sex, or dignity. . . . God, who produces and gives breath to men, willed that all should be equal. . . . In his sight, no one is a slave, no one a master; for all have the same father, by an equal right we are all children.[14]

Between the fall of Rome and the early Enlightenment, the color-blind legacy of pagan antiquity, combined with the Christian belief in a shared humanity embodied in the doctrine of monogenesis, stood as a powerful barrier to the rise of racial thinking, categories, hierarchies, and conflict. Indeed, races later to be reviled in the West were honored. One of the wise men who presented their gifts to the infant Christ was usually depicted as being dark-skinned; early Christians celebrated the conversion of Africans as evidence of the spiritual equality of all human beings; and during the late Middle Ages, a favorable image of blacks was expressed in the idea of "le bon Nègre."[15] Black was beautiful, and race-blind behavior expressed race-blind attitudes. To be sure, some black Africans were forcibly brought to Europe or shipped to America, but others traveled freely as ambassadors and pilgrims, or collaborated with Europeans in the slave trade itself. This was not the only way in which slavery remained race-blind: for more than a millennium, from the Vikings to the Ottomans, the trade in slaves was overwhelmingly in *white* people, from eastern Europe and Asia. As such, it was geography, not race, that determined who was a slave; this was equally true in the Spanish and Portuguese colonies in America, where marriages between colonizers and indigenes were commonplace.[16]

But there were also countervailing developments, and it was in medieval times that racial stereotypes and displays of hostility first became conspicuous. In late antiquity, Africans were popularly deemed to be descended from Canaan via Ham, and since Canaan had dishonored *his* father, Noah, their descendants were cursed and condemned to be dark-skinned and servile, as the hewers of wood and the drawers of water. Notions of "purity of blood" (notably in the Iberian world as "limpieza de sangre") became widespread on a continent thought to be under siege by Islam. Among those deemed to lack such purity and to be accomplices of the devil were the Jews. A thousand years of religious objection had hardened into a racial animus, as the Jews came to be seen as a people apart, who could be neither converted nor assimilated into a broader humanity; and such discriminatory thinking also seemed to furnish divine sanction for employing black Africans as slaves.[17] The result was that there were many violent outbursts against Jews, ranging from attacks by Crusaders in the Holy Land from 1096 to their expulsion from Spain four hundred years later; and from the mid-fifteenth century, the Portuguese began to enslave black Africans, shipping some back to work in Europe, and transporting others across the Atlantic to labor in their American empire. Such were the beginnings of European racial attitudes and categories, which would persist into the twentieth century, establishing by reason of blood or skin the inferiority of all other peoples to white Christian Europeans.[18]

Yet for every tendency toward a modern conception of race, there was an equal and opposite tendency to undercut it, which prevented race from emerging as a central organizing concept of Western intellectual life, a major component of political culture, or a significant means of structuring human identities and differences before the middle of the eighteenth century.[19] By then, however, racial categories, rankings, and identities *were* becoming more sharp, fixed, and significant, and there were a number of explanations for this development. It was partly a manifestation of the neoclassical sensibility of the Enlightenment, deriving from ancient Greece and Rome, which demonstrated an exclusive preference for white-skinned people. It was partly a consequence of the increasing travel and encounters between Europeans and peoples in Africa and South Asia, whose existence (and appearance) the biblical story of monogenesis and the curse of Canaan did not necessarily explain. There was also the expanding Atlantic slave trade, in which by now many European nations were participating, and which established and institutionalized the connection between freedom, superiority, and whiteness on the one hand, and servitude, inferiority, and blackness on the other. By the second half of the eighteenth century, these racial taxonomies were also becoming more pronounced on America's eastern seaboard and in the Caribbean, where the slave-owning societies and slave-labor economies placed whites over blacks in binary opposition.[20]

The view that the peoples of the world were divided by the categories and identities of race may seem to run counter to the rational currents of Enlightenment thought, but it was fairly common among Enlightenment thinkers. In 1753, David Hume observed that "the negroes" were now regarded as being "naturally inferior to the whites," and Immanuel Kant made the same point twenty years later, in *The Different Races of Mankind:* "whites and negroes," he argued, "are not two different kinds of species, but nevertheless two different races."[21] Here was a significant (and unintended?) consequence of the European Enlightenment, whose leading lights had sought to overthrow and supersede religion, belief, and superstition and replace them with reason, observation, and science. But in undermining (and often ridiculing) the tenets of established religion, Enlightenment thought also challenged the basic, time-hallowed Christian doctrines of monogenesis and common humanity. Experience and observation seemed rather to ratify the notion that there were many different peoples inhabiting the globe, who belonged to diverse races, and whose forebears may have originated at different times and in different parts of the world. Hence the new doctrine of polygenesis, embraced in Britain and France, the Caribbean, and the United States by such rationalists as Lord Kames and Voltaire.[22] This lent support to what was seen as the unbridgeable division between peoples who were black and those who were white: "for monogenists, race could be considered chance variations; for polygenists, differences were bound to be absolute."[23]

This was not the only way in which the Enlightenment led to an intensification of racial thought and divisions, for if the peoples of the globe had originated in separate parts of it, and were immutably different from one another, then it should be possible to assign them distinctive natures and separate identities and to rank them according to their collective sophistication, or lack thereof. The Swedish botanist Carolus Linnaeus, celebrated for pioneering modern taxonomy, is also often credited with inaugurating this practice, when in 1735 he divided and ordered humankind into four distinct races: white European, red American, dark Asiatic, and black negro. Although he did not explicitly rank them, Linnaeus's description of the races clearly indicated his preferences: he describes Europeans as "acute, inventive . . . [and] governed by laws," whereas the Africans were "crafty, indolent, negligent . . . [and] governed by caprice."[24] Meanwhile, Linnaeus's contemporary, Georges-Louis Leclerc, Comte de Buffon, preferred a sixfold classification: Lapp polar, Tartar, South Asian, European, Ethiopian, and American, but he likewise assumed that Europeans were intellectually superior to the others, especially Africans, whom he dismissed as "simple and stupid."[25] Johann Friedrich Blumenbach's *On the Natural Variety of Mankind*, published in 1775, and twice revised, eventually concluded that there were five races: Caucasian—a term he coined to indicate a superior racial lineage unique to the inhabitants of central and western Europe—along with lesser groupings he described as Mongolian, Ethiopian, American, and Malay.[26]

At a time of such pervasive racial language, identities, and hierarchies, the contradiction went generally unremarked when Britain's American colonists rebelled and established a nation dedicated to "the proposition that all men are created equal," but excluded from this declaration the fifth of its people who were black African slaves. "What then," asked J. Hector St. John de Crèvecoeur at just this time, "is the American, this new man?" His answer was clear: "a mixture of English, Scotch, Irish, French, Dutch, Germans and Swedes. . . . He is either a European or a descendant of a European."[27] This view of the new nation's racial hierarchy was affirmed by Thomas Jefferson, who insisted that "the difference" between blacks and whites was "fixed in nature," and not susceptible to alteration or adjustment.[28] Accordingly, when the U.S. Congress passed the Naturalization Act of 1790, it restricted American citizenship to those superior specimens of humanity described as "free white persons," and this legislation would remain in force for the next eighty years. (In the *Dred Scott* decision of 1857, Chief Justice Roger B. Taney would later uphold this understanding and assert that blacks could not be American citizens because they "had no rights which the white man was bound to respect," and were debarred by their race from being part of the American "political family," which remained restricted to whites.)[29]

The establishment of racial attitudes, identities, and rankings across the Western world during the second half of the eighteenth century was reinforced by the growth in a range of pseudoacademic endeavors later described as "scientific racism." During the 1770s, Peter Camper of the Netherlands and Johann Kaspar Lavater of Switzerland suggested that human beings could be racially classified and ranked on the basis of the varied dimensions, differing angles, and volumetric capacities of their skulls; thus was inaugurated the new field of craniometry, which soon became popular across Europe and the United States.[30] The result was the proliferation of publications purporting to demonstrate that the foreheads of negroes receded more than those of whites, and that their cranial capacity was thus significantly smaller, suggesting their brains were too, which could only mean they were less intelligent—conclusive proof that blacks belonged to a different and inferior race. Craniometry flourished into the early decades of the nineteenth century, and these years also witnessed the heyday of the cognate discipline of phrenology, whose practitioners made even more systematic attempts to correlate mental capacity with the contours of the skull, though reaching the same conclusion that white people possessed larger brains and greater intelligence than black people.[31] Here was seemingly irrefutable evidence that distinct races *did* exist, and that they could be separated and ranked in permanent hierarchies.

During the first half of the nineteenth century, racial categories, rankings, and identities became increasingly important in Western thought, politics, and culture, and practitioners of subjects as varied as linguistics, anthropology, ethnography, philology, biology, phrenology, and craniometry were preoccupied with observing, measuring, ordering, and explaining what they believed were these all-pervasive racial types.[32] Yet for all this apparent certainty and objectivity, and notwithstanding the belief that "race was everything," it was (like class, only more so) a concept and category on which agreement proved to be impossible.[33] There was no consensus as to whether the origins (and thus the races) of humankind could be better explained in terms of monogenesis or polygenesis. From the late eighteenth century, the general trend in informed thought was away from the former and toward the latter, but neither Linnaeus nor Buffon nor Blumenbach believed in polygenesis. This confusion about how (and where) humanity began also meant there was no agreement as to the precise number of races.[34] Were there two, namely white and black, which subsumed all the others (as Jefferson and Kant believed)? Or were there three (Gobineau), or four (Linnaeus), or five (Blumenbach) or six (Buffon), or were there many more (as Knox thought)? Were such racial characteristics as skin color, the size of the skull, or the angle of the forehead the result of biology (in which case they could not be changed), or had they evolved in response to the environment in keeping with the new insights of Darwin (in which case perhaps they might be)? Should races be classified by such physical features, or by their mental attainments and cultural attributes, or both?[35]

By now there was also uncertainty as to whether races were separate and distinct, or intermingled and interbred, thereby hybridizing and melding imperceptibly into one another. The reality in the Caribbean and the Spanish Americas was that the "white" and "black" races regularly intermarried, which meant people of mixed race—variously called mestizos or half-breeds—were widespread. Between 1776 and 1789, Médéric Louis Elie Moreau de Saint-Méry produced a detailed survey of the nuances of race and elaborate gradations of color to be found in the French colony of Saint-Domingue (later Haiti), which cast doubt on the view that the world was divided between "pure" whites and "pure" blacks, and even some of the early pioneers of racial taxonomies, such as Johann Blumenbach, accepted that their limited number of specified races were no more than ideal types, and that in practice there was a human continuum, as the races merged one into another by insensible degrees.[36] This was enough to move the likes of Gobineau, the American slaveholder Josiah Nott, and Professor James Reddie of Edinburgh University to condemn race-mixing and miscegenation as a "filthy" practice; they noted that such mongrel peoples were "doomed to perish," going the way of the ancient Egyptians and the Carthaginians. And there were some, like Knox's protégé James Hunt, who believed the state had an obligation to enforce racial separateness and purity by passing restrictive laws to "regulate the intermixture of the races of man."[37]

A further unresolved issue was the relationship between these recently discerned racial identities and the simultaneous rise of national identities: were they mutually reinforcing or mutually exclusive? There were those like Robert Knox who argued that Europe had always been a racial melting pot, that the races were hopelessly mixed up, and that they would always remain so, resulting in the sort of antagonisms that had erupted across the continent during 1848. From this perspective, aligning national identities with racial identities was unrealistic and impossible. Alternatively, there were those like Johann Gottfried von Herder who combined the "scientific" view of race with a mystical belief in the unchanging spirit of the people ("Volksgeist"), expressed in their culture, history, and language, in the hope that there could be established a pure, unsullied collective "volkish" identity. Such an outcome was especially attractive to those who believed in the Aryan race, whose origins were traced back by philologists, via ancient Greece and Rome, to India; and the superiority of the Aryans over all other races would be proclaimed by (among others) Richard Wagner, offering powerful validation to those who believed that the great task of nineteenth-century German statesmanship must be to align the racial identity of the "Volk" with an appropriate unit of political jurisdiction, bringing together blood and soil, race and nation.[38]

There was also disagreement as to whether races were becoming more or less pure, stronger or weaker, were progressing or degenerating.[39] Gobineau feared that the "unnatural" mixing and miscegenation meant the weaker races (with darker skins and smaller brains) were undermining and would eventually overwhelm the stronger races (with white skins and bigger brains), thereby subverting and eventually overturning what ought to be the permanent racial hierarchy.[40] But this gloomy interpretation was challenged by a more optimistic view of racial prospects, derived from the work of Charles Darwin, especially his *Origin of Species* (1859) and *Descent of Man* (1871). Darwin did not believe in rigid racial identities, but thought they "graduate into each other," which meant it was "hardly possible to discover clear distinctive characters between them." Yet his argument that evolution was based on the survival of the fittest was taken by some to mean that life was a struggle for existence among races, and that those with greater energy and intelligence would triumph by reason of natural selection over those lesser breeds who were enervated and stupid and thus doomed to extinction. From this so-called social Darwinist perspective, races must be getting stronger not weaker, and the purpose of statecraft should be to facilitate this process of human evolution by intervening in the preordained conflicts between the races, thereby ensuring the eventual triumph of the superior races and the necessary subjugation (even the elimination) of the lesser ones.[41]

Since "scientific racism" was riven by inaccuracies and internal contradictions, this lent support to the alternative, traditionalist view: namely, that the attempt to undermine the traditional biblical teachings of monogenesis and common humanity by dividing and ordering people on the basis of their skin color was not only intellectually flawed but also morally wicked. Such was the opinion of those who campaigned to abolish slavery, who believed that all human beings were created equal in the image of God. In Britain, the conviction that slavery was an unacceptable affront to this religiously hallowed idea of common humanity was vividly conveyed in the ceramic badge manufactured by Josiah Wedgwood, on which a kneeling, manacled black slave cries out, perhaps in despair, perhaps in hope, "Am I not a man and a brother?"[42] In the United States, similar sentiments were expressed by Theodore Dwight Weld: "no condition of birth, no shade of colour, no misfortune of circumstances" could "annul the birthright charter, which God has bequeathed to every being upon whom he has stamped his own image," by which he meant the freedom and equality all humans should enjoy. Any society based on the race hierarchy of slavery was an affront to the creator. "The real battleground between liberty and slavery," agreed Samuel Cornish, who had established the first black newspaper in New York City, "is prejudice against colour."[43]

To be sure, the many abolitionists in many lands had many motives for wishing to see the end of slavery, but the progress of that cause and its success in Britain (1833), the Netherlands (1863), the United States (1865), Spain (1886), and Brazil (1888) owed much to the moral conviction that its continued existence was an affront to the claim that all men were created equal by God.[44] These views also underlay the steps taken in the United States to reorder its polity in the aftermath of Emancipation, by dismantling the legal sanctions that had upheld the slave-society hierarchy based on the "narrow bounds of race." The Fourteenth Amendment, ratified in 1868, wrote equal citizenship for all people born in the United States (except "Indians not taxed"), into the Constitution, thereby nullifying the *Dred Scott* decision; the Fifteenth Amendment, ratified two years later, prohibited individual states from making race a qualification for voting. The result was that American whites and blacks were for the first time deemed to be equal members of the human race and of the American body politic, as the color line previously maintained between them was legally dismantled and constitutionally abolished. In the words of William Curtis, the editor of *Harper's Weekly*, the Civil War and Emancipation had transformed America from being a nation "for white men" only into one "for mankind" as a whole.[45]

Yet despite its intrinsic inconsistencies and contradictions, and notwithstanding the abolition of slavery, racialist thought and identities, reinforced by social Darwinist ideas of race struggle, became *more* influential in the Western world during the years of high imperialism. In Britain, the historian E. A. Freeman celebrated the triumph of the Anglo-Saxons, whose capacity for self-government he thought unrivaled, and whose superiority over all other races he constantly proclaimed.[46] Sir Charles Dilke in *Greater Britain* (1868) and Sir John Seeley in *The Expansion of*

England (1883) thought of the British Empire primarily in terms of the "white" parts of it, namely Canada, Australia, New Zealand, and South Africa. By the early twentieth century, this "enlarged" British identity was articulated by figures such as James Bryce, in his lectures on race proclaiming transoceanic Anglo-Saxon superiority, and by Cecil Rhodes, who believed the English were "the finest race in the world, and that the more of the world we inhabit, the better it is for the human race." Hence the Rhodes Scholarships, designed "to promote the unity and extend the influence of the English-speaking race" by bringing Britons from the overseas dominions to study at Oxford University.[47] As such, the British Empire was an essentially Anglo-Saxon enterprise, and when Rudyard Kipling urged the Americans to adopt a similarly assertive policy, he did so in a poem that exhorted its readers to "take up the white man's burden."[48]

Kipling's verses were addressed to Theodore Roosevelt, and when he became American president he enthusiastically accepted the challenge. Like Bryce, Roosevelt had been influenced by the writings of E. A. Freeman, and he believed in Anglo-Saxon racial destiny and superiority, dismissing native Americans as "savages" and blacks as "wholly unfit for the suffrage"; these views were widely shared among the governing elite by such figures as Henry Cabot Lodge and Woodrow Wilson, and by many white Americans who continued to regard blacks as intrinsically inferior.[49] The preoccupation with racial identities and rankings only intensified as immigrants poured into the United States from central, southern, and eastern Europe and threatened the traditional dominance of white Anglo-Saxon Protestants. One response, in William Z. Ripley's *The Races of Europe* (1899) and by the *Dictionary of Races and Peoples* (produced in 1911 by the U.S. Immigration Commission), was to specify more elaborate racial rankings, inserting Jews, Italians, and Hungarians between the Anglo-Saxons at the top and the blacks and Native Americans at the bottom. A second and more anxious reaction, as proclaimed by E. A. Ross in *The Old World in the New* (1914) and by Madison Grant in *The Passing of the Great Race* (1916), was to warn that the influx of these new immigrants meant that pure Anglo-Saxon Americans would be overwhelmed by lesser, alien races.[50]

In Germany, racial thought and categories also hardened, once the Reich had been created in 1870, with the aim of aligning the boundaries of political authority with those of racial identity: the cult of Aryan superiority intensified, as did the belief in "volkish" nationalism that owed much to Herder and Wagner. Less than a decade after unification, works were appearing such as William Marr's *Jewry's Victory over Teutonism* (1879) and Eugen Dühring's *The Jewish Question* (1881), which took a hostile attitude to their subject, encapsulated in the observation of the historian Heinrich von Treitschke that "the Jews are our misfortune."[51] The result was a growing fear (or hope) that there must be a race war between the Aryans and the Jews, in which the forces of light and darkness would fight to the death for world domination, and which the Aryans must win. This view was put forward by Georges de Lapouge in his book *The Aryan: His Social Role* (1899), and more vividly by Houston Stewart Chamberlain in his *Foundations of the Nineteenth Century* (also 1899), which became a best seller in Germany in the years before 1914. Chamberlain was English by birth, but had settled in Germany, where he married Wagner's daughter. He was a passionate believer in the importance of race identities and in Aryan superiority as embodied in the pan-German "Volk," and he loathed the Jews, whom he regarded as the epitome of evil, against whom the Aryans must wage an unrelenting, Manichean struggle.[52]

The racial identities and antagonisms being proclaimed in Britain, the United States, and Germany were paralleled in many parts of Europe, from the Russia of the Jewish pogroms to the France of the Dreyfus Affair to the Austria where the young Adolf Hitler was growing up in the anti-Semitic environment of fin-de-siècle Vienna. But race thought in Great Britain, the American Republic, and the German Reich was distinguished by a growing sense that these countries shared a common identity transcending the boundaries of their separate nations. One version of this community was the "English-speaking peoples," encompassing the Anglo-Saxon stock of Britain, plus the four dominions of Canada, Australia, New Zealand, and South Africa, and the United States: indeed, Cecil Rhodes sought to "promote the unity and extend the influence of the English-speaking race," and his scholarship scheme included awards for Americans as well as those from the British Empire.[53] A more extended version of the Anglo-Saxon brotherhood included the Aryan or Teutonic races of Germany, descended from the same racial stock as the British and the Americans, and who shared the same gifts for self-government. The Rhodes Scholarships also recognized the existence of this greater racial community and sought to strengthen it: in a codicil to his will, Rhodes granted five awards to Germany, in addition to those already assigned to the British Empire and the United States.[54]

THE RULE OF RACE

During the decades before the First World War, the identities built around the collectivities and consciousnesses of race were widely believed to be more significant than those constructed on the alternative basis of religion, gender, or class, while in Britain, the United States, and Germany the global potentialities of race identities went beyond the limited boundaries of the nation-state. The result was that the century from the 1880s witnessed many attempts to create structures of rule and authority on the basis of racial identities and hierarchies, and these efforts took two forms, the inclusionary and the exclusionary. The inclusionary variant permitted the incorporation and coexistence of different races within a nation or empire, on the basis of a rigid hierarchy, which was enforced to keep the races ranked and separate; the exclusionary denied that different racial groups should coexist within the same polity, and sought to expel those who belonged to unwanted inferior stock, or prevent them from gaining entry in the first place.[55] The inclusionary variant characterized regimes in which whites asserted their superiority over indigenous blacks; the exclusionary characterized anti-Semitic regimes, which sought to exclude (and even exterminate) Jews, who were a threat to racial purity and thus could not be tolerated. Either way, political power was employed to promote one (superior) race over other (inferior) races, and to this end, inclusionary and exclusionary measures were often employed together.[56]

To a marked degree, the European powers created empires

that proclaimed "the omnipresence of racial differences," for one underlying presumption was the superiority of the white man over those whom Kipling described as "lesser breeds without the law," and who were invariably dark-skinned.[57] One of the ways in which Canada, Australia, New Zealand, and South Africa proclaimed their sense of national identity was as "white man's countries." Their ruling elites believed the colored races were intrinsically different and inferior, that they should live separate lives in separate areas, and that they were unsuited to politics and government. As a result, native peoples were dispossessed of their lands, and were either disenfranchised or prevented from holding the vote, ostensibly because of their limited literacy and command of English, but in practice because they had the wrong skin color. [58] In Australia, the Commonwealth Franchise Act of 1902 denied Aboriginal men and women the vote, and when the Union of South Africa was created in 1910 it was on the basis of a de facto all-white franchise. One of the Union's architects was the young Afrikaner J. C. Smuts, who did not "believe in politics for them," namely black people, and insisted that whites and blacks should be separated, because "racial blood mixture is an evil." It was in South Africa that the politics of racial exclusion culminated in the Native Land Act of 1913, which confined black Africans, who formed the great majority of the population, to 7 percent of its territory, and prevented them from owning or leasing land in areas set aside for whites.[59]

At the same time that these race hierarchies were being domestically embedded, the policies of racial exclusion were increasingly embraced in the British dominions to ensure they continued to be "white men's countries," by restricting immigration of blacks, South Asians, and (especially) Chinese. The fear of cheap "Asiatic" labor was common to white settler societies bordering the Pacific, where the Chinese were willing to work for lower wages than white men. These immigrant populations were tiny, but as the global economy turned down during the late nineteenth century, such foreigners were often made the scapegoat, and the rights of white labor mutated into the entrenching of racial privilege. In the Australian colonies, for instance, immigration was closely restricted during the 1880s.[60] New Zealand moved in step, and successive prime ministers were determined to have "the purity of our race maintained." In Canada, similar legislation was passed in British Columbia against Chinese migrants who had come to build the Canadian Pacific Railway. On confederation in 1901, the Australian parliament expelled Pacific Islanders and prevented "non-whites" from entering the country to settle, thereby inaugurating the "White Australia" policy, and in 1913 South Africa carried an Immigration Restriction Act, consolidating legislation earlier passed in Cape Colony, Natal, the Transvaal, and the Orange Free State.[61]

From this perspective, the British Empire was a white man's empire, in which inferior people of color were denied political and legal rights where they lived, and were prevented from moving from one part of the empire to another. In 1901, the Australian attorney general, Alfred Deakin, defending the White Australia policy, described the motive for establishing this great racial divide as "the instinct of self preservation," for it was "nothing less than the national manhood, the national character and the national future that are at stake."[62] To be a colored person in these white men's countries was demeaning, humiliating, and degrading. Mahatma Gandhi would never forget the insults he suffered when he visited Natal in 1893; appalled at the segregation between whites and blacks, on trains and in hotels and even in public baths, he concluded that the whole colony was afflicted by "the deep disease of colour prejudice."[63] And what was true of the British Empire was no less true of the French or Belgian or German empires at the same time. In the latter case, and uniquely among early-twentieth-century Western imperial powers, marriages between German colonists and nonwhites (including those of mixed blood and "Christian half-castes") were banned.[64]

There were similar developments in the United States, where in the aftermath of the Civil War and Emancipation, the issues, identities, and hierarchies of race became, paradoxically, *more* pronounced and more central to American public discourse. This was partly because in the era of social Darwinism and high imperialism, race thought and talk and the desire to reaffirm racial divisions and rankings were widespread; but it was also that with the formal end of Reconstruction in 1877, the position of blacks got worse, not better, as southern whites ruthlessly reasserted their collective racial supremacy, while the federal government, refusing to commit sufficient resources or apply enough force to overcome violent white resistance, failed to enforce civic and political equality for blacks.[65] In the South, one of the unintended consequences of Emancipation was that black males were no longer depicted as childlike innocents, who needed firm but benevolent guidance; instead they were increasingly regarded as subhuman beasts who were widely believed to be sexual predators, lusting after white women, and who deserved to be lynched or burned alive in the interests of natural justice.[66] Here was a new racist culture, of negative stereotyping, as embodied in "white supremacism" and the Ku Klux Klan. The result was that in the American South, the forty years after Reconstruction witnessed the most sustained and coherent effort yet made to order society on the basis of racial identities and divisions, hierarchies, and subordination.

Although they were unable to resurrect the slave system, southern whites soon devised legal and extralegal measures that deprived blacks of their recently won rights to vote, hold public office, and engage in politics. By the 1890s, segregation was the law and the custom in towns and cities throughout the South, encompassing all aspects of public living (and dying), for it was enforced in hotels, prisons, schools, restaurants, stores, factories, hospitals, buses, trains, toilets—and cemeteries. The majority of blacks were systematically reduced to positions of dependency, poverty, and restricted aspirations in a brutally bifurcated social order: intermarriage between blacks and whites was prohibited, and during the 1880s and 1890s white lynchings of blacks averaged 150 a year.[67] The segregation and subordination of blacks was accompanied by political disenfranchisement. Beginning in Mississippi in 1890, all southern states enacted legislation that meant only whites would be eligible to vote in Democratic primaries, which effectively excluded blacks from the political process, for the white supremacist Democrats were the majority party across the South. The Supreme Court might have declared such racist laws unconstitutional, but it failed to protect blacks from this new form of what became known as "Jim Crow" discrimination, which effectively nullified the Fourteenth and Fifteenth Amendments in the South.[68]

This determination to subordinate blacks was accompanied by renewed efforts by the Anglo-Saxons to reassert that America was a "white man's country." The first was the decision to join with Canada, New Zealand, and Australia in restricting Asian immigrants, and in 1882 the Chinese Exclusion Act, which passed after loud demands from organized labor, barred any sizable immigration of Chinese workers. The second was the parallel demand to limit the new immigrants pouring in from southern and eastern Europe, peoples who were dismissed by the economist Francis Amasa Walker in 1890 as "beaten men from beaten races, representing the worst failures in the struggle for existence." One bill to keep such people out of the United States was vetoed by President Grover Cleveland in 1897, but a second became law in 1924, and thereafter immigration from southern and eastern Europe was severely limited (and it was barred from Asia altogether). "America must be kept American," declared President Calvin Coolidge: the "huddled masses, yearning to be free" now had to try their luck elsewhere.[69] The third development was the growing racial assertiveness of the United States overseas. As one American soldier put it, having participated in the conquest of the Philippines, "we all wanted to kill 'niggers.'" The result of these policies was what the historian Eric Foner has termed the "re-racialization of America" and "the resurgence of an Anglo-Saxonism that fused patriotism, xenophobia and an ethno-cultural definition of nationhood in a renewed rhetoric of racial exclusiveness."[70]

In Germany, the anti-Semitism preached by writers such as Lapouge and Chamberlain would eventually lead to even worse horrors than those seen in the American South. Throughout the North German Federation from 1869, and across the entire Reich two years later, Jews only formed 1 percent of the population, and they enjoyed full rights of citizenship. But those who had not become Christians were often denied access to jobs in the civil service, academe, and the military. By the late nineteenth century, however, as German politics moved decisively to the right, there was a marked rise in "volkish nationalism" and popular anti-Semitism, especially among the lower middle class.[71]

Defeat in the First World War led to a search for explanations, and the Jews, with their alleged internationalist conspiracies and their rootless disloyalty to the Reich, were for many the obvious scapegoats. During the 1920s, German nationalists continued to believe that the "Volk" defined their nation as a unique and exclusive community, one that should incorporate all Germans inside and outside the formal frontiers of their recently reduced territory, but deny the German nationality of anyone who was not of the "Volk," even if formally a German citizen. Popular social biology lent support to such views, by reinforcing the Aryan myth that all authentic Germans, whether living in the fatherland or outside it, shared a common physical origin, which explained their cultural distinctiveness, spiritual affinity—and racial homogeneity.[72]

The young Adolf Hitler had fully assimilated these inclusionist and exclusionist racial views, and he would later implement them with unique intensity, fanaticism, belligerence, and terror.[73] Each nation, Hitler believed, should be made up of "a multitude of more or less similar beings," who were thus "linked by blood" and by a shared racial consciousness. Because races and nations were (or should be) thus aligned, it followed that the world was divided into two distinct categories: the "higher races," imbued with the urge for self-preservation and continuance, and capable of creating and sustaining a superior culture; and the "lower races," destined for biological degeneration, cultural sterility, and ultimate disappearance. Accordingly, Hitler's nations were collective communities that were racially based and locked in permanent confrontation and perpetual struggle, they were exclusive and belligerent from nature and necessity, and the Aryan nation or "Volk" was the supreme form of racial awareness and expression of racial superiority.[74] The state, in Hitler's view, must be coterminous with the nation, the "Volk," and the race, and its purpose was to promote and protect the biological purity of its population, to raise levels of racial consciousness, and to consolidate a greater Germany by incorporating those Aryans who lived beyond its own borders.

From 1933 to 1945, Hitler sought to define, preserve, extend, and defend the racially pure German "Volk": "the aim of German policy," he observed in November 1937, "is to make secure and to preserve the racial mass and to enlarge it."[75] The essence of this racial bond was a common racial blood ("Volksblut"), and from the beginning of his dictatorship, legislation was carried laying down who was and who was not a racial German. In 1935, he passed an act "for the protection of German blood and German honor," which meant Germans could marry only Germans; he also enacted a new citizenship law, which defined who Germans were—and were not. By this definition, non-Germans could not be full members of Hitler's "Germanic state of the German nation."[76] At the same time that Hitler was defining the German nation in terms of blood, he was also defining—and extending—it in terms of territory, as he sought to create a greater, racially homogeneous Reich by incorporating those Germans living beyond its borders in the former Habsburg Empire; hence the occupation of the Rhineland, the annexation of Austria and Czechoslovakia, and the attack on Poland. In October 1939, Hitler named Heinrich Himmler as the Reich Commissioner for the Strengthening of the German Race, and he soon established a German Racial Register as the first step in identifying anyone living outside the Reich who might qualify on the basis of blood as being authentically German.[77]

Hitler also sought to purify the Reich by excluding the Jews: biologically inferior, devoid of territorial roots or a geographical homeland, they might be international capitalists obsessed with profits, or Communists espousing global revolution. But whatever their agenda, they were the malevolent and incorrigible enemy of the racial state, sucking its culture dry, polluting its biological heritage, and undermining its collective willpower.[78] In the six years from March 1933, more than 250 laws and decrees were passed, depriving Jews of their German citizenship, expelling them from professional life, forbidding them from marrying Germans or having sexual relations with them, and expropriating their assets. The idea that Germany should be cleansed of Jews was a cardinal axiom of Nazi policy: "the Jews must get out of Germany," Hitler told Joseph Goebbels in November 1937, "in fact out of the whole of Europe."[79] Two years later, he empowered Himmler to deport all Jews from Greater Germany to the east, and from expulsion to elimination was but a step: in the summer of 1941, Hermann Göring authorized Reinhard Heydrich to find a "Final Solution" to the problem of the Jewish population, and the way was open for "the biological extermination," as one Nazi put it, "of the whole of European Jewry." Just as Lenin had believed it was his duty to assist the preordained historical process by helping to bring about the proletarian revolution against the Russian bourgeoisie, so Hitler believed he must throw the power and weight of the German state behind the Aryan race to ensure its predestined victory in its Manichean struggle for world mastery against the Jews.[80]

In the same way that Hitler's regime lethally implemented the racial thought that had intensified in Germany during the forty years before the First World War, so too did the Afrikaner leaders of South Africa appropriate the pre-1914 racial theories of white empire and turn them into virulent public policies, based on the idea of an authentic and homogeneous (and embattled) Afrikaner "Volk" standing against the lesser black race. The initial impetus for more complete segregation was the migration of blacks from the countryside to the cities during and after the First World War, which resulted in the imposition of "influx controls" on migrants, along with confinement to segregated townships or compounds for those allowed to remain in urban industrial areas. Beginning in 1924, laws were passed giving working-class whites a measure of security against black competition: "industrial colour bars" were constructed, setting the wages of whites at artificially high levels and giving them exclusive access to skilled jobs. Further repression of blacks soon followed: the Masters and Servants Act imposed greater controls on the nonwhite workforce; the Immorality Act declared intercourse between white and nonwhite a criminal offense; and the Native Administration Act allowed the government to deport any African who was judged to be promoting hostility between blacks and whites.[81]

In 1948, the victory of the Nationalist Party ushered in the culminating era of South Africa's white-dominated politics. Many of the Nationalist Party's leaders had opposed going to war with Nazi Germany, and some had remained sympathetic to Hitler throughout the conflict. The result was that South Africa embarked on the construction of what the historian George M. Fredrickson has described as "the most comprehensive racist regime meant to be a permanent structure that the world has ever seen," as new laws were introduced to complete the machinery of segregation.[82] The Mixed Marriage Act of 1949 banned unions between whites and all non-Europeans, while the Immorality Act of 1950 declared illegal any form of sexual relations between men and women across the color line. Soon afterward, the Suppression of Communism Act allowed the government to proceed against anyone who sought to bring about political, industrial, social, or economic change "by the promotion of disturbance and disorder," which effectively outlawed any form of black political protest against white supremacy, and the Illegal Squatters Act gave the government power to remove Africans from any chosen area.[83] These were draconian powers, and for almost forty years they would be ruthlessly wielded. "Our view," Prime Minister J. G. Strydom explained in 1952, "is that in every sphere the Europeans must retain the right to rule the country and keep it a white man's country."[84]

Despite the biblical doctrines of monogenesis and common humanity, the legislative entrenchment of apartheid from the late 1940s was given religious sanction by the Dutch Reformed Church, which insisted that God had instituted the boundary lines between the races. This meant, as the South African prime minister D. F. Malan explained to the African National Congress, that racial identities were "permanent and not man-made," since Afrikanerdom was "but a creation of God," and that "our history is the highest work of the Architect of the Centuries." Likewise, the minister for Bantu administration, De Wet Nel, insisted apartheid was "not a mere abstraction which hangs in the air. It is a divine task which has to be implemented and fulfilled systematically."[85] To give effect to these views, children in South African schools were taught "Christian National thought," a bizarre amalgam of extreme neo-Calvinism, intense scientific racism, and nostalgic neo-Nazism. Even Smuts, whose views on race were—and are—controversial, thought apartheid "a crazy concept, born of prejudice and fear."[86] Small wonder that to Sir John Maud, British high commissioner to South Africa from 1959 to 1962, such views combined the confessional bigotry of the European wars of religion with racist opinions reminiscent of Nazi Germany: Prime

Minister Hendrik Verwoerd's government, he said, owed "more to the seventeenth century than to the twentieth century," and there was "an ominous Hitlerian smell about it," while he found the minister for external affairs, Eric Louw, "disturbingly reminiscent of Dr. Goebbels."[87]

Such were the attempts made by white men to construct nations and empires on the basis of racial identities and hierarchies; but since the racial theories and categories on which they were based were both mistaken and contradictory, it is scarcely surprising that in practice it proved difficult to "regulate the intermixture of the races of man." It bears repeating that no late-nineteenth-century nation was inhabited by a single, homogeneous racial group: the United Kingdom was populated by Celts as well as Anglo-Saxons; the United States, in addition to being a nation of blacks and whites (and Native Americans), was becoming a multiracial melting pot; and the German Reich not only contained Aryans and Jews, but also many non-Aryans, while many Germans were living outside the fatherland in the Austro-Hungarian Empire. It was equally impossible to realize the larger, transoceanic racial groupings being advocated at this time. The shared sense of Anglo-Saxon solidarity or "Britannic ethnicity" between the metropolis and the "white" dominions was undercut by the growing demands of the settlers to establish their own national identities. The transatlantic feelings of Anglo-Saxon brotherhood were undermined by British anxieties about America's industrial and financial might, and by its isolationist tendencies and residual hostility to the British Empire. And the Teutonic fellowship linking the Anglo-Saxons of America, Britain, and Germany did not survive the First World War, one indication of which was that the Rhodes Scholarships awarded to Germans were abolished and redistributed to the British Empire.[88]

Moreover, the expanding empires of the late nineteenth century were complex phenomena, driven and governed by many varied and contradictory impulses, of which race was only one. The projection of European (and latterly American) force overseas was an uncertain matter, which meant that in the tropical "colonies of rule" the imperial powers were obliged to govern with and through indigenous hierarchies: in reality, empire was often more of a collaborative endeavor with dark-skinned rulers than the strident rhetoric of racial superiority suggested.[89] Race thought and categories were also challenged by the countervailing policy of imperial trusteeship, which insisted that the point of empire was not to proclaim and assert the superiority of white people but to put colored people first. This was partly a religious and ethical impulse, underscored by the missionary belief in the God-given unity of all humankind, and it was partly political in that the British Empire's official position was that the interests of the natives were "paramount," and took precedence over those of white settlers or "immigrant races." And the measures passed by the dominions to make them "white men's countries" were greeted with skepticism and disapproval in London, where the needs of white settlers formed only one element in a complex imperial equation, and where the official view remained, as the colonial secretary Joseph Chamberlain explained in 1897, that the empire made "no distinction in favour of, or against, race or colour."[90]

The idea that there was a single, binary division in the European empires between the superior (white) colonizers and the inferior (dark-skinned) colonizers was also too simplistic to fit the facts. In the four great "white" dominions of the British Empire, there were distinct Scottish and Irish identities (there were also distinct Protestant Irish and Catholic Irish identities), and there were significant Jewish enclaves in big cities from Johannesburg to Sydney. Even more significant, and divisive, were the (largely Catholic) French in the province of Quebec, Canada, and the Afrikaners in South Africa, against whom the British had fought, and with whom reconciliation was never more than partial. There were other divisions among whites: between civil servants and businessmen, financiers and entrepreneurs, soldiers and settlers, capitalists and workers.[91] It was the same with those lumped together under the implausibly monolithic identity of "black." There were myriad tribes in Africa, some of whom were dark-skinned, but others that were Arabs, and there were many different castes and races in South Asia. Moreover, colonizer and colonized interacted, regularly fraternized, and even married across these allegedly impermeable boundaries of racial identity.

Whatever its ideology, empire could never have existed in practice as a simple subjugation of nonwhites: colonizer and colonized collaborated and commingled in various ways.[92]

The undoubted reality of this imperial mingling explains why several of the most strident European proponents of race thought, categories, and superiority were opposed to European overseas expansion. From their perspective, empire was *not* the preordained vehicle for the assertion of white dominance, but rather a slippery slope to white degeneration. Among mid-nineteenth-century writers, the likes of Robert Knox and the Comte de Gobineau were highly skeptical of the virtues of imperial acquisitiveness. Likewise, when the United States became an imperial power, many advocates of racial segregation in the South, and of the restriction of immigrants from Europe and Asia, opposed annexing the Philippines, arguing that the nation already had its hands full in coping with inferior races at home, and should not get involved with other such wretched peoples abroad. At least to some extent, Adolf Hitler also shared these views: in *Mein Kampf*, he was retrospectively critical of Germany's decision to join the Scramble for Africa and to acquire colonies. Following the arguments advanced by Knox and Gobineau, he thought the Aryans should avoid tropical regions inhabited by non-Europeans.[93]

Even in the American South, where the line between whites and blacks was legally sanctioned, the reality was more complex than the letter of Jim Crow would suggest. In part this was because the "black experience" was becoming more varied. Agricultural laborers remained preponderant, but there was the beginning of an urban black middle class, with its own newspapers, businesses, churches, and banks. Blacks were also migrating to the rapidly industrializing North, where the pay was better and there were opportunities to become pastors, teachers, or doctors, and this trend intensified during the First World War. Despite the de facto discrimination in the North, many states tolerated intermarriage, public facilities remained legally unsegregated, and blacks could vote.[94] The notion of a unified, monolithic white race was also being eroded and undercut: by the widespread anti-Semitism especially marked on the East Coast, by the continued hostility of the Anglo-Saxons to the recently arrived immigrants from Ireland and central and eastern Europe, by the disenfranchisement of poor whites as well as blacks in the South, and by uncertainty about the racial status of Hispanics in the southern and western territories acquired by the United States from Mexico. When California entered the Union in 1850, such people were deemed to be white, but in New Mexico they were regarded as Native Americans, and statehood was delayed until 1912, long after the qualifying number of inhabitants had been reached.[95]

The attempt to establish clear-cut racial boundaries in Germany between Aryans and Jews was equally problematic. In Bismarck's Reich, the fit between the "Volk" and the nation had never been exact, and Germany's defeat in the First World War, with a subsequent loss of territory, reignited these issues.[96] Borderlands containing sizable German minorities were handed over to France, Denmark, and Poland. Millions of Germans from the former Habsburg Empire now lived under Czech or Italian rule, and formed the majority in the newly created state of Austria. During the 1920s, attempts were made to produce a map of what a true and complete German nation would look like, encompassing all of the "Volk," but the results were inconclusive, and it bears repeating that the union of Germany with Austria was forbidden at Versailles.[97] Moreover, Aryans and Jews were often mixed up together, in both their professional and private lives. Beginning in 1871, the founding father of German anthropology, Rudolf Virchow, undertook a survey of six million schoolchildren in the Reich, recording the color of their eyes, hair, and skin, and he concluded that "pure" and separate Aryan and Jewish races did not exist. And this reality became more pronounced thereafter: the proportion of Jews marrying non-Jews had risen from almost 8 percent in the period 1901–04 to just under 23 percent in 1929. The result was that many Jews resembled the Aryan archetype, being tall, fair-haired, and blue-eyed, while many Nazi leaders did not, including Goebbels, Himmler—and Hitler himself.[98]

Intermarriage, and the more general desire for assimilation, which led many Jews (among them the young Nikolaus Pevsner) to regard themselves as Germans first and Jews a distant second, made it difficult for the Nazis to draw a simple, clear-cut line between Aryan and Jew. Any German with three Jewish grandparents was deemed to be automatically Jewish, whereas those who were one-fourth or even one-half Jewish in ancestry could be considered German citizens if they did not practice Judaism or marry Jews or other part-Jews.[99] But this was an arbitrary standard, and it was virtually impossible to produce a precise definition of who did (and did not) possess the "German blood," even though a great deal of SS-sponsored "scientific" effort was devoted to trying to do so. The geography of race was no better delineated than the biology, as later attempts to map the full extent of "volkish" territory under the Third Reich were no more successful than the efforts made in the 1920s.[100] In reality, Nazi designations of Aryans and Jews were random and inconsistent, and their policies were no different from those applied by Karl Lueger, an earlier mayor of Vienna, an anti-Semite but with Jewish friends: "I decide who is a Jew." Even as the German Reich expanded by conquest, and one and a half million Europeans were interrogated, measured, photographed, and medically examined to see whether they satisfied the biological criteria of Aryan racial purity, the final "judgment about race," recorded in Himmler's Racial Register, remained confused, contradictory—and arbitrary.[101]

It was the same in South Africa, where once again the allegedly monolithic and polarized racial categories did not stand up to serious biological or genealogical scrutiny. Just as in Germany it was impossible to draw a single line between Aryans and Jews, so it was impossible in South Africa to define a clear boundary between blacks and whites. There were those categorized as "Asians," immigrants (like Gandhi) from British India who were neither black nor white. There was also another intermediary category, namely the "Coloureds," a substantial population of mixed origin that had developed in the western Cape out of the interaction of Europeans, Asians, Khoikhoi ("Hottentots"), and black Africans in the seventeenth and eighteenth centuries. They were essentially Afrikaner in language and culture, but under apartheid they were increasingly segregated and discriminated against. The Immorality, Group Marriage, and Urban Areas Acts had made it illegal for Coloureds to have sex, intermarry, or live in the same neighborhood with whites, and by the 1960s they found themselves reduced from a status intermediate between whites and

Africans to one that was closer to the latter than the former. This was not an arrangement congenial to all Afrikaners, who wanted a much more clear-cut division, and there were others who, on account of their pro-Nazi leanings, were unhappy with the decision to categorize Jews as whites, on the grounds that they were not part of the authentic Afrikaner "volk."[102]

As the South African economy became the most industrialized on the continent, it proved more difficult to maintain these simplified, artificial boundaries. By the early 1960s, Sir John Maud was convinced that apartheid must collapse because it was "inconceivable that in this multi-racial state the criterion of advancement will forever remain the colour of your skin." The attempt to keep whites and blacks separate, insisting on the superiority of the former and the inferiority of the latter, must give way, "for the simple reason that it is not only evil, but cannot be made to fit the facts." The South African economy, Maud believed, could not in the long run work on the basis of apartheid, any more than the American economy could have survived on the basis of slavery. He was also convinced that the perverted religious teachings of the Dutch Reformed Church, lending bogus legitimation to racist doctrines by spuriously claiming divine sanction, would not prevail against the traditional biblical injunctions stressing the equality and brotherhood of man, which had underpinned the campaigns to abolish the slave trade and slavery more than a century before. "Christianity," Maud concluded, in his valedictory dispatch to the British government, "is a much more serious threat than Communism to white supremacy." In the end, he was sure, common humanity would prevail over racial divisions.[103]

THE FALL OF RACE

The attempts to establish empires and nations on the basis of unambiguous racial identities, distinctions, rankings, inclusions, and exclusions were undertaken on the assumption that there was no such thing as a humanity common to all people: indeed, according to those proponents of racialist schemes in the European empires, or the American South, or Nazi Germany, or South Africa, the objects of oppression belonged to races so alien, inferior, and reprehensible as to be barely human. Yet even the most fiercely enforced of these views, policies, and polities, whether based on religious, biological, or historical evidence, have ultimately proved unstable and unsustainable, resting as they did on intellectual foundations that were at best uncertain and contradictory, and at worst plain wrong. Even as these regimes were being created, their policies and presumptions were subjected to ever more critical analysis and scrutiny, and from a variety of perspectives. Some of the earliest and most persuasive defiance of racialist thought came from Christians who believed that racial hierarchies and identities could not be reconciled with the religious teaching that all people were equal in the sight of God. Among them was Sir John Maud, who believed that racist policies violated the teachings of the Bible. Evangelical whites in the American South, Hitler's stooges among the German clergy, and fellow travelers in the Dutch Reformed Church of South Africa might piously claim otherwise, but they were in a minority; and the hostility of the Christian churches to the treatment of the Jews by the Nazis, and to that of nonwhites in South Africa, would prove decisive in mobilizing opinion against those regimes. As the fourth assembly of the World Council of Churches would put it in 1968, racism "denies our common humanity in creation and our belief that all men are made in God's image."[104]

But it was not the Christian churches alone that deplored attempts to divide the world into superior and inferior races; their resistance was reinforced by academics on both sides of the Atlantic. Some French scholars, unimpressed by a century of taxonomical confusions and inconsistencies, contended that there were no "pure" races, and in the United States the anthropologist Franz Boas urged that the whole notion of an anatomically unchanging racial hierarchy, established on the allegedly "scientific" measurement of different skulls, was inaccurate and misleading.[105] In the aftermath of Germany's aggression and defeat during the First World War, many writers sought to disprove the earlier claims concerning "volkish" preeminence and Teutonic superiority. In 1922, the Belgian Théophile Simar argued that the concept of race had been devised for political purposes and lacked all scientific validity, and that the claims of German superiority over other

European races was utterly wrong. Four years later, the American sociologist Frank H. Hankins mounted another attack on the theory of Nordic supremacy and the doctrines of "race purity and superiority" that supported it. And in a book published posthumously as *Racism* in 1938, the German-Jewish sexologist Magnus Hirschfeld set out to provide a history and a refutation of the racial doctrines of the Nazis. "If it were practicable," he wrote, "we should certainly do well to eradicate the term 'race' as far as subdivisions of the human species are concerned."[106]

The rise of Hitler and the application of Nazi racial policies created widespread consternation in academic circles, and work denouncing "scientific racism" gained increasing scholarly traction.[107] In 1936, at a joint meeting of the Anthropology and Zoology sections of the British Association for the Advancement of Science, the distinguished geneticist H. J. Fleurie declared that pure races did not exist; in the same year, E. A. Ross, who had deplored the arrival of immigrants to America from central and eastern Europe before the First World War, now admitted that "*difference of race* means far less to me now than it once did."[108] Franz Boas remained an influential figure among an older generation of American anthropologists, and in 1937 the young cultural critic Jacques Barzun published a book entitled *Race: A Study in Modern Superstition*, in which he insisted that "a satisfactory definition of race is not to be had," that it lumped people together "on the most superficial, unverified grounds of similarity," that it was "a superstition on a par with the belief in witchcraft and horoscopes," and that "a prudent man" would suspend judgment on the whole subject "until genetics can offer a more complete body of knowledge."[109] (It was a prescient prediction.) Four years later, at the annual gathering of the American Association of Physical Anthropologists, similar views were expressed by the anthropologist Ashley Montagu, who declared that the accepted view of race was artificial and did not agree with the facts.[110]

There were also political activists who defied racialist regimes. Booker T. Washington, although devoted to the advancement of blacks in the postbellum American South, did not believe they should mobilize against white supremacists, but rather that they should talk, cooperate, and come to terms with them, on the grounds of political prudence as well as in the name of common humanity. In fact, he urged that his fellow blacks eschew politics; cultivate the habits of thrift, honesty, and sobriety; and concentrate on the acquisition of a Christian character and a good education, in the hope that they might make a modest living and achieve some degree of economic security. Washington opposed inciting conflict between the two races, seeking instead to "cement the races and bring about a hearty co-operation between them," and he offered whites "the patient, sympathetic help of my race."[111] This doctrine of accommodationism proposed one version of how blacks and whites might get along with each other; Mahatma Gandhi offered another. Unlike Washington, Gandhi *did* believe in protest and mobilization (albeit of a nonviolent kind), but although he is best remembered as the figure who decried the racism he had encountered in South Africa, and as the nationalist leader who harassed the British and humbled their empire, Gandhi saw these specific South African and South Asian issues in terms of humanity as a whole.[112] In 1906, he took a vow of celibacy to free himself to care for *all* humanity as his own family; his teachings and politics drew on Christianity as well as Hinduism; and while seeing them as opponents, Gandhi was eager to engage in conversations with representatives of the British Raj across the boundaries of race. He believed in forgiving his enemies, in the underlying interconnectedness of life, and in a single, shared "authentic humanity."[113]

But rather than denying the importance of race, attacks on the racialist status quo in other countries reaffirmed it. In 1893, Charles Pearson, a Liberal Australian politician, published a book entitled *National Life and Character: A Forecast*, predicting the overthrow of Anglo-Saxon racial hegemony, because white men would be "elbowed and hustled and perhaps even thrust aside" by their supposed inferiors in Africa and Asia. This was also the view of the American intellectual W. E. B. DuBois, who asserted at the Pan-African Congress in London in 1900 that the great issue of the twentieth century would be "the problem of the colour line," by which he meant "the relation of the darker to the lighter races of men in Asia and Africa, in America and the islands of the sea"—a relation that he too believed was soon bound to change.[114] Pearson and DuBois shared the Anglo-Saxonist view that the world was divided between the monolithic identities of white and colored races, inevitably fated to struggle; but where they differed from it was in their conviction that the colored people, not the whites, would emerge victorious, thereby inverting the traditional racial hierarchy. Even before 1914, then, it was clear that the appeal to racial identities could be used as much against Europe's hegemony as on its behalf.[115]

DuBois was a university-educated northerner, who believed his fellow college graduates should organize and agitate blacks, to radicalize their politics, and to secure manhood suffrage, the eradication of distinctions based on color, equal employment opportunities, and equal rights. He regarded racial pride and the assertion of a distinct racial consciousness as essential prerequisites for black advancement, and he thought Africans and African Americans shared a common culture and racial identity, becoming one of the founding fathers of Pan-Africanism. In 1915, he published *The Negro*, a sweeping account of the alleged racial unity of the African peoples and of the glories of the continent's ancient kingdoms.[116] DuBois believed in a black identity that transcended the boundaries of Africa and the American South, and these internationalist views were further developed during the 1920s by the Jamaican immigrant Marcus Garvey, who celebrated "race distinction" and urged the creation of an independent state in Africa to which American negroes should be free to return. His aims were "to make the negro race conscious" and "to champion negro nationhood by redemption in Africa," and he too repeatedly called for international black solidarity. Indeed, on one occasion, Garvey compared the aims of the (spectacularly resurgent) Ku Klux Klan in America with his own aims in Africa: the Klan wanted to make America exclusively a white man's country; he wanted to make Africa exclusively a black man's country.[117]

There was another part of the world where the conventional racial hierarchies were attacked by those who nevertheless believed in the concept of race, namely Japan, a nation that had industrialized rapidly during the closing decades of the nineteenth century, defeated and shamed the Chinese, concluded an alliance with Britain, vanquished and humiliated Russia, and established its own Asiatic empire. Here was a country undergoing "astonishing development," and that seemed increasingly Western in its attitudes, attainments, and ambitions; yet the people of Japan had "yellow" skins and did not fit on either side of the alleged white-black racial divide. In 1902, the French government wrote to the British Foreign Office to inquire whether the Japanese should be categorized as white or nonwhite. The British could not decide, but the Japanese were convinced they were so superior to such lesser races as "Kanakas, Negroes, Pacific Islanders, Indians or other Eastern peoples" that "to refer to them in the same terms cannot but be regarded in the light of a reproach, which is hardly warranted by the fact of the shade of the national complexion." During the 1890s and 1900s, Japan regularly protested that the restrictions on Asiatic immigration recently established in the United States, Canada, and Australia insulted their nation by placing it on the same level in the racial hierarchy as inferior peoples such as the Chinese and Koreans.[118]

One Japanese response to such humiliation, exemplified by the newspaper proprietor Tokutomi Soho, was to give up trying to obtain acceptance by the white nations and to urge all "coloured people" to "combine and crush Albinocracy. We must make the whites realize that there are others as strong as they."[119] But after the First World War, having joined the entente against Germany and its allies, the Japanese strategy at the Paris Peace Conference was again to try for such acceptance, by lobbying for a clause in the Covenant of the League of Nations proclaiming the equality of all the races of the world; but that effort was defeated by an alliance of the "white" dominions of the British Empire, the United States, and Britain itself. This "Anglo-Saxon dominance in defiance of racial equality," along with the U.S. Immigration Act of 1924, which specifically excluded the Japanese, was a further rebuff that long rankled popular and official opinion in Japan, and it stiffened the resolve of those who advocated more aggressive nationalist policies. It also helps explain why, in the aftermath of Pearl Harbor, the Japanese would present their imperialist conquest of the indigenous peoples of the Pacific Islands and Asia as something very different, namely as a war for liberation—indeed, as the first serious attempt to overthrow the white empires of America and Europe.[120]

Such were the varied arguments about racial identities and rankings advanced between the 1900s and the 1930s: some contended there were no races, some that there were two, and some that there were more. These inconsistencies had emerged early at the Universal Race Congress, held in London in 1911.[121] Its aim was to "discuss, in the light of science and the modern conscience," the relations between the "so-called white and so-called coloured peoples," with a view "to encouraging between them a fuller understanding, the most friendly feelings, and a heartier co-operation." This was scarcely a coherent manifesto, by turns proclaiming the existence of race, expressing doubts about the "so-called" binary categories of white and colored, but also hoping the races might get along better with each other. There was much resort to the rhetoric of Christian universalism, and insistence that the peoples of the world were "to all intents and purposes essentially equals in intellect, enterprise, morality and physique," but some delegates took different views. As a social Darwinist, Felix von Luschan, professor of anthropology at Berlin, conceded that "the brotherhood of man" might be "a good thing," but thought "the struggle for life is a far better one." Races were different and antagonistic, and conflict between them was an essential precondition for human progress. From another perspective, Baron d'Estournelles de Constant regretted that "the white man" in Africa or Asia felt himself "to be more or less master, with power to act as he will" over all lesser peoples, while W. E. B. DuBois insisted that the key issue in America was "whether at last the Negro will gain full recognition as a man, or be utterly crushed by superior numbers."

Thereafter, as attacks on the twentieth-century race regimes gathered force, their contradictions became more apparent. As an advocate of aggressive black mobilization against whites, W. E. B. DuBois deplored the accommodationism of Booker T. Washington, which he regarded as a narrow and pessimistic policy of betrayal and submission; yet DuBois's belief in a unified, coherent, monolithic black consciousness ignored the increasing variety of the black experience in the United States, and made even less sense when extended to the Caribbean and Africa.[122] Moreover, the idea that there was a single color line, with a "white" race on one side and a "black" race on the other, might have been shared by white supremacists who wanted to keep things as they were, and by black activists who wanted to change things radically, but both were at fault in claiming the existence of these two homogeneous, inevitably antagonistic identities, and in ignoring the many conversations, encounters, and interactions that took place across these allegedly impermeable racial boundaries. And what of those other races that did not fit this polarized, dichotomized, black-and-white world? What, for instance, of the Jews: were they absolutely and loathsomely non-Aryan, as Hitler insisted, or were they part of the white South African "volk," as some champions of apartheid claimed? And where did the "yellow races" of China and Japan, or those who belonged to the "brown races" of North Africa and the Middle East, fit into this oversimplified, Manichean picture?

These inconsistencies were largely rendered moot during the Second World War, by a widespread repudiation of racialist thought and identities that was partly a matter of conviction and partly one of strategic necessity. President Franklin D. Roosevelt insisted that his "four freedoms" should be enjoyed by people of "every creed and every race, wherever they live"; the Allies claimed to be fighting for a liberty that was opposed to Aryan superiority and Japanese racial intolerance; and where politics and public opinion led, the academy followed. Horrified by the uses to which the Nazis and the Japanese had put the idea of inborn racial difference, physical and social scientists now retreated headlong from the claims that racial categories, identities, and hierarchies were the best way to understand the peoples of the world. The writings of Franz Boas, his student Ruth Benedict, and anthropologists critical of the link between race, culture, and ability now began to reach a mass audience.[123] Benedict's *Races and Racism*, published in 1942, dismissed race thought as "a travesty of scientific knowledge"; in the same year, Ashley Montagu's *Man's Most Dangerous Myth: The Fallacy of Race* became a best seller; and in 1944 the Swedish sociologist Gunnar Myrdal published *An American Dilemma*, which concluded that Jim Crow segregation in the

South was unjustified and un-American. By the end of the Second World War, the notion that race was the most significant form of collective human identity, consciousness, and ranking had been stripped of any serious claim to intellectual respectability. It was no longer the "everything" that earlier authorities from Knox to Hitler had claimed.[124]

Yet even as the idea of race, and the binary divisions built around it, were being intellectually undermined, evidentially discredited, and politically invalidated, the politics of racial identities and antagonisms were being given fresh impetus from a variety of developments. There was the Atlantic Charter, agreed by Winston Churchill and Franklin Roosevelt in 1941, which recognized "the rights of all peoples to choose the form of government under which they will live," a provision with serious implications for the European empires, where millions of dark-skinned people lived under authorities they had not chosen.[125] There was also the Japanese success in conquering vast swaths of the British, French, and Dutch empires, thus destroying the notion of the white man's innate superiority and ushering in a new world where Asiatic peoples had to be taken seriously and treated as equals rather than inferiors. And there was the critical reaction to the high-minded claims made in the United States that it had gone to war in 1941 to fight racial prejudice, discrimination, and genocide, all of which sounded distinctly implausible given the persistence of Jim Crow and the crude American racial stereotyping of the Japanese as rats, dogs, gorillas, and snakes. How could the Roosevelt administration condemn other regimes constructed on the basis of racial identities, inequality, and discrimination, given white America's own prejudices against blacks?[126] Was the Second World War a conflict of racial liberation—or merely of one racist dominion against another?

It was in this atmosphere of contradictions that the United Nations established its Educational, Scientific and Cultural Organization (UNESCO), one of whose aims was to counter the "ignorance and prejudice" that had underpinned the belief in the "doctrine of [the] inequality of men and of races." It convened a panel of scientists, chaired by Ashley Montagu, to produce a definitive verdict on race.[127] Their first statement was issued in

1950. "Scientists," it began, "have reached general agreement in recognizing that mankind is one: that all men belong to the same species, *Homo Sapiens*." Genes responsible for the "hereditary differences between men" were "always few when compared to the whole genetic constitution of man and the vast number of genes common to all human beings regardless of the population to which they belong." It followed that "the likenesses among men are far greater than their differences," and that "national, religious, geographic, linguistic and cultural groups do not necessarily coincide with racial groups." The panel urged it would be best "to drop the term 'race' altogether," since "for all practical purposes, 'race' is not so much a biological phenomenon as a social myth." It concluded with a ringing endorsement of the reality of common humanity: "Biological studies lend support to the ethic of universal brotherhood; for man is born with drives towards co-operation. . . . In this sense, every man is his brother's keeper." A year later, a second UNESCO group reaffirmed these findings, insisting that there were "no scientific grounds whatsoever for the belief that there were pure races or a hierarchy of superior and inferior human groups."[128]

Underlying these words was the widespread revulsion at the Jewish Holocaust, but the defeat of Germany had vanquished that most terrifying of racist polities, and during the next half century the remaining regimes that had been constructed on the basis of racialist thought, identities, superiority, subordination, segregation, and exclusion also disappeared. The end of the British Raj in India, of Dutch rule in the East Indies, and of French dominion in Indochina portended the termination of all the European empires in Asia, Africa, and the West Indies, and decolonization was virtually complete by the 1980s. During the same period, the "white" dominions of Canada, Australia, and New Zealand abandoned their policies of racial discrimination, ended their restrictions on immigration, sought to atone for earlier acts of genocide and dispossession, and embraced multiculturalism. At the same time, the Jim Crow laws and customs of the American South were toppled: civil rights legislation ended discrimination and gave blacks the vote, while the Supreme Court nullified state laws banning marriage or sexual relations across the boundaries of race, and the

1924 immigration law was effectively repealed.[129] Nor could the apartheid regime in South Africa endure indefinitely against what was becoming a global repudiation of racialist thinking. In 1990, President F. W. de Klerk announced that the discriminatory laws and state apparatus enforcing apartheid would be abandoned and that Nelson Mandela would be freed. Four years later Mandela was elected president, leading a government that was a "rainbow coalition" including blacks, Coloureds, Asians, and whites.[130]

This breathtaking survey of events might seem to vindicate the view that the house of cards constructed on racialist thought and racial identities had finally collapsed after the Second World War. But the underlying thinking did not melt away so easily. As the historian David Reynolds has noted, the extra-European assault on white racism after 1945 was "mounted in the name of another invented category, 'blackness,'" with "the ironic effect of entrenching racial conceptions still further."[131] Many African nationalist leaders of the postwar period, fighting for freedom against imperial dominion, were concerned to proclaim racial identities, to raise black consciousness, and to urge white Europeans to get out of their countries. It was the same in the United States, where Malcolm X propounded the doctrine of "black nationalism" while castigating the "devil race" of white men and "angrily" demanding black power and black separation, and where many American universities established departments of African American studies that sought to explore (and help create?) a shared sense of transatlantic African American identity and black consciousness. Even Martin Luther King Jr. sometimes spoke of the "marvelous new militancy which has engulfed the negro community," while Nelson Mandela for a time embraced violence as the only way to bring apartheid to an end.[132] In Africa and the United States, the color line remained strongly in evidence, and demands for independence and civil rights looked like the declaration of a race war the blacks in America and Africa were determined to win.

Yet the claim that there was a single, united, all-encompassing black consciousness being mobilized against European colonial oppression in Africa and white supremacists in America was belied and contradicted by much of the evidence. It bears repeating that many of the "black" agitations against imperial rule in Africa were fissured by divisions between different tribes, between those who lived in the countryside and the town, and between the traditional forces of collaborating authority and the new forces of middle-class nationalism: in the case of Southern Rhodesia, for example, there were deep divisions between those Africans led by Robert Mugabe and those who followed Joshua Nkomo. The result was that independence often ushered in more divisive battles as rival tribes, parties, and factions struggled over who would obtain the spoils of the postcolonial state: as in the former Belgian Congo, where the province of Katanga soon broke away, and where civil war continues to this day; as in Rwanda, where in the 1994 genocide between half a million and one million Tutsi were exterminated by the Hutu; and as in the Sudan, where the south broke away from the north, but where another long-running civil war nevertheless continued.[133] Moreover, the struggles for independence against the "white" European empires were not only carried on by "black" Africans but also by Arabs in North Africa and the Middle East, as well as by the inhabitants of South Asia and Indochina, none of whom could possibly be described as black.

In the deimperializing twentieth century, as in the imperializing nineteenth, there was no one single global color line dividing all the peoples of the world into blacks and whites. The same was true in the United States, where by the 1950s the range of black circumstances was more varied than ever, divided between North and South, country and town, working class and middle class. Some blacks, trapped in the ghettoes of big cities, rioted and rampaged; others joined the nonviolent protests against segregation in the South. Some of them, such as the parents of Condoleezza Rice, did not buy into arguments about collective mobilization, but preferred to embrace the individual ethic of self-help and accommodationism; and whether black civil rights leaders were confrontationalist or conciliatory, they were invariably male, and they gave very little recognition to the role of women.[134] And after a generation in which university departments had been devoted to tracing and studying (and often proclaiming) the unity, coherence, and victimhood of the African American experience and identity, that experience and identity, fissured by geography and gender, class and culture, had turned out to be very difficult to discern. The result, in the words of Cornel West, was that "there is no such thing as having one identity or of there being one essential identity that fundamentally defines who we actually are." Reginald McKnight agreed: "we are not a race," he wrote, "not even simply an agglomeration of individuals." Depending on the circumstances or purposes, he argued, "we are at times a 'We' and a 'Them,' an 'Us' and 'The Other.'"[135]

But while such claims to an all-encompassing black identity and consciousness were in some ways too inflated, they were also too limited, for like the white supremacists against whom they were mobilizing, they denied the common humanity that was more than ever being scientifically verified.[136] Two figures, inspired by Gandhi, embraced this broader picture—not always, and not always successfully, but in ways that were nevertheless inspirational and transformative. The first was Martin Luther King Jr., who drew on the Christian teachings of the unity of humankind and sought to stress human connections and affinities in a "network of mutuality." "Many of our white brothers," he declared in Washington, D.C., in August 1963, "have come to realize that their destiny is tied up with our destiny." So he dreamed of a time when "the sons of former slaves and the sons of former slave-owners will be able to sit down together at a table of brotherhood," when "little black boys and black girls will be able to join hands with little white boys and white girls as sisters and brothers," and when there would be a redeemed America encompassing "all of God's children, black men and white men, Jews and Gentiles, Protestants and Catholics."[137] The second figure was Nelson Mandela, whose views were close to King's, though he was not a practicing Christian. He espoused "harmony" between "all persons," in conversation and operation across the boundaries of racial identity, and in the importance of forgiveness and reconciliation in the postapartheid South Africa, which should be a country "of which all humanity will be proud." He recognized the greater and more compelling identity of "the entire human race," and he personified it with such charisma and moral force that he became someone who "transcended colour" and was "above race."[138]

BEYOND RACE?

As with the solidarities of class, so with the identities of race, the twentieth century ended very differently from how it began. The destruction of Nazi Germany, the fall of the European colonial empires, the de-racing of civil rights in the United States, and the end of apartheid in South Africa were as much a repudiation of the view that "race is everything" as the collapse of the Communist regimes was a rejection of the proposition that the history of all hitherto existing societies had been primarily one of class identity and class struggle. The passing of those regimes based on racial identities and hierarchies lent credibility to Barack Obama's assertion in 2004 that "there's not a black America and white America and Latino America and Asian America. There's the United States of America."[139] In so saying, Obama was also acknowledging a significant development in the American academy since the 1980s, namely the proposition that race was of "declining significance." One explanation, associated with the work of William Julius Wilson, to which Obama was indebted, was that the continued growth and consolidation of a black bourgeoisie meant race had become less important than class in explaining blacks' life chances; another was the increased number of interracial marriages; and the result was a plethora of books asserting that race as a form of collective identity mattered less in American society than before.[140] Here was a new "postracial" America, of which Obama was, appropriately, the first "postracial" president.

Yet the notion of race lingers as a form of identity and ranking that stubbornly refuses to die. Since the 1960s, there have been sporadic efforts to rehabilitate the nineteenth-century notion that races can be identified and ordered.[141] African leaders such as Robert Mugabe continue to play the "race card," denouncing white Western colonialism and neoimperialism. Some Americans lament that the color line persists, and that the country has by no means gotten beyond race; Obama's position is more equivocal than his eloquent exhortations to get beyond a black-and-white view of the United States suggests; and Randall Kennedy is surely correct to argue that everything about Obama's alleged "postracial presidency" is "widely, insistently, almost unavoidably interpreted through the prism of race."[142] One indication of the persistence of race as a category of human identity, but also of the serious doubts concerning its validity, can be found in the U.S. Census, which requires respondents to declare their racial identity from a list of options that in recent decades has changed frequently, inexplicably, and arbitrarily. In the 1930 census, Mexicans were deemed to belong to a separate race, but not in subsequent ones. In the same census and again in 1940, "Hindu" appeared as a separate race category, but then it too disappeared. In 1970, Indian Americans and Pakistani Americans were declared to be "white," but in 1980 they were reclassified as "Asian." In 2000, respondents were asked to describe themselves as belonging to one or more of fifteen "racial" identities, and if they refused to do so, their racial identity would be imputed and assigned by the Census Bureau.[143]

Thus, however mutably, does race persist; but as these taxonomical fluctuations suggest, it *has* significantly declined in plausibility as the most all-embracing category of human identity—not just in the United States but around the world. For the sustained undermining of racial solidarities and rankings by anthropologists has been corroborated (as Jacques Barzun presciently anticipated) by geneticists, building on the discovery by James Watson and Francis Crick of the structure of DNA. According to the findings of the Human Genome Project, people of all backgrounds, locations, and "races" share more than 99.9 percent of their DNA, and in the case of the remaining 0.1 percent, there is more variation *within* stereotypical racial groups than *between* them. This means that 99.9 percent of the genes of a "black" person are the same as those of a "white" person, and that the genes of any "black" person may be more similar to the genes of a "white" person than to another "black" person. Thus understood, race is a biologically meaningless concept and category, literally no more than skin deep. It is also neither innate nor permanent, for skin color can change dramatically from one generation to another as the result of mixed-race marriages.[144]

Thus has scientific research undermined those who urged that humanity had many, polygenic origins, which explained why there were so many different (and unequal) races, and thus has it supported earlier biblical arguments built around the belief in a monogenic creation, which stressed the essential unity and equality of humankind.[145] Nor is this the only way in which, as President Bill Clinton puts it, "modern science" has corroborated "ancient faiths," for many paleoanthropologists insist that *Homo sapiens* evolved once, in Africa, between 120,000 and 150,000 years ago. Thereafter, the new species migrated "out of Africa" (as this theory is known), and eventually spread across the whole of the habitable globe. If this is right (the argument is persuasive, but not conclusive), then it follows, as Stephen Jay Gould has written, that "all modern humans," regardless of their skin color, "form an entity united by physical bonds of descent from a recent African root," which reinforces the view that the idea of common humanity and the reality of human unity "is no idle political slogan or tenet of mushy romanticism."[146] Like the competing identities allegedly constructed around religion, nation, class, and gender, the claims of race to be the most important way of understanding who we are do not survive serious scrutiny. What, then, of the claims made by President Clinton's successor, who insisted that the abiding division of peoples into different and antagonistic civilizations was the most all-encompassing and the most important collective identity of all?

SIX

Civilization

Civilisation will not last, freedom will not survive, peace will not be kept, unless a very large majority of mankind unites together to defend them and show themselves possessed of a constabulary power before which barbaric and atavistic forces will stand in awe.

—Winston Churchill,
"Civilisation," in R. S. Churchill, ed.,
*Into Battle: Speeches of the Right
Hon. Winston S. Churchill CH, MP*

When we look at the history of the world, it is very important to recognize that we are not looking at the history of different civilizations truncated and separated from each other. Civilizations have a huge amount of contact, and there is a kind of inter-connectedness. I have always thought of the history of the world, not as a history of civilizations, but as a history of world civilizations evolving in often similar, often diverse, ways, always interacting with each other.

—Amartya Sen, quoted in N. MacGregor,
A History of the World in 100 Objects

IN 1749, almost exactly one hundred years before Robert Knox went on his lecture tour in the north of England touting the overwhelming significance of racial identities, the British philosopher David Hartley published his *Observations on Man*, in which he contrasted "barbarity and ignorance" on the one side with "instruction and civilization" on the other.[1] So far as is known, this is the first time these two identities, which would soon be regarded as the ultimate form of collective aggregation and human antagonism, had been thus juxtaposed and contrasted. Almost a quarter of a century later, on March 23, 1772, James Boswell made an entry in his diary. That morning, he had found his friend Samuel Johnson working on a revised edition of his celebrated dictionary, and they had discussed a new word by then in circulation that the "great lexicographer" had been considering for possible inclusion, but which he had on reflection decided to reject. "He would," Boswell regretfully noted, "not admit *civilization*, but only *civility*"; yet with "great deference" to Johnson, Boswell "thought *civilization*, from to *civilize*, better in the sense [that it was] opposed to *barbarity*, than *civility*."[2] Samuel Johnson may have rejected the word "civilization," but it soon received a kind of formal recognition, in the pages of *Ash's Dictionary*, in 1775. By then, "civilization" was being freely used in polite and educated circles in England and Scotland, both as a description of the highest state to which society might aspire and as a collective identity opposed to the more venerable solidarity of barbarism.

From the very outset, "civilization" as a noun, a concept, and an identity was a word that had behind it what the cultural critic Raymond Williams termed "the general spirit of the Enlightenment." It had come into common currency in France at an even earlier date, and its subsequent adoption seems to have been a clear example of British cultural borrowing, so it was scarcely surprising that the patriotically insular Dr. Johnson was not exactly enamored of it.[3] But even without his enthusiasm for it, "civilization" soon became established as part of the everyday vocabulary on both sides of the Channel, and in France as in Britain, it was often deployed to indicate the highest stage of collective human identity, development, and achievement, not only in politics but also in culture and society. Yet in the German-speaking lands of Europe, where the word "Zivilisation" also came into use at this time, it did not signify such an exalted state of existence or group identity: it was a "second-rank term," referring to external appearances and superficialities, which were subordinate to the more weighty German concept of "Kultur." So while the British and the French might see *themselves* as the embodiment of a cosmopolitan European civilization, German speakers knew better, and while the British and the French (and later the Italians) came to contrast the accomplishments and identities of their civilization with barbarism, the Germans related to both of these concepts and identities rather differently and more circumspectly.[4]

This Enlightenment antithesis, between the embattled collectivities of civilization and barbarism, was historically asymmetrical, for while "civilization" was a relatively recent concept, the term "barbarism," to which it was now contrasted, had been common currency on the continent for more than two millennia.[5] It had originally been used by the ancient Greeks to describe those aliens who spoke some other language: indeed, "barbarian" was an onomatopoeic rendering of what sounded to the Greek ear as their inane babbling ("bar bar"), and "barbarian" was taken up in due course by the Romans to identify those savage unfortunates who resided outside their empire and did not speak Latin. Thereafter, the word was employed as a commonplace derision by western Christians who regarded themselves as cultivated, superior, and refined, in contrast to those aliens beyond their ken whom they loathed as crude, violent, heathen, inferior, and ill-educated; and it was in this sense that "barbarian" was widely used in medieval and early modern Europe, when it was variously applied to the Slavs, Magyars, Vikings, Saracens, Arabs, Tartars, and Turks.[6] It was later adopted by the ruling elites of Renaissance Italy, who saw themselves as the heirs of imperial Rome, to denounce the "northern barbarians" invading from France and Germany during the fourteenth and fifteenth centuries. (The sack of Rome by the German soldiers of the emperor Charles V in 1527 was likened to the alleged fall of the city to the Goths in 476 CE, and the last chapter of Machiavelli's *The Prince* was famously entitled "Exhortation to Liberate Italy from the Barbarians.")[7]

Before the eighteenth century, then, and insofar as there was an antonym to what was already by then the venerable collective category of "barbarian," it was not another generalized solidarity, but a sequence of place- and time-specific societies and cultures, whether it be ancient Greece, imperial Rome, Christian Europe, or Renaissance Italy. As such, "barbarian" was an identity, and generally an inferiority, ascribed to successive alien groups by those regarding themselves as "superior." The latter felt no need to define themselves collectively, only to describe and disparage those whom they regarded as a hostile, threatening, and predatory "other," and in so doing they projected onto successive cohorts of "barbarians" a shared identity and a common consciousness that was not necessarily felt or accepted. They also furnished historical accounts of barbarian development, and delivered moral judgments on barbarian behavior, which were at best oversimplified and at worst deeply misleading. "Each man," Montaigne rightly observed, "calls barbarism whatever is not his own practice."[8] During the second half of the eighteenth century, however, these asymmetrical polarities and identities were transformed by the more balanced and all-encompassing antithesis between "barbarism" and "civilization," and this new formulation received its most celebrated, influential, and enduring (but also misunderstood and misapplied) elaboration from Edward Gibbon, to whom we now return.

CIVILIZATION AND BARBARISM

As befitted a work of Enlightenment rationality indebted to contemporary Scottish thinkers, Gibbon's *Decline and Fall of the Roman Empire* was constructed around contrasts, antitheses, and dichotomies, of which two were particularly significant. The first was between "pagans" and "Christians," but the second was that between the civilized Romans and the barbarian hordes beyond their borders, who would eventually overwhelm and vanquish the empire. "In the second century of the Christian era," Gibbon famously began his opening chapter, "the empire of Rome comprehended the fairest part of the earth, and the most civilized portion of mankind."[9] As he saw it, Rome had conferred upon a large portion of humanity a unique blend of civic virtue and personal freedom, the blessings of order, justice, prosperity, and individual rights, and an unrivaled cultural heritage of poetry, oratory, history, philosophy, and art; and the word that he used to describe that achievement in its entirety was the very one that Dr. Johnson had recently rejected, namely "civilization." For Gibbon, barbarism was the negation of civilization, and he equated it with savagery. The Goths, for instance, were pastoral nomads, they had no notion of fixed, landed property, nor of the laws required to regulate it, and they were "unacquainted with the use of letters," which meant that, far from being a "civilized people," they were merely a "herd of savages, incapable of knowledge or reflection," and they were naturally inclined to war. (Perhaps not surprisingly, Gibbon did not learn German, because he thought it was too "barbarous" a language.)[10]

Yet despite the immeasurable superiority of Rome, neither its vast empire nor its remarkable achievements were lastingly established, for according to Gibbon, their imperium was overwhelmed not only by "Christianity," which vanquished "paganism," but also by "barbarism," which triumphed over "civilization." During the late fourth century, he argued, external pressure on Rome's distant frontiers, which was itself in response to the invasive force exerted farther east by the Huns, became irresistible, as the Goths crossed the Danube in 376 CE, and defeated the imperial legions at Adrianople two years later. But this was only the beginning: in the first decade of the fifth century, the Vandals forded the Rhine into the empire, and subsequently advanced over the Pyrenees into Spain, and the Goths invaded Italy, sacking Rome in 410. There was worse to come: the Vandals captured Carthage in 439, they pillaged Rome sixteen years later, and the last emperor in the west, Romulus Augustulus, was deposed in 476. Within scarcely a hundred years, according to Gibbon, "the Roman world was overwhelmed by a deluge of barbarians"; new kingdoms were established by the Visigoths in Spain and southern Gaul, by the Franks in northern Gaul, by the Ostrogoths in Italy, and by the Vandals in North Africa; the once-great city of Rome was left a shattered and wasted ruin; and "the barriers which had so long separated the savage and the civilized nations of the earth were . . . leveled to the ground."[11]

For Gibbon, the outcome of this titanic but unequal struggle between the opposed identities of civilization and barbarism was a huge regression in the course of human history, as the western Roman Empire fell victim to the "vicissitudes of fortune, which spares neither man nor the proudest of his works, which buries empires and cities in a common grave." The crude, brutal Germanic tribes had obliterated the hard-won gains of Graeco-Latin civilization, and their devastating intrusions and destructive conquests had ushered in a dark age of ruin and decay, from which it took Europe centuries to recover. For Gibbon, these terrible times were characterized in the West by the "lowest ebb of primitive barbarism" among the empire's successor kingdoms, while in the East the wounded, beleaguered empire of Byzantium somehow survived, even though Gibbon regarded it as being incorrigibly moribund, parochial, and corrupt—so much so that its later history presented "a tedious and uniform tale of weakness and misery." There might be occasional revivals and reconquests, as under the emperor Justinian, but its long-term trajectory was toward oblivion, as its dominions were eroded by successive waves of eastern barbarians: by the Persians, the Slavs, the Arabs, by Seljuk Turks, and eventually by the Ottoman Turks, who vanquished the "second Rome" when they sacked Constantinople in 1453.[12]

Yet for all its apparent heroic simplicities, Gibbon's dichotomy of civilized and barbarian was (like his polarity of pagan and Christian) hedged with many caveats and qualifications that have often been overlooked. To begin with, and as befitted someone of his ironic disposition, he never believed that the Romans were unreservedly virtuous and that the barbarians were utterly without redeeming qualities. As he saw it, the high point of Roman civilization had come in the earlier time of the republic, whereas the later eras of imperial despotism were characterized by "immoderate greatness," when corruption, luxury, excess, and enervation weakened resolve, sapped liberty, and subverted freedom.[13] Not surprisingly, Gibbon sometimes conceded that decayed and degenerate Rome both needed and deserved to be vanquished then reinvigorated by the hordes pressing inexorably on the empire's borders, which might be savage and warlike, but which were also brave, energetic, and, in their own fashion, believers in the sort of freedom on which Rome had long since given up. Thus understood, the central paradox of *The Decline and Fall* was that the barbarians invaded and conquered a great empire only to find that they in turn were overwhelmed by the idea of a civilization that they had seemingly vanquished, but that they eventually reenergized and renewed and liberated.[14] The result was a gradual evolution from "primitive barbarism" to "the full tide of modern civilization," which meant the Europe of Gibbon's time was "secure from any future irruption of barbarism," and that the threat it had represented was over—at least on his own continent, although not necessarily elsewhere.[15]

Moreover, while Rome may for a time have embodied "civilization," Gibbon recognized that it was neither monolithic nor unchanging, and he preferred the republic's spirited freedom to the "immoderate greatness" of the empire or the decayed lethargy of Byzantium.[16] Nor did the coherence of his other and opposing category of "barbarian" hold up to closer scrutiny, for the external forces that assailed and eventually destroyed the empire came in varied and distinct guises, in terms of their origins, aims, behavior, and beliefs. There were those emanating from Asia, successively the Huns under Attila, the Mongols under Genghis Khan, and the Timurids under Tamerlane, whose westward expansion put powerful indirect pressure on the boundaries of the empire. There were the Vandals, the Franks, the Visigoths, and the Ostrogoths, who in retreating before Attila's Asiatic hordes smashed their way through the borders of the Western Empire, bringing chaos and ruin, even though eventually followed by freedom and liberty. Finally, there were the Persians, the Arabs, and the Turks, who assailed the Roman Empire on its eastern frontiers: they were more inclined to enervation, corruption, and oriental despotism than their vigorous northern counterparts, and in the case of the Arabs, they were also powerfully motivated by a crusading religion. From this more nuanced Gibbonian perspective, "barbarian" was too simplistic a collective category to encompass all Rome's many enemies across a thousand years, for as their varied histories and attributes suggested, they possessed no shared sense of unity, identity, mission, or purpose.[17]

On closer inspection, then, Gibbon's celebrated dichotomy between the collective identities of "civilization" and "barbarism" was less clear-cut than a cursory reading of *The Decline and Fall* might suggest, yet since his day, the same polarities and warring antagonisms have been projected in many times and places. For the Comte de Ségur, the French ambassador to the court of Catherine the Great, the identities Gibbon had discerned in the world of late antiquity were still in being, but they were now to be found in Russia, where the westward-facing capital of St. Petersburg was

a confused amalgam of "the age of barbarism and that of civilization, the tenth and the eighteenth centuries, the manners of Asia
and those of Europe."[18] But for the Chinese emperor Qianlong,
receiving a British delegation led by Lord Macartney in 1793, it
was the Europeans who were the barbarians, whereas the Asiat-
ics were civilized. He was unimpressed by the gifts and gadgets
Macartney brought as an indication of his nation's technological superiority, and he dismissed George III's "humble desire to
partake of the benefits of our civilization." Macartney's delegation thought the Chinese arrogant, xenophobic, authoritarian,
and backward, but the Chinese remained convinced they were the
civilized ones and that the Europeans (like everyone else beyond
their own borders) were the savages. Six decades later, in the
aftermath of the destruction by the British and the French of the
Old Summer Palace in imperial Peking, an outraged and embarrassed Victor Hugo offered another variant: "We Europeans are
the civilized ones, and for us the Chinese are barbarians. This is
what civilization has done to barbarism."[19]

But Gibbon's resonant, if oversimplified, dichotomy was not
only extended, adapted, and even reversed during the course of
the late eighteenth and nineteenth centuries: it was also stripped
of its adversarial aspects by those who insisted that barbarism and
civilization were not antagonistic identities locked in a mortal
Manichean conflict, but were the extreme positions on a continuous and continuing spectrum of political, social, intellectual,
moral, and aesthetic development. They were not Gibbon's clashing aggregations, doomed to primordial and perpetual confrontation; rather, they were the beginning and end points of the long
journey of human evolution. Reformulated in this way, civilization was not a collective and embattled entity, always at war with
the barbarians, but a continuing *process*, which had reached its
zenith with the advanced nations of nineteenth-century Europe.
It was this view that underlay such works as François Guizot's
Histoire de la civilisation en Europe and his *Histoire de la civilisation
en France*, Jacob Burckhardt's *The Civilization of the Renaissance in
Italy*, and H. T. Buckle's *Introduction to the History of Civilization
in England*.[20] It was this sense of ultimate attainment on the part
of some Europeans that also inspired the "civilizing mission" of

nineteenth-century imperialism, where the avowed aim was to lift up those peoples at a lower stage of human development.[21] And this view achieved its fullest articulation in the work of the émigré sociologist Norbert Elias, who published *The Civilizing Process* in German in 1939, the very year when it seemed to many that that process had come to a terrible halt.[22]

Because of the strong claims made to it by France and Britain, and sometimes by Italy, European "civilization" in the nineteenth and twentieth centuries did not necessarily encompass the whole continent, and the relations of the German-speaking peoples to the concept and the collectivity remained in question. From one perspective, deriving from a careful reading of *The Decline and Fall,* there were Germans who took pride in not being "civilized" at all. For Johann Gottfried von Herder, writing at the beginning of the nineteenth century, and developing an argument Gibbon had made only en passant, it was the Teutonic "barbarians" who had been brave, energetic, and freedom-loving: they were "northern giants, to whom the enervated Romans appeared as dwarfs; they ravaged Rome, and infused new life into expiring Italy."[23] Thereafter, many German writers and politicians followed Herder, insisting it was the so-called barbarians who had always been the morally superior peoples, plucking the lamp of civilization away from decadent and declining Rome; and this inverted dichotomy was widely embraced by late-nineteenth-century German scholars, who saw the Anglo-Saxon-Teutonic race as the great energizing and reforming force in Western history, sweeping away Latin degeneracy and corruption. The same interpretation was advanced in Britain by Thomas Hodgkin, a Quaker banker and historian, whose *Italy and Her Invaders* appeared a century after *The Decline and Fall.* Hodgkin was more sympathetic to German language and culture than Gibbon, and he urged that Gibbon had underestimated the achievements of the "barbarians" in transforming a decaying empire into thriving and vigorous kingdoms.[24]

From another perspective, however, the collective German superiority over western European civilization in the nineteenth century did not derive from the greater vigor of "barbarism" in opposition to "civilization," but from the greater refinement of "Kultur," which articulated identities in intellectual, artistic, and spiritual terms, compared to Anglo-French "Zivilisation," which was deemed to be more concerned with (baser) political, social, and economic matters. For Friedrich Nietzsche, writing a commentary revealingly entitled *Kultur contra Zivilisation*, "Civilisation is altogether something different than Culture will allow: it is perhaps its inverse." And civilization was also its inferior: as Thomas Mann later put it, "culture equals true spirituality, while civilization means mechanization."[25] Thus regarded, German "Kultur" was greatly superior to European (which meant essentially Anglo-French-Italian) "civilization." Not surprisingly, those who were placed on the far side of this divide did not agree, even when certain military and political events seemed to justify such an ordering. When Victor Hugo, who was not unaware of the ambiguities of the terms "civilization" and "barbarism," addressed the French National Assembly in 1871, following his nation's recent crushing defeat in the Franco-Prussian War, he insisted on contrasting the "barbarism" of German "Kultur" with the "light" that was French civilization, which meant for Hugo that despite France's military humbling and humiliation, it was still the superior nation.[26]

By the end of the nineteenth century, the European categories and identities relating to civilization were thus so varied and inconsistent as to be far beyond Gibbon's initial, resonant, and easily vulgarized identities and antitheses of civilized or barbarian. And yet these basic terms were frequently resorted to and constantly reworked by the belligerents during the First World War, which would see a multiplication of identity rhetoric, behavioral stereotyping, and opposing groups, but all of them founded on the same simple dichotomy.[27] The leaders and propagandists of the Anglo-French Entente insisted they were fighting to defend Christian European "civilization" from the aggression, pillage, and ruin of the Austrian and German "barbarians," who were, after all, descended from the Goths and the Huns, and from whom decency and chivalry could thus not be expected. When Britain and France were (belatedly) joined by Italy, the argument was further strengthened that the Entente was the embodiment and defender of European civilization. As their governments put it in a note of January 1917 addressed to President Woodrow

Wilson, among their war aims was "the expulsion from Europe of the Ottoman Empire, which has proved itself so radically alien to Western civilization." But this was only an incoherent formulation, since for much of the war, the British, French, and Italians were also allied with the Russians, and the Slavs had often been regarded by inhabitants of western Europe as "barbarians," not least by Queen Victoria herself.[28]

The wartime propaganda of the Austrians and the Germans was no less contradictory. Projecting one familiar collective identity, they insisted they were fighting to defend their "Kultur," which was more important and admirable than Anglo-French "civilization"; but they also contended that Anglo-French "civilization" had become decadent and degenerate, in need of being vanquished, to be revived—a bracing and historic dose of Teutonic "barbarism" rather than of "Kultur" was their prescription. (This had earlier been Nietzsche's plea and prediction, before he lapsed into madness in the 1890s.)[29] And so both the Entente and the Central Powers saw the latter as the side of "barbarism" during the First World War. But the identity had diametrically opposed moral and behavioral terms to each: it meant virtue and vigor from a German-speaking perspective, the embodiment of everything vile and violent according to the British, the French, and the Italians. Either way, Gibbon's confident prediction that barbarism no longer represented an external threat to European civilization had been confounded from within. Instead of being "irruptions" from beyond the continent, the barbarians were now as much inside Europe as outside, though the implications were not immediately recognized. Writing ten years after the Armistice, Clive Bell noted that "since from August 1914 to November 1918 Great Britain and her allies were fighting for civilization, it cannot, I suppose, be impertinent to inquire precisely what civilization may be." Yet there was little geographical or historical precision in the pages that followed, and Bell fell back on a familiar and glib appropriation from *The Decline and Fall:* "no characteristic of a barbarous society can possibly be a peculiarity of civilized societies."[30]

These clashing (and contradictory) collective identities were again projected by the opposing sides during the Second World

War. As a young man, Winston Churchill had read Gibbon, and he regularly used the simple distinction between "civilization" and "barbarism" in his books and speeches, most resonantly in his wartime broadcasts in 1940, when he contrasted the "Christian civilization," for which he believed the British Empire and people stood and would fight, with the "long night" of Nazi "barbarism" and the new "dark age" with which it threatened not only Europe but also the United States.[31] Yet even for Churchill, matters were rarely this clear-cut. He regretted that Italy had abandoned its historic bonds with France and Britain as the guardian of European civilization to throw its lot in with Nazi barbarism. "Down the ages and above all other calls," he had written to Mussolini shortly after becoming prime minister, "comes the cry that the joint heirs of Latin and Christian civilization must not be ranged against one another in mortal strife."[32] It was an appeal to a shared historic collective identity, recently reaffirmed during the First World War, but Il Duce ignored it. Moreover, Churchill would later find himself in alliance with Stalin's Russia—an even worse embodiment of Slav barbarism than the tsarist autocracy that had preceded it. He had detested the "foul baboonery" of Bolshevism since the October Revolution, and he would have been neither surprised nor encouraged by the words of Mikhail Tukhachevsky, the best general in the first Red Army, who boasted that his aim was to "reduce civilization to ruin" and to make Moscow "the centre of the world of the barbarians."[33]

Like many belligerent Germans before him, Adolf Hitler took Gibbon's familiar categories and inverted them. "Yes, we are the barbarians!" he had declared in 1933, shortly after the Reichstag fire. "We want to be barbarians! It is an honourable title. We shall rejuvenate the world!" It was, he believed, an "historical necessity" that the Germans invade decadent and effete civilizations to snatch the flame of life from their dying embers.[34] But looking eastward, the "German people" had often seen themselves as the defenders of European civilization against the Slav and Russian barbarians, and the invasions of Yugoslavia and of the Soviet Union during the Second World War were justified by Hitler on precisely that contradictory basis.[35] As for the French, when peace was restored in 1945, their historians of the ancient world would later write about the fall of Rome in terms that had been influenced by their own experience of defeat in 1940, when the triumphant conquering Germans had seemed neither rejuvenating barbarians nor the harbingers of a civilizing mission. This hostile perspective informed the writing of André Piagnol, when he noted that "Roman civilization did not pass peacefully away. It was assassinated." And Pierre Courcelle was also thinking of 1940 as much as the fifth century CE when he excoriated the earlier German invaders as "barbares," "hordes," and "envahisseurs"; their passage through the empire had been marked by "incendies," "ravages," "sacs," and "massacres"; and they had left behind "ruines désertes" and "régions dévastées."[36]

Thus was Gibbon's distinction between civilization and barbarism perpetuated, though not as he had meant and applied it, for Europe itself had become the scene of these clashes, and since Freud's meditation *Civilization and Its Discontents*, that has increasingly become the conventional wisdom.[37] Half a century later, Eric Hobsbawm wrote an article entitled "Barbarism: A User's Guide," insisting that "civilization receded between the Treaty of Versailles and the fall of the bomb on Hiroshima," while "barbarism has been on the increase for most of the twentieth century, and there is no sign that this increase is at an end."[38] Soon afterward, Bernard Wasserstein completed "a history of Europe in our own time," to which he gave the faux-Gibbonian title *Barbarism and Civilization*. "There is," he began, quoting Walter Benjamin, "no document of civilization that is not simultaneously a document of barbarism," and in his concluding paragraph he cited Friedrich Engels to the same effect: "the more civilization advances, the more it is compelled to cover the evils it necessarily creates." Thus regarded, civilization and barbarism were to be found not in separate peoples or different places, but within the same individuals and societies. Who, Wasserstein concluded, could contemplate the violence and cruelty, genocide and torture, mass murder and holocaust of recent times "without acknowledging the barbarism deeply implanted in the heart of our civilization?"[39]

Yet while Gibbon's dichotomy has enjoyed an afterlife such as he would never have imagined,[40] since the 1980s, historians of "late antiquity" have been rethinking the collective and antagonistic solidarities allegedly existing during Rome's "decline and fall," and they have generally reinforced his qualifications and more nuanced perspectives. They no longer write of "waves" of "barbarians" "confronting," "invading," and "flooding" the Roman Empire and "overturning" its "civilization": instead, they urge that accounts depicting "a violent and antagonistic encounter between sharply contrasting adversaries whose collective identities are clear and easily grasped" are "too theatrical to jibe with the known incidents of Roman-barbarian encounter in the fourth to sixth centuries." On closer inspection, the "Germanic" tribes loosely labeled "barbarians" were varied and diverse, and lacking any sense of cohesion, unity, or identity; their set-piece battles with the imperial legions were the exception rather than the rule; "at no time in antiquity, early or late, was there a collective hostility of barbarians toward the empire or a collective purpose to tear it down"; and accommodation and assimilation were generally more in evidence than confrontation and conflict. Thus regarded, the "underlying theme of relations between Rome and the barbarians in the late antiquity was not antagonism and strife but mutual need and co-operation," and such encounters as did take place were between people "as individuals not collectivities."[41]

Accordingly, "late antiquity" is now widely regarded as a place where "transformation" and assimilation rather than "confrontation" and cataclysm prevailed, where "Romans" and "barbarians" were in practice often difficult to tell apart, where it was generally believed that "an able Goth wants to be like a Roman," and where many works of art expressed these accommodations and conversations in stylistic syntheses negating any such "ancient polarities."[42] To be sure, some scholars still insist this revisionist version of "late antiquity" presents too static and serene a picture, and they continue to maintain that Roman civilization *did* collapse into a new dark age after a century of crisis, trauma, and confrontation.[43] Nevertheless, it seems generally recognized that "the myth that the fall of the west was a titanic and ideological struggle between two great united forces, Rome and 'the barbarians,'" is no longer a sustainable view, and the result is that the traditional (and oversimplified) Gibbonian paradigm has largely "vanished" from current scholarly discussion, though not yet from popular consciousness. And since this polarity of "civilized" and "barbarian" identities can no longer be convincingly applied to the subject and period for which originally conceived, we should be very circumspect about discerning similar collectivities and antagonisms in other eras and in circumstances that Gibbon never intended or imagined.[44]

THE RISE AND FALL OF CIVILIZATIONS

In any case, by the early twentieth century, another way of looking at collective human identities had come into being, no longer constructed around the antagonisms of civilization and barbarism, but around the concept of a plurality of *civilizations*. One explanation for this new perspective was the growth of such disciplines as archaeology, philology, oriental studies, and sociology, which suggested there had been many other civilizations in addition to "the West" or "Europe," which no longer seemed to be the high point and the end point toward which all lesser societies might strive to progress. As Emile Durkheim and Marcel Mauss put it in 1913, "if there does not exist one human civilization, there have been and there still are diverse civilizations which dominate and develop the collective life of each people."[45] The academic developments their article summarized were reinforced by the First World War, from which one widely drawn conclusion was that European civilization was neither as admirable nor as unified as some had previously thought, and that it might be better (and more humbly) understood as one civilization among the many that had existed across human history and around the globe. But while it seemed more plausible to urge that the essence of human existence and identity might be found among all these "great collective personalities," and not solely in one of them, such a pluralistic view also raised several questions: how many of these civilizations had there been? How might they be defined and described? What were the relations among them? And what (if any) were their future prospects?[46]

One scholar who was stimulated by the First World War to address these issues was a long since forgotten historian named Frederick J. Teggart, who taught at the University of California at

Berkeley. In April 1918, he published *The Processes of History*, which began by deploring "that inevitable human propensity to classify all those who are in any way unlike ourselves, or who merely lie outside our own group, as "'fiends,' 'aliens,' and 'barbarians,'" and also by recognizing that the First World War had lessened "the exclusiveness and self-confidence of the western European, and has induced in him an awakening appreciation of the manhood and common human quality of out-lying peoples."[47] Traditional narrative history, Teggart argued, was inadequate to the urgent and demanding task of understanding how "civilizations have arisen and decayed, to be followed by other civilizations," and in order to do justice to these "pluralistic" pasts, he insisted that "the analytical study of history" must be founded upon a comparison of the "particular histories of all human groups," including those beyond Europe and the Near East such as India and China. Teggart also believed these civilizations were not hermetically sealed off from one another, but interacted creatively, and that this borrowing and cross-fertilization was the key to progress: "human advancement," he wrote, "is the outcome of the co-mingling of ideas through the contact of different groups." "Civilization," he concluded, "is everywhere the result of the stimulus evoked by the friction of one group upon another."[48]

While Teggart was writing *The Processes of History*, the German historian and philosopher Oswald Spengler was at work on a much larger scholarly enterprise, published in two volumes between 1918 and 1922; it appeared in English translation as *The Decline of the West*.[49] Spengler's thoughts were vague and mystical, and his central, pseudobiological thesis was banal and unconvincing, namely that civilizations were like living organisms, which meant they were born, grew up, and flourished, but also that they were destined to decay and die.[50] Like most Germans, Spengler accepted the difference between "Kultur" and "Zivilisation," and also the superiority of the former over the latter, but he offered an ingenious and evolutionary connection between them. As he saw it, the most brilliant, fertile, and creative phase in the development of these large collective groups took place during the first part of their history, and when writing of this period he called them "cultures." But all such cultural collectivities were doomed to fall and to fail, and it was to this second, deteriorated, protracted stage that he gave the name "civilization." "The culture," he wrote, "suddenly hardens, it mortifies, its blood congeals, its force breaks down, and it becomes civilization." To Spengler, then, civilizations were not the acme of collective human achievement and identity; rather, they were "the organic-logical sequel, fulfillment and finale of a culture," they were "a conclusion, the thing-become succeeding the thing-becoming, death following life, rigidity following expansion. . . . They are an end, irrevocable yet by inward necessity reached again and again."[51]

Despite his pretentious prose, Spengler made a serious case, namely that it was only by abandoning the deludedly linear and incorrigibly parochial story of the European past that a broader (but also a more somber) world-historical perspective might be obtained, and in *The Decline of the West* he sketched and tabulated the evolution of six culture-civilizations: the Egyptian, the Indian, the Classical, the Chinese, the Arabian, and the Western.[52] Thus understood, Classical Greece had been a "culture," but in the aftermath of Alexander the Great, Classical Rome, by contrast, had been merely a "civilization." Indeed, for Spengler, the Romans were barely that: standing "between Hellenic culture and nothingness," they were a "negative phenomenon," the "barbarians who did not *precede* but *closed* a great development."[53] (Here was a complete and audacious inversion of Edward Gibbon's founding premise.) In the same way, Spengler insisted, Western "culture" had declined and rigidified into Western "civilization" during the nineteenth century, with the excesses of the French Revolution and Napoleon.[54] Accordingly, the trajectory of the West was "not a limitless tending upwards and onwards for all time," since "the nineteenth and twentieth centuries, hitherto looked on as the highest point of an ascending straight line of world history," were "in reality a stage of life which may be observed in every culture that has ripened to its limit." The "future which is still in store for us" was thus a dark and doom-laden prospect in which "the history of West-European mankind will be definitely *closed*."[55]

In seeing "world-history" as the successive rise and fall of large collective groups to which he gave the name of "cultures" and "civilizations," Spengler shared Teggart's view that there was more to the human past and to human identities than the trajectory of Europe.[56] He further agreed with Teggart that all cultures and civilizations were, in some fundamental sense, parallel, analogous, contemporary, and philosophically equivalent, for they unvaryingly followed the same course in conformity with a fixed timetable. Yet Spengler also insisted, in direct contradiction of Teggart, that cultures were so separate, autonomous, and profoundly different from one another that communication between them was virtually impossible, and in a chapter entitled "The Relations Between Cultures" he concluded there were none: "between the souls of two cultures the screen is impenetrable."[57] While they were growing and developing, cultures were by definition impermeable to outside influences: there was "an impassable barrier against all contacts on the deeper levels," and their creative force came from within, not from the "barbarians" outside. Only when a culture decayed and degenerated into the lingering death of a civilization did it seek (or succumb) to external contacts, ranging from the mixing and interchange of ideas to military confrontation and imperial dominion (or subordination); but to the interconnections and interactions between cultures or between civilizations Spengler devoted little attention.[58]

Neither Teggart nor Spengler much influenced the popular perception in the interwar Anglophone world that civilizations were the most significant form of human identity, but another historian who did, and who recognized his indebtedness to these pioneers, was the Winchester- and Oxford-educated academic Arnold J. Toynbee.[59] In 1922, he published *The Western Question in Greece and Turkey*, which was subtitled *A Study in the Contact of Civilisations*. Toynbee sought to offer an evenhanded account of the conflict that had broken out between the Greeks and the Turks in Anatolia following the collapse of the Ottoman Empire, but this challenging exercise in contemporary history was framed by a much broader treatment.[60] Civilizations, Toynbee affirmed, following Spengler and Teggart, were "the most real and fundamental forms of human society." But despite his subtitle, it was his belief that when they were growing and flourishing, they were self-contained and impermeable: "so long as a civilization is fulfilling its potentialities and developing in accordance with its genius, it is a universe in itself." Only when they were declining did they come into contact with other civilizations, as with the enfeebled remnants of the Near Eastern (Greece) and the Middle Eastern (Turkey) civilizations, which had both absorbed Western ideas of nationalism during the nineteenth and early twentieth centuries, leading to the recent confrontation between them, and its "destructive" rather than "constructive" results.[61]

Toynbee's key insight, which he took from Spengler, was that the "smallest intelligible fields of historical study" were "a limited number of *separate* and *autonomous* civilizations" (my italics). The "endless cross-currents among persons, localities, regions and continents" mattered little to him: he did not think they influenced civilizations on the way up, which he believed were isolated and impermeable, and although he thought civilizations on the way down did become interlinked and permeable, the consequences were usually deforming and disastrous.[62] Condemning the failure to take account of the distinctiveness and independence (and also equivalence) of civilizations—the qualities that he believed made them the irreducible units of human history and human identity—Toynbee, in his conclusion, was moved to disparage and "confute" the "false antitheses" that were "so deeply rooted in the Western mind" between Christianity and Islam, between Europe and Asia, and between civilization and barbarism (which he dismissed as "the greatest nonsense of all"). Yet as often in his work, his meaning was not altogether plain: earlier in the book, he had also averred, in words that seem hard to fathom but that apparently paid contradictory homage to the famous dichotomies of *The Decline and Fall*, that "civilizations, like individuals, spring from two parents, and in all new civilizations whose parentage we can trace, the heritage from the civilized mother has been more important than that from the barbarian who violated her."[63]

By the time *The Western Question* appeared, Toynbee had already sketched out a more comprehensive work, which he would publish in twelve volumes between 1934 and 1961 as *A Study of History*, in which he identified twenty-one major civilizations (including not only Western, Hellenic, Arabic, and Hindu, but also Egyptian, Andean, Sinic, and Yucatec), as well as four "abortive" civilizations (Far Western Christian, Far Eastern Christian, Scandinavian, and Syriac), and also five "arrested" civilizations (Polynesian, Eskimo, Nomadic, Ottoman, and Spartan).[64] These civilizations were the "intelligible units" of human history and of identity, and they were much more significant than the nation-state, which was a relative newcomer to the historical scene. Toynbee described in detail the stages through which all twenty-one civilizations passed, from genesis and growth, via a "time of troubles," to a "universal state" and eventually to breakdown and disintegration. These cycles were not inevitable, organic, and preordained, as Spengler had insisted; rather, they depended on the responses (and nonresponses) by "creative minorities" to the challenges with which their civilizations were beset during the course of their existence.[65] When such people rose to these challenges, their civilizations grew and flourished, but when they failed to do so, their civilizations declined into nationalism, militarism, imperialism, and the tyranny of a once-creative elite that had degenerated into a despotic minority. At all stages, civilizations were driven by this internal dynamic, rather than by their external contacts, which meant they invariably ended the same way—not because of violent confrontations with one another, but because of the inability of their decaying elites to solve internal problems and surmount internal difficulties. "Civilizations," Toynbee concluded, "die from suicide, not by murder."[66]

Like many of his generation, Toynbee had read Gibbon early in life, but he disliked his cool, skeptical rationalism and his mockery of the Christian faith, and he did not share Gibbon's (admittedly qualified) admiration for Rome's imperial civilization.[67] To be sure, Toynbee's account of the decline and fall of the Roman Empire seemed Gibbonian in its concepts and categories. He wrote of an "internal proletariat," which took up and propagated the new religion of Christianity that swept across the empire, and he wrote of an "external proletariat," which successfully pressed on Rome's borders, and which was merely a fancy name for the barbarian invaders. But Toynbee insisted that Gibbon had misunderstood both "barbarism and religion" in arguing that they were the agents of the empire's collapse. Pace the account offered in *The Decline and Fall*, Christian religion did not "destroy" Rome, since Hellenic civilization was long since dead by then; on the contrary, Christianity was the creative harbinger of the new (and better) European civilization that was gradually coming to fruition. Nor, as Gibbon alleged, were the barbarians responsible for the empire's demise: they were merely in at the death, feasting on the corpse of Hellenic civilization like vultures, but as "heroes without a future," they made no lasting contribution to the new Western civilization that Christianity was already bringing into being.[68] Here was the full elaboration of an interpretation Toynbee had earlier sketched, namely that as new civilizations came into being, they owed more to the virtuous mother who had brought them to birth than to the barbarian who had violated her.

A Study of History was not well received by professional historians, and almost without exception they rejected Toynbee's claim that the key understanding to the human past, present, and future lay in treating the rise and fall of civilizations as the most important and capacious of all collective human identities.[69] He never adequately defined what he meant by civilization ("a movement and not a condition, a voyage and not a harbour," he once bafflingly wrote) or by identity, and his treatment of these vague constructions was often more mystical and metaphysical than scholarly or academic.[70] He arbitrarily separated out some civilizations (such as Sumerian and Babylonian, both of which were surely Mesopotamian), whereas he no less arbitrarily lumped others together (such as Greek and Roman, in the single category of Hellenic). He did not convince in his efforts to force the varied histories of all civilizations into the rigid trajectory of "rise and fall," and in his claims that this was the result of empirical inquiry undistorted by any prior presuppositions. He placed too much stress on civilizations as autonomous, self-contained entities, and (like Spengler) he gave little attention to how they interacted, delaying his treatment of that subject until the eighth and ninth volumes, where he discussed "affiliations" and "apparentations" seemingly as an afterthought.[71] And by the time he published his final volumes, Toynbee had abandoned his earlier approach, by downgrading civilizations to a subordinate place in human history, while promoting religious identities and teleologies above them, thereby fatally undermining his initial model and method.[72]

Despite a cascade of professional criticism, Toynbee was lion-ized among the reading public and in the media as the greatest historian of his day, and he was also acclaimed as someone who had important *and encouraging* things to say about the present prospects and future direction of Western civilization. For while according to Toynbee all other great collectivities had either disappeared or were in advanced decline (in this second category came the Far Eastern, the Hindu, the Eastern Orthodox, and the Islamic civilizations), Western civilization was very much *alive*, and Toynbee believed that revival and renewal were possible, provided those in authority embraced some form of higher "spiritual truth," which would combine Christianity, Hinduism, Buddhism, and Islam. Decline, he seemed to be saying, could be not only postponed, but perhaps averted altogether: "our future depends largely upon ourselves. We are not just at the mercy of an inexorable fate."[73] With the coming of the Cold War, this reading of Toynbee proved especially popular in the postwar United States, and in 1947 he was taken up by Henry Luce, the publisher of *Time*, *Life*, and *Fortune* magazines. Luce thought Toynbee was offering a powerful historical defense of Western civilization, and that he was calling for a renewal of religious faith, especially in the United States, as it faced the unprecedented challenge from the Communist barbarians for the control of the deimperializing, bipolar world. "Our civilization," *Time* insisted in March 1947, in an issue that pictured Toynbee on the cover and profiled him inside, "is not inexorably doomed."[74]

The idea that Toynbee had written *A Study of History* to proclaim the continued viability of Western civilization under transatlantic leadership found a ready response in America for well over a decade after 1945. After the nation's decisive participation in the First World War, there had developed a growing sense that the United States was evolving into the world's preeminent agent and exemplar of civilization, and this view would be expounded across the ensuing decades in such influential books as *The Rise of American Civilization* (1927) by Charles A. and Mary R. Beard and *America as a Civilization* (1957) by Max Lerner. And as the West faced the unprecedented challenges of the subsequent Great Depression and the Second World War, American colleges and universities offered new courses tracing the history of

Western civilization, from ancient Greece and Rome, via medieval, Renaissance, and modern Europe, to contemporary America, and a plethora of textbooks were written for this burgeoning market, among them *A Survey of European Civilization* (1939) by Wallace K. Ferguson and Geoffrey Brunn, and *A History of Western Civilization* (1941) by Arthur Watts.[75] In the years after 1945, these courses, in what became known as "Western civ," reached a rapidly expanding undergraduate audience; they proclaimed and championed the uniquely liberal, tolerant, and progressive values of Europe and the United States; they reinforced the view that the leadership and defense of the West was now America's responsibility and opportunity; and they created a reading public that was eager to read Toynbee's volumes and to find in them reinforcement for these views.

In fact, Toynbee never believed most of the things Americans imputed to him in the decade or so after 1945. To be sure, he had initially supported the Marshall Plan, the establishment of NATO, and the sending of troops to Korea, but he generally distrusted American democracy, believing the country too secular (like most of the West), and he did not share what soon became the prevailing American hostility to Russia: "western imperialism," he wrote in 1952, "not Russian Communism is Enemy No 1 today for the majority of the human race, and the west hasn't woken up to this."[76] Nor did he agree with Henry Luce that the United States was predestined to succeed Britain as the leader of the free, civilized world against Communist tyranny, Stalinist dictatorship, and Russian barbarism: indeed, Toynbee had long entertained an "animus against western civilization" (though not its classical predecessor), and he thought America was no more than a peripheral part of that uninspiring collectivity, believing its "alarming," "colonial," and "militaristic" prosecution of the war in Vietnam to be part of its mistaken pursuit of "the mythical monster 'World Communism.' "[77] As for the future prospects of Western civilization, Toynbee hedged his bets more than his transatlantic audience was willing to recognize. It might, he admitted, rally and recover and reassert itself. But all other civilizations had already "broken down and gone to pieces," and "no child of this civilization who has been born in our generation can easily imagine that our own society is immune from the danger of suffering the common fate."[78]

Between them, Teggart, Spengler, and Toynbee had sought to make the case that humanity should be best understood as being divided up into a plurality of civilizations and identities. But they did not agree as to how many civilizations there had been, they could not define them or describe their trajectories satisfactorily, they disagreed as to whether civilizations interacted with each other or not, and they were uncertain as to how (and how many) civilizations would evolve in the future. In short, the proposition that civilization had always been the most significant and self-conscious human aggregation, subsuming all other, lesser solidarities, could not be convincingly demonstrated or consistently verified. Yet once Toynbee's *Study of History* was completed, sociologists and political scientists eagerly embraced his approach, which seemed far less parochial than most historical writing of the time, and during the 1960s they produced a succession of books, providing lists and typologies of civilizations, setting out their rise-and-fall parabolas, and offering explanations as to when, how, and why they came and went.[79] Most of them were vulnerable to the same criticisms that had already been leveled at Toynbee himself, and predictably they found little favor with most professional historians. But by the third quarter of the twentieth century, when the Cold War was at its height, the notion that the world might best be understood in terms of a plurality of civilizations, which interacted antagonistically, had become one of the conventional wisdoms of the time.

THE CLASH OF CIVILIZATIONS

But when the Berlin Wall fell, and the Soviet Union collapsed in 1991, the idea that the world should be understood in terms of a battle of identities and ideologies, between Western civilization on the one side and Communism on the other, suddenly seemed to be part of a history that was now over; and in the "new world order" that the first President George Bush welcomed and proclaimed, where freedom, democracy, and capitalism had apparently prevailed over totalitarianism, dictatorship, and state planning, it no longer seemed appropriate to understand the world in terms of competing or conflicting civilizations based on antagonistic identities and opposed beliefs. But President Bush also put together a coalition against Saddam Hussein of Iraq, and this was for some a sign and a portent of new collective identities, which would soon be hardening, and of confrontations between them. Scarcely a decade later, during the presidency of the second George Bush, in what suddenly and ominously seemed to be a *re*polarized world, the view that humanity should be understood not just in terms of different civilizations but also in terms of latent confrontations—or actual "clashes"—between them again attracted widespread support among many policymakers in London and Washington. But whereas Gibbon and Toynbee had written as historians about civilizations and identities, never expecting their interpretations to make any impact on those in power, the most recent scholarship on these matters came from the disciplines of politics, sociology, and government, some of its practitioners determined to influence policy, as one of them undoubtedly did.

By coincidence, the phrase "clash of civilizations" had first been launched into the public consciousness as the subtitle to a book appearing in the same decade that Arnold J. Toynbee had produced his own work on the "contact of civilizations" (although it bears repeating that this subject never interested him much). In 1926, Basil Mathews published *Young Islam on Trek: A Study in the Clash of Civilizations*, which may have been a deliberate play on Toynbee's earlier choice of words. Mathews was an American missionary who disliked the militaristic urge to conquest that he regarded as the hallmark of Islam, and although he hoped Christianity might eventually prevail, he feared these two civilizations were more likely to confront each other in war than to seek together a common future.[80] But Mathews's book made little impact, and his phrase only began to attain its recent popularity and resonance in 1990, when the Middle Eastern expert Bernard Lewis published an article entitled "The Roots of Muslim Rage," in which he argued that Muslims were increasingly threatened (and often outraged) by Western ideas of secularism and modernism, and that this made "a clash of civilizations" between these two collectivities ever more likely in the near future.[81] Lewis's words were subsequently taken up by the Harvard political scientist Samuel P. Huntington, initially as the title (albeit with a question mark attached) for an article that appeared in the journal *Foreign Affairs* in the summer of 1993. So great was the interest in and reaction to his essay that three years later Huntington restated and elaborated his thesis (now abandoning the question mark) for what would become a best seller: *The Clash of Civilizations and the Remaking of the World Order.*[82]

Huntington was clearly indebted to Bernard Lewis for his title, as well as drawing on Lewis's work when discussing the history and politics of the Middle East. Nevertheless, his general thesis, which he hoped would be both "meaningful to scholars and useful to policymakers," was more wide-ranging geographically (although less extended historically). For Huntington's aim was to offer "an interpretation of the evolution of global politics after the Cold War," and the unit of identity around which he constructed his interpretation was civilization. "Human history," he insisted, "is the history of civilizations. It is impossible to think of the development of humanity in any other terms. . . . Throughout history civilizations have provided the broadest identifications for people."[83] He believed civilizations subsumed and encompassed all lesser group solidarities and collective identities, be they tribes, ethnic groups, religious confessions, or even nation-states, and that it was essential for those in government to understand "the nature, identity and dynamics of civilizations" when making future policy. In all, he discerned "seven or eight major civilizations" currently in existence around the globe. Those he named Western, Latin American, Islamic, Sinic (which he had termed "Confucian" in his original article), Hindu, Japanese, and Orthodox were relatively easy to locate and identify, and to them, with less certainty, he added African ("possibly") and Buddhist (though he admitted it was not "a major civilization").[84]

In depicting the world in these multicivilizational terms, Huntington was setting himself against those myopic triumphalists who, after the United States had vanquished Soviet Russia in the Cold War, had embraced the "widespread and parochial conceit that the European civilization of the west is now the universal civilization of the world." But this, he insisted, was not how things were, for power was "shifting from the long-predominant west to non-western civilizations," which meant it was essential to understand *all* these great global groupings of humanity. As Huntington defined them, civilizations were best understood in terms of culture, and especially in terms of their increasingly active and assertive religions, which he believed were their "central defining characteristic."[85] They differed markedly from one another in their beliefs, their organizations, their relations to secular authority, and the extent of their proselytizing aims and expansionist ambitions. As a result, "the predominant patterns of political and economic development" also varied "from civilization to civilization," which meant that "the key issues on the international agenda involve differences among civilizations." If these differences were recognized, accepted, and managed, Huntington urged, peaceful coexistence among these civilizations was possible. But if not, the prospect was bleak, and "the fault lines between civilizations" would become "the battle lines of the future." Hence Huntington's conclusion that in the emerging era "an international order based on civilizations" was "the surest safeguard against world war," while it was the growing likelihood of clashes among civilizations that constituted "the greatest threat to world peace." And even these clashes might be no more than a stage on the way to the climactic struggle to come, namely "the greater clash, the global 'real clash,' between civilization and barbarism."[86]

In light of these general observations, Huntington offered some specific prescriptions for survival in the multipolar post–Cold War world, where he believed "states increasingly define their interests in civilizational terms." In the West, there were serious tasks of "renewal" ahead: it must recognize it was no longer the global hegemon it had once been, but was now merely one civilization among several, and it must also revitalize its spiritual strength by rejecting multiculturalism and by reasserting the importance of the Christian religion and the uniqueness of its traditional liberties and democratic values.[87] These tasks were made all the more necessary—and all the more urgent—because of the growing power and determination of an ever more hostile Islam, and also because of the threat that China increasingly posed to the

West; as a result of these widening fault lines, conflict between the West and Islam, or a war between the West and China, could not be ruled out. "The dangerous clashes of the future," Huntington warned, "are likely to arise from the inter-action of Western arrogance, Islamic intolerance, and Sinic assertiveness."[88] Ideally, these three civilizations should try to live at peace and seek to reach mutual accommodations, by respecting each other's differences, and by dividing the globe into well-defined spheres of influence. But this could not be guaranteed, since one form that "Western arrogance" might take was "intervention in the affairs of other civilizations," which Huntington deplored and feared as "probably the single most dangerous source of instability and potential global conflict in a multi-civilizational world."[89]

Huntington's article and book provoked a great deal of journalistic and academic comment, but although some of it was favorable, much of it was critical. While writing in a Toynbee-like manner about civilizations rising and falling, Huntington provided no convincing, long-term historical account as to how or when or why his seven (or eight) "major civilizations" had come into being or had so recently become so prominent. In 1920, he claimed, the world had been divided between the Western imperial powers and the rest, and in the 1960s between the "free world" and the "Communist bloc," albeit with many "unaligned nations" in South Asia, Africa, and South America. But somehow, suddenly, the world of the 1990s had become defined and dominated by "civilizations," which had clearly been around a long time, even though they had not seemed significant in the preceding decades. This was scarcely an historically plausible version of global history during the twentieth century. Moreover, Huntington's civilizations, and the collective identities that they purportedly embodied and articulated, turned out on closer inspection to be based on little more than overaggregated statistics (which concealed at least as much as they revealed), on the mistaken assumption that one hegemonic variable determined both individual and collective identity (to the neglect of all the others), and on a map of the world that made them seem monolithic and hermetically sealed off from one another (when even the author conceded the boundaries between them were often vague and ill-defined).[90]

By Huntington's own admission, *The Clash of Civilizations* was written to provide a "simplified map of reality," but on many occasions he had oversimplified the cartography (both literally and metaphorically) to the point where reality scarcely seemed to matter or intrude at all.[91] Like Spengler and Toynbee before him, many of Huntington's civilizations seem on closer inspection to be little more than arbitrary groupings and idiosyncratic personal constructs. Sweden and Spain were part of the West, whereas Greece was not; Sinic civilization included Korea but excluded Japan, and encompassed Vietnam but left out Laos; Latin America "could be considered either a sub-civilization within western civilization or a separate civilization closely affiliated to the west and divided as to whether it belongs to the west"; African civilization extended across all the sub-Saharan continent, but tribal identities were still "pervasive," and it had not yet "cohered" into "a distinct civilization"; and Buddhism, "although a major religion, has not been the basis of a major civilization," since it had adapted, assimilated, or been suppressed in China, Korea, and Japan, and had survived only in Sri Lanka, Burma, Tibet, Bhutan, Mongolia, and parts of Indochina. Such vague collective groupings and "cultural entities" carry little conviction, and the global historian Felipe Fernández-Armesto was surely right in observing that Huntington "could not fully satisfy the demand for a definition or classification of civilizations to match the importance he gave them."[92]

This deficiency is well illustrated in the case of the Republic of India, which Huntington claimed formed a distinct and separate "Hindu civilization." In fact, India has been a secular democracy since its independence from Britain in 1947, which means there has never been a "Hindu" component to its constitution—much to the dismay and disappointment of the more intransigent elements in the Hindutva movement.[93] To be sure, Hindus have always been a numerical majority, but there are also more Muslims in India (in excess of 140 million) than in any other country in the world, with the exception of Indonesia and, marginally, Pakistan; and nearly every country that forms part of Huntington's "Islamic civilization" contains fewer Muslims than those millions living in India. (Elsewhere, in an admission by turns contradictory and inaccurate, Huntington argued that India was not a unitary civilization at all, but a "cleft country" divided by the "civilizational fault-line" between Muslims and Hindus.)[94] Moreover, across the centuries, Christians, Parsees, Jains, Sikhs, Jews, and Buddhists, as well as atheists and agnostics, have all lived (and often thrived) in India; one indication of this long tradition of religious pluralism was that in 2005 the nation's president was a Muslim, its prime minister was a Sikh, and the head of the ruling party was a Christian. Under these circumstances, to categorize India and its civilization as "just a Hindu country" is, as Amartya Sen notes, "a fairly bizarre idea."[95]

Similar criticisms have been made of Huntington's signature concepts of "Western" and "Islamic" civilizations. For many nations in the allegedly monolithic "West," ranging from Canada and the United States to France and Germany, are ethnically very diverse: should African Americans be included by virtue of their American citizenship, or are they a transatlantic offshoot of "African" civilization? The constitutional arrangements and political cultures of these countries are similarly varied: the United States is a transcontinental federation, the United Kingdom an unusual mixture of monarchy, union, and devolution, France a powerfully centralized state, and so on. The claim that the West has always been the unique repository of reason, freedom, and liberty betrays a deep historical ignorance, not only of the West itself, but also of anywhere (or, indeed, everywhere) else.[96] And the range of religious faiths that can be subsumed beneath the Western, Christian umbrella is also astonishingly wide, while what many Americans most deplore about Europe is that it is too secular. The same objections apply to the depiction of "Islam" as a mirror-image unitary civilization, for it, too, is a very varied religion in terms of its tenets and practices, and like Christianity again, it has its own share of conservatives, moderates, radicals—and extremists. Moreover, it is impossible to treat the Middle East as a distinct or as a monolithic or as a unified region, because there is "no one 'Islam'": Jordan and Iran, Saudi Arabia and Egypt, Iraq and the Sudan, Morocco and Turkey are very different countries, with correspondingly different histories, political cultures, constitutional arrangements, and international profiles.[97]

Underlying these specific criticisms is a more general objection that should scarcely need belaboring by this stage. In defining his civilizations exclusively in religious terms, Huntington assumed that faith and belief were the preeminent and overwhelming criteria of human identity and solidarity. But at no stage did he successfully demonstrate this, and it is difficult to see how he could have done so, for it bears repeating that while a particular religious faith may be shared by many individuals, it is only one identity among others that any person may claim. And while for some people it may be the most important, for many others it is not. In any case, how any individual may self-identify—in what order he or she may rank his or her group affiliations—surely varies to such an extent that no single affiliation will in the long run be more commanding than any other.[98] This applies with particular force to the claim that civilization is the largest and most all-encompassing category of collective human identity, for the notion that these vast transcontinental aggregations, often taking in hundreds of millions of people, can be defined in terms of one single and shared affiliation, which overrides all others, is to carry oversimplification to the point of absurdity. Yet the more complex and varied these so-called civilizations are rightly recognized to be, the more difficult it becomes to define and distinguish and weigh them, let alone to claim they are the most important identity of all. Here is a fundamental paradox about collective identities that Huntington neither addressed nor resolved.

Not surprisingly, then, he also misunderstood—indeed, disregarded—the many overlaps, interactions, and interconnections between civilizations that his maps represented as being sealed off, protected, and clearly and impermeably bounded. To be sure, Huntington admitted that in practice, land borders were rarely this precisely or clearly demarcated, but he did not draw the obvious conclusion, namely that such places, where one formal jurisdiction melds and merges imperceptibly into another, may be transnational or transcultural zones of engagement and interaction as much as they may be potential areas of confrontation and conflict.[99] And like many maps, Huntington's division of the world into separate terrestrial authorities misled in another way, for it failed to represent the massive cross-land flows and transoceanic movements in people, in goods, in money, in services, in information, and in ideas—flows and movements that connect all but the most isolated regions on earth, and that are doing so to a greater degree than ever before in human history. To the extent that Huntington conceded the ever-increasing interconnectedness of the globe, he thought it reinforced particular civilizational identities and fueled intercivilizational conflict; but the evidence suggests it is at least as likely that such varied, increasing, and multifarious encounters draw peoples and nations and civilizations closer together in a revived and intensified sense of shared experiences, common identities, and global cosmopolitanism.[100]

Detailed research, undertaken since the appearance of Huntington's article and book, confirms these early doubts.[101] In political terms, most nations still act primarily in their own self-interest, rather than as a constituent or subordinate part of any greater collectivity: states' individual concerns and priorities continue to be more important to their leaders and citizenry than any higher sense or call of civilizational unity. Since they have always been difficult to describe or define, it is scarcely surprising that civilizations are incapable of acting with unified, coherent, and directed purpose, which undermines Huntington's claim that it is the "differences among civilizations" that "have generated the most prolonged and the most violent conflicts."[102] More particularly, the notion that a clash between the West and Islam (or between the West and China) is *bound* to occur because their histories are so antagonistic, and their values are so different, will scarcely bear careful scrutiny. A great deal of evidence has already been adduced in an earlier chapter suggesting that in the long term, relations between Christianity and Islam have been characterized as much by accommodation and conversation as by antagonism and confrontation, and recent surveys make plain that there are shared values, including the idea and ideal of democracy, which is as attractive to many Muslims as to Christians.[103] In any case, since 1945, both during and after the Cold War, conflicts have broken out between states belonging to the *same* civilization (as defined by Huntington) on many more occasions than they have between states belonging to *different* civilizations, which scarcely supports his prediction that it is between civilizations that future conflicts are most likely to occur.[104]

Despite, or perhaps because of, these major errors and limitations, Huntington's book appealed powerfully to those neoconservative politicians, intellectuals, and evangelical Christians who, by the late 1990s, were hoping that the scandal-beset presidency of Bill Clinton would be followed by a more assertive Republican administration. They found its "simplified paradigms or maps" to be appealing and convincing, and they happily regarded them as "indispensable to human thought and action."[105] They shared Huntington's insistence on the importance of religion in determining the largest collective identities; they agreed that the West needed to rediscover its sense of identity and purpose; and (up to a point) they appreciated the guidance he gave, and the warnings he furnished, concerning the future relations between the West and the rest of the world. But just as Gibbon and Toynbee had been misunderstood or oversimplified by pundits and politicians who invoked their names to justify their own views and policies, so Huntington would also (at least in part) be misinterpreted or misrepresented by those on the American right. For he repeatedly insisted that the post–Cold War world was multipolar, and that the most pressing task facing the West, whose global influence was diminishing by the day, was not to provoke confrontation but to reach some form of accommodation with those other civilizations that were becoming increasingly important. By such means, Huntington hoped, the "clash of civilizations," which he thought "improbable but not impossible," might be averted. So while to the neoconservatives Huntington's work was a manifesto justifying confrontation and unilateralism, in reality it was a much less bellicose admonition.

On their initial publication, Huntington's arguments were well received by such foreign policy luminaries from the "realist" school as Henry A. Kissinger, but with limited popular notice. It was not until years later, with the events of 9/11, that his "clash of civilizations" thesis would become, seemingly overnight, the most influential explanation of what had just occurred, and of what must happen in the future. Three groups in particular embraced what they believed to be the Huntington interpretation of events with great vehemence and enthusiasm. The first were the American media, which "automatically, implicitly and unanimously," and with little serious reflection or analysis, decided Huntington's analysis of two civilizations locked in a mortal global clash was correct.[106] The second was President George W. Bush and his supporters, ranging from such neoconservative intellectuals as William Kristol, Richard Perle, and Robert Kagan, to the British prime minister, Tony Blair, along with most of his cabinet and the House of Commons, who responded by urging a new "Crusade" to "save civilization itself." Hence the invasions of Iraq and Afghanistan, and the Manichean rhetoric about the "war on terror" as the great struggle between the forces of light and the "axis of evil," between Judeo-Christian freedom and democracy on the one hand and Islamic despotism and tyranny on the other.[107] And the third group to embrace the Huntington thesis, although from the opposite side, was the followers of Osama bin Laden himself, who gleefully agreed that Al Qaeda was leading the Islamic world in a clash with the West, a holy war against the great, wicked, monstrous, and degenerate Satan, the head of the serpent being the United States.[108]

For a time, it did seem possible to contend that the world was threatened and sundered by an apocalyptic "clash" in the way Huntington had analyzed and predicted: "our civilization," the late Christopher Hitchens observed, "must be fought for and barbarism must be defeated."[109] But almost from the outset, it was clear that neither side was as united or as homogeneous as these formulated polarities suggested. It soon emerged that several hundred of those who died when the twin towers collapsed were Muslims, while Saddam Hussein's regime in Iraq, however brutal, was by the norms of the Arab world a notably secular regime, with little sympathy for the militant Islamism of Osama bin Laden, let alone his ambition to establish a Muslim caliphate.[110] These were inconvenient facts for those who wished to depict a deep, divisive conflict between the Christian West and the Islamic world, and they were but a foretaste of what was to come. The "war on terror" would soon become highly unpopular on both sides of the Atlantic, and the impatient denunciations by Donald Rumsfeld, the U.S. secretary of defense, of "old Europe" suggested that

"Christian civilization" was less monolithic or enthusiastic than the overwrought rhetoric of Bush or Blair repeatedly claimed. And on what was supposed to be the "other side," many Arab governments denounced the attack on the World Trade Center, urging that it was no proper, much less consensual, expression of Islam, which they were at pains to identify as a religion of peace. Meanwhile, many divisions within that faith, chiefly between Sunni and Shiite, once little remarked by outsiders, would come to prominence following the invasion of Iraq.[111]

Yet both Bush and Blair continued to insist they were engaged in a Manichean conflict, defining and defending civilization against the forces of barbarism, terror, darkness, and evil. As a born-again Christian, George W. Bush appropriated the formulation in the Gospel of Matthew that you were either with America or you were against it, and Tony Blair expressed equally fervent certainty: "I don't believe," he observed, "that what is happening in Iraq today is anything other than an absolutely visceral, profound struggle between what is right and what is wrong." Neither leader had any time for nuance, compromise, dialogue, or accommodation, and Roy Jenkins's words on Blair applied equally well to Bush: "the Prime Minister, far from lacking conviction, has almost too much, particularly when dealing with the world beyond Britain. He is a little Manichean for my perhaps now jaded taste, seeing matters in stark terms of good and evil, black and white, contending with each other, and with a consequent belief that if evil is cast down, good will inevitably follow."[112] Yet neither Bush nor Blair succeeded in convincing the majority of people in "the West" that the attack on the World Trade Center was the first blow in a global struggle resembling the hot war against Fascism or the Cold War against Communism. At the very least, they should have read Huntington more carefully, for despite the shortcomings of his analysis of civilizations as the ultimate unit of collective human identity, he had consistently urged accommodation rather than confrontation, and he had explicitly counseled against preemptive military action. Indeed, in the aftermath of 9/11, he refused to support the idea of a "war on terror" or the American-led invasion of Iraq.[113]

Not surprisingly, then, the Bush-Blair view of the world, in which "the battle lines are drawn" in a "simple binary struggle" between "good and evil," has been very publicly rejected by their successors.[114] Determined to "seek a new beginning" in the relations between the West and Islam, President Barack Obama discarded the "clash of civilizations" as an explanation of the woes of the world, and urged the merits—and the precedents—of conversation and conciliation. He made this plain in Turkey in 2009, when he told his audience that their country "is not where East and West divide: this is where they come together," and he developed his argument in a later speech at Cairo University.[115] He noted that "the relationship between Islam and the West" had sometimes been characterized by "conflict and religious wars," but that there had also been "centuries of coexistence and cooperation." On balance, he was convinced that "the interests we share as human beings are far more powerful than the forces that drive us apart," and he called for a dialogue between Christianity and Islam based on "a sustained effort to listen to each other, to learn from each other, to respect one another, and to seek common ground." He spoke of Islam's great achievements in mathematics, medicine, architecture, poetry, and music, to which the West was indebted. He urged Americans and Muslims to abandon their crude stereotypes of each other, to focus on "finding the things we share" rather than on "seeing what is different," and to "recognize our common humanity."[116]

CIVILIZATION AND ITS DISCONTENTS

Ever since the late eighteenth century, the notion that civilizations (and, sometimes, barbarians) constitute the ultimate, most capacious, and most significant form of collective human identity has been an arresting and appealing one, because it offers the most comprehensive yet also the most simplified account of the diversity and complexity of the peopled past. Such a view of human identity was shared in the nineteenth century by the British philosopher John Stuart Mill and the French statesman and historian Fran-çois Guizot, and since then it has been especially arresting and appealing to pundits, policymakers, and political leaders seeking to mobilize popular support for a particular international cause or overseas venture: in defense of civilization against barbarism, or in defense of one version of civilization against another.[117] But across the last two hundred years, the evidence is clear that when political leaders derive their aggregated categories from authors such as those discussed here, they invariably compound the original literary licenses and scholarly liberties that had been taken by adding further simplifications of their own. The resulting collective identities are almost invariably misleading to the point where they may, as in the case of the so-called clash of civilizations, be simultaneously convincing to some while wholly unconvincing to others, and the accumulated evidence strongly suggests that the skeptics are more correct than the believers.[118]

To be sure, the notion that civilizations and barbarisms, or civilizations and civilizations, are predestined to confront each other and go to war with each other, as the ultimate manifestation of competing human identities, consciousnesses, and agencies, is one that can be easily articulated, both rhetorically and cartographically. The Manichean simplicities of "us" versus "them," and of "good" versus "bad," can be inflated to a global scale by messianic wordsmiths, and they look good on paper, as depicted on visually persuasive maps of the world. Yet if there are such entities as civilizations, this is not, pace Gibbon, Toynbee, and Huntington, how they function and interact with each other in the long run. And even if such entities as civilizations actually do exist, there is little evidence that they are, pace Gibbon, Toynbee, and Huntington, self-confined or prone to clash in the long run. As Felipe Fernández-Armesto writes in his own study of the subject, "Even when locked in what appears to be mutual hostility—like Ancient Rome and Persia, or medieval Christendom and Islam—civilizations tend to develop relationships which are mutually acknowledging and sometimes mutually sustaining. . . . Though there are occasional exceptions," he concludes, "it seems to be hard for any civilization to survive at a high level of material achievement, except in contact with others."[119] With civilizations, as with religions, nations, classes, genders, and races, we neglect at our peril the conversations that go on across what some mistakenly think to be impermeable boundaries.

Indeed, in recent years the United Nations has deliberately

sought, in the name of promoting a global sense of common humanity, to encourage such transcivilizational dialogues and encounters, an endeavor that culminated in November 2006 in the publication of a report entitled *The Alliance of Civilizations*. The history of relations between cultures, it concluded, was not only characterized by "wars and confrontation"; it was also a "history of mutual borrowing and constant cross-fertilization," since civilizations "overlap, interact and evolve in relationship with one another." In its humane internationalism and its well-intentioned liberalism, such a document seems light-years away from the belligerent unilateralists who appropriated—and corrupted—Huntington's "clash of civilizations" thesis.[120] Yet in one significant sense, made plain in its very title, the UN document shared the presumptions of Huntington and those who had invoked his work to justify the "war on terror," namely that the world *was* divided into different civilizational groups that constituted the highest form of collective human identity. While diverging from the neocons over whether civilizations clashed or conversed, they concurred with them in the belief that civilizations undoubtedly did exist.[121]

But did they, and do they, exist? After making thirteen television programs on the subject, the art historian Sir Kenneth Clark concluded that civilization was extremely difficult to define and describe. [122] How right he was—and is. Despite the uncounted scholars from many disciplines who have tried their hand at the question, there is no agreement as to how many civilizations there have been in the past, or how many exist today. Just as it is clearly inadequate to define an individual on the basis of only one criterion, such as religion, so, too, do civilizations defy such reduction; yet to define them on the basis of many criteria avails a meaningless category for the very opposite reason. Still, despite its deep flaws as the largest and most inclusive form of collective human solidarity, civilization has continued to appeal to those who wish to sort reality into the simplest possible categories and identities—categories and identities that retain their currency so long as their incoherence and contradictions are not betrayed by practical experience. It would be flying in the face of the evidence to hope that a word in such ready common usage for two hundred years might now be given up. But future world leaders who invoke "civilization" ought to be more circumspect about doing so than many who have recently and irresponsibly been bandying it around to such baleful effect. Of all collective forms of human identity, civilization is the most nebulous, and it is this very vagueness that makes it at once so appealing and so dangerous. As Dr. Johnson realized, it is a word, a concept, a category, and a version of human aggregation and conflict we would be much better off without.[123]

Conclusion

"Wasn't it the chronic danger of our time, not only practical, but intellectual, to let the world get divided into two halves?"

—C. P. Snow, *The Affair*

There has not, so far as I know been any previous age in which the common humanity of all human beings, just in virtue of our all being human, has been so widely recognized and acted upon as it is today.

—Arnold J. Toynbee, *Experiences*

DESPITE THEIR UNDENIABLE DIFFERENCES and variations, the collective identities investigated in this book share significant characteristics. A first is that each is invoked and deployed to promote particular group interests: religions compete in their claims to uniquely privileged access to their respective deities; every nation stresses its special characteristics and admirable virtues vis-à-vis any or all others; classes go to war to decide which of them should enjoy the greater share of the profits of the means of production; women do battle with men to undo centuries of exploitation and discrimination; whites enforce their supremacy over blacks, and blacks fight to free themselves from it; and civilizations clash on the basis of differing perceptions as to which are good and evil. A second is that many leaders and writers have claimed that one of these six solidarities is both more homogeneous and more important than any other form of human aggregation, thereby resembling a winning squash or a victorious turnip or a triumphant pumpkin in a horticultural competition, being bigger, better, and more important than any of its rivals. A third is that these identities are presented as being so innate, intrinsic, adversarial, and confrontational that the world must properly be understood in Manichean terms, as a cosmic battleground between religions or nations or classes or genders or races or civilizations.

A fourth shared characteristic is that these battling solidarities are sustained by affirming memories, reinforcing stories, and historical accounts that reject any greater sense of common humanity.

As the foregoing pages often concede, tensions and conflicts have indeed arisen across the centuries between different groups that have sought to define themselves, or else have been defined in relation to, one of the six categories of identity explored here.[1] Battles have been fought and conflicts have been waged to protect or promote religions or nations or civilizations, and class, gender, and race have given rise to a host of social and political upheavals, from civil disobedience to civil wars. But it is also the case that these aggregations, constructed and pitted against one another, and often accompanied by extravagant claims as to their primacy and significance, need to be treated with healthier skepticism than they all too often receive. To begin with, they are rarely as homogeneous, monolithic, or all-encompassing, or as naturally belligerent and as adversarially entrenched, as their leaders and apologists, propagandists and historians like to claim: how often, it behooves us to ask, have (for example) most Christians, most Germans, most workers, most women, most blacks, or most inhabitants of the West felt a common identity against most pagans, most Frenchmen, most employees, most men, most whites, or most barbarians? Claims made for the homogeneity, the unanimity, and the innate bellicosity of such groupings invariably break down under scrutiny, into myriad fragments, significant exceptions, and many alternative competing identities. The combative mobilization of such collective categories has always depended on making totalizing claims to uniformity and all-inclusiveness that are never actually true, and these identities belong to those "fictions" that seem regrettably inseparable from the processes of politics and realities of government.[2]

As for the claims made by figures ranging from Marx and Engels, via Robert Knox, to Germaine Greer and George W. Bush, to the effect that one of these six identities is paramount, trumping and incorporating the others as *the* explanation of human behavior, past, present, and future: it follows, self-evidently, that these claims cannot *all* be true. Conceivably, one of them is right, and the other five are wrong, but to judge by the ample evidence against each of them, it seems more plausible to conclude, in the spirit of W. S. Gilbert's aphorism, "When everyone is somebody, then no-one's anybody," that *no* exclusive and hegemonic assertion made on behalf of *any* of these six aggregations is *ever* true. Both individually and collectively, we are all creatures of multiple rather than single identities, we inhabit many different and diverse groupings at the same time, and they vary in their significance, and in their claims on our attention, depending on particular contexts and specific circumstances. As Amartya Sen has rightly observed, it is an "odd presumption" that "people of the world can be uniquely categorized according to some singular and overarching system of partitioning," and this misguidedly "solitarist" approach to the many identities we all simultaneously possess is not only intrinsically wrong and empirically incorrect, but it also disregards and undermines the broader and more encompassing collective category of our "shared humanity."[3]

Such claims also mistakenly assume that the world is divided and polarized between single, all-encompassing collectivities. Yet it cannot be too often repeated that while conflicts between those whom Matthew Arnold famously described as "ignorant armies" clashing by night "on a darkling plain" are undeniably a significant part of the story of humanity, the Manichean view of the world frequently deployed to proclaim, ignite, and promote confrontations between "us" and "them," between the "good guys" and the "bad guys," and between the forces of light and those of darkness, fails to recognize or describe the messy, complex, contingent, multifaceted, interconnected, joined-up reality of human relations.[4] As these pages have shown time and again, conversations across these allegedly unbridgeable divides—between (for example) Christians and pagans, or Germans and Frenchmen, or workers and capitalists, or women and men, or blacks and whites, or the West and the rest—make up a substantial, perhaps even preponderant, part of the whole human experience. Whether envisaged individually or collectively, the reality of the human past has always been informed by dialogue, interaction, connection, borrowing, blending, and assimilation, at least as much as it has been by disagreement, hostility, belligerence, conflict, separation, or unlikeness. That our sense of the past, and of the present, has been too often dominated by an exaggerated insistence on the importance of confrontation and difference is not only a disservice to the cause of knowledge but also misrepresents the nature of the human condition, and misidentifies the best paths by which that condition has been improved—and may be further improved.

Among the partisans and proponents of divided humanity, there is often an easy presumption of cause and effect between the agitation and articulation of group identities, the resulting pressure exerted on those in power, and the furtherance of human progress: as colonial nationalists battle for freedom from imperial control, or as women worldwide seek to gain liberties and equality, or as blacks in the United States campaigned for their civil rights. But while some collective groupings are built around such virtuous claims, and achieve such admirable outcomes, not all of them are, and not all of them do, as evident in the mobilization of Aryans against Jews, or of white supremacists against blacks, for very different (and very deplorable) ends. There is an additional assumption that such mobilizations invariably achieve their aims, but the processes whereby colonies became independent, or women's circumstances were improved, or civil rights were won for American blacks, or apartheid was ended in South Africa, were clearly much more complex than that.[5] The mobilizations may well have played a part—but only a part. Moreover, some of the most successful leaders of these causes achieved their ends through appeals *across* these divides, rather than on the basis of adversarial identities: Martin Luther King Jr. promoted the interests of blacks that they might enjoy civil rights with whites, not at their expense; Betty Friedan sought to involve men as well as women in the pursuit of her feminist agenda; and in denouncing apartheid, Nelson Mandela was motivated by a concern not just for blacks, but for humanity as a whole.

Even those who have sometimes advocated sectional interests, particular identities, and group antagonisms have on occasions seen the force, wisdom, and justification of a more generous, all-embracing, and inclusive view. One such individual was Rudyard Kipling, successively acclaimed and denounced as the racist poet who declared the white man's burden and advocated the white man's supremacy. But in a very different mood, he would urge a broader perspective on humanity, in which the differences were ultimately dissolved in the similarities:

> *All good people agree*
> *And all good people say,*
> *All nice people, like Us, are We*
> *And everyone else is They:*
> *But if you cross the sea,*
> *Instead of over the way,*
> *You may end (think of it!) by looking on We*
> *As only a sort of They!*[6]

And one such institution of which the same may be said has been Christianity, which for much of its history has been belligerently and intolerantly opposed to alternative religions, as well as to heretical and heterodox versions of itself, but which has also been a powerful force in the twentieth century against such evils as racism and the mistreatment of women, in the cause of proclaiming a common humanity.[7]

Yet what V. S. Naipaul once called "that missing large idea of human association" has received little attention from historians, even in our own time when world history, global history, and transnational history are more advocated and more popular than ever before.[8] This is partly because the deeds and attitudes that constitute and exemplify our common humanity tend to be to historians what good news is to journalists: the default mode of human activity, a quotidian reality that rarely merits headlines, being somehow either unworthy or uninteresting.[9] And this lack of appeal is evident across the political as well as the scholarly spectrum. On the left, the preferred model of human behavior and association remains that of collective identities heroically mobilized by charismatic leaders to achieve virtuous ends through struggle and conflict against implacable forces and evil foes. On the right, the vision of common humanity is also occluded, by stressing the primacy of struggle and competition among individuals, an atomistic (and antagonistic) view immortalized by Margaret Thatcher's observation that there is no such thing as society. Neither of these perspectives leaves any room for the greater claims or larger subject of our shared humanity beyond our differences. Yet the human past needs to be approached, understood, explained, and written not just in terms of competing individuals and the survival of the fittest, or of group identities latently or actually in conflict with each other, but also in terms of the concerns, activities, and achievements that transcend these divisions. "History and humanity," one American scholar notes, "are not in fact enclosed in boxes, whether national, ethnic, local or continental. Good history ought to reflect this truth."[10]

As the late J. H. Plumb once remarked, history "is neither pagan nor Christian, it belongs to no nation or class, it is universal; it is human in the widest sense of the term."[11] Thus understood, the primary job of the historian is not to assist in constructing the artifice of discrete, self-contained, self-regarding, and mutually exclusive groups. This enterprise has been a priority too long unexamined to the detriment of a more complex, dynamic, and ultimately more compelling understanding based on the multiplicity of identities, by turns individual and collective, separate and shared, that animate all of us in unique and changing ways. A history that dwells only on divided pasts denies us the just inheritance of what we have always shared, namely a capacity to "live together in societies sufficiently harmonious and orderly not to be constantly breaking apart." Surely, then, it is at least as worthwhile to take as our starting point humanity's essential (but under-studied) unity as it is to obsess on its lesser (but over-studied) divisions?[12]

Late in his life, having done with *A Study of History*, that became Arnold J. Toynbee's view, as expressed in his words quoted above, and that wider and wiser perspective has been eloquently and appropriately reaffirmed by his biographer, Professor William H. McNeill:

> Humanity entire possesses a commonality which historians may hope to understand just as firmly as they can comprehend what unites any lesser group. Instead of enhancing conflicts, as parochial historiography inevitably does, an intelligible world history might be expected to diminish the lethality of group encounters by cultivating a sense of indi-

vidual identification with the triumphs and tribulations of humanity as a whole. This, indeed, strikes me as the moral duty of the historical profession in our time.[13]

In this McNeill is undoubtedly correct: the history of humankind is at least as much about cooperation as it is about conflict, and about kindness to strangers as about the obsession with otherness and alterity. To write about the past no less than to live in the present, we need to see beyond our differences, our sectional interests, our identity politics, and our parochial concerns to embrace and to celebrate the common humanity that has always bound us together, that still binds us together today, and that will continue to bind us together in the future.[14]

ACKNOWLEDGMENTS

Although I had been brooding on this subject for a long time, the immediate stimulus to get some preliminary thoughts down on paper was the invitation to give the George Macaulay Trevelyan Lectures, which I delivered under the auspices of the History Faculty of the University of Cambridge during the Lent Term of 2007. I am grateful to Professor Quentin Skinner and to the board of electors for asking me, to Professor Richard J. Evans for urging me to tackle a large topic that might appeal to undergraduates, and to the Master and Fellows of Christ's College, Cambridge, for their generous hospitality during my visit. Having already written Trevelyan's biography, I was delighted to be given this opportunity to pay him another form of homage, and it was a particular pleasure to do so exactly fifty years since the lectures established in his honor had been inaugurated. This book is an expanded and rewritten version of my original texts, incorporating much new material and more fully developed argumentation, and I have deleted my original opening remarks about Trevelyan's life, work, and family, which seemed appropriate to the local Cambridge setting, but not to a publication that I hope will reach, as Trevelyan's own writings so often did, a much wider audience.

In tackling this subject, I have drawn upon a broad range of literature far beyond my limited sphere of knowledge, and I am indebted to many friends who have helped me in areas of the past (and present) that are not my own: Anthony Appiah, Robert Attenborough, Christopher Bayly, David Bell, the late Isaiah Berlin, Glen Bowersock, Judith M. Brown, Peter Brown, Richard Bulliet, Owen Chadwick, John Darwin, John Elliott, Felipe Fernández-Armesto, Eric Foner, Roy Foster, Timothy Garton Ash, Anthony Grafton, John Hall, Henry Hardy, the late Eric Hobsbawm, Brooks Hosfield, Michael Howard, Ronald Hyam, Jonathan Israel, the late Tony Judt, Stephen Lamport, Nomi Levy-Carrick, Anthony Low, Neil MacGregor, Kirsten MacKenzie, Alastair MacLachlan, Peter Mandler, Phil Nord, Nel Irvin Painter, the late Simon Price, David Reynolds, Duncan Robinson, Daniel T. Rodgers, Emma Rothschild, Stuart Schwartz, Hamish Scott, Amartya Sen, Christine Stansell, Shirley Tilghman, Sean Wilentz, and Adrian Young. I have also been greatly helped by reading the many books on diverse subjects that have come my way as a judge of the Wolfson History Prize, and by stimulating discussions with my co-judges, Keith Thomas, Averil Cameron, Richard J. Evans, and Julia Smith. Earlier versions of some of these chapters were delivered to gatherings at the Institute of Historical Research in London, to the Council in the Humanities at Princeton University, as the Rushton Lecture at the University of Virginia, to the Australian National University in Canberra, and at the Festival of Ideas in Melbourne.

I undertook the initial work for the Trevelyan Lectures while I was Queen Elizabeth the Queen Mother Professor of British History at the Institute of Historical Research in the University of London, and I completed the reading for this book as Whitney J. Oates Senior Research Scholar in the Council of the Humanities at Princeton University. I am grateful to many colleagues and friends in both institutions for their help, support, and encouragement, in particular to Miles Taylor, Elaine Walters, Helen McCarthy, Jennifer Wallis, and Martha Vandrei in London, and to Jeremy Adelman, Anthony Grafton, Harold James, William Chester Jordan, Phil Nord, Carol Rigolot, and Gideon Rosen in Princeton. Most of this book was written while I was Fletcher Jones Foundation Distinguished Fellow at the Huntington Library in San Marino, California, and a Director's Visitor at the Institute for Advanced Study at Princeton. I owe a large debt to Roy Ritchie and Susie Karasnoo at the Huntington, and to Peter Goddard at the Institute, for giving me such a warm welcome, and for providing ideal surroundings for sustained thought and uninterrupted writing.

I am grateful, as ever, to my agents, Gill Coleridge in London and Michael Carlisle in New York, for smoothing the bumpy path from original idea to manuscript to publication, and I am indebted to the help, wisdom, and guidance of my two transatlantic editors and friends, Simon Winder at Penguin and George Andreou at Alfred A. Knopf, with both of whom it has again been a joy and a pleasure to work. I also wish to thank Juhea Kim for having overseen the production of the book with great alertness and efficiency, Roland Ottewell for his meticulous copyediting of the text, and Sara Brooks for her help with the proofs. Linda Colley has, as before, made life worth living and books worth writing, and I once more offer up to her my thanks and love. I dedicate this work to two dear friends, whose lives in medicine and music, and in so much else besides, are a constant reminder, embodiment, and celebration of the humanity that all of us share. And I offer this book in the hope that it may contribute to a greater awareness, appreciation, understanding, and recognition of that broader existence we all have in common, that lies beyond the single identities, the exaggerated differences, and the polarized animosities that too easily and too often loom too large, too distorting, and too damaging in all of our lives.

David Cannadine
Norfolk, England
July 10, 2012

NOTES

INTRODUCTION

1. For the formative elements of George W. Bush's worldview, see M. Lind, *Made in Texas: George W. Bush and the Southern Takeover of American Politics* (New York, 2002). For three recent examples of this Manichean formulation, see D. Berreby, *Us and Them: Understanding Your Tribal Mind* (New York, 2005); C. Jennings, *Them and Us: The American Invasion of British High Society* (London, 2007); W. Hutton, *Them and Us: Politics, Greed and Inequality—Why We Need a Fair Society* (London, 2010).

2. Quoted in E. Luce, "A Tragedy of Errors," *Financial Times*, January 19, 2009.

3. T. Todorov, *The Fear of Barbarians: Beyond the Clash of Civilizations* (Chicago, 2010), pp. 91, 100–101, 104.

4. D. Bell, "Class Consciousness and the Fall of the Bourgeois Revolution," *Critical Review* 16 (2004): 336–38; P. Novick, *That Noble Dream: The "Objectivity Question" and the American Historical Profession* (Cambridge, 1988), pp. 469–521.

5. M. Guibernan, *The Identity of Nations* (Cambridge, 2007), p. 173.

6. C. Geertz, "What Is a State If It Is Not a Sovereign?: Reflections on Politics in Complicated Places," *Current Anthropology* 45 (2004): 584; F. Nussbaum, "The Politics of Difference," *Eighteenth-Century Studies* 23 (1990): 375–86; S. Collini, *English Pasts: Essays in History and Culture* (Oxford, 1999), p. 264; C. Hall, "Introduction: Thinking the Postcolonial, Thinking the Empire," in C. Hall, ed., *Cultures of Empire: A Reader* (Manchester, 2000), p. 16; K. Wilson, "Introduction: Histories, Empires, Modernities," in K. Wilson, ed., *Cultures, Identity and Modernity in Britain and the Empire, 1660–1840* (Cambridge, 2004), p. 5. For a recent attempt to write global history employing the concept of "difference" as the organizing principle, see J. Burbank and F. Cooper, *Empires in World History: Power and the Politics of Difference* (Princeton, 2010).

7. L. Colley, "Britishness and Otherness: An Argument," *Journal of British Studies* 31 (1992): 309–29; W. H. McNeill, "Mythistory, or Truth, Myth, History, and Historians," *American Historical Review* 91(1986): 5.

8. M. Nussbaum, *Not for Profit: Why Democracy Needs the Humanities*

(Princeton, 2010), pp. 28–29, 35–36; A. Appiah, *Cosmopolitanism: Ethics in a World of Strangers* (New York, 2006), pp. xx–xxi. See also A. Ryan, "Cosmopolitans," *New York Review of Books*, June 22, 2006, pp. 46–48.

9. M. Angelou, "Human Family," in *I Shall Not Be Moved* (New York, 1990), p. 5.

10. T. Garton Ash, "Obama's Beijing Balancing Act Points to the New Challenge for the West," *Guardian*, November 18, 2009; Garton Ash, "Obama Must Wish He Were Cameron," *Guardian*, July 22, 2010; N. MacGregor, "The Whole World in Our Hands," *Guardian, Review*, July 24, 2004; MacGregor, "Britain Is at the Centre of a Conversation with the World," *Guardian*, April 19, 2007; MacGregor, *A History of the World in 100 Objects* (London, 2011), pp. xviii, xxv.

11. Bill Clinton, "World Without Walls," *Guardian, Saturday Review*, January 26, 2002; Clinton, "My Vision for Peace," *Observer*, September 8, 2002.

12. Todorov, *Fear of Barbarians*, p. 197. Raymond Aron once made a similar point when he observed that life "is never a struggle between good and evil, but between the preferable and the detestable": quoted in T. Judt, *The Burden of Responsibility* (Chicago, 1998), p. 182.

13. For a rare and honorable exception to this generalization, see M. Macmillan, *Dangerous Games: The Uses and Abuses of History* (New York, 2009), esp. pp. 54–90.

14. J. Goody, *Production and Reproduction: A Comparative Study of the Domestic Domain* (Cambridge, 1976), p. ix; M. B. Finocchiaro, "Science, Religion, and the Historiography of the Galileo Affair: On the Undesirability of Oversimplification," *Osiris* 16 (2001): 116.

15. B. Bailyn, "How England Became Modern: A Revolutionary View," *New York Review of Books*, November 19, 2009, p. 44; L. Putnam, "To Study the Fragments/Whole: Microhistory and the Atlantic World," *Journal of Social History* 39 (2006): 617.

16. K. V. Thomas, *The Ends of Life: Roads to Fulfillment in Early Modern England* (Oxford, 2009), p. 6.

17. P. Vallely, "Blair's Glinting Eye Turns to Iran," *Independent on Sunday*, January 23, 2011. See also the Angolan freedom fighter Artur Carlos Maurício Pestana dos Santos (Pepetela), *Mayombe* (London, 1983), p. 2.

ONE: RELIGION

1. Matthew 25:31–46.

2. P. Brown, *The World of Late Antiquity from Marcus Aurelius to Mohammad* (London, 1971), pp. 54–55.

3. A. Pagden, *Worlds at War: The 2,500-Year Struggle Between East and West* (Oxford, 2008), pp. 124–27.

4. R. Lane Fox, *Pagans and Christians* (Harmondsworth, 1996), pp. 561–71; H. Katouzian, *The Persians: Ancient, Medieval and Modern Iran* (London, 2009), pp. 49–58.

5. M. E. Marty, *When Faiths Collide* (Oxford, 2005), p. 159; W. Lippman, *A Preface to Morals* (New York, 1929), p. 76; Matthew 12:30.

6. Matthew 25:35.

7. Marty, *When Faiths Collide*, p. 134.

8. J. Wolffe, introduction to J. Wolffe, ed., *Religion in History: Conflict, Conversion and Coexistence* (Manchester, 2004), pp. 5–6.

9. H. R. Trevor-Roper, *The Rise of Christian Europe* (London, 1965).

10. J. G. A. Pocock, *Barbarism and Religion*, vol. 3, *The First Decline and Fall* (Cambridge, 2003), pp. 71–74; G. Clark, *Christianity and Roman Society* (Cambridge, 2004), pp. 9–10.

11. G. A. Bonnard, ed., *Edward Gibbon: Memoirs of My Life* (London, 1966 ed.), p. 147; Pocock, *First Decline and Fall*, p. 497.

12. J. W. Swain, *Edward Gibbon the Historian* (London, 1966), pp. 62–70; P. Brown, "Gibbon's Views on Culture and Society in the Fifth and Sixth Centuries," in G. W. Bowersock, J. Clive, and S. R. Graubard, eds., *Edward Gibbon and the Decline and Fall of the Roman Empire* (Cambridge, Mass., 1977), pp. 43–45.

13. R. Porter, *Gibbon* (London, 1988), pp. 1, 112–15.

14. D. P. Jordan, *Gibbon and His Roman Empire* (Urbana, Ill., 1971), p. 106.

15. Porter, *Gibbon*, pp. 105–6; J. W. Burrow, *Gibbon* (Oxford, 1985), pp. 52–55.

16. Porter, *Gibbon*, p. 119.

17. Burrow, *Gibbon*, p. 53.

18. P. B. Craddock, *Edward Gibbon, Luminous Historian, 1772–1794* (Baltimore, 1989), pp. 60–63.

19. Porter, *Gibbon*, pp. 121–23.

20. L. Gossman, *The Empire Unpossess'd: An Essay on Gibbon's "Decline and Fall"* (Cambridge, 1981), pp. 33, 47; Jordan, *Gibbon and His Roman Empire*, p. 106; Burrow, *Gibbon*, p. 51.

21. Porter, *Gibbon*, pp. 125–29.

22. Ibid., p. 117.

23. Jordan, *Gibbon and His Roman Empire*, pp. 106, 112; Porter, *Gibbon*, p. 115; Burrow, *Gibbon*, p. 63.

24. Swain, *Gibbon the Historian*, p. 66; Craddock, *Gibbon, Luminous Historian*, p. 63.

25. J. G. A. Pocock, *Barbarism and Religion*, vol. 1, *The Enlightenments of Edward Gibbon, 1737–1764* (Cambridge, 1999), p. 283; Porter, *Gibbon*, p. 116; Bonnard, *Edward Gibbon*, p. 136; Burrow, *Gibbon*, p. 66.

26. Burrow, *Gibbon*, p. 53.

27. Clark, *Christianity and Roman Society*, p. 35; J. Huskinson, "Pagan and

Christian in the Third to Fifth Centuries," in Wolffe, *Religion in History*, p. 15.

28. R. A. Markus, *The End of Ancient Christianity* (Cambridge, 1990), pp. 21–22; Burrow, *Gibbon*, p. 56.

29. Jordan, *Gibbon and His Roman Empire*, p. 107.

30. Porter, *Gibbon*, pp. 124–28.

31. Lane Fox, *Pagans and Christians*, p. 592; Brown, *World of Late Antiquity*, p. 104.

32. B. Caseau, "Sacred Landscapes," in G. W. Bowersock, P. Brown, and O. Grabar, eds., *Interpreting Late Antiquity: Essays on the Postclassical World* (Cambridge, Mass., 2001), pp. 34–35; C. Kelley, "Empire Building," in ibid., pp. 184–85; M. Beard, J. North, and S. Price, *Religions of Rome*, vol. 1, *A History* (Cambridge, 1998), pp. 364–75; Lane Fox, *Pagans and Christians*, pp. 609–62; Clark, *Christianity and Roman Society*, p. 14.

33. A. Cameron, *The Mediterranean World in Late Antiquity, AD 395–600* (London, 1993), pp. 7–8; M. Vessey, "The Demise of the Christian Writer and the Re-Making of 'Late Antiquity': From H.-I. Marrou's *Saint Augustine* (1938) to Peter Brown's *Holy Man* (1983)," *Journal of Early Christian Studies* 6 (1998): 377–411.

34. P. Brown, "Christianization and Religious Conflict," in A. Cameron and P. Garnsey, eds., *The Cambridge Ancient History*, vol. 13, *The Late Empire, A.D. 337–425* (Cambridge, 1998), p. 641.

35. Wolffe, introduction to *Religion in History*, pp. 6–8; Beard, North, and Price, *Religions of Rome*, p. 388.

36. Clark, *Christianity and Roman Society*, pp. 38–53; G. W. Bowersock, *Martyrdom and Rome* (Cambridge, 1995), pp. 2, 18, 41–43.

37. Huskinson, "Pagan and Christian," pp. 21–22.

38. K. Shelton, *The Esquiline Treasure* (London, 1988), pp. 72–75.

39. B. Caseau, "Sacred Landscapes," pp. 29–30.

40. J. Sandwell, "Christian Self-Definition in the Fourth Century AD: John Chrysostom on Christianity, Imperial Rule and the City," in J. Sandwell and J. Huskinson, eds., *Culture and Society in Later Roman Antioch* (Oxford, 2003), pp. 35–58.

41. Huskinson, "Pagan and Christian," pp. 29–31.

42. Brown, "Christianization and Religious Conflict, pp. 632–35; Lane Fox, *Pagans and Christians*, pp. 586, 607–8; Markus, *End of Ancient Christianity*, p. 28; Clark, *Christianity and Roman Society*, p. 10.

43. Huskinson, "Pagan and Christian," p. 35.

44. Introduction to Bowersock, Brown, and Grabar, *Interpreting Late Antiquity*, p. xi.

45. Clark, *Christianity and Roman Society*, pp. 11, 14.

46. Brown, *World of Late Antiquity*, pp. 70–72; Markus, *End of Ancient Christianity*, p. 110.

47. Clark, *Christianity and Roman Society*, p. 1; Cameron, *Mediterranean World*, p. 144. See also R. Bartlett, "Reflections on Paganism and Christianity in Medieval Europe," *Proceedings of the British Academy* 101 (1998): 55–76.

48. Porter, *Gibbon*, pp. 85, 132.

49. ibid., pp. 4, 85, 104–7, 144–45; Burrow, *Gibbon*, pp. 49–51; D. J. Geanakopolos, "Edward Gibbon and Byzantine Ecclesiastical History," *Church History* 35 (1966): 170–85; S. Runciman, "Gibbon and Byzantium," in Bowersock, Clive, and Graubard, *Gibbon and the Decline and Fall of the Roman Empire*, pp. 53–60.

50. Porter, *Gibbon*, pp. 130–31; Burrow, *Gibbon*, pp. 77–78.

51. A. Cameron, "Thinking with Byzantium," *Transactions of the Royal Historical Society*, 6th. ser., 21 (2011): 54.

52. R. W. Bulliet, *The Case for Islamo-Christian Civilization* (New York, 2004), pp. 1–45.

53. Brown, *World of Late Antiquity*, p. 194; R. Fletcher, *The Cross and the Crescent: The Dramatic Story of the Earliest Encounters Between Christians and Muslims* (London, 2004), pp. 11–15, 42–44.

54. R. Crowley, *Empires of the Sea: The Final Battle for the Mediterranean, 1521–1580* (London, 2008); B. Rogerson, *The Last Crusaders: The Hundred-Year Battle for the Centre of the World* (London, 2009).

55. N. Housley, *Fighting for the Cross: Crusading to the Holy Land* (London, 2009), pp. 208–37; B. J. Kaplan, *Divided by Faith: Religious Conflict and the Practice of Toleration in Early Modern Europe* (Cambridge, Mass., 2007), pp. 300–12.

56. J. Riley-Smith, *The Crusades, Christianity and Islam* (New York, 2008), pp. 1–7; H. Kennedy, *The Great Arab Conquests: How the Spread of Islam Changed the World We Live In* (London, 2007), p. 50; S. O'Shea, *Sea of Faith: Islam and Christianity in the Medieval Mediterranean World* (London, 2006), p. 173.

57. A. Wheatcroft, *Infidels: The Conflict Between Christendom and Islam, 638–2002* (London, 2003), pp. 275–309.

58. H. Pirenne, *Muhammad and Charlemagne* (London, 1939), pp. 151–53, 165–66, 183–85, 284.

59. Wheatcroft, *Infidels*, pp. xxxi, 5, 39, 48, 59, 157, 309. See, more recently, for a similar argument, A. Wheatcroft, *The Enemy at the Gate: Habsburgs, Ottomans and the Battle for Europe* (London, 2008).

60. Pagden, *Worlds at War*, pp. 1–31, 137–38, 171, 176–77.

61. Wheatcroft, *Infidels*, p. 314.

62. Ibid., pp. xxxi, 5–6, 38, 202; Pagden, *Worlds at War*, pp. xiv, xx.

63. D. MacCulloch, *The Reformation: A History* (New York, 2004), p. 676; A. Walsham, *Charitable Hatred: Tolerance and Intolerance in England, 1500–1700* (Manchester, 2009), p. 238.

64. Fletcher, *Cross and the Crescent*, pp. 18, 20; R. Bonney, *Jihad: From Qur'an to bin Laden* (London, 2004), pp. 1–14, 395–423; O'Shea, *Sea of Faith*, pp. 15, 171–72; Z. Karabell, *People of the Book: The Forgotten History of Islam and the West* (London, 2007), pp. 4, 20, 26.

65. H. Goddard, *Christians and Muslims: From Double Standards to Mutual Understanding* (London, 1995), pp. 103–24.

66. O'Shea, *Sea of Faith*, pp. 111, 269.

67. Karabell, *People of the Book*, pp. 181–82.

68. Ibid., pp. 82–83; I. Almond, *Two Faiths, One Banner: When Muslims Marched with Christians across Europe's Battlegrounds* (London, 2009), esp. pp. 8–12.

69. O'Shea, *Sea of Faith*, pp. 141, 156; T. S. Ashbridge, "The 'Crusader' Community at Antioch: The Impact of Interaction with Byzantium and Islam," *Transactions of the Royal Historical Society*, 6th ser., 9 (1999): 319–21. For another example of how polarized Crusading identities were undercut, see P. E. Chevedden, "The Islamic View and the Christian View of the Crusades: A New Synthesis," *History* 93 (2008): 181–200.

70. D. M. Varisco, *Reading Orientalism: Said and the Unsaid* (Seattle, 2007), p. 123; Rogerson, *Last Crusaders*, p. 4.

71. Fletcher, *Cross and the Crescent*, pp. 20–21; N. Matar, "John Locke and the Turbanned Nations," *Journal of Islamic Studies* 2 (1991): 67–77; Karabell, *People of the Book*, pp. 158–79; O'Shea, *Sea of Faith*, pp. 277–83; M. Mazower, *Salonica, City of Ghosts: Christians, Muslims and Jews, 1430–1950* (New York, 2005), p. 24.

72. Fletcher, *Cross and the Crescent*, pp. 60–65; Karabell, *People of the Book*, pp. 6, 101–14; O'Shea, *Sea of Faith*, p. 233.

73. F. Braudel, *The Mediterranean and the Mediterranean World in the Age of Philip II*, 2 vols. (London, 1972), vol. 2, pp. 757–835; D. Abulafia, *The Great Sea: A Human History of the Mediterranean* (London, 2011), pp. 258–70.

74. Fletcher, *Cross and the Crescent*, pp. 38–39, 57–58, 116–30; J. Lyons, *The House of Wisdom: How Arabs Transformed Western Civilization* (London, 2009), pp. 4–5.

75. W. Dalrymple, "The Truth About Muslims," *New York Review of Books*, November 4, 2004, p. 32; J. H. Elliott, "A Question of Coexistence," *New York Review of Books*, August 13, 2009, pp. 38–39, 42.

76. O'Shea, *Sea of Faith*, pp. 131–40; M. R. Menocal, *The Ornament of the World: How Muslims, Jews, and Christians Created a Culture of Tolerance in Medieval Spain* (New York, 2002), pp. 17–49; H. Kennedy, *The Court*

of the Caliphs: The Rise and Fall of Islam's Greatest Dynasty (London, 2004), esp. pp. 112–44.

77. J. Mather, *Pashas: Britons in the Middle East, 1550–1850* (London, 2009), pp. 89–99, 166–67; M. Greene, *A Shared World: Christians and Muslims in the Early Modern Mediterranean* (Princeton, 2000), esp. pp. 3–12; A. Lebor, *City of Oranges: Arabs and Jews in Jaffa* (London, 2006), pp. 11–14; P. Mansel, *Levant: Splendour and Catastrophe on the Mediterranean* (London, 2010), pp. 1–3, 356; D. Quataert, *The Ottoman Empire, 1700–1922* (Cambridge, 2000), pp. 172–79; Mazower, *Salonica*, pp. 10, 23.

78. D. Howard, *Venice and the East* (London, 2000); Institut du Monde Arabe, *Venise et l'Orient, 828–1797* (Paris, 2006); L. Jardine and J. Brotton, *Global Interests: Renaissance Art Between East and West* (London, 2000); G. MacLean, ed., *Re-Orienting the Renaissance: Cultural Exchanges with the East* (London, 2005).

79. J. Cuno, *Who Owns Antiquity? Museums and the Battle over Our Ancient Heritage* (Princeton, 2008), pp. 68–70, and references cited there; N. Matar, *Islam in Britain, 1558–1685* (Cambridge, 1998); Matar, *Turk, Moors and Englishmen in the Age of Discovery* (Cambridge, 1999); Matar, *In the Lands of the Christians: Arabic Travel Writing in the Seventeenth Century* (London, 2003).

80. O'Shea, *Sea of Faith*, pp. 8–9.

81. N. Z. Davis, *Trickster Travels: A Sixteenth-Century Muslim Between Worlds* (New York, 2006). For a similar (Jewish) example of such mobility, from about half a century later, see M. Garcia-Arenal and G. Wiegers, *A Man of Three Worlds: Samuel Pallache, a Moroccan Jew in Catholic and Protestant Europe* (Baltimore, 2003).

82. C. Geertz, "Among the Infidels," *New York Review of Books*, March 23, 2006, pp. 23–24.

83. Elliott, "Question of Coexistence," pp. 39, 42; Karabell, *People of the Book*, pp. 8, 279–81.

84. Sir S. Runciman, *A History of the Crusades*, vol. 3, *The Kingdom of Acre* (Cambridge, 1955), p. 480.

85. Fletcher, *Cross and the Crescent*, p. 158.

86. For two recent examples of such a more measured approach, see T. Ashbridge, *The Crusades: The War for the Holy Land* (London, 2009); J. Phillips, *Holy Warriors: A Modern History of the Crusades* (London, 2009).

87. Karabell, *People of the Book*, p. 8; Dalrymple, "Truth About Muslims," p. 34; Bulliet, *Islamo-Christian Civilization*, p. 45.

88. F. Fernández-Armesto, "Struggle, What Struggle?" *Sunday Times, Culture*, May 4, 2003, p. 43.

89. Porter, *Gibbon*, p. 132.

90. S. Freud, *Civilization and Its Discontents* (New York, 1989 ed.), p. 72; P. Baldwin, *The Narcissism of Minor Differences: How America and Europe Are Alike* (Oxford, 2009), p. 10.

91. Kaplan, *Divided by Faith*, pp. 2, 128–29.

92. G. Parker, ed., *The Thirty Years War* (New York, 1984), pp. 210–11; P. H. Wilson, *Europe's Tragedy: A History of the Thirty Years War* (London, 2008), pp. 779–821; MacCulloch, *The Reformation*, pp. xx–xxi, 485, 671–72; J. H. Elliott, *Europe Divided, 1559–1598* (London, 1968), pp. 388–97.

93. S. Clark, *Thinking with Demons: The Idea of Witchcraft in Early Modern Europe* (Oxford, 1997), pp. 64, 377.

94. Kaplan, *Divided by Faith*, pp. 26, 34–38, 47.

95. Wilson, *Europe's Tragedy*, p. 465.

96. K. V. Thomas, "Speak of the Devil," *New York Review of Books*, April 27, 2006, p. 34.

97. E. Cameron, *Interpreting Christian History: The Challenge of the Church's Past* (Oxford, 2005), pp. 131–44.

98. J.-L. Quantin, *The Church of England and Christian Antiquity: The Construction of a Confessional Identity in the Seventeenth Century* (Oxford, 2009); P. Kewes, ed., *The Uses of History in Early Modern England* (San Marino, Calif., 2006); S. Ditchfield, *Liturgy, Sanctity and History in Tridentine Italy: Pietro Maria Campi and the Preservation of the Particular* (Cambridge, 1995). For suggestive treatments of the Protestant and Catholic histories of the English Reformation see, respectively, R. O'Day, *The Debate on the English Reformation* (London, 1986); J. Vidmar, *English Catholic Historians and the English Reformation, 1585–1954* (Brighton, 2005).

99. Kaplan, *Divided by Faith*, p. 102.

100. Ibid., pp. 150–51.

101. Ibid., p. 130.

102. MacCulloch, *The Reformation*, pp. 226–31, 302–3; P. Matheson, *Cardinal Contarini at Regensburg* (Oxford, 1972); D. Nugent, *Ecumenism in the Age of the Reformation: The Colloquy of Poissy* (Cambridge, Mass., 1974); E. Tongle, "A Mini–'Colloquy of Poissy' in Brittany: Inter-confessional Dialogue in Nantes in 1562," in L. Racaut and A. Ryrie, eds., *Moderate Voices in the European Reformation* (Aldershot, 2005), pp. 51–69.

103. L. Racaut and A. Ryrie, "Introduction: Between Coercion and Persuasion," in ibid., pp. 2, 12.

104. Kaplan, *Divided by Faith*, pp. 15–22; H. R. Guiggisberg, *Sebastian Castellio, 1515–1563: Humanist and Defender of Religious Toleration in a Confessional Age* (Aldershot, 2003).

105. M. Greengrass, "Conclusion: Moderate Voices: Mixed Messages," in

Racaut and Ryrie, *Moderate Voices in the European Reformation*, pp. 208–11; Q. Skinner, *The Foundations of Modern Political Thought*, 2 vols. (Cambridge, 1978), vol. 2, p. 249.

106. Kaplan, *Divided by Faith*, pp. 111–12.

107. MacCulloch, *The Reformation*, pp. 262–63, 343–44, 471–73, 677.

108. Wilson, *Europe's Tragedy*, pp. 9–10, 377; Wilson, "Dynasty, Constitution, and Confession: The Role of Religion in the Thirty Years War," *International History Review* 30 (2008): 473–514.

109. MacCulloch, *The Reformation*, pp. 495–501.

110. Wilson, *Europe's Tragedy*, pp. 758–62.

111. Kaplan, *Divided by Faith*, p. 12.

112. R. W. Scribner, "Preconditions of Tolerance and Intolerance in Sixteenth-Century Germany," in O. P. Grell and R. W. Scribner, eds., *Tolerance and Intolerance in the European Reformation* (Cambridge, 1996), pp. 34, 38.

113. Kaplan, *Divided by Faith*, p. 131; C. Ginzburg, *The Cheese and the Worms: The Cosmos of a Sixteenth-Century Miller* (Baltimore, 1992), pp. 9–10, 49–51, 62.

114. Ibid., p. 76.

115. Walsham, *Charitable Hatred*, pp. 11, 20–21, 26–30, 207–8.

116. R. Muchembled, introduction to E. Andor and I. G. Toth, eds., *Frontiers of Faith: Religious Exchange and the Constitution of Religious Identities, 1400–1750* (Budapest, 2001), p. 4.

117. Kaplan, *Divided by Faith*, pp. 134–35, 144–48, 172–90; Kaplan, *Calvinists and Libertines: Confession and Community in Utrecht, 1578–1620* (Oxford, 1995), p. 27.

118. Kaplan, *Divided by Faith*, pp. 217–45.

119. Ibid., p. 251.

120. Ibid., pp. 254–93.

121. Walsham, *Charitable Hatred*, p. 12.

122. S. B. Schwartz, *All Can Be Saved: Religious Tolerance and Salvation in the Iberian Atlantic World* (London, 2008), pp. 84–87.

123. Elliott, "Question of Coexistence," p. 42.

124. M. Macmillan, *Dangerous Games: The Uses and Abuses of History* (New York, 2009), pp. 73–78.

125. V. Smith, *Akbar: The Great Mogul* (Oxford, 1917), p. 257; A. Sen, *The Argumentative Indian: Writings on Indian History, Culture and Identity* (London, 2005), pp. xii, 17–19, 76, 274, 287–93.

126. D. Barenboim, *Everything Is Connected: The Power of Music* (London, 2008), pp. 43–44, 60–74. See also J. Goldberg, *A Muslim and a Jew Across the Middle East Divide* (New York, 2006).

127. Sen, *Argumentative Indian*, p. 25.

128. J. Wolffe, "Contentious Christians: Protestant-Catholic Conflict Since the Reformation," in Wolffe, *Religion in History*, p. 98.

129. Karabell, *People of the Book*, p. 182. Ironically enough, given his view of the all-encompassing religious confrontations between "Christianity" and "Islam," Andrew Wheatcroft grudgingly agrees: "Very few, in the East or in the West, in the past as in the present," he notes, "voluntarily lived their lives *wholly* according to the Holy Books and the Laws. Most people spent their days in conformity to the mores of their own group and community." In this, at least, he is surely correct. Wheatcroft, *Infidels*, p. 308, emphasis in original text.

130. J. Fulton, *The Tragedy of Belief: Division, Politics and Religion in Ireland* (Oxford, 1991), pp. 176–77, 180; M. Elliott, *The Catholics of Ulster: A History* (London, 2000), pp. 458–60; D. H. Akenson, *Intolerance: The E-Coli of the Human Mind* (Canberra, 2004), p. 60.

131. Fulton, *Tragedy of Belief*, pp. 180–81.

132. Elliott, *Catholics of Ulster*, p. 459.

133. Fulton, *Tragedy of Belief*, p. 187.

134. M. Elliott, *When God Took Sides: Religion and Identity in Ireland— Unfinished History* (Oxford, 2008), p. 4.

135. See, for example, Ginzburg, *Cheese and the Worms*, pp. 37–39.

TWO: NATION

1. C. de Gaulle, *Memoirs of Hope: Renewal, 1958–62; Endeavour, 1962–* (London, 1971), pp. 3–4, 301. For France's "natural" yet "altering" boundaries, see P. Sahlins, "Natural Frontiers Revisited: France's Boundaries Since the Seventeenth Century," *American Historical Review* 95 (1990): 1423–51.

2. M. Howard, *War and the Nation State* (Oxford, 1978), pp. 11, 15; D. Cannadine, *Making History Now and Then: Discoveries, Controversies and Explorations* (London, 2008), pp. 173–74; E. J. Hobsbawm, *The Age of Empire, 1875–1914* (London, 1987), pp. 142–64.

3. For this essentially "modernist" interpretation, see especially B. Anderson, *Imagined Communities: Reflections on the Origin and Spread of Nationalism* (London, 1983), pp. 46, 81, 191; E. Gellner, *Nations and Nationalism* (Oxford, 1983), pp. 25, 35–38, 51–55; Gellner, *Nationalism* (London, 1997), p. 13; E. J. Hobsbawm, *Nations and Nationalism Since 1780: Programme, Myth, Reality* (2nd ed., Cambridge, 1992), pp. 5, 9–10, 14; J. Breuilly, *Nationalism and the State* (2nd ed., Manchester, 1993), p. 85. For the nineteenth century as the century of "nation making," see W. Bagehot, *Physics and Politics* (London, 1887), chs. 3 and 4.

4. G. M. Trevelyan to John Maynard Keynes, February 1905, quoted in

D. Cannadine, *G. M. Trevelyan: A Life in History* (London, 1992), p. 63; I. Tyrrell, *Transnational Nation: United States History in Global Perspective since 1789* (London, 2007), p. 3.

5. F. Braudel, *The Identity of France*, vol. 1, *History and Environment* (London, 1988), pp. 18–19, 21–22; S. Berger, "A Return to the National Paradigm? National History Writing in Germany, Italy, France and Britain from 1945 to the Present," *Journal of Modern History* 77 (2005): 654–55; J. H. Elliott, *National and Comparative History* (Oxford, 1991), p. 20.

6. Braudel, *History and Environment*, pp. 15, 17, 18–19, 23–25; S. L. Kaplan, "Long-Run Lamentations: Braudel on France," *Journal of Modern History* 63 (1991): 341.

7. F. Braudel, *On History* (Chicago, 1980), p. 191; J. Jackson, "Historians and the Nation in Contemporary France," in S. Berger, M. Donovan, and K. Passmore, eds., *Writing National Histories: Western Europe Since 1800* (London, 1999), pp. 241–42.

8. F. Braudel, *The Mediterranean and the Mediterranean World in the Age of Philip II*, 2 vols. (London, 1972), vol. 2, p. 901.

9. Kaplan, "Long-Run Lamentations," p. 342; L. Hunt, "French History in the Last Twenty Years: The Rise and Fall of the *Annales* Paradigm," *Journal of Contemporary History* 21 (1986): 209–13; S. Kinser, "*Annaliste* Paradigm? The Geohistorical Structuralism of Fernand Braudel," *American Historical Review* 86 (1981): 63–105.

10. For recent surveys, see Berger, Donovan, and Passmore, *Writing National Histories*.

11. For another such definition, see J. J. Kellas, *The Politics of Nationalism and Ethnicity* (London, 1992), pp. 2–3.

12. For a discussion of the differing views of those scholars who see nations and national identity as coterminous with "modernity," and those who believe them to be "perennial," see A. D. Smith, "National Identities: Modern and Medieval?" in S. Forde, L. Johnson, and A. V. Murray, eds., *Concepts of National Identity in the Middle Ages* (Leeds, 1995), pp. 22–24; C. Kidd, *British Identities Before Nationalism: Ethnicity and Nationhood in the Atlantic World, 1600–1800* (Cambridge, 1999), pp. 1–6.

13. E. J. Hobsbawm, *Interesting Times: A Twentieth-Century Life* (London, 2002), p. 310. There has also been a massive outpouring of books on nationalism and national identity by pundits, sociologists, and political scientists; for one such work, which defines national identity almost exclusively in political terms, see W. Norman, *Negotiating Nationalism: Nation-Building, Federalism and Secession in the Multinational State* (Oxford, 2006), pp. 33–37.

14. L. Johnson, "Imagining Communities: Medieval and Modern," in

Forde, Johnson, and Murray, *National Identity in the Middle Ages*, pp. 1–20; S. Reynolds, "The Idea of the Nation as a Political Community," in L. Scales and O. Zimmer, eds., *Power and the Nation in European History* (Cambridge, 2005), pp. 54–66; A. Hastings, *The Construction of Nationhood: Ethnicity, Religion and Nationalism* (Cambridge, 1997), pp. 1–13; T. C. W. Blanning, *The Culture of Power and the Power of Culture: Old Regime Europe, 1660–1789* (Oxford, 2002), pp. 15–25; T. Turville-Petre, *England the Nation: Language, Literature and National Identity, 1290–1340* (Oxford, 1996), p. v; C. Hirsch, *The Origins of Nationalism: An Alternative History from Ancient Rome to Early Modern Germany* (Cambridge, 2011), pp. 1–33.

15. Smith, "National Identities: Modern and Medieval?" pp. 29–32, 46; S. Grosby, *Nationalism: A Very Short Introduction* (Oxford, 2005), pp. 57–72.

16. Hastings, *Construction of Nationhood*, p. 18.

17. Ibid., p. 186; Blanning, *Culture of Power*, p. 23.

18. H. Koht, "The Dawn of Nationalism in Europe," *American Historical Review* 52 (1947): 266.

19. M. T. Clanchy, *England and Its Rulers, 1066–1307* (Oxford, 2006 ed.), pp. 240–41.

20. R. R. Davies, "The Peoples of Britain and Ireland, 1100–1400: I. Identities," *Transactions of the Royal Historical Society*, 6th ser., 4 (1994): 4–5.

21. Ibid., p. 7; S. Foot, "The Making of Angelcyn: English Identity before the Norman Conquest," *Transactions of the Royal Historical Society*, 6th ser., 6 (1996): 28.

22. G. R. Elton, *The English* (Oxford, 1993), pp. 27–28; J. Campbell, "The Late Anglo-Saxon State: A Maximum View," *Proceedings of the British Academy* 87 (1995): 47; A. P. Smyth, "The Emergence of English Identity, 700–1000," in A. P. Smyth, ed., *Medieval Europeans: Studies in Ethnic Identity and National Perspectives in Medieval Europe* (London, 1998), pp. 24–52; Foot, "Making of Angelcyn," pp. 37, 49.

23. R. R. Davies, "The Peoples of Britain and Ireland, 1100–1400: II: Names, Boundaries and Regnal Solidarities," *Transactions of the Royal Historical Society*, 6th ser., 5 (1995): 12; Davies, "The Peoples of Britain and Ireland, 1100–1400: IV: Language and Historical Mythology," *Transactions of the Royal Historical Society*, 6th ser., 7 (1997): 12, 19–20; J. Gillingham, *The English in the Twelfth Century: Imperialism, National Identity and Political Values* (Woodbridge, 2000), pp. xvi, 113–44; Turville-Petre, *England the Nation*, p. 216; Hastings, *Construction of Nationhood*, pp. 15, 35–38, 47–48. But cf. D. Pearsall, "Chaucer and Englishness," *Proceedings of the British Academy* 101 (1998): 77–99.

24. S. Reynolds, *Kingdoms and Communities in Western Europe, 900–1300*, 2nd ed. (Oxford, 1997), pp. lix, 250–92.

25. Blanning, *Culture of Power*, p. 21; Koht, "Dawn of Nationalism," p. 277; L. Scales, *The Shaping of German Identity, Authority and Crisis, 1245–1414* (Cambridge, 2012), passim.

26. Blanning, *Culture of Power*, p. 21; M. G. Dietz, "Patriotism," in T. Ball, J. Farr, and R. L. Hanson, eds., *Political Innovation and Conceptual Change* (Cambridge, 1989), p. 181.

27. Davies, "Identities," p. 10.

28. J. Gillingham, "1066 and All That Elton," *Transactions of the Royal Historical Society*, 6th ser., 7 (1997): 330; Gillingham, *English in the Twelfth Century*, p. xvi.

29. Davies, "Identities," pp. 19–20; Davies, "Names, Boundaries, and Regnal Solidarities," pp. 16–17; Reynolds, "Idea of the Nation," p. 58.

30. Blanning, *Culture of Power*, p. 21; Koht, "Dawn of Nationalism," p. 279; P. Sahlins, *Boundaries: The Making of France and Spain in the Pyrenees* (Los Angeles, 1989), p. 271.

31. O. Ranum, introduction to O. Ranum, ed., *National Consciousness, History and Political Culture in Early-Modern Europe* (Baltimore, 1975), p. 1.

32. T. C. W. Blanning, *The Pursuit of Glory: Europe, 1648–1815* (London, 2007), pp. 306–07.

33. Ranum, introduction to *National Consciousness*, p. 5; Hastings, *Construction of Nationhood*, pp. 99, 114.

34. Hastings, *Construction of Nationhood*, pp. 56–57; L. Greenfield, *Nationalism: Five Roads to Modernity* (Cambridge, Mass., 1992), pp. 60–70. There is, of course, a problem about Shakespeare's claim that England occupied the whole of the "sceptered isle" of Great Britain, since large parts of it were inhabited by the Scots and the Welsh.

35. Blanning, *Culture of Power*, p. 22; J. O. Bartley, *Teague, Shenkin, and Sawney: Being an Historical Study of the Earliest Irish, Welsh and Scottish Characters in English Plays* (Cork, 1954), passim.

36. M. J. Rodriguez-Salgado, "Christians, Civilized and Spanish: Multiple Identities in Sixteenth-Century Spain," *Transactions of the Royal Historical Society*, 6th ser., 8 (1998): 237–38.

37. Blanning, *Culture of Power*, pp. 290–301; Blanning, *Pursuit of Glory*, pp. 305, 310–12.

38. For which see Greenfield, *Nationalism*, chs. 2–4; Blanning, *Culture of Power*, chs. 6–7.

39. Schulze, *States, Nations and Nationalism*, pp. 111–12; but cf. D. Bell, *The Cult of the Nation in France: Inventing Nationalism, 1680–1800* (Cambridge, Mass., 2001), pp. 5–6.

40. Ranum, introduction to *National Consciousness*, pp. 12–13; Blanning, *Pursuit of Glory*, p. 307.

41. But cf. Turville-Petre, *England the Nation*, p. 40.

42. Hastings, *Construction of Nationhood*, pp. 185–200.

43. J. H. Elliott, *Spain, Europe and the Wider World, 1500–1800* (London, 2009), pp. 3–24.

44. Blanning, *Pursuit of Glory*, p. 307.

45. Ranum, introduction to *National Consciousness*, pp. 2–5, Elliott, *Spain, Europe and the Wider World*, p. xvi.

46. C. Tilly, "Reflections on the History of European State-Making," in C. Tilly, ed., *The Formation of National States in Western Europe* (Princeton, 1975), p. 15.

47. M. Howard, *War in European History*, 2nd ed. (Oxford, 2009), pp. 11, 20–21.

48. Ibid., pp. 20–37, 70–73, 110–11.

49. Ibid., pp. 72–73.

50. R. Bartlett, *The Making of Europe: Conquest, Colonization, and Cultural Change, 950–1350* (Princeton, 1993), p. 196.

51. R. J. W. Evans, *The Language of History and the History of Language* (Oxford, 1998), pp. 13–20.

52. Bell, *Cult of the Nation*, pp. 16, 171–73; Blanning, *Culture of Power*, pp. 234–36.

53. D. Armitage and M. Braddick, introduction to D. Armitage and M. Braddick, eds., *The British Atlantic World, 1500–1800* (Basingstoke, UK, 2002), pp. 6–7; Elliott, *Spain, Europe and the Wider World*, pp. 173–210; Rodriguez-Salgado, "Multiple Identities in Sixteenth-Century Spain," pp. 238–51.

54. Blanning, *Pursuit of Glory*, pp. 319–21; Bell, *Cult of the Nation*, pp. 9–14; Elliott, *Spain, Europe and the Wider World*, pp. 211–29; J. Adelman, "An Age of Imperial Revolutions," *American Historical Review* 113 (2008): 319–40.

55. Howard, *War in European History*, pp. 93–115.

56. C. S. Maier, "Consigning the Twentieth Century to History: Alternative Narratives for the Modern Era," *American Historical Review* 105 (2000): 807–8.

57. Ibid., p. 814.

58. Ibid., pp. 816, 819, 823.

59. E. W. Anderson, "Geopolitics: International Boundaries as Fighting Places," *Journal of Strategic Studies* 22 (1999): 127–28; Lord Curzon of Kedleston, *Frontiers: The Romanes Lecture of 1907* (Oxford, 1908), p. 7.

60. Maier, "Consigning the Twentieth Century to History," pp. 820–21; N. Faith, *The World the Railways Made* (London, 1990), pp. 58–70.

61. G. L. Mosse, *The Nationalization of the Masses: Political Symbolism and Mass Movements in Germany from the Napoleonic Wars Through the Third Reich* (New York, 1975), esp. pp. 1–3; E. Weber, *Peasants into Frenchmen: The Modernization of Rural France, 1870–1914* (Stanford, 1975), esp. pp. ix–xi, 485–86.

62. Hobsbawm, *Age of Empire*, pp. 84–111, 142–64; Howard, *War in European History*, pp. 110–11; Howard, *War and the Nation State*, pp. 8–12.

63. Cannadine, *Making History Now and Then*, pp. 173–78; G. G. Iggers, "Nationalism and Historiography, 1789–1996: The German Example in Historical Perspective"; B. Stuchtey, "Literature, Liberty and the Life of the Nation: British Historiography from Macaulay to Trevelyan"; C. Crossley, "History as a Principle of Legitimation in France (1820–48)"; P. Bahners, "National Unification and Narrative Unity: The Case of Ranke's *German History*," all in Berger, Donovan, and Passmore, *Writing National Histories*, pp. 15–29, 30–46, 49–56, 57–68; Elliott, *National and Comparative History*, pp. 17–24.

64. Blanning, *Culture of Power*, p. 20; Grosby, *Nationalism*, p. 76; H. Schulze, *States, Nations and Nationalism: From the Middle Ages to the Present* (Oxford, 1996), pp. 95–96; A. D. Smith, "Memory and Modernity: Reflections on Ernest Gellner's Theory of Nationalism," *Nations and Nationalism* 2 (1996): 383; Smith, *The Ethnic Origins of Nations* (Oxford, 1986), p. 2; P. Geary, *The Myth of Nations: The Medieval Origins of Europe* (Princeton, 2002), pp. 15–40.

65. Hobsbawm, *Age of Empire*, p. 149; R. N. Bellah, "Civil Religion in America," *Daedalus* 96 (1967): 1–21; Bellah, "American Civil Religion," in R. E. Richey and D. G. Jones, eds., *American Civil Religion* (New York, 1974), pp. 255–72.

66. Schulze, *States, Nations and Nationalism*, p. 104; Bell, *Cult of the Nation*, p. 6.

67. Hobsbawm, *Nations and Nationalism*, pp. 44, 60–61; Schulze, *States, Nations and Nationalism*, p. 161; Weber, *Peasants into Frenchmen*, pp. 67–70.

68. Evans, *Language of History*, pp. 25–28; I. Deak, *Beyond Nationalism: A Social and Political History of the Habsburg Officer Corps, 1848–1918* (Oxford, 1990), pp. 56–58, 99–102; Hobsbawm, *Nations and Nationalism*, pp. 94–100.

69. In which regard, see A. J. P. Taylor, *English History, 1914–1945* (Harmondsworth, 1970), p. 25: "Until August 1914, a sensible, law-abiding Englishman could pass through his life and hardly notice the existence of the state, beyond the post office and the policeman." But cf. Hobsbawm, *Nations and Nationalism*, pp. 80–81, where he argues that "a family would have to live in some very inaccessible place if some member or other were not to come into regular contact with the national state and its agents."

70. D. Rodgers, *Atlantic Crossings: Social Politics in a Progressive Age* (Cambridge, Mass., 1998), pp. 35–36; N. Blewett, "The Franchise in the United Kingdom, 1885–1908," *Past and Present* 32 (1965): 27–56; Reynolds, "Idea of the Nation," p. 56.

71. Hobsbawm, *Nations and Nationalism*, pp. 105–6. For another example, see O. Zimmer, *A Contested Nation: History, Memory and Nationalism in Switzerland, 1761–1891* (Cambridge, 2003).

72. Schultz, *States, Nations and Nationalism*, p. 231.

73. J. Darwin, *The Empire Project: The Rise and Fall of the British World-System, 1830–1970* (Cambridge, 2009), pp. 144–79.

74. J. L. Garvin, *The Life of Joseph Chamberlain* (London, 1934), vol. 6, p. 564.

75. C. A. Bayly, The *Birth of the Modern World, 1780–1914* (Oxford, 2004), pp. 451–87.

76. Faith, *World the Railways Made*, pp. 254–56, 279–81, 326–29.

77. D. Cannadine, "The Context, Performance and Meaning of Ritual: The British Monarchy and the "Invention of Tradition," c. 1820–1977," in E. J. Hobsbawm and T. Ranger, eds., *The Invention of Tradition* (Cambridge, 1983), pp. 120–38; Hobsbawm, *Nations and Nationalism*, pp. 84–85.

78. D. Cannadine, "Kaiser Wilhelm II and the British Monarchy," in T. C. W. Blanning and D. Cannadine, eds., *History and Biography: Essays in Honour of Derek Beales* (Cambridge, 1996), pp. 188–94.

79. N. Ferguson, *The World's Banker: The History of the House of Rothschild* (London, 1998), pp. 1–33.

80. D. E. D. Beales, *From Castlereagh to Gladstone, 1815–1885* (London, 1969), p. 294.

81. J. Auerbach, *The Great Exhibition of 1851: A Nation on Display* (London, 1999), pp. 159–89.

82. C. A. Jones, *International Business in the Nineteenth Century: The Rise and Fall of a Cosmopolitan Bourgeoisie* (Brighton, 1987), p. 88.

83. Quoted in Tyrrell, *Transnational Nation*, p. 6.

84. This argument has been made with particular force in recent years in regard to the United States: see Tyrrell, *Transnational Nation*, pp. 1–9; T. Bender, *A Nation Among Nations: America's Place in World History* (New York, 2006), pp. 1–14; Rodgers, *Atlantic Crossings*, pp. 1–3.

85. Rodgers, *Atlantic Crossings*, p. 44; M. Harper, "Migration from Africa, Asia and the South Pacific," in A. Porter, ed., *The Oxford History of the British Empire*, vol. 3 (Oxford, 1999), pp. 73–100; Bayly, *Birth of the Modern World*, pp. 134–43.

86. Rodgers, *Atlantic Crossings*, pp. 33–52.

87. N. Faires, "Immigrants and Industry: Peopling the 'Iron City,' " in S. P. Hays, ed., *City at the Point: Essays in the Social History of Pittsburgh* (Pittsburgh, 1989), p. 10; Rodgers, *Atlantic Crossings*, p. 50.

88. Rodgers, *Atlantic Crossings*, p. 59.

89. Ibid., pp. 61–62.

90. F. J. Turner, "The Significance of History," in R. A. Billington, ed.,

Frontier and Section: Selected Essays of Frederick Jackson Turner (Englewood Cliffs, N.J., 1961), pp. 20–21.

91. Quoted in I. Tyrrell, "Making Nations/Making States: American Historians in the Context of Empire," *Journal of American History* 86 (1999): 1031; Bender, *Nation Among Nations*, p. 299.

92. R. Reinalda, *The Routledge History of International Organizations* (London, 2009); J. F. Chown, *A History of Monetary Unions* (London, 2003); C. Moorehead, *Dunant's Dream: War, Switzerland, and the History of the Red Cross* (London, 1998); P. T. Marsh, *Bargaining on Europe: Britain and the First Common Market, 1860–1892* (New Haven, 1999).

93. Further examples of internationalist collaboration are fully explored in M. Mazower, *Governing the World: The History of an Idea* (London, 2012); A. Swenson, *The Rise of Heritage: Preserving the Past in France, Germany and England, 1789–1914* (Cambridge, 2013).

94. Z. Steiner, *The Lights That Failed: European International History, 1919–1933* (Oxford, 2005), pp. 1–6.

95. Ibid., pp. 9, 36–37, 84.

96. Ibid., p. 69; M. MacMillan, *The Peacemakers: The Paris Peace Conference of 1919 and Its Attempt to End War* (London, 2001), p. 19.

97. Steiner, *Lights That Failed*, pp. 91–92.

98. M. Heimann, *Czechoslovakia: The State That Failed* (London, 2009), p. 47; Steiner, *Lights That Failed*, pp. 51–53, 96, 151–52; Hobsbawm, *Nations and Nationalism*, pp. 131–33.

99. Steiner, *Lights That Failed*, p. 109.

100. E. Rogan, *The Arabs: A History* (London, 2009), p. 191.

101. Steiner, *Lights That Failed*, p. 105.

102. Hobsbawm, *Nations and Nationalism*, p. 165.

103. Steiner, *Lights That Failed*, p. 40.

104. Ibid., pp. 602–32; C. Mulley, *The Woman Who Saved the Children: A Biography of Eglantyne Jebb, Founder of Save the Children* (London, 2009), p. 274.

105. W. R. Louis, *Imperialism at Bay: The U.S. and the Decolonization of the British Empire, 1941–1945* (New York, 1978); D. Mack Smith, *Mussolini's Roman Empire* (New York, 1976); M. Mazower, *Hitler's Empire: How the Nazis Ruled Europe* (New York, 2008).

106. S. Williams, R. Holland, and T. A. Berringer, preface to R. Holland, S. Williams, and T. A. Berringer, eds., *The Iconography of Independence: "Freedoms at Midnight"* (London, 2009), pp. xi–xix.

107. Hastings, *Construction of Nationhood*, pp. 160–62; Hobsbawm, *Nations and Nationalism*, p. 153; C. Geertz, *The Interpretation of Cultures* (New York, 1973), pp. 234–310.

108. R. L. Watts, *New Federations: Experiments in the Commonwealth* (Oxford, 1966), passim.

109. D. Cannadine, "Introduction: Independence Day Ceremonials in Historical Perspective," in Holland et al., *Iconography of Independence*, p. 8; Hobsbawm, *Nations and Nationalism*, p. 154.

110. T. Garton Ash, "1919!" *New York Review of Books*, November 5, 2009, pp. 4–8; M. Kramer, "The Collapse of East European Communism and the Repercussions Within the Soviet Union (Part I)," *Journal of Cold War Studies* 5 (2003): 217–24; A. L. Brown, *The Rise and Fall of Communism* (London, 2009), pp. 564–65.

111. Hobsbawm, *Nations and Nationalism*, pp. 166–67.

112. Kramer, "Collapse of East European Communism (Part I)," pp. 205–16; T. Judt, *Postwar: A History of Europe Since 1945* (London, 2005), pp. 644–46; S. Rausing, *History, Memory, and Identity in Post-Soviet Estonia: The End of a Collective Farm* (Oxford, 2004), pp. 146–52.

113. Brown, *Rise and Fall of Communism*, pp. 532–33, 549–50, 588, 592–93; D. Priestland, *The Red Flag: Communism and the Making of the Modern World* (London, 2009), pp. 518–19, 548.

114. Judt, *Postwar*, pp. 650–51, 659.

115. Heimann, *Czechoslovakia*, pp. 307–24; Hastings, *Construction of Nationhood*, pp. 124–47; Hobsbawm, *Nations and Nationalism*, p. 179.

116. Maier, "Consigning the Twentieth Century to History," pp. 814–15, 823–25.

117. For the growth in the number of multinational agencies since 1945, see Hobsbawm, *Nations and Nationalism*, p. 181; Cannadine, *Making History Now and Then*, pp. 178–79.

118. Cannadine, *Making History Now and Then*, p. 179.

119. S. Berger and C. Lorenz, eds., *The Contested Nation: Ethnicity, Class, Religion and Gender in National Histories* (Basingstoke, 2008); Berger, "Return to the National Paradigm?" pp. 672–78; T. Todorov, *The Fear of Barbarians: Beyond the Clash of Civilizations* (Chicago, 2010), pp. 74–75; D. T. Rodgers, *Age of Fracture* (Cambridge, Mass., 2011), pp. 228–29; C. A. Bayly, "Ireland, India and the Empire, 1780–1914," *Transactions of the Royal Historical Society*, 6th. ser., 10 (2000): 377.

120. N. Davies, *Vanished Kingdoms: The History of Half-Forgotten Europe* (London, 2011).

121. J. Darwin, *After Tamerlane: The Global History of Empire* (London, 2007), p. 23; D. Reynolds, *America, Empire of Liberty: A New History* (London, 2009), pp. 578–80. For recent books on this subject, see N. Ferguson, *Colossus: The Rise and Fall of the American Empire* (London, 2005); C. S. Maier, *Among Empires: American Ascendancy and Its Predecessors* (Cambridge, Mass., 2006); B. Porter, *Empire and Superempire: Britain, America and the World* (London, 2006).

122. Bell, *Cult of the Nation*, pp. 211–17; Judt, *Postwar*, pp. 701–7, 773–74;

Todorov, *Fear of Barbarians*, p. 79; H. James, *A German Identity: 1770 to the Present Day* (London, 2000), pp. 230–32.

123. J. Cuno, *Who Owns Antiquity? Museums and the Battle over Our Ancient Heritage* (Princeton, 2008), p. 80.

124. S. Radcliffe and S. Westwood, *Remaking the Nation: Place, Identity and Politics in Latin America* (London, 1996), pp. 9–28, 160–72.

125. Hobsbawm, *Nations and Nationalism*, p. 186; Todorov, *Fear of Barbarians*, p. 67.

126. For two contrasting opinions on the future of the (European) nation and national identities, see A. S. Milward, *The European Rescue of the Nation-State* (London, 1992), pp. 4, 45; M. Burgess, *Federation and European Union: The Building of Europe, 1950–2000* (London, 2000), pp. 56–76. For more balanced views, see N. O'Sullivan, "Visions of European Unity Since 1945," *Proceedings of the British Academy* 94 (2007): 119–20; Judt, *Postwar*, pp. 796–99. For a broader and more skeptical perspective, see P. Kennedy, "Things Fall Apart," *Financial Times*, September 28, 2012.

127. C. Geertz, *Available Light: Anthropological Reflections on Philosophical Topics* (Princeton, 2000), pp. 229–30.

128. Schulze, *States, Nations and Nationalism*, pp. 97–98.

129. E. Renan, "What Is a Nation?" in S. Woolf, ed., *Nationalism in Europe, 1818 to the Present: A Reader* (London, 1996), p. 50; Hobsbawm, *Nations and Nationalism*, p. 12.

130. M. MacMillan, *Dangerous Games: The Uses and Abuses of History* (New York, 2009), pp. 39, 71.

131. Bayly, *Birth of the Modern World*, p. 363.

132. Hobsbawm, *Nations and Nationalism*, p. 176; Geary, *Myth of Nations*, p. 54; Galatians 3:28; Matthew 18:18.

133. Hastings, *Construction of Nationhood*, pp. 31–34.

134. Hobsbawm, *Nations and Nationalism*, p. 123.

135. B. Harrison, *Seeking a Role: The United Kingdom, 1951–70* (Oxford, 2009), p. xviii; Hastings, *Construction of Nationhood*, pp. 113, 183.

136. Davies, "Identities," p. 1; Hastings, *Construction of Nationhood*, p. 32.

THREE: CLASS

1. T. Hunt, *The Frock-Coated Communist: The Revolutionary Life of Friedrich Engels* (London, 2009), pp. 65–66, 119.

2. Ibid., pp. 119–21; G. Stedman Jones, introduction to K. Marx and F. Engels, *The Communist Manifesto* (London, 2002 ed.), pp. 70–73; D. R. Kelley, "The Metaphysics of Law: An Essay on the Very Young Marx," *American Historical Review* 83 (1978): 350–67.

3. Hunt, *Engels*, pp. 120, 123; Stedman Jones, introduction to *The Communist Manifesto*, pp. 50–53.

4. A. Briggs, *Victorian Cities* (Berkeley, 1993 ed.), p. 87; Hunt, *Engels*, pp. 78–102.

5. Stedman Jones, introduction to *The Communist Manifesto*, p. 64; Hunt, *Engels*, pp. 131–34.

6. Marx and Engels, *The Communist Manifesto*, pp. 196, 219, 258.

7. The intellectual borrowings, indebtednesses, adaptations, and denials are comprehensively discussed in Stedman Jones, introduction to *The Communist Manifesto*, pp. 50–177; G. Lichtheim, *Marxism: An Historical and Critical Study*, 2nd ed. (London, 1964), pp. 33–62; E. J. Hobsbawm, *How to Change the World: Marx and Marxism, 1840–2011* (London, 2011), pp. 16–47.

8. Stedman Jones, introduction to *The Communist Manifesto*, pp. 99–119.

9. Hunt, *Engels*, pp. 14–17, 61.

10. Lichtheim, *Marxism*, pp. 3–20, 45; D. Priestland, *The Red Flag: Communism and the Making of the Modern World* (London, 2009), p. 45.

11. Hunt, *Engels*, pp. 41–46, 54–56, 123–25, 131–33; Stedman Jones, introduction to *The Communist Manifesto*, pp. 8–9, 38, 81–119, 140–44.

12. M. Howard, *War and the Nation State* (Oxford, 1978), pp. 9–11.

13. Marx and Engels, *Communist Manifesto*, pp. 223, 234, 241.

14. H. Schulze, *States, Nations, and Nationalism: From the Middle Ages to the Present* (Oxford, 1996), p. 257.

15. This paragraph is based on D. Cannadine, *Class in Britain* (London, 1998), pp. 2–3, 54–56, and the references cited there.

16. K. Marx and F. Engels, *The German Ideology* (New York, 1947), pp. 48–49.

17. Cannadine, *Class in Britain*, p. 3.

18. R. W. Miller, "Social and Political Theory: Class, State, Revolution," in T. Carver, ed., *The Cambridge Companion to Marx* (Cambridge, 1992), p. 56.

19. G. Lukács, *History and Class Consciousness* (Cambridge, Mass., 1971 ed.), pp. 46–82; Priestland, *Red Flag*, pp. 110–11; Cannadine, *Class in Britain*, pp. 3–4.

20. Marx and Engels, *Communist Manifesto*, pp. 222, 258.

21. Ibid., pp. 220, 226; Miller, "Social and Political Theory," p. 56.

22. Marx and Engels, *Communist Manifesto*, pp. 233, 244.

23. W. G. Runciman, *Great Books, Bad Arguments: "Republic," "Leviathan," and "The Communist Manifesto"* (Princeton, 2010), pp. 90–95.

24. Ibid., pp. 98–99.

25. Cannadine, *Class in Britain*, pp. 8–9.

26. Miller, "Social and Political Theory," p. 62.

27. Ibid., pp. 96–97.

28. Cannadine, *Class in Britain*, pp. 9–10.

29. Marx and Engels, *Communist Manifesto*, p. 224.

30. Miller, "Social and Political Theory," pp. 63–65.

31. Marx and Engels, *Communist Manifesto*, pp. 231, 247.

32. Ibid., p. 235.

33. S. Maza, *The Myth of the French Bourgeoisie: An Essay in the Social Imaginary, 1750–1850* (Cambridge, Mass., 2003), pp. 2–6, 180, 194–95; D. Bell, "Class, Consciousness, and the Fall of the Bourgeois Revolution," *Critical Review* 16 (2004): 323–51.

34. Runciman, *Great Books, Bad Arguments*, pp. 105–7; D. Wahrman, *Imagining the Middle Class: The Political Representation of Class in Britain, c. 1780–1840* (Cambridge, 1995), pp. 273–89, 411–13.

35. Hunt, *Engels*, p. 115.

36. Historians have often been divided on political lines in their assessment of the veracity of Engels's account. For an admiring view, see E. J. Hobsbawm, introduction to F. Engels, *The Condition of the Working Class in England* (London, 1969 ed.), p. 15. For a hostile view, see W. H. Chaloner and W. O. Henderson, eds., *The Condition of the Working Class in England* (Oxford, 1958), pp. xxx–xxxi. For more balanced views, see Briggs, *Victorian Cities*, pp. 105–17; Hunt, *Engels*, pp. 103–17.

37. Marx and Engels, *Communist Manifesto*, pp. 199, 233; Miller, "Social and Political Theory," pp. 62–63; Hunt, *Engels*, pp. 149–51.

38. Stedman Jones, introduction to *The Communist Manifesto*, p. 8.

39. Ibid., p. 15; Marx and Engels, *Communist Manifesto*, p. 258.

40. Runciman, *Great Books, Bad Arguments*, p. 91; A. Brown, *The Rise and Fall of Communism* (London, 2009), p. 20.

41. Marx and Engels, *Communist Manifesto*, p. 244.

42. Lichtheim, *Marxism*, pp. 373–75; Runciman, *Great Books, Bad Arguments*, pp. 15–16, 87–89.

43. *The Red Republican*, November 9, 1850, pp. 161–62.

44. Stedman Jones, introduction to *The Communist Manifesto*, pp. 14–19, 39–49; Marx and Engels, *Communist Manifesto*, p. 218; Hobsbawm, *How to Change the World*, pp. 176–80.

45. Stedman Jones, introduction to *The Communist Manifesto*, p. 25; Marx and Engels, *Communist Manifesto*, p. 203; Hunt, *Engels*, p. 279.

46. H. and J. M. Tudor, eds., *Marxism and Social Democracy: The Revisionist Debate, 1896–1898* (Cambridge, 1988), pp. 85, 168–69; Lichtheim, *Marxism*, pp. 259–300; Brown, *Rise and Fall of Communism*, pp. 38–39.

47. Stedman Jones, introduction to *The Communist Manifesto*, pp. 18–21.

48. Priestland, *Red Flag*, pp. 59–60; Runciman, *Great Books, Bad Arguments*, pp. 107–8.

49. E. J. Hobsbawm, *Nations and Nationalism Since 1780: Programme, Myth, Reality*, 2nd ed. (Cambridge, 1992), p. 130.

50. Marx and Engels, *Communist Manifesto*, p. 211.

51. Brown, *Rise and Fall of Communism*, pp. 1–10.

52. Marx and Engels, *Communist Manifesto*, p. 196; Lichtheim, *Marxism*, pp. 325–28; Hunt, *Engels*, pp. 273–76; H. Wada, "Marx and Revolutionary Russia," in T. Shanin, ed., *The Late Marx and the Russian Road* (London, 1983), pp. 40–75; D. R. Kelley, "The Science of Anthropology: An Essay on the Very Old Marx," *Journal of the History of Ideas* 45 (1984): 245–62.

53. Priestland, *Red Flag*, p. 29; Brown, *Rise and Fall of Communism*, p. 49. The evolution of Lenin's thought on these matters can be traced in *The Development of Capitalism in Russia* (1899), *What Is to Be Done?* (1902), and *One Step Forward, Two Steps Back* (1904).

54. Lichtheim, *Marxism*, pp. 330–43; Brown, *Rise and Fall of Communism*, pp. 32–41; Priestland, *Red Flag*, pp. 76–77.

55. Brown, *Rise and Fall of Communism*, pp. 51–52.

56. K. Kautsky, *The Dictatorship of the Proletariat* (Ann Arbor, 1964 ed.), pp. 19–20, 140; Hunt, *Engels*, p. 360; Lichtheim, *Marxism*, p. 270; Brown, *Rise and Fall of Communism*, pp. 52–54, 78.

57. S. Davies, *Popular Opinion in Stalin's Russia: Terror, Propaganda and Dissent, 1934–1941* (Cambridge, 1997), p. 139; Brown, *Rise and Fall of Communism*, pp. 59, 67; Priestland, *Red Flag*, pp. 93–94, 170.

58. Priestland, *Red Flag*, pp. xxvi, 139, 157–60, 206; Brown, *Rise and Fall of Communism*, pp. 2, 60–64.

59. J. Riddell, ed., *Founding the Communist International: Proceedings of the First Congress, March 1919* (New York, 1987), pp. 222–32; Priestland, *Red Flag*, p. 113.

60. Priestland, *Red Flag*, p. 107; Brown, *Rise and Fall of Communism*, pp. 78–84.

61. C. S. Maier, *Recasting Bourgeois Europe: Stabilization in France, Germany, and Italy in the Decade After World War I* (Princeton, 1975), passim.

62. Hobsbawm, *How to Change the World*, pp. 344–84.

63. Priestland, *Red Flag*, pp. 454, 462, 480; T. Judt, *Ill Fares the Land* (New York, 2010), p. 236.

64. D. Cannadine, ed., *The Speeches of Winston Churchill* (Harmondsworth, 1990), pp. 303, 339.

65. M. Leffler, *For the Soul of All Mankind: The United States, the Soviet Union and the Cold War* (New York, 2007), p. 98; E. Foner, *The Story of American Freedom* (New York, 1998), p. 253; Priestland, *Red Flag*, pp. xxiv, 230, 233, 325, 379.

66. D. Cannadine, *Making History Now and Then: Discoveries, Controversies and Explorations* (London, 2008), pp. 97–100.

67. Priestland, *Red Flag*, pp. xix–xx.

68. R. Mitter, *A Bitter Revolution: China's Struggle with the Modern World*

(Oxford, 2004), p. 159; Marx and Engels, *Communist Manifesto*, p. 263, note 25; Priestland, *Red Flag*, pp. 252–58; Brown, *Rise and Fall of Communism*, p. 100.

69. Priestland, *Red Flag*, p. 237; Judt, *Ill Fares the Land*, pp. 88–90.

70. *Hansard*, House of Lords, July 6, 1966, column 1136; Priestland, *Red Flag*, pp. 328–35, 342; Brown, *Rise and Fall of Communism*, pp. 240–43, 268–77.

71. Priestland, *Red Flag*, pp. 353–57, 375, 383, 391–98.

72. J. H. Kautsky, *Communism and the Politics of Development: Revisionist Myths and Changing Behavior* (New York, 1968), p. 216; Brown, *Rise and Fall of Communism*, pp. 3, 606–7.

73. R. Aldous, *Reagan and Thatcher: The Difficult Relationship* (New York, 2012), p. 179; M. Thatcher, *The Downing Street Years* (London, 1993), p. 463.

74. Runciman, *Great Books, Bad Arguments*, pp. 13–14, 95.

75. Brown, *Rise and Fall of Communism*, pp. 10, 616; Runciman, *Great Books, Bad Arguments*, pp. 91, 113–14.

76. Cannadine, *Class in Britain*, p. 2; Stedman Jones, introduction to *The Communist Manifesto*, p. 5.

77. E. J. Hobsbawm, *Interesting Times: A Twentieth-Century Life* (London, 2002), pp. 56, 127.

78. V. Kiernan, "Notes on Marxism in 1968," in R. Miliband and J. Saville, eds., *The Socialist Register, 1968* (London, 1968), pp. 190–95. Initially, this generation also included such figures as the young J. H. Plumb and the young Hugh Trevor-Roper, who "accepted certain fundamental tenets of Marxist dogma, believing in the omnipotence of economics and the inevitability of class struggle." A. Sisman, *Hugh Trevor-Roper: The Biography* (London, 2010), p. 202.

79. E. J. Hobsbawm, "The Historians' Group of the Communist Party," in M. Cornforth, ed., *Rebels and Their Causes* (London, 1978), pp. 21–47; R. Samuel, "British Marxist Historians, 1880–1980," *New Left Review*, no. 120 (1980): 42–55; H. Kaye, *The British Marxist Historians: An Introductory Analysis* (Cambridge, 1984), pp. 7–22; Kaye, *The Education of Desire: Marxists and the Writing of History* (London, 1992), pp. 18–30.

80. A. L. Morton, *A People's History of England* (London, 1938); M. Dobb, *Studies in the Development of Capitalism* (London, 1946). See also Kaye, *Education of Desire*, pp. 116–24; Kaye, *British Marxist Historians*, pp. 23–50; P. M. Sweezy, ed., *The Transition from Feudalism to Capitalism: A Symposium* (New York, 1954); R. H. Hilton, ed., *The Transition from Feudalism to Capitalism* (London, 1976).

81. Hobsbawm, "Historians' Group," p. 23. For two other influential books published at this time, which treated particular episodes in English history from a Marxist perspective, see H. Fagan, *Nine Days*

That Shook England: An Account of the People's Uprising in 1381 (London, 1938); H. Holorenshaw, *The Levellers and the English Revolution* (London, 1939). Holorenshaw was a pseudonym for Joseph Needham.

82. E. P. Thompson, *The Making of the English Working Class* (Harmondsworth, 1968), p. 11.

83. Kaye, *Education of Desire*, pp. 68, 70; E. J. Hobsbawm, "Marxist Historiography Today," in C. Wickham, ed., *Marxist History-Writing for the Twenty-First Century* (Oxford, 2007), p. 180.

84. R. Hilton and H. Fagan, *The English Rising of 1381* (London, 1950); R. H. Hilton, *Bond Men Made Free: Medieval Peasant Movements and the English Rising of 1381* (London, 1973); Hilton, *Class Conflict and the Crisis of Feudalism: Essays in Medieval Social History* (London, 1985); Kaye, *British Marxist Historians*, pp. 81–95.

85. C. Hill, *The English Revolution of 1640* (London, 1940); Hill, *The Century of Revolution, 1603–1714* (London, 1961); and for a similar argument, see also R. H. Tawney, "The Rise of the Gentry, 1558–1640," *Economic History Review* 11 (1941), pp. 1–38. For discussion and analysis, see Kaye, *British Marxist Historians*, pp. 103–16; P. Zagorin, "The Social Interpretation of the English Revolution," *Journal of Economic History* 19 (1959): 376–401; L. Stone, *The Causes of the English Revolution, 1529–1642* (London, 1972), pp. 26–43; R. C. Richardson, *The Debate on the English Revolution Revisited* (London, 1988), pp. 98–133.

86. Thompson, *The Making of the English Working Class*, p. 11. For a similar argument, see J. Foster, *Class Struggle and the Industrial Revolution: Early Industrial Capitalism in Three English Towns* (London, 1974).

87. E. J. Hobsbawm, "The Formation of British Working-Class Culture" and "The Making of the Working Class, 1870–1914," both in his *Worlds of Labour: Further Studies in the History of Labour* (London, 1984), pp. 176–213.

88. Hilton, *Bond Men Made Free*, p. 112; Kaye, *British Marxist Historians*, pp. 75–76.

89. E. J. Hobsbawm, "The Crisis of the Seventeenth Century," in T. H. Aston, ed., *Crisis in Europe, 1560–1660* (London, 1965), pp. 5–58; Hobsbawm, "The Seventeenth Century in the Development of Capitalism," *Science and Society* 24 (1960): 97–112.

90. G. Rude, *Revolutionary Europe, 1783–1815* (London, 1964); Rude, *Europe in the Eighteenth Century: Aristocracy and the Bourgeois Challenge* (London, 1972); Rude, *The French Revolution* (London, 1988).

91. E. J. Hobsbawm, *The Age of Revolution: Europe, 1789–1848* (London, 1962).

92. G. Lefebvre, *The Coming of the French Revolution, 1789* (Princeton, 1947); Lefebvre, *The French Revolution*, 2 vols. (New York, 1962–64); A. Souboul, *The Parisian Sans-Culottes and the French Revolution, 1793–4*

(Oxford, 1964); Souboul, *The French Revolution, 1787–1799* (London, 1974); Souboul, *A Short History of the French Revolution, 1789–1799* (London, 1977). For a helpful survey, see G. Ellis, "The 'Marxist Interpretation' of the French Revolution," *English Historical Review* 93 (1978): 353–76.

93. Bell, "Class, Consciousness, and the Fall of the Bourgeois Revolution," pp. 331, quoting J. P. Bertaud, *La Révolution armée: Les Soldat-Citoyens et la Révolution Française* (Paris, 1979), p. 31.

94. Stone, *Causes of the English Revolution*, pp. ix, 36–39; Cannadine, *Making History Now and Then*, pp. 237–42; E. Hobsbawm, "May 1968," in Hobsbawm, *Uncommon People: Resistance, Rebellion and Jazz* (London, 1998), pp. 213–22; B. Moore, *Social Origins of Dictatorship and Democracy: Lord and Peasant in the Making of the Modern World* (Boston, 1966).

95. G. Katsiaficas, *The Imagination of the New Left: A Global Analysis of 1968* (Boston, 1987); G. Stedman Jones, "The Meaning of the Student Revolt," in A. Cockburn and R. Blackburn, eds., *Student Power: Problems, Diagnosis, Action* (Harmondsworth, 1969), pp. 25–56; Stedman Jones, *Outcast London: A Study in the Relationship Between Classes in Victorian London* (Harmondsworth, 1984 ed.), pp. xii–xiv; C. Lin, *The British New Left: A Cultural History, 1957–77* (Edinburgh, 1993); D. Dworkin, *Cultural Marxism in Post-War Britain: History, the New Left and the Origins of Cultural Studies* (Durham, N.C., 1977).

96. See especially G. E. M. de Ste. Croix, *The Class Struggle in the Ancient Greek World from the Archaic Age to the Arab Conquests* (London, 1981).

97. M. Mollat and P. Wolff, *The Popular Revolutions of the Late Middle Ages* (New York, 1973); R. Cazelles, "The Jacquerie," and S. K. Cohn Jr., "Florentine Insurrections, 1342–1385, in Comparative Perspective," both in R. H. Hilton and T. H. Aston, eds., *The English Rising of 1381* (Cambridge, 1984), pp. 74–83, 143–64; S. K. Cohn Jr., "Popular Insurrection and the Black Death: A Comparative View," in C. Dyer, P. Coss, and C. Wickham, eds., *Rodney Hilton's Middle Ages: An Exploration of Historical Themes* (Oxford, 2007), pp. 188–204; C. Wickham, "Memories of Underdevelopment: What Has Marxism Done for Medieval History, and What Can It Still Do?," in Wickham, *Marxist History-Writing*, pp. 37–38.

98. R. Hilton, introduction to T. H. Aston and C. H. E. Philpin, eds., *The Brenner Debate: Agrarian Class Structure and Economic Development in Pre-Industrial Europe* (Cambridge, 1985), pp. 5–9.

99. Wickham, "What Has Marxism Done for Medieval History?," p. 42; P. Anderson, *Passages from Antiquity to Feudalism* (London, 1974); Anderson, *Lineages of the Absolutist State* (London, 1974). For a similar Marxist interpretation, see also V. Kiernan, *State and Society in Europe, 1550–1650* (Oxford, 1980).

100. P. Anderson, "The Notion of Bourgeois Revolution," in his *English Questions* (London, 1992), pp. 105–8; R. B. Morris, "Class Struggle and the American Revolution," *William and Mary Quarterly*, 3rd ser., 19 (1962): 3–29.

101. H. Gutman, *Work, Culture, and Society in Industrializing America: Essays in American Working-Class and Social History* (New York, 1976); Gutman, *Power and Culture: Essays on the American Working Class* (New York, 1987); M. H. Frisch and D. J. Walkowitz, eds., *Working-Class America: Essays on Labor, Community and American Society* (Urbana, Ill., 1983); S. Wilentz, *Chants Democratic: New York and the Rise of the American Working Class* (New York, 1984); Wilentz, "Against Exceptionalism: Class Consciousness and the American Labor Movement, 1790–1920," *International Labor and Working Class History* 26 (1984): 1–24; G. McNall, *The Road to Rebellion: Class Formation and Populism, 1865–1900* (Chicago, 1988); L. Fink, *In Search of the American Working Class: Essays in American Labor History and Political Culture* (Urbana, Ill., 1994).

102. S. E. Ross, *Francisco I Madero: Apostle of American Democracy* (New York, 1955); C. C. Cumberland, *The Mexican Revolution: Genesis Under Madero* (Austin, 1952); J. Womack, *Zapata and the Mexican Revolution* (New York, 1968); J. M. Hart, *Revolutionary Mexico* (Berkeley, 1987); A. Knight, "Revisionism and Revolution: Mexico Compared to England and France," *Past and Present*, no. 134 (1992): 164–65.

103. D. Koenker, *Moscow Workers and the 1917 Revolution* (Princeton, 1981); S. A. Smith, *Red Petrograd: Revolution in the Factories, 1917–1918* (Cambridge, 1983); R. G. Suny, *The Baku Commune, 1917–1918: Class and Nationality in the Russian Revolution* (Princeton, 1917); Suny, "Toward a Social History of the October Revolution," *American Historical Review* 88 (1983): 31–52.

104. See, for example: A. Walder, "The Re-Making of the Chinese Working Class, 1949–1981," *Modern China* 10 (1984): 3–48; I. Katznelson and A. R. Zolberg, eds., *Working-Class Formation: Nineteenth-Century Patterns in Western Europe and the United States* (Princeton, 1986); Z. Lockman, "Imagining the Working Class: Culture, Nationalism and Class Formation in Egypt, 1899–1914," *Poetics Today* 15 (1994): 157–90.

105. E. J. Hobsbawm, "From Social History to the History of Society," in Hobsbawm, *On History* (London, 1997), pp. 85–87; Hobsbawm, "Marxist Historiography Today," p. 187.

106. By 1950, Hugh Trevor-Roper had concluded that "Marxism has been a great stimulus to historical study, but by now it has long succumbed to intellectual sclerosis": Sisman, *Trevor-Roper*, p. 202.

107. M. Taylor, "The Beginnings of Modern British Social History," *History Workshop* 43 (1997): 155–76.

108. R. Porter and C. R. Whittaker, "States and Estates," *Social History* 1 (1976): 367–76; P. Anderson, "Origins of the Present Crisis," *New Left Review*, no. 23 (1964): 26–51; E. P. Thompson, "The Peculiarities of the English," in R. Miliband and J. Saville, eds., *The Socialist Register, 1965* (London, 1965), pp. 311–62; A. J. Mayer, *The Persistence of the Old Regime: Europe to the First World War* (London, 1981); G. Stedman Jones, "Working-Class Culture and Working-Class Politics in London, 1870–1900: Notes on the Re-Making of a Working Class," in his *Languages of Class: Studies in English Working-Class History, 1832–1982* (Cambridge, 1983), pp. 179–238. For broader discussions of disagreements, see P. Anderson, *Considerations on Western Marxism* (London, 1976); Anderson, *Arguments Within English Marxism* (London, 1980).

109. Runciman, *Great Books, Bad Arguments*, pp. 102–3; P. A. Brunt, "A Marxist View of Roman History," *Journal of Roman Studies* 72 (1982): 157–63; P. Lekas, *Marx on Historical Antiquity: Problems of Historical Methodology* (New York, 1988); A. Girdina, "Marxism and Historiography: Perspectives on Roman History," in Wickham, *Marxist History-Writing*, pp. 20–21.

110. Wickham, "What Has Marxism Done for Medieval History?," p. 41; Marx and Engels, *Communist Manifesto*, p. 219; Runciman, *Great Books, Bad Arguments*, p. 101.

111. Zagorin, "Social Interpretation of the English Revolution," pp. 389–90; L. Stone, "The Bourgeois Revolution of Seventeenth-Century England Revisited," *Past and Present* 109 (1985): 44–54; Stone, *Causes of the English Revolution*, pp. 36, 40, 54–56; C. Russell, *Un-Revolutionary England, 1603–1642* (Hambledon, 1990); A. MacLachlan, *The Rise and Fall of Revolutionary England: An Essay on the Fabrication of Seventeenth-Century History* (Basingstoke, 1996); H. R. Trevor-Roper, "The General Crisis of the Seventeenth Century," in Aston, *Crisis in Europe*, pp. 59–95; J. H. Elliott, "Revolution and Continuity in Early Modern Europe," in Elliott, *Spain and Its World, 1500–1700* (London, 1989), pp. 92–113; Elliott, "The General Crisis in Retrospect: A Debate Without End," in Elliott, *Spain, Europe and the Wider World, 1500–1800* (London, 2009), pp. 52–73.

112. A. Cobban, *The Myth of the French Revolution* (London, 1955); Cobban, *The Social Interpretation of the French Revolution* (Cambridge, 1964); Cobban, *Aspects of the French Revolution* (London, 1968); G. Cavanaugh, "The Present State of Revolutionary Historiography: Alfred Cobban and Beyond," *French Historical Studies* 7 (1972): pp. 587–606; S. Schama, *Citizens: A Chronicle of the French Revolution* (London,

1989), p. xiv. For other revisionist accounts, see W. Doyle, *Origins of the French Revolution* (Oxford, 1980); Doyle, *The Oxford History of the French Revolution* (Oxford, 1989); Doyle, *Origins of the French Revolution*, 3rd ed. (Oxford, 1999); F. Furet, *Interpreting the French Revolution* (Cambridge, 1981); T. C. W. Blanning, *The French Revolution: Aristocrats Versus Bourgeois?* (London, 1987); P. R. Hanson, *Contesting the French Revolution* (Oxford, 2009); W. G. Runciman, introduction to Wickham, *Marxist History-Writing*, pp. 5–6.

113. R. M. Hartwell and R. Currie, "The Making of the English Working Class," *Economic History Review*, 2nd ser., 18 (1965): 633–43; C. Calhoun, *The Question of Class Struggle* (Chicago, 1982), pp. 60–94.

114. W. Reddy, *Money and Liberty in Modern Europe: A Critique of Historical Understanding* (Cambridge, 1987), p. 195.

115. R. Ruiz, *The Great Rebellion: Mexico, 1905–1924* (New York, 1980); P. V. N. Henderson, *Felix Díaz, the Porfirians and the Mexican Revolution* (Lincoln, Neb., 1981); P. Vanderwood, *Disorder and Progress: Bandits, Police and Mexican Development* (Lincoln, Neb., 1991); Knight, "Revisionism and Revolution," pp. 165–97; Knight, "The Mexican Revolution: Bourgeois? Nationalist? Or Just a 'Great Rebellion'?" *Bulletin of Latin American Research* 4 (1985): 1–37.

116. L. H. Haimson, "The Problem of Social Identities in Early Twentieth-Century Russia," *Slavic Review* 47 (1988): 1–20; E. Acton, *Rethinking the Russian Revolution* (London, 1990); R. Pipes, *The Russian Revolution* (New York, 1990); R. G. Suny, "Revision and Retreat in the Historiography of 1917: Soviet History and Its Critics," *Russian Review* 53 (1994): 165–82; L. H. Siegelbaum and R. G. Suny, "Class Backwards? In Search of the Soviet Working Class," in L. H. Siegelbaum and R. G. Suny, eds., *Making Workers Soviet: Power, Class and Identity* (Ithaca, N.Y., 1994), pp. 1–26; O. Figes, *A People's Tragedy: The Russian Revolution, 1891–1924* (London, 1997); S. Smith, *Revolution and the People in Russia and China: A Comparative History* (Cambridge, 2008), pp. 1–15.

117. A. Kessler-Harris, "A New Agenda for American Labor History," in J. Carroll Moody and A. Kessler-Harris, eds., *Perspectives in American Labor History: The Problems of Synthesis* (DeKalb, Ill., 1989), p. 219; D. T. Rodgers, *Age of Fracture* (Cambridge, Mass., 2011), p. 93. See also D. Brody, "The Old Labor History and the New: In Search of the New American Working Class," *Labor History* 20 (1979): 111–26; M. Frisch, "Sixty Characters in Search of Authority," *International Labour and Working Class History* 27 (1985): 100–103; M. J. Buhle, "The Future of American Labor History: Towards a Synthesis?" *Radical Historians Newsletter*, no. 44 (1984): 1–2; D. Montgomery, *The Fall*

of the House of Labor (New York, 1987); Smith, *Revolution and the People in Russia*, pp. 1–15.

118. Kaye, *Education of Desire*, pp. 169–72; Kaye, "E. P. Thompson, the British Marxist Historical Tradition and the Contemporary Crisis," in H. J. Kaye and K. McClelland, eds., *E. P. Thompson: Critical Perspectives* (Philadelphia, 1990), pp. 252–75; G. Eley and W. Hunt, eds., *Reviving the English Revolution: Reflections and Elaborations on the Work of Christopher Hill* (London, 1988); R. Brenner, "Bourgeois Revolution and the Transition to Capitalism," in A. L. Beier, D. Cannadine, and J. M. Rosenheim, eds., *The First Modern Society: Essays in English History in Honour of Lawrence Stone* (Cambridge, 1989), pp. 271–304; Brenner, *Merchants and Revolution: Commerical Change, Political Conflict, and London's Overseas Traders, 1550–1663* (Cambridge, 1993); G. C. Comninel, *Rethinking the French Revolution: Marxism and the Revolutionary Challenge* (London, 1987); E. J. Hobsbawm, *Echoes of the Marseillaise: Two Centuries Look Back on the French Revolution* (London, 1990); C. Jones, "Bourgeois Revolution Revivified: 1789 and Social Change," in C. Lucas, ed., *Rewriting the French Revolution* (Oxford, 1991), pp. 69–118; H. Heller, *The Bourgeois Revolution in France (1789–1815)* (London, 2006); R. McKibbin, *Classes and Cultures: England, 1918–1951* (Oxford, 1998); G. Eley and K. Neild, eds., *The Future of Class in History: What's Left of the Social?* (Ann Arbor, Mich., 2007); MacLachlan, *Rise and Fall of Revolutionary England*, pp. 298–325.

119. Rodgers, *Age of Fracture*, p. 253.

120. Stone, *Causes of the English Revolution*, pp. 40, 43; C. Hill, *Intellectual Origins of the English Revolution* (Oxford, 1965), p. 3; Hill, "A Bourgeois Revolution?" in J. G. A. Pocock, ed., *Three British Revolutions: 1641, 1688, 1776* (Princeton, 1980), pp. 109–39; Hill, *The Experience of Defeat: Milton and Some Contemporaries* (New York, 1984).

121. Hobsbawm, *On History*, p. 239; Hobsbawm, "Marxist Historiography Today," p. 187.

122. E. P. Thompson, "The Making of a Ruling Class," *Dissent* (Summer 1993): 380; Cannadine, *Class in Britain*, p. 16; P. Joyce, *Democratic Subjects: The Self and the Social in Nineteenth-Century England* (Cambridge, 1995), p. 2.

123. V. Kiernan, "Revolution and Reaction, 1789–1848," *New Left Review*, no. 19 (1963): 75.

124. Hunt, *Engels*, p. 343; Stedman Jones, introduction to *The Communist Manifesto*, p. 143.

125. Judt, *Ill Fares the Land*, pp. 140–42; Stedman Jones, introduction to *The Communist Manifesto*, p. 9; Hobsbawm, *On History*, pp. 237–38; Runciman, *Great Books, Bad Arguments*, pp. 115, 120; R. Samuel, *The Lost*

World of British Communism (London, 2007), p. 51; R. H. S. Crossman, in A. Koestler et al., *The God That Failed* (London, 1965), pp. 5–6.

126. G. Best, review of Thompson, *Making of the English Working Class*, *Historical Journal* 8 (1965): 278; Runciman, *Great Books, Bad Arguments*, pp. 109–10. Even Victor Kiernan, who was more aware than his fellow Marxists of the importance of religion, had little time for or understanding of the importance of the nation: Kaye, *Education of Desire*, pp. 82–83, and references cited there.

127. I. Deutscher, "The Wandering Jew as Thinker and Revolutionary," *Universities and Left Review* 4 (1958): 13; R. Miliband, "The Politics of Contemporary Capitalism," *New Reasoner* 5 (1958), p. 47; S. Hall, "A Sense of Classlessness," *Universities and Left Review* 5 (1958): 30.

128. Hobsbawm, *Nations and Nationalism Since 1780*, esp. pp. 177–92; Hobsbawm, *On History*, pp. 5–9, 266–77; Hobsbawm, "Marxist Historiography Today," pp. 184–85.

129. Hunt, *Engels*, pp. 308–13; Stedman Jones, introduction to *The Communist Manifesto*, p. 4.

130. J. W. Scott, "Women in *The Making of the English Working Class*," in Scott, *Gender and the Politics of History* (New York, 1988), pp. 68–90; A. Clark, *The Struggle for the Breeches: Gender and the Making of the British Working Class* (London, 1995); P. A. Custer, "Reconfiguring Jemima: Gender, Work and Politics in Lancashire, 1770–1820," *Past and Present*, no. 195 (2007): 127–58; Hobsbawm, *On History*, p. 71.

FOUR: GENDER

1. W. Thompson, *Appeal of One-Half of the Human Race, Women, Against the Pretensions of the Other Half, Men, to Retain Them in Political, and Thence in Civil and Domestic Slavery* (London, 1825; reprinted, London, 1983), pp. xxi–xxii; B. Taylor, *Eve and the New Jerusalem: Socialism and Feminism in the Nineteenth Century* (New York, 1983), pp. 22–24.

2. M. Walters, *Feminism: A Very Short Introduction* (Oxford, 2005), pp. 43–45; D. Wahrman, " 'Middle-Class' Domesticity Goes Public: Gender, Class and Politics from Queen Anne to Queen Victoria," *Journal of British Studies* 32 (1993): 410–14.

3. T. Ball, "Utilitarianism, Feminism, and the Franchise: James Mill and His Critics," *History of Political Thought* 1 (1980): 110–12.

4. Thompson, *Appeal of One-Half of the Human Race*, pp. 39, 77.

5. Ibid., pp. 17, 35, 53, 61, 68–69.

6. J. W. Scott, *Gender and the Politics of History* (New York, 1988), pp. 2, 32.

7. B. Friedan, *The Feminine Mystique* (New York, 2001 ed.), pp. 511–12; G. Greer, *The Female Eunuch* (New York, 2008 ed.), p. 131.

8. A. D. Smith, *National Identity* (Harmondsworth, 1991), p. 4.

9. S. de Beauvoir, *The Second Sex* (New York, 1989 ed.), p. xxv.

10. J. W. Scott, "Fantasy Echo: History and the Construction of Identity," *Critical Inquiry* 27 (2001): 286–87.

11. M. Dowd, *Are Men Necessary? When Sexes Collide* (New York, 2005), pp. 7, 80, 199–200.

12. C. Stansell, *The Feminist Promise: 1792 to the Present* (New York, 2010), p. 39; L. Brizendine, *The Female Brain* (New York, 2006), pp. 7–8.

13. The classic Aristotelian texts are reprinted in R. Agonito, ed., *History of Ideas on Woman: A Source Book* (New York, 1977), pp. 43–54; J. English, ed., *Sex Equality* (Engelwood Cliffs, N.J., 1977), pp. 20–31. For recent feminist attempts to "recover" Aristotle, see C. A. Freedland, ed., *Feminist Interpretations of Aristotle* (University Park, Pa., 1998).

14. Stansell, *Feminist Promise*, pp. 4–5.

15. 1 Timothy 2:12–15; O. Hufton, *The Prospect Before Her: A History of Women in Western Europe*, vol. 1, *1500–1800* (New York, 1996), pp. 30–33; S. Mendelson and P. Crawford, *Women in Early Modern England, 1550–1720* (Oxford, 1998), pp. 32–34.

16. English, *Sex Equality*, pp. 42–47; Stansell, *Feminist Promise*, p. 14; J. Rendall, *The Origins of Modern Feminism: Women in Britain, France and the United States, 1780–1860* (London, 1985), pp. 7–32.

17. T. Paine, *Rights of Man, Common Sense and Other Political Writings* (New York, 1995, ed.), p. 11; Agonito, *History of Ideas on Woman*, pp. 249–63; C. Darwin, *The Descent of Man*, in P. H. Barrett and R. B. Freeman, eds., *The Works of Charles Darwin* (London, 1986), vol. 21, pp. 556, 564, 605, 614.

18. Agonito, *History of Ideas on Woman*, pp. 265–69, 297–322; P. Gay, *The Bourgeois Experience: Victoria to Freud*, vol. 2, *The Tender Passion* (New York, 1986), p. 85; C. Thompson, *Psychoanalysis: Evolution and Development* (New York, 1950), pp. 131–33; S. Freud, *New Introductory Lectures on Psychoanalysis* (New York, 1933), pp. 170ff.

19. J. Gray, *Men Are from Mars, Women Are from Venus: The Definitive Guide to Relationships* (London, 1992), esp. pp. 1–5, 7, 10.

20. S. Baron-Cohen, *The Essential Difference* (London, 2003), pp. 1–6, 78–80, 129.

21. For similar arguments to those of Baron-Cohen (and Gray), see Brizendine, *Female Brain*; S. Pinker, *The Sexual Paradox: Men, Women and the Gender Gap* (New York, 2008).

22. G. Greer, *The Whole Woman* (New York, 2000), pp. 70–80.

23. Gray, *Men Are from Mars*, p. 7; A. Kessler-Harris, "Gender and Work: Possibilities for a Global Overview," in B. Smith, ed., *Women's History in Global Perspective*, 3 vols. (Urbana, Ill., 2004–5), vol. 1, pp. 147–51.

24. K. V. Thomas, "The Double Standard," *Journal of the History of Ideas* 20 (1959): 195–216.

25. H. L. Smith, *All Men and Both Sexes: Gender, Politics and the False Universal in England, 1640–1832* (University Park, Pa., 2002), pp. 1–38.

26. Quoted in S. Jones, *Y: The Descent of Man* (London, 2002), p. xv.

27. B. Hill, *Women, Work and Sexual Politics in the Eighteenth Century* (Oxford, 1990), pp. 24–68, offers an approving summary of these views.

28. For the United States, see N. F. Cott, *The Bonds of Womanhood: Woman's Sphere in New England, 1780–1835* (New Haven, 1977); M. Ryan, *Cradle of the Middle Class: The Family in Oneida County, New York, 1790–1865* (Cambridge, 1981). For the United Kingdom, see C. Hall, "The Early Formation of Domestic Ideology," in S. Burman, ed., *Fit Work for Women* (London, 1979), pp. 15–32; L. Davidoff and C. Hall, *Family Fortunes: Men and Women of the English Middle Class, 1780–1850* (Chicago, 1987).

29. T. Laqueur, *Making Sex: Body and Gender from the Greeks to Freud* (Cambridge, Mass., 1990); M. McKeon, "Historicising Patriarchy: The Emergence of Gender Difference in England, 1660–1760," *Eighteenth Century Studies* 28 (1995): 295–322; T. Hitchcock, "Redefining Sex in Eighteenth-Century England," *History Workshop Journal* 41 (1996): 72–90; Hitchcock, *English Sexualities, 1700–1800* (Basingstoke, 1997), esp. p. 49.

30. A. Vickery, "Golden Age to Separate Spheres? A Review of the Categories and Chronology of English Women's History," *Historical Journal* 36 (1993): 385; Cott, *Bonds of Womanhood*, pp. 160–206; C. Smith-Rosenberg, "The Female World of Love and Ritual: Relations Between Women in Nineteenth-Century America," *Signs* 1 (1975): 9–10; M. Vicinus, *Independent Woman: Work and Community for Single Women, 1850–1920* (London, 1985), p. 3; M. Shanley, *Feminism, Marriage and the Law in Victorian England* (London, 1989), pp. 6–7.

31. Vickery, "Golden Age to Separate Spheres?," pp. 383, 388; Davidoff and Hall, *Family Fortunes*, pp. 11, 454.

32. Reprinted in Agonito, *History of Ideas on Woman*, pp. 397–402.

33. M. Hines, *Brain Gender* (Oxford, 2004), esp. pp. 222–23, 226–28.

34. Plato's classic text is reprinted in Agonito, *History of Ideas on Woman*, pp. 23–39; English, *Sex Equality*, pp. 13–19. For Plato as a feminist, see J. Annas, "Plato's Republic and Feminism," *Philosophy* 51 (1976): 307–21; N. Tuana, ed., *Feminist Interpretations of Plato* (University Park, Pa., 1995). In other contexts, however, Plato does not maintain this view of women, as in the *Laws* or in the *Timaeus*: see C. G. Allen, "Plato on Women," *Feminist Studies* 2 (1975): 131–38; M. Canto, "The Politics of Women's Bodies: Reflections on Plato," in S. R. Suleiman, ed., *The Female Body in Western Culture* (Cambridge, Mass., 1986), pp. 339–53. For a judicious appraisal of these issues, see G. Vlastos,

"Was Plato a Feminist?," *Times Literary Supplement*, March 17–23, 1989, pp. 276, 288–89.

35. Stansell, *Feminist Promise*, p. 6; K. Offen, *European Feminisms, 1700–1950: A Political History* (Stanford, 2000), p. 34.

36. Stansell, *Feminist Promise*, p. 15; Offen, *European Feminisms*, p. 57.

37. Hufton, *Prospect Before Her*, pp. 461–62; J. W. Scott, "French Feminists and the Rights of 'Man': Olympe de Gouge's Declarations," *History Workshop Journal*, no. 28 (1989): 1–21; Scott, *Only Paradoxes to Offer: French Feminists and the Rights of Man* (Cambridge, Mass., 1996), p. 42.

38. Hufton, *Prospect Before Her*, pp. 453–55; Stansell, *Feminist Promise*, pp. 20, 23; M. Wollstonecraft, *A Vindication of the Rights of Woman* (New York, 1988 ed.), p. 175.

39. Colossians 3:18; Galatians 3:28; Mendelson and Crawford, *Women in Early Modern England*, p. 31.

40. Stansell, *Feminist Promise*, pp. 42, 45–46.

41. R. J. Evans, *The Feminists: Women's Emancipation Movements in Europe, America and Australasia, 1840–1920* (London, 1977), pp. 46–47.

42. Stansell, *Feminist Promise*, pp. 69–71; A. S. Rossi, ed., *The Feminist Papers: From Adams to de Beauvoir* (Boston, 1973), pp. 413–21.

43. English, *Sex Equality*, pp. 54–65; Agonito, *History of Ideas on Woman*, pp. 223–48; Evans, *The Feminists*, pp. 18–22.

44. H. Ibsen, *A Doll's House and Other Plays* (New York, 1965, ed.), p. 228. This play has become a canonical feminist text: see Beauvoir, *Second Sex*, pp. 464, 478, 616; Friedan, *Feminist Mystique*, pp. 140–41; Greer, *Female Eunuch*, p. 22; Stansell, *Feminist Promise*, p. 143.

45. T. Hunt, *The Frock-Coated Communist: The Revolutionary Life of Friedrich Engels* (London, 2009), pp. 309–14; F. Engels, *The Origin of the Family, Private Property and the State* (New York, 1942, ed.), esp. pp. 128–29, 134–39; Agonito, *History of Ideas on Woman*, pp. 273–88.

46. S. Steinbach, *Women in England, 1760–1914: A Social History* (London, 2004), p. 273.

47. Stansell, *Feminist Promise*, p. 173; C. A. Lunardini and T. J. Knock, "Woodrow Wilson and Woman Suffrage: A New Look," *Political Science Quarterly* 95 (1980–81): 655–56.

48. Stansell, *Feminist Promise*, pp. 154, 162; E. Goldman, *Anarchism and Other Essays* (New York, 1969 ed.), p. 239.

49. Stansell, *Feminist Promise*, pp. 194–95; Beauvoir, *Second Sex*, pp. xxi–xxii, 267.

50. A. Oakley, *Sex, Gender and Society* (London, 1972), p. 170; L. Segal, *Why Feminism? Gender, Psychology, Politics* (London, 1999), p. 39.

51. L. Davidoff, "Gender and the Great Divide: Public and Private in British Gender History," *Journal of Women's History* 15 (2003): 11–27; M. P. Ryan, "The Public and the Private Good: Across the Great Divide in

Women's History," *Journal of Women's History* 15 (2003): 10–27; Ryan, *Women in Public Between Banners and Ballots, 1825–1880* (Baltimore, 1990).

52. Vickery, "Golden Age to Separate Spheres?" pp. 402–14; O. Hufton, "Women in History: Early Modern Europe," *Past and Present* 51 (1983): 126; J. Bennett, "History That Stands Still: Women's Work in the European Past," *Feminist Studies* 14 (1988): 269–83; Bennett, "Medieval Women, Modern Women: Across the Great Divide," in D. Aers, ed., *Culture and History, 1350–1600: Essays on English Communities, Identities and Writing* (London, 1992), pp. 147–75; B. Hill, "Women's History: A Study in Change, Continuity, or Standing Still," *Women's History Review* 2 (1993): 5–22; J. Bennett, "Women's History: A Reply to Bridget Hill," *Women's History Review* 2 (1993): 173–84.

53. Davidoff and Hall, *Family Fortunes*, pp. 29–30; D. Cannadine, *Making History Now and Then: Discoveries, Controversies and Explorations* (London, 2008), pp. 97–109.

54. Wahrman, " 'Middle-Class' Domesticity Goes Public," pp. 399–403; A. Clark, *The Struggle for the Breeches: Gender and the Making of the British Working Class* (London, 1995), pp. 179–273; J. Melching, "Advice to Historians on Advice to Mothers," *Journal of Social History* 9 (1979): 44–63; L. Kerber, "Separate Sphere, Female Worlds, Woman's Place: The Rhetoric of Women's History," *Journal of American History* 75 (1988): 9–39; J. Bennett, "Medieval Women in Modern Perspective," in Smith, *Women's History in Global Perspective*, vol. 2, p. 170; J. Cadden, *Meanings of Sex Difference in the Middle Ages: Medicine, Science and Culture* (New York, 1993); K. Harvey, "The Substance of Sexual Difference: Change and Persistence in Representations of the Body in Eighteenth-Century England," *Gender and History* 14 (2002): 202–23; Harvey, "The Century of Sex? Gender, Bodies and Sexuality in the Long Eighteenth Century," *Historical Journal* 45 (2002): 899–916.

55. Vickery, "Golden Age to Separate Spheres?" pp. 385–90; P. Branca, "Image and Reality: The Myth of the Idle Victorian Woman," in M. Hartman and L. Banner, eds., *Clio's Consciousness Raised: New Perspectives on the History of Women* (New York, 1974), pp. 179–91; M. J. Peterson, "No Angels in the House: The Victorian Myth and the Paget Women," *American Historical Review* 89 (1984): 693; L. Colley, *Britons: Forging the Nation, 1707–1837* (London, 1992), pp. 237–81; M. Berg, "Women's Property and the Industrial Revolution," *Journal of Interdisciplinary History* 24 (1993): 235–50.

56. Vickery, "Golden Age to Separate Spheres?" p. 392; S. Alexander, "Women, Class and Sexual Differences in the 1830s: Some Reflections on the Writing of Feminist History," *History Workshop Journal* 18 (1984): 130–31.

57. Bennett, "Medieval Women in Modern Perspective," p. 158.

58. J. T. Wood, "A Critical Response to John Gray's Mars and Venus Portrayals of Men and Women," *Southern Communication Journal* 67 (2002): 203–5; T. Hames, "The Message for Earthlings: Men Aren't Martians and Women Aren't Venusians," *Times* (London), September 5, 2005.

59. *Guardian Unlimited*, May 3, 2003; N. Walter, "Prejudice and Evolution," *Prospect* (June 2005): 34–39; C. Fine, *Delusions of Gender: How Our Minds, Society and Neurosexism Create Difference* (London, 2005); R. Jordan-Young, *Brain Storm: The Flaws in the Science of Sex Differences* (Cambridge, Mass., 2010).

60. G. Bock, "Challenging Dichotomies: Perspectives on Women's History," in K. Offen, R. R. Pierson, and J. Rendall, eds., *Writing Women's History: International Perspectives* (Bloomington, Ind., 1991), p. 7.

61. Beauvoir, *Second Sex*, pp. xxiv–xxv; Hines, *Brain Gender*, pp. 213–14.

62. Wood, "Critical Response," pp. 205–6; D. T. Rodgers, *Age of Fracture* (Cambridge, Mass., 2011); p. 153; S. M. Evans, *The Tidal Wave: How Women Changed America at Century's End* (New York, 2003), p. 153.

63. G. Vlastos, "Does Slavery Exist in Plato's Republic?," *Classical Philology* 63 (1968): 291–95; E. V. Spelman, "Hairy Cobblers and Philosopher-Queens," in B.-A. Bar On, ed., *Engendering Origins: Critical Feminist Readings in Plato and Aristotle* (Albany, N.Y., 1994), pp. 3–24.

64. E. V. Spelman, "Who's Who in the Polis," in Bar On, *Engendering Origins*, pp. 99–125.

65. R. W. Connell, "The Big Picture: Masculinities in Recent World History," *Theory and Society* 22 (1993): 597–623; Connell, *Masculinities* (Cambridge, 1995), esp. pp. 77–81; E. A. Rotundo, *American Manhood: Transformations in Masculinity from the Revolution to the Modern Era* (New York, 1993); J. Tosh, "What Should Historians Do with Masculinity? Reflections on Nineteenth-Century Britain," *History Workshop Journal* 38 (1994): 179–202; G. L. Mosse, *The Image of Man: The Creation of Modern Masculinity* (New York, 1996).

66. A. Shepard, *Meanings of Manhood in Early Modern England* (Oxford, 2003), pp. 2–3; author's emphasis.

67. E. Power, "The Position of Women," in C. G. Crump and E. F. Jacob, eds., *The Legacy of the Middle Ages* (Oxford, 1926), pp. 401–33; Bennett, "Medieval Women in Modern Perspective," pp. 143–48.

68. D. G. Neal, *The Masculine Self in Late Medieval England* (Chicago, 2008), pp. 1–11, 241–53; D. M. Hadley, "Introduction: Medieval Masculinities," in Hadley, ed., *Masculinity in Medieval Europe* (London, 1999), pp. 6–8.

69. Hufton, *Prospect Before Her*, pp. 492–513; Mendelson and Crawford, *Women in Early Modern England*, pp. 301–44.

70. Shepard, *Meanings of Manhood*, pp. 1–5; K. Harvey, "The History of Masculinity, Circa 1650–1800," *Journal of British Studies* 44 (2005): 296–311.

71. Vickery, "Golden Age to Separate Spheres?," p. 390; J. Tosh, "Masculinities in an Industrializing Society: Britain, 1800–1914," *Journal of British Studies* 44 (2005): 337.

72. Greer, *Female Eunuch*, pp. 25, 369.

73. N. Jay, "Gender and Dichotomy," *Feminist Studies* 7 (1981): 38–56; Bock, "Challenging Dichotomies," pp. 1–23; M. Wiesner-Hanks, "World History and the History of Women, Gender, and Sexuality," *Journal of World History* 18 (2007): 55.

74. J. M. Faragher, *Women and Men on the Overland Trail* (New Haven, 1979), pp. xi, 3, 14–15; Faragher, "History from the Inside Out: Writing the History of Women in Rural America," *American Quarterly* 33 (1981): 537–57.

75. Beauvoir, *Second Sex*, pp. xx–xxi.

76. Scott, "Fantasy Echo," pp. 285–87.

77. Walters, *Feminism*, p. 90; R. Milkman, "Women's History and the Sears Case," *Feminist Studies* 12 (1986): 394–95; M. Minow, "Learning to Live with the Dilemma of Difference: Bilingual and Special Education," *Law and Contemporary Problems* 48 (1984): 160; J. W. Scott, *Parité! Sexual Equality and the Crisis of French Universalism* (Chicago, 2005), pp. 51–58.

78. Alexander, "Women, Class and Sexual Differences," p. 126; Rodgers, *Age of Fracture*, pp. 148–49; S. Kent, "Worlds of Feminism," in Smith, *Women's History in Global Perspective*, vol. 3, p. 275.

79. Scott, *Gender and the Politics of History*, pp. 167–69.

80. Friedan, *Feminist Mystique*, pp. 525–26; Greer, *Female Eunuch*, pp. 13–26, 353–71; Greer, *Whole Woman*, pp. 236–43; Stansell, *Feminist Promise*, pp. 253–54.

81. Hufton, *Prospect Before Her*, p. 495.

82. Evans, *The Feminists*, pp. 15–16; Offen, *European Feminisms*, pp. 50–76; B. G. Smith, *Changing Lives: Women in European History Since 1700* (Lexington, Mass., 1989), pp. 93–133; O. Hufton, "Women in Revolution, 1789–96," *Past and Present*, no. 53 (1971): 90–108; Hufton, *Prospect Before Her*, pp. 462–90, 495.

83. Evans, *The Feminists*, pp. 23–32; D. Reynolds, *One World Divisible: A Global History Since 1945* (New York, 2000), pp. 308–9; J. S. Chafez and A. G. Dworkin, *Female Revolt: Women's Movements in World and Historical Perspective* (Totowa, N.J., 1986), p. 218.

84. E. Sarah, "Towards a Reassessment of Feminist History," *Women's Studies International Forum* 5 (1982): 519–24.

85. Smith, *Changing Lives*, pp. 348–49; Stansell, *Feminist Promise*, pp. 108–9, 121–22.
86. Offen, *European Feminisms*, pp. 144–81; Smith, *Changing Lives*, pp. 349–50; Evans, *The Feminists*, pp. 246–53.
87. Evans, *The Feminists*, pp. 211–28.
88. Ibid., pp. 46–47; Stansell, *Feminist Promise*, pp. 123–24.
89. Steinbach, *Women in England*, pp. 273–74; S. S. Holton, *Feminism and Democracy: Women's Suffrage and Reform Politics in Britain, 1900–1918* (Cambridge, 1986), p. 7.
90. Steinbach, *Women in England*, pp. 285–92.
91. Ibid., p. 269.
92. Ibid., pp. 224–25, 270.
93. Ibid., pp. 250–59.
94. Evans, *The Feminists*, pp. 124–37; Steinbach, *Women in England*, pp. 249, 276; Stansell, *Feminist Promise*, pp. 136–37.
95. Smith, *Changing Lives*, pp. 302–13; L. A. Tilly, "Women's Collective Action and Feminism in France, 1870–1914," in L. A. Tilly and C. Tilly, eds., *Class Conflict and Collective Action* (Beverly Hills, Calif., 1981), pp. 207–31.
96. Evans, *The Feminists*, pp. 250–52; Offen, *European Feminisms*, pp. 257–61; Smith, *Changing Lives*, pp. 365–68; H. H. Alonso, introduction to J. Addams, E. G. Balch, and A. Hamilton, *Women at The Hague: The International Conference of Women and Its Results* (Urbana, Ill., 2003 ed.), pp. v–xl.
97. Evans, *The Feminists*, pp. 188–231; Reynolds, *One World Divisible*, p. 308.
98. Reynolds, *One Word Divisible*, p. 309; Stansell, *Feminist Promise*, pp. 179–81.
99. Friedan, *Feminine Mystique*, pp. 423–27; J. Meyerowitz, "Beyond the Feminine Mystique: A Reassessment of Postwar Mass Culture, 1946–1958," *Journal of American History* 79 (1993): 1455–82.
100. L. Segal, *Is the Future Female?* (New York, 1987), pp. 43–55.
101. B. Linden-Ward and C. H. Green, *Changing the Future: American Women in the 1960s* (New York, 1993), p. 79.
102. Walters, *Feminism*, pp. 110–12.
103. R. Morgan, "Introduction: The Women's Revolution," in Morgan, ed., *Sisterhood Is Powerful: An Anthology of Writings from the Women's Liberation Movement* (New York, 1970), p. xiii; R.-M. Lagrave, "A Supervised Emancipation," in F. Thebaud, ed., *A History of Women in the West*, vol. 5 (Cambridge, Mass., 1994), pp. 466–77.
104. L. B. Iglitizin and R. Ross, eds., *Women and the World, 1975–1985: The Woman's Decade* (Santa Barbara, Calif., 1986).

105. Stansell, *Feminist Promise*, pp. 355–56; D. Russell and N. van de Ven, preface to Russell and van de Ven, eds., *The Proceedings of the International Tribunal on Crimes Against Women* (Millbrae, Calif., 1976), p. xv; R. Morgan, "Prefatory Note and Methodology," in Russell and van de Ven, ed., *Sisterhood Is Global: The International Women's Movement Anthology* (New York, 1984), p. xii.

106. Reynolds, *One World Divisible*, pp. 686–88.

107. Scott, *Gender and the Politics of History*, pp. 2–3, 15–27; Steinbach, *Women in England*, pp. 3–4; R. Morgan, "Introduction: New World Women," in Morgan, ed., *Sisterhood Is Forever: The Women's Anthology for a New Millennium* (New York, 2003), p. lv.

108. Stansell, *Feminist Promise*, pp. 21–22, 195–96, 206.

109. Scott, *Gender and the Politics of History*, pp. 188–89; L. F. Brown, *Apostle of Democracy: The Life of Lucy Maynard Salmon* (New York, 1943), p. 256.

110. Greer, *Female Eunuch*, p. 11.

111. Reynolds, *One World Divisible*, p. 312.

112. Rodgers, *Age of Fracture*, p. 150.

113. Walters, *Feminism*, p. 105; bell hooks, *Feminist Theory from Margin to Center* (Boston, 1984).

114. Stansell, *Feminist Promise*, pp. xii, xvii.

115. Greer, *Female Eunuch*, pp. 12–13, 77–78; Friedan, *Feminist Mystique*, pp. 519–26; Stansell, *Feminist Promise*, pp. 213–16, 234–36, 253–58; Reynolds, *One World Divisible*, pp. 311–12.

116. J. Olcott, "Preface to The Greatest Consciousness-Raising Event in History: International Women's Year and the Challenge of Transnational Feminism" (unpublished paper, Shelby Cullom Davis Center for Historical Studies, Princeton University, February 26, 2010).

117. Walters, *Feminism*, p. 117.

118. Stansell, *Feminist Promise*, p. xvii.

119. Rodgers, *Age of Fracture*, p. 178; J. Dean, *Solidarity of Strangers: Feminism After Identity* (Berkeley, 1996), p. 1.

120. See, for example, the varied views expressed in AHR Forum, "Revisiting 'Gender: A Useful Category of Historical Analysis,'" *American Historical Review* 113 (2008): 1344–1430.

121. Scott, *Only Paradoxes to Offer*, p. 160; Scott, "Fantasy Echo," pp. 285–90.

122. Bennett, "Medieval Women," p. 171.

123. M. Nussbaum, "The Professor of Parody," *New Republic*, February 22, 1999, pp. 37–45; Walters, *Feminism*, pp. 140–41.

124. Rodgers, *Age of Fracture*, pp. 11, 61–64, 146, 1564–56; Scott, *Only Paradoxes to Offer*, pp. 11–13, 172–75; Stansell, *Feminist Promise*, p. 395;

J. Halley, *Split Decisions: How and Why to Take a Break from Feminism* (Princeton, 2006), p. 10.

125. Beauvoir, *Second Sex*, p. xx.

126. D. Haraway, "A Manifesto for Cyborgs: Science, Technology and Socialist Feminism in the 1980s," in L. Nicholson, ed., *Feminism/Postmodernism* (London, 1990), p. 197.

127. Greer, *Whole Woman*, pp. 4, 13.

128. For some suggestive comments on this subject in the British case, see B. Harrison, *Finding a Role? The United Kingdom, 1970–1990* (Oxford, 2010), pp. 237–39.

129. Stansell, *Feminist Promise*, p. xix.

130. Rodgers, *Age of Fracture*, pp. 164–74.

131. Reynolds, *One World Divisible*, pp. 318–29, 400–401, 660; Walters, *Feminism*, pp. 123–31; N. R. Keddie, "Women in the Middle East Since the Rise of Islam," in Smith, *Women's History in Global Perspective*, vol. 3, pp. 94–106.

132. Greer, *Whole Woman*, pp. 3–20.

133. Morgan, *Sisterhood Is Forever*, p. lv; Reynolds, *One World Divisible*, pp. 686–87; A. Wolf, "Working Girls," *Prospect*, April 2006, pp. 28–33.

FIVE: RACE

1. R. Knox, *The Races of Men: A Fragment* (London, 1850). The enlarged edition of 1862 is revealingly subtitled *A Philosophical Inquiry into the Influence of Race over the Destinies of Nations*. For Knox's life and career, see I. Rae, *Knox: The Anatomist* (London, 1964); K. Stephen, *Robert Knox* (London, 1981). For Knox's thought, see M. D. Biddiss, "The Politics of Anatomy: Dr. Robert Knox and Victorian Racism," *Proceedings of the Royal Society of Medicine* 69 (1976): 245–50; E. Richards, "The 'Moral Anatomy' of Robert Knox: The Interplay Between Biological and Social Thought in Victorian Societal Thought," *Journal of the History of Biology* 22 (1989): 373–436; P. Mandler, "The Problem with Cultural History," *Cultural and Social History* 1 (2004): 96–103; Mandler, *The English National Character: The History of an Idea from Edmund Burke to Tony Blair* (London, 2006), pp. 40, 74.

2. R. Richardson, *Death, Dissection and the Destitute* (London, 1987), pp. 131–43.

3. Knox, *Races of Men*, p. v; G. L. Mosse, *Toward the Final Solution: A History of European Racism* (New York, 1978), pp. 67–70.

4. Knox, *Races of Men*, pp. 65–66, 245; Biddiss, "Politics of Anatomy," p. 250.

5. R. Blake, *Disraeli* (London, 1966), pp. 201–5, 258–60; B. Disraeli, *Tan-*

306 / Notes to Pages 176–180

cred, or the New Crusade (London, 1882 ed.), p. 149; Disraeli, speech of February 1, 1849, quoted in H. Odom, "Generalizations on Race in Nineteenth-Century Physical Anthropology," *Isis* 58 (1967): 9.

6. Mosse, *Toward the Final Solution*, pp. 51–58.
7. N. Painter, *The History of White People* (New York, 2010), pp. 182, 195.
8. I. Berlin, *Four Essays on Liberty* (London, 1969), p. 106; M. Biddiss, introduction to Biddiss, ed., *Images of Race* (Leicester, 1970), p. 12.
9. Compare, for example, Mosse, *Toward the Final Solution*, pp. xi–xvi; G. M. Fredrickson, *Racism: A Short History* (Princeton, 2002), pp. 17–47.
10. D. Brion Davis, *The Problem of Slavery in Western Culture* (Ithaca, N.Y., 1966), pp. 70–72; Brion Davis, *Inhuman Bondage: The Rise and Fall of Slavery in the New World* (Oxford, 2006), pp. 40–47.
11. F. M. Snowden Jr., *Blacks in Antiquity: Ethiopians in the Greco-Roman Experience* (Cambridge, Mass., 1970); Snowden, *Before Color Prejudice: The Ancient View of Blacks* (Cambridge, Mass., 1983); L. A. Thompson, *Romans and Blacks* (London, 1989); E. S. Gruen, *Rethinking the Other in Antiquity* (Princeton, 2011); I. Hannaford, *Race: The History of an Idea in the West* (Washington, D.C., 1996), pp. 17–85.
12. C. Kidd, *The Forging of Races: Race and Scripture in the Protestant Atlantic World, 1600–2000* (Cambridge, 2006), p. 3; Acts of the Apostles 17:26.
13. Quoted in Hannaford, *Race*, p. 96.
14. Quoted in N. Stepan, *The Idea of Race in Science: Great Britain, 1800–1960* (London, 1982), pp. 1–2.
15. Kidd, *Forging of Races*, pp. 25–26; Fredrickson, *Racism*, pp. 17–19, 26–28.
16. D. Abulafia, *The Great Sea: A Human History of the Mediterranean* (London, 2011), pp. 216–19, 477–83, 569–70; K. J. P. Lowe, "Introduction: The Black African Presence in Renaissance Europe," in T. F. Earle and K. J. P. Lowe, eds., *Black Africans in Renaissance Europe* (Cambridge, 2005), p. 2; K. J. P. Lowe, "Representing Africa: Ambassadors and Princes from Christian Africa to Renaissance Italy and Portugal, 1402–1606," *Transactions of the Royal Historical Society*, 6th. ser., 17 (2007): 401–28; Painter, *White People*, pp. 34–39.
17. Fredrickson, *Racism*, pp. 18–22, 29–33, 43–45.
18. Ibid., p. 6.
19. J. Chaplin, "Race," in D. Armitage and M. Braddick, eds., *The British Atlantic World, 1500–1800* (Basingstoke, 2002), pp. 154–66; Kidd, *Forging of Races*, p. 54.
20. Fredrickson, *Racism*, p. 64.
21. D. Hume, *Essays, Moral, Political and Literary* (Indianapolis, 1987 ed.), pp. 208 fn, 629–30; Kidd, *Forging the Races*, pp. 93–94; Mosse, *Toward*

the *Final Solution*, p. 30; J. Israel, *Democratic Enlightenment: Philosophy, Revolution and Human Rights, 1750–1790* (Oxford, 2011), pp. 738–39.

22. C. Bolt, *Victorian Attitudes to Race* (London, 1971), p. 9; Stepan, *Idea of Race*, p. 29; Painter, *White People*, pp. 114–15; Israel, *Democratic Enlightenment*, pp. 250–53.

23. Mosse, *Toward the Final Solution*, p. 33.

24. Quoted in E. C. Eze, ed., *Race and the Enlightenment: A Reader* (Cambridge, Mass., 1997), p. 13; Fredrickson, *Racism*, p. 56.

25. S. Peabody, *"There Are No Slaves in France": The Political Culture of Race and Slavery in the Ancien Régime* (New York, 1996), p. 66.

26. Hannaford, *Race*, pp. 202–13; Painter, *White People*, pp. 72–90.

27. J. H. St. J. de Crèvecoeur, *Letters from an American Farmer* (New York, 1981 ed.), p. 69; E. Foner, *The Story of American Freedom* (New York, 1998), p. 39.

28. T. Jefferson, *Notes on the State of Virginia* (Chapel Hill, N.C., 1982 ed.), pp. 138–39; Chaplin, "Race," p. 165.

29. Foner, *American Freedom*, p. 75; Fredrickson, *Racism*, pp. 80–81; J. H. Kettner, *The Development of American Citizenship, 1608–1870* (Chapel Hill, N.C., 1978), pp. 235–46; E. P. Hutchinson, *Legislative History of American Immigration Policy, 1798–1865* (Philadelphia, 1981), pp. 405–33.

30. Painter, *White People*, pp. 64–68; Mosse, *Toward the Final Solution*, pp. 21–25.

31. Bolt, *Victorian Attitudes to Race*, p. 15; Biddiss, introduction to *Images of Race*, p. 15; Painter, *White People*, pp. 190–94; S. J. Gould, *The Mismeasure of Man*, rev. ed. (New York, 1996), pp. 105–41.

32. Bolt, *Victorian Attitudes to Race*, p. 4; Mosse, *Toward the Final Solution*, pp. 70–71; P. Stock, " 'Almost a Separate Race': Racial Thought and the Idea of Europe in British Encyclopedias and Histories, 1771–1830," *Modern Intellectual History* 8 (2011): 3–29; E. Barkan, *The Retreat of Scientific Racism: Changing Concepts of Race in Britain and the United States Between the World Wars* (Cambridge, 1992), pp. 3–4.

33. Bolt, *Victorian Attitudes to Race*, p. xi; Biddiss, introduction to *Images of Race*, pp. 11, 16; Painter, *White People*, pp. 213–14; Mosse, *Toward the Final Solution*, pp. 121–22; J. Darwin, *After Tamerlane: The Global History of Empire Since 1405* (London, 2007), p. 348.

34. Mosse, *Toward the Final Solution*, pp. 32–33.

35. Ibid., pp. 11, 17–20, 30; Biddiss, introduction to *Images of Race*, p. 15.

36. Kidd, *Forging of Races*, pp. 7–8; Painter, *White People*, pp. 195–98; Fredrickson, *Racism*, p. 57.

37. Painter, *White People*, pp. 195–98; Bolt, *Victorian Attitudes to Race*, pp. xii, 10, 23.

38. Fredrickson, *Racism*, pp. 8, 70–71; Mosse, *Toward the Final Solution*, pp. 36–41, 102.

39. D. Pick, *Faces of Degeneration: A European Disorder, c. 1848–c. 1918* (Cambridge, 1989), pp. 11–27.

40. Mosse, *Toward the Final Solution*, pp. 54–55.

41. Barkan, *Retreat of Scientific Racism*, pp. 17–18; Biddiss, introduction to *Images of Race*, pp. 18–20.

42. R. Hyam, *Understanding the British Empire* (Cambridge, 2010), pp. 25–26, 161–68; Brion Davis, *Inhuman Bondage*, p. 239; L. Colley, *Britons: Forging the Nation, 1707–1837* (2nd. ed., London, 2005), pp. 354–55.

43. Brion Davis, *Inhuman Bondage*, pp. 252–53; Foner, *American Freedom*, p. 88.

44. Brion Davis, *Inhuman Bondage*, pp. 238–39.

45. Foner, *American Freedom*, pp. 89, 98, 105–7.

46. M. Lake and H. Reynolds, *Drawing the Global Colour Line: White Men's Countries and the International Challenge of Racial Equality* (Cambridge, 2008), pp. 50–53, 59–60, 89–90; T. Koditschek, *Liberalism, Imperialism, and the Historical Imagination: Nineteenth-Century Visions of a Greater Britain* (Cambridge, 2011), pp. 240–50.

47. Lake and Reynolds, *Global Colour Line*, pp. 11, 72–74, 95–113; J. Bryce, *The Relations of the Advanced and the Backward Races of Mankind* (Oxford, 1902), passim; D. Bell, *The Idea of Greater Britain: Empire and the Future of World Order, 1860–1900* (Princeton, 2007), pp. 7–9; J. Darwin, *The Empire Project: The Rise and Fall of the British World-System, 1830–1970* (Cambridge, 2009), p. 147; P. Ziegler, *Legacy: Cecil Rhodes, The Rhodes Trust and Rhodes Scholarships* (London, 2008), pp. 13–14.

48. D. Gilmour, *The Long Recessional: The Imperial Life of Rudyard Kipling* (London, 2002), pp. 126–32; Fredrickson, *Racism*, pp. 107–8.

49. Foner, *American Freedom*, p. 186; Lake and Reynolds, *Global Colour Line*, pp. 95–113; T. G. Dyer, *Theodore Roosevelt and the Idea of Race* (Baton Rouge, 1980), pp. 16–19, 70–80, 100–109.

50. Painter, *White People*, pp. 201–56, 289–308; Foner, *American Freedom*, p. 187; J. Stein, "Defining the Race, 1890–1930," in W. Sollors, ed., *The Invention of Ethnicity* (New York, 1989), pp. 70–80.

51. Mosse, *Toward the Final Solution*, pp. 99–101, 120, 148–9, 165–66; Fredrickson, *Racism*, pp. 72–78.

52. Mosse, *Toward the Final Solution*, pp. 105–10; Hannaford, *Race*, pp. 348–56; Painter, *White People*, pp. 311–16; Fredrickson, *Racism*, pp. 89–91.

53. B. Perkins, *The Grand Rapprochement: England and the United States, 1895–1914* (New York, 1968); S. Anderson, *Race and Rapprochement:*

Anglo-Saxonism and Anglo-American Relations, 1895–1904 (Madison, N.J., 1981); P. A. Kramer, "Empires, Exceptions, and Anglo-Saxons: Race and Rule Between the British and United States Empires," *Journal of American History* 88 (2002): 1315–53; P. Clarke, "The English-Speaking Peoples Before Churchill," *Britain and the World* 4 (2011): 199–231.

54. Ziegler, *Legacy*, pp. 8, 13, 17.

55. J. P. Greene, "Introduction: Empire and Liberty," in Greene, ed., *Exclusionary Empire: English Liberty Overseas, 1600–1900* (Cambridge, 2010), p. 24.

56. Fredrickson, *Racism*, pp. 9–10.

57. Hyam, *Understanding the British Empire*, p. 30.

58. Ibid., p. 223.

59. G. M. Fredrickson, *White Supremacy: A Comparative Study in American and South African History* (Oxford, 1981), pp. 239–44; Lake and Reynolds, *Global Colour Line*, pp. 155, 222–37; Hyam, *Understanding the British Empire*, pp. 351, 359 n. 24; C. Saunders, "The Expansion of British Liberties: The South African Case," in Greene, *Exclusionary Empire*, p. 285.

60. Lake and Reynolds, *Global Colour Line*, pp. 30–45; Darwin, *Empire Project*, pp. 162–64, 167.

61. Lake and Reynolds, *Global Colour Line*, pp. 137–65, 178–79, 315; J. Stenhouse and B. Moloughney, " 'Drug-Besotted Sin-Begotten Sons of Filth'; New Zealanders and the Oriental Other," *New Zealand Journal of History* 33 (1999): 43–64.

62. Lake and Reynolds, *Global Colour Line*, pp. 139–40.

63. Ibid., pp. 114–19; M. K. Gandhi, *An Autobiography* (London, 2001 ed.), pp. 114, 160.

64. Fredrickson, *Racism*, pp. 102, 112–13; H. Bley, *South-West Africa Under German Rule, 1894–1914* (Evanston, Ill., 1971), pp. 163–64, 207, 212–13.

65. Foner, *American Freedom*, pp. 131–33; C. Vann Woodward, *Origins of the New South, 1877–1913* (Baton Rouge, 1951); Woodward, *The Strange Career of Jim Crow* (New York, 3rd ed., 1974); M. Perman, *Struggle for Mastery: Disenfranchisement in the South, 1888–1908* (Chapel Hill, N.C., 2001).

66. Fredrickson, *Racism*, pp. 82–83.

67. J. Williamson, *The Crucible of Race: Black-White Relations in the American South Since Emancipation* (New York, 1984), pp. 111–223; L. F. Litwack, *Trouble in Mind: Black Southerners in the Age of Jim Crow* (New York, 1998), pp. 117–18, 185.

68. Fredrickson, *Racism*, p. 82, 110–11; Foner, *American Freedom*, p. 131.

69. Lake and Reynolds, *Global Colour Line*, pp. 129–31; Foner, *American Freedom*, pp. 131, 189; Painter, *White People*, pp. 209–11, 234, 238, 322–23.

70. S. C. Miller, *"Benevolent Assimilation": The American Conquest of the Philippines, 1899–1903* (New Haven, 1982), p. 188; Hyam, *Understanding the British Empire*, p. 127; Lake and Reynolds, *Global Colour Line*, pp. 106–13; Foner, *American Freedom*, pp. 131–32, 137, 188–89.

71. Fredrickson, *Racism*, pp. 77–88; P. Pulzer, *The Rise of Political Anti-Semitism in Germany and Austria* (Cambridge, Mass., 1988), pp. 83–119.

72. R. Overy, *The Dictators: Hitler's Germany and Stalin's Russia* (London, 2004), p. 549.

73. Mosse, *Toward the Final Solution*, pp. 99–100, 110–11, 204–5; M. Burleigh and W. Wippermann, *The Racial State: Germany, 1933–1945* (Cambridge, 1991), pp. 23–43; R. J. Evans, *The Coming of the Third Reich* (New York, 2005), pp. 450–51.

74. Overy, *The Dictators*, p. 552.

75. Ibid., pp. 570–71.

76. Burleigh and Wippermann, *Racial State*, p. 49.

77. R. J. Evans, *The Third Reich at War* (New York, 2009), pp. 28–29.

78. Fredrickson, *Racism*, pp. 118–22.

79. Overy, *The Dictators*, pp. 583–84; R. J. Evans, *The Third Reich in Power* (New York, 2006), pp. 506–79.

80. Burleigh and Wippermann, *Racial State*, p. 102; Overy, *The Dictators*, pp. 552–53; Evans, *Third Reich at War*, pp. 216–318.

81. Lake and Reynolds, *Global Colour Line*, pp. 327–30; Fredrickson, *Racism*, pp. 116–17.

82. Fredrickson, *Racism*, p. 133.

83. Lake and Reynolds, *Global Colour Line*, p. 354; Fredrickson, *Racism*, p. 124.

84. W. H. Vatcher, *White Laager: The Rise of Afrikaner Nationalism* (New York, 1965), p. 160.

85. Fredrickson, *Racism*, pp. 135–36; G. M. Carter, *The Politics of Inequality: South Africa Since 1948* (London, 1958), p. 370; T. D. Moodie, *The Rise of Afrikanerdom: Power, Apartheid and the Afrikaner Civil Religion* (Berkeley, 1975), p. 265.

86. For differing views on Smuts and race see Hyam, *Understanding the British Empire*, pp. 342–60; S. Marks, "White Masculinity: Smuts, Race and the South African War," *Proceedings of the British Academy* 111 (2001): 199–223; N. Garson, "Smuts and the Idea of Race," *South African Historical Journal* 57 (2007): 153–78; S. Dubow, "Smuts, the United Nations, and the Rhetoric of Race and Rights," *Journal of Contemporary History* 43 (2008): 45–73.

87. Hyam, *Understanding the British Empire*, pp. 353–55.

88. Darwin, *Empire Project*, pp. 147, 177; Ziegler, *Legacy*, pp. 88–90; Painter, *White People*, p. 317.
89. D. Cannadine, *Ornamentalism: How the British Saw Their Empire* (London, 2001).
90. M. Adas, *Machines as the Measure of Men: Science, Technology, and Ideologies of Western Dominance* (Ithaca, N.Y., 1989), pp. 199–210, 271–75; Darwin, *Empire Project*, p. 168; Hyam, *Understanding the British Empire*, pp. 31, 222–29; Lake and Reynolds, *Global Colour Line*, pp. 123–24, 131.
91. Darwin, *Empire Project*, p. 178.
92. M. Vaughan, "Liminal," *London Review of Books*, March 23, 2006, pp. 15–16, taking issue with A. Memmi, *The Coloniser and the Colonised* (London, 2003).
93. Fredrickson, *Racism*, pp. 108–9; Mosse, *Toward the Final Solution*, pp. 51–57; Bolt, *Victorian Attitudes to Race*, p. 22; M. Banton, *Racial Theories* (2nd ed., Cambridge, 1998), pp. 73–74; M. D. Biddiss, *Father of Racist Ideology: The Social and Political Thought of Count Gobineau* (London, 1970), pp. 253–54.
94. Foner, *American Freedom*, pp. 173–74; Fredrickson, *Racism*, pp. 102–3, 116.
95. Foner, *American Freedom*, pp. 78–79.
96. Overy, *The Dictators*, p. 547.
97. G. H. Herb, *Under the Map of Germany: Nationalism and Propaganda, 1918–1945* (London, 1997), pp. 136–39.
98. Mosse, *Toward the Final Solution*, pp. 91–93; Fredrickson, *Racism*, pp. 124–25.
99. S. Harries, *Nikolaus Pevsner: The Life* (London, 2011), pp. 38–40, 47, 125.
100. Overy, *The Dictators*, p. 573; Herb, *Under the Map of Germany*, pp. 132–40.
101. Mosse, *Toward the Final Solution*, pp. 141–42; Overy, *The Dictators*, pp. 576–78; Evans, *Third Reich in Power*, p. 545.
102. Fredrickson, *Racism*, pp. 132, 136–37.
103. Hyam, *Understanding the British Empire*, pp. 353–54.
104. Kidd, *Forging of Races*, p. 275.
105. Painter, *White People*, pp. 228–32, 237–38.
106. Fredrickson, *Racism*, pp. 158–63.
107. Stepan, *Idea of Race*, pp. 140–69; Barkan, *Retreat of Scientific Racism*, pp. 279–340.
108. Lake and Reynolds, *Global Colour Line*, p. 350; Painter, *White People*, p. 329; emphasis in original.
109. Hannaford, *Race*, pp. 371–72, 374–76; Barkan, *Retreat of Scientific Racism*, pp. 76–95; Fredrickson, *Racism*, pp. 163–64; J. Barzun, *Race: A Study in Superstition*, rev. ed. (New York, 1965), pp. 15–16.

110. A. Montagu, *Race, Science and Humanity* (Princeton, 1963 ed.), pp. 1–2, 8.

111. Foner, *American Freedom*, p. 135; J. White, *Black Leadership in America: From Booker T. Washington to Jesse Jackson* (2nd ed., London, 1990), pp. 29–30.

112. R. J. Terchek, "Conflict and Nonviolence," in J. M. Brown and A. Parel, eds., *The Cambridge Companion to Gandhi* (Cambridge, 2011), p. 118; J. M. Brown, introduction to M. Gandhi, *The Essential Writings* (Oxford, 2008), pp. xxvii–xxviii.

113. J. M. Brown, "Gandhi and Human Rights: In Search of True Humanity," in A. J. Parel, ed., *Gandhi, Freedom and Self-Rule* (Lanham, Md., 2000), pp. 87–94.

114. Lake and Reynolds, *Global Colour Line*, pp. 1–2, 75–94.

115. Darwin, *After Tamerlane*, p. 349.

116. White, *Black Leadership*, pp. 51–65; J. Parker and R. Rathbone, *African History: A Very Short Introduction* (Oxford, 2007), p. 36.

117. Kidd, *Forging of Races*, pp. 256–57; Foner, *American Freedom*, pp. 174–75; White, *Black Leadership*, pp. 79, 84.

118. Lake and Reynolds, *Global Colour Line*, pp. 9–10, 104, 145–49, 155, 168–78.

119. Ibid., pp. 273–78.

120. Ibid., pp. 11, 284–305, 320–24, 339–40.

121. M. D. Biddiss, "The Universal Races Congress of 1911," *Race* 13 (1971): 37–46; R. J. Holton, "Cosmopolitanism or Cosmopolitanisms? The Universal Races Congress of 1911," *Global Networks* 2 (2002): 153–70; Lake and Reynolds, *Global Colour Line*, pp. 251–62.

122. White, *Black Leadership*, pp. 38–42.

123. J. W. Dower, *War Without Mercy: Race and Power in the Pacific War* (New York, 1986), pp. 3–14; Foner, *American Freedom*, p. 223; Painter, *White People*, pp. 332–42.

124. Barkan, *Retreat of Scientific Racism*, pp. 279–85; Foner, *American Freedom*, p. 239; Fredrickson, *Racism*, pp. 165–67.

125. A. Sampson, *Mandela: The Authorised Biography* (London, 1999), p. 39.

126. Foner, *American Freedom*, pp. 240–42; C. Thorne, "Racial Aspects of the Far Eastern War of 1941–1945," *Proceedings of the British Academy* 66 (1980): 360–77.

127. Lake and Reynolds, *Global Colour Line*, p. 351; Barkan, *Retreat of Scientific Racism*, pp. 341–42; K. Malik, *Man, Beast and Zombie: What Science Can and Cannot Tell Us About Human Nature* (London, 2000), pp. 16, 134–35.

128. Hannaford, *Race*, pp. 385–86; UNESCO, *Conference for the Establishment of the United Nations Educational, Scientific and Cultural Organization* (Paris, 1945), p. 93; L. Kuper, ed., *Race, Science and Society*

(London, 1975), pp. 343–53; M. Brittain, "Race, Racism and Antiracism: UNESCO and the Politics of Presenting Science to the Postwar Public," *American Historical Review* 112 (2007): 1386–1413.

129. Foner, *American Freedom*, pp. 280–82.

130. Sampson, *Mandela*, pp. 402,

131. D. Reynolds, *One World Divisible: A Global History Since 1945* (New York, 2000), p. 201.

132. White, *Black Leadership*, pp. 150–66; Kidd, *Forging of Races*, pp. 268–70; Foner, *American Freedom*, pp. 283–84; Painter, *White People*, pp. 374–77; Sampson, *Mandela*, pp. 140–59; M. Marable, *Malcolm X: A Life of Reinvention* (New York, 2011), pp. 167–79, 198–203, 480–85.

133. Reynolds, *One World Divisible*, pp. 213–19, 598–608.

134. White, *Black Leadership*, p. 141; P. Stothard and N. Danziger, "What Condi Did First," *Times Magazine* (London), April 1, 2006, p. 19.

135. C. West, quoted in J. Rajchman, ed., *The Identity in Question* (New York, 1995), p. 15; R. McKnight, "Confessions of a Wannabe Negro," in G. Early, ed., *Lure and Loathing: Essays on Race, Identity, and the Ambivalence of Assimilation* (New York, 1993), p. 112; P. Alexander and R. Halpern, eds., *Racialising Class, Classifying Race: Labour and Difference in Britain, the USA and Africa* (Basingstoke, 2000).

136. For surveys of this literature see F. B. Livingstone, "On the Non-Existence of Human Races," *Current Anthropology* 3 (1962): 279–81; G. A. Harrison, "The Race Concept in Human Biology," *Journal of Biosocial Science*, supplement no. 1 (1969): 129–42.

137. Foner, *American Freedom*, p. 279; A. E. Meier, E. Rudwick, and F. L. Broderick, eds., *Black Protest Thought in the Twentieth Century* (2nd ed., New York, 1971), pp. 49–50; D. Wells, ed., *We Have a Dream: African-American Visions of Freedom* (New York, 1993), pp. 168–72.

138. Sampson, *Mandela*, pp. 27, 47, 79, 193, 493, 520, 582–85; K. Asmal, D. Chichester, and W. James, eds., *Nelson Mandela: In His Own Words* (London, 2003), esp. pp. 313–59.

139. T. J. Sugrue, *Not Even Past: Barack Obama and the Burden of Race* (Princeton, 2010), p. 53.

140. W. J. Wilson, *The Declining Significance of Race: Blacks and Changing American Institutions* (Chicago, 1978); Wilson, "The Declining Significance of Race: Revisited and Revised," *Daedalus* (Spring 2011): 55–69; Sugrue, *Not Even Past*, pp. 73–80. See also D. J. Dickerson, *The End of Blackness* (New York, 2004), pp. 3–26.

141. For example, C. Coon, *The Origin of Races* (New York, 1963); J. R. Baker, *Race* (Oxford, 1974); R. Herrnstein and C. Murray, *The Bell Curve: The Reshaping of American Life by Difference in Intelligence* (New York, 1994); but see the devastating reviews by, respectively, A. Montagu, "What Is Remarkable About Varieties of Man Is Likenesses,

Not Differences," *Current Anthropology* 4 (1963): 361; J. B. Birdsell, *Annals of Human Biology* 2 (1975): 208–10; Gould, *Mismeasure of Man*, pp. 367–90.

142. Sugrue, *Not Even Past*, pp. 92–137; W. J. Wilson and R. P. Taub, *There Goes the Neighborhood: Racial, Ethnic and Class Tensions in Four Chicago Neighborhoods and Their Meaning for America* (New York, 2006), p. 161; B. Obama, *The Audacity of Hope: Thoughts on Reclaiming the American Dream* (New York, 2006), pp. 227–69; R. Kennedy, *The Persistence of the Color Line: Racial Politics and the Obama Presidency* (New York, 2011), p. 3.

143. Painter, *White People*, pp. 384–86.

144. Ibid., pp. 390–91, 395–96.

145. Malik, *Man, Beast and Zombie*, pp. 17–18.

146. Painter, *White People*, p. 392; S. J. Gould, "Honorable Men and Women," *Natural History* 97 (1988): 16–20; Gould, *Mismeasure of Man*, p. 399.

SIX: CIVILIZATION

1. D. Hartley, *Observations on Man, His Frame, His Duty and His Expectations, Part the Second* (London, 1749), p. 355.

2. R. Williams, *Keywords* (London, 1976), p. 48; emphasis in Boswell's original.

3. L. Wolff, *Inventing Eastern Europe: The Map of Civilization on the Mind of the Enlightenment* (Stanford, 1994), pp. 12–13; L. Febvre, "Civilisation: Evolution of a Word and a Group of Ideas," in P. Burke, ed., *A New Kind of History: From the Writings of Febvre* (New York, 1973), pp. 219–57; F. Braudel, *On History* (Chicago, 1980), p. 180.

4. B. Bowden, "The Ideal of Civilisation: Its Origins and Socio-Political Character," *Critical Review of International and Political Philosophy* 7 (2004): 28–34, 36–41; N. Elias, *The Civilising Process* (Oxford, 2000 ed.), pp. 10, 24–27.

5. T. Todorov, *The Fear of Barbarians: Beyond the Clash of Civilizations* (Chicago, 2010), pp. 14–28.

6. W. R. Jones, "The Image of the Barbarian in Medieval Europe," *Comparative Studies in Society and History* 13 (1971): 376–407; A. Pagden, *The Fall of Natural Man: The American Indian and the Origins of Comparative Ethnology* (Cambridge, 1986 ed.), pp. 15–26; Pagden, *Worlds at War: The 2,500-Year Struggle Between East and West* (Oxford, 2008), pp. 32–34, 61–62.

7. Wolff, *Inventing Eastern Europe*, pp. 4–5.

8. M. de Montaigne, *Essays* (Harmondsworth, 1991 ed.), pp. 231,

1114–15; C. Geertz, *Available Light: Anthropological Reflections on Philosophical Topics* (Princeton, 2000), p. 45.

9. F. Furet, "Civilization and Barbarism in Gibbon's *History*," in G. W. Bowersock, J. Clive, and S. R. Grubard, eds., *Edward Gibbon and the Decline and Fall of the Roman Empire* (Cambridge, Mass., 1977), pp. 159–66; J. W. Burrow, *Gibbon* (Oxford, 1985), pp. 39–40, 80, 84.

10. J. G. A. Pocock, *Barbarism and Religion*, vol. 4, *Barbarians, Savages and Empires* (Cambridge, 2005), pp. 2, 158–61; R. Porter, *Gibbon* (London, 1988), p. 5.

11. Burrow, *Gibbon*, pp. 39–40, 67–69, 81; Porter, *Gibbon*, pp. 136, 138–40.

12. Porter, *Gibbon*, pp. 143–45.

13. Burrow, *Gibbon*, pp. 42–51, 86–87.

14. Porter, *Gibbon*, p. 81; Pocock, *Barbarians, Savages and Empires*, p. 92.

15. Porter, *Gibbon*, pp. 145, 152–53.

16. S. Runciman, "Gibbon and Byzantium," in Bowersock et al., *Gibbon and the Decline and Fall of the Roman Empire*, pp. 53–60.

17. Burrow, *Gibbon*, p. 76; Pocock, *Barbarians, Savages and Empires*, pp. 11–22, 96, 133.

18. Wolff, *Inventing Eastern Europe*, pp. 13, 357.

19. For brief recent accounts, see J. Spence, *The Chan's Great Continent: China in Western Minds* (London, 1998), pp. 56–61; K. Teltscher, *The High Road to China: George Bogle, the Panchen Lama, and the First British Expedition to Tibet* (New York, 2006), pp. 247–50; J. Lovell, *The Great Wall: China Against the World, 1000 BC–AD 2000* (London, 2006), pp. 2–12; H. G. Gelber, *The Dragon and the Foreign Devils: China and the World, 1100 BC to the Present* (London, 2007), pp. 160–65. For earlier, anniversary accounts, see A. Singer, *The Lion and the Dragon: The Story of the First British Embassy to the Court of the Emperor Qianlong in Peking, 1792–1794* (London, 1992); A. Peyrefitte, *The Collision of Two Civilisations: The British Expedition to China, 1792–94* (London, 1993, trans. J. Rothschild). The Chinese word "yi," often translated as the pejorative "barbarian," is thought by some scholars, in certain circumstances, to be more inclusive than confrontational, and that it should be translated descriptively and nonpejoratively as "the foreign peoples," or "outsiders," or "strangers": see J. L. Hevia, *Cherishing Men from Afar: Quuing Guest Ritual and the Macartney Embassy of 1793* (Durham, N.C., 1995), pp. 120–21. I am grateful to Professor Susan Naquin for this reference.

20. J. S. Mill, *Essays on Politics and Culture* (London, 1962 ed.), pp. 51–52; Bowden, "Ideal of Civilisation," p. 34; P. Mandler, *History and National Life* (London, 2002), p. 42.

21. J. P. Parry, *The Politics of Patriotism: English Liberalism, National Identity, and Europe, 1830–1886* (Cambridge, 2006), pp. 20–22, 187, 248;

J. Osterhammel, *Europe, the "West" and the Civilizing Mission* (London, 2006).

22. N. Elias, *Über den Prozess der Zivilisation*, 2 vols. (Basel, 1939).

23. J. G. Herder, *Outlines of a Philosophy of History* (London, 1800), p. 421.

24. T. Newark, introduction to T. Hodgkin, *Huns, Vandals and the Fall of the Roman Empire* (London, 1996 ed.), pp. xxii–xxiv; T. S. Brown, "Gibbon, Hodgkin and the Invaders of Italy," in R. McKitterick and R. Quinault, eds., *Edward Gibbon and Empire* (Cambridge, 1997), pp. 148–54.

25. Braudel, *On History*, pp. 181–82; Bowden, "Ideal of Civilisation," pp. 39–40.

26. Bowden, "Ideal of Civilisation," pp. 40–41.

27. P. Fussell, *The Great War and Modern Memory* (Oxford, 1975), pp. 75, 79, 82.

28. A. J. Toynbee, *The Western Question in Greece and Turkey: A Study in the Contact of Civilisations* (London, 1922), p. 328; Wolff, *Inventing Eastern Europe*, p. 366. For Spanish versions of these characterizations of the Central and Entente powers during the First World War, see R. Carr, *Modern Spain, 1875–1980* (Oxford, 1980), pp. 81–82.

29. Bowden, "Ideal of Civilisation," p. 40; A. Kuper, *Culture: The Anthropologists' Account* (Cambridge, Mass., 1999), p. 8; W. A. Kaufmann, *Nietzsche: Philosopher, Psychologist, Antichrist* (Princeton, 1950), pp. 87, 316–17, 339, 362.

30. C. Bell, *Civilization: An Essay* (New York, 1928), pp. 3, 15, 17.

31. R. Quinault, "Winston Churchill and Gibbon," in McKitterick and Quinault, *Edward Gibbon and Empire*, pp. 317–32; W. Churchill, "Civilisation," in R. S. Churchill, ed., *Into Battle: Speeches by the Rt. Hon. Winston S. Churchill CH, MP* (London 1941), pp. 35–36.

32. R. A. Butler, *The Art of the Possible* (London, 1971), p. 85.

33. Quoted in F. Fernández-Armesto, *Civilizations: Culture, Ambition, and the Transformation of Nature* (New York, 2001), p. 20.

34. Newark, introduction to *Huns, Vandals*, p. xxiv; H. Rauschning, *Hitler Speaks* (London, 1939), p. 87.

35. Wolff, *Inventing Eastern Europe*, pp. 369–70.

36. A. Piganiol, *L'Empire chrétien (325–395)* (Paris, 1947), p. 422; P. Courcelle, *Histoire littéraire des grandes invasions germaniques* (Paris, 1948), passim. Nor were such views confined to French scholars, for British historians writing in the aftermath of the Second World War also saw the fall of the Roman Empire through the lens of their perceptions of 1939–45. In 1952, J. M. Wallace-Hadrill, who had interrogated high-ranking German prisoners, published a book entitled *The Barbarian West, 400–1000*, which began with a chapter sketching out the "civilization" that was "threatened" by the "barbarians." Having

surveyed the secure achievements of the Roman Empire, the author ended, apocalyptically (and autobiographically), "upon such a world, the Huns fell": J. M. Wallace-Hadrill, *The Barbarian West, 400–1000* (3rd ed., London, 1967), pp. 9, 20.

37. S. Freud, *Civilization and Its Discontents* (New York, 1961 ed.), pp. 66–71; Todorov, *Fear of Barbarians*, pp. 24–25. Another proponent of this view was the historian George Macaulay Trevelyan, who, like his near contemporary Winston Churchill, had also read Gibbon as a young man. But his conclusion at the end of the Second World War was more somber, for while he rejoiced in the eventual Allied victory, he was convinced that the long and devastating war had "cooked the goose of civilization" and that humanity was now living in "an age steadily lapsing and finally rushing into barbarism." See D. Cannadine, *G. M. Trevelyan: A Life in History* (London, 1992), pp. 168, 175.

38. E. J. Hobsbawm, "Barbarism: A User's Guide," *New Left Review* 206 (1994): 45, 49.

39. W. Benjamin, *Illuminations* (London, 1970 ed.), p. 258; B. Wasserstein, *Barbarism and Civilization: A History of Europe in Our Time* (Oxford, 2007), pp. 1, 793.

40. Here is one recent example, its title full of sub-Gibbonian vocabulary: B.-H. Lévy, *Life in Dark Times: A Stand Against the New Barbarism* (New York, 2008). In fact, Lévy was criticizing the anti-Americanism that he believed characterizes much of the contemporary European left, and it was to this group that he gave the title "new barbarians." See also M. B. Salter, *Barbarians and Civilization in International Relations* (London, 2002).

41. W. Goffart, *Barbarians and Romans, AD 48–54: The Techniques of Accommodation* (Princeton, 1980), esp. pp. 3–39; Goffart, "Rome, Constantinople and the Barbarians," *American Historical Review* 86 (1981): pp. 275–306; Goffart, "The Theme of 'the Barbarian Invasions,'" in E. Chrysos and A. Schwartz, eds., *Das Reich und die Barbaren* (Veroffentlichungen des Instituts fur österreichische Geschichtsforschung, 29; Vienna, 1989), pp. 87–107; both reprinted in Goffart, *Rome's Fall and After* (London, 1989).

42. P. Brown, *The World of Late Antiquity, AD 150–750* (London, 1971), pp. 122–23; H. Wolfram, *History of the Goths* (Berkeley, 1988), esp. pp. 158–59; P. Amory, *People and Identity in Ostrogothic Italy, 489–554* (Cambridge, 1997), pp. xi, 1–6, 13–14; J. M. H. Smith, "Did Women Have a Transformation of the Roman World?" *Gender and History* 12 (2000): 553–54; Smith, *Europe After Rome: A New Cultural History, 500–1000* (Oxford, 2005), pp. 7–9, 253–67; P. S. Wells, *Barbarians to Angels: The Dark Ages Reconsidered* (New York, 2008), pp. xi–xv.

43. B. Ward-Perkins, *The Fall of Rome and the End of Civilization* (Oxford,

2005); P. Heather, "The Huns and the End of the Roman Empire in Western Europe," *English Historical Review* 110 (1995): 4–41; Heather, *The Fall of the Roman Empire* (London, 2005).

44. Ward-Perkins, *Fall of Rome*, p. 181; P. Brown, G. Bowersock, and A. Cameron, "The World of Late Antiquity Revisited," *Symbolae osloenses* 72 (1997): 5–90; G. Bowersock, "The Vanishing Paradigm of the Fall of Rome," in Bowersock, *Selected Papers on Late Antiquity* (Bari, 2000), pp. 187–97. For recent attempts to synthesize these opposing views, see G. Halsall, *Barbarian Migrations and the Roman West, 376–568* (Cambridge, 2007), esp. pp. 19–22; C. Wickham, *After Rome* (London, 2009), ch. 4. For a broader view of these recent disagreements, see N. Etherington, "Barbarians Ancient and Modern," *American Historical Review* 116 (2011): 31–57.

45. E. Durkheim and M. Mauss, "Note on the Notion of Civilization," *Social Research* 38 (1971), p. 812; the article was originally published in *L'Année sociologique* 12 (1913): 46–50.

46. Fernández-Armesto, *Civilizations*, p. 18. For some of the interwar writing on civilization, see E. Huntington, *Civilization and Climate* (New Haven, 1922); A. Schweitzer, *The Decay and Restoration of Civilization* (London, 1932); V. G. Childe, *Man Makes Himself* (London, 1936).

47. F. J. Teggart, *The Processes of History* (New Haven, 1918), pp. 4, 6.

48. Ibid., pp. 13–14, 37, 112, 119, 151; W. H. McNeill, *Arnold J. Toynbee: A Life* (Oxford, 1989), pp. 100–101.

49. H. Stuart Hughes, *Oswald Spengler: A Critical Estimate*, rev. ed. (New York, 1962), pp. 36–64.

50. O. Spengler, *The Decline of the West*, 2 vols. (London, 1934), vol. 1, p. 107; Hughes, *Spengler*, p. 11.

51. Spengler, *Decline of the West*, vol. 1, pp. 31, 106, 355; Hughes, *Spengler*, p. 72; Braudel, *On History*, pp. 182, 188; Fernández-Armesto, *Civilizations*, p. 18.

52. Spengler, *Decline of the West*, vol. 1, Tables i–iii. In vol. 2, Spengler added three more culture-civilizations: the Babylonian, the Mexican, and the Russian.

53. Ibid., vol. 1, pp. 32, 36.

54. Ibid., vol. 1, p. 151.

55. Ibid., vol. 1, pp. 38–39, 167; Hughes, *Spengler*, p. 7.

56. Ibid., vol. 2, pp. 159–73.

57. Ibid., vol. 2, pp. 55–83, 171.

58. Ibid., vol. 2, pp. 38–42, 162–63, 332; McNeill, *Toynbee*, p. 101.

59. For one cogent contemporary critique of Spengler, see R. G. Collingwood, "Oswald Spengler and the Theory of Historical Cycles," *Antiquity* 1 (1927): 311–25, 435–46; for a contemporary popularization, see

E. H. Goddard and P. A. Gibbons, *Civilisation or Civilisations: An Essay in the Spenglerian Philosophy of History* (London, 1926).

60. McNeill, *Toynbee*, pp. 98–109.

61. Toynbee, *Western Question*, pp. 22, 36, 362–63.

62. Ibid., p. 334; A. J. Toynbee, *A Study of History*, 2 vol. abridgment by D. C. Somervell (London, 1947–57), vol. 1, p. 35; McNeill, *Toynbee*, pp. 102, 110; A. J. Toynbee, *Civilization on Trial* (Oxford, 1948), pp. 9–10.

63. Toynbee, *Western Question*, pp. 12, 327–46.

64. McNeill, *Toynbee*, pp. 99–100, 110–12.

65. For Toynbee's criticism of Spengler on this score, see Toynbee, *Study of History*, vol. 1, pp. 210–11, 248–51.

66. Ibid., vol. 1, pp. 275–76.

67. A. J. Toynbee, *Experiences* (New York, 1969), pp. 10, 200–203. For Toynbee's disagreements with Gibbon, see W. H. Walsh, "The End of a Great Work," in A. Montagu, ed., *Toynbee and History: Critical Essays and Reviews* (Boston, 1956), pp. 125–26.

68. Toynbee explicitly criticizes Gibbon along these lines in *Study of History*, vol. 1, pp. 260–62; vol. 2, pp. 19, 77–79; Toynbee, *Civilization on Trial*, pp. 226–31. For "vultures" (and "maggots"), see Toynbee, *Study of History*, vol. 1, p. 14. See also McNeill, *Toynbee*, p. 177; Editorial, "Vicisti, Galilaee," *Times Literary Supplement*, August 19, 1939, p. 491.

69. McNeill, *Toynbee*, pp. 164–65, 254–61. For contemporary anthologies of criticisms of Toynbee, see P. Geyl, A. J. Toynbee, and P. A. Sorokin, *The Pattern of the Past: Can We Determine It?* (Boston, 1949); Montagu, *Toynbee and History*; E. T. Gargan, ed., *The Intent of Toynbee's History* (Chicago, 1961). For other critiques, see also Braudel, *On History*, pp. 189–97; R. Davenport-Hines, ed., *Letters from Oxford: Hugh Trevor-Roper to Bernard Berenson* (London, 2006), pp. 234–37, 243.

70. Toynbee, *Civilization on Trial*, p. 55.

71. McNeill, *Toynbee*, p. 166; W. Kaufmann, "Toynbee and Super-History," in Montagu, *Toynbee and History*, pp. 306–10.

72. Toynbee, *Study of History*, vol. 2, pp. 87–93, 109–13; Toynbee, *Civilization on Trial*, pp. 213–52. See also E. Voegelin, "Toynbee's *History* as a Search for Truth," in Gargan, *Intent of Toynbee's History*, pp. 183–98; P. Geyl, "Toynbee as Prophet," in Montagu, *Toynbee and History*, pp. 360–77.

73. Toynbee, *Study of History*, vol. 1, pp. 551–54; Toynbee, *Civilization on Trial*, p. 41.

74. McNeill, *Toynbee*, pp. 205–61.

75. D. A. Segal, " 'Western Civ' and the Staging of History in American Higher Education," *American Historical Review* 105 (2000): 779–83,

785–88; G. Allardyce, "The Rise and Fall of the Western Civilization Course," *American Historical Review* 87 (1982): 695–96, 703–16.

76. McNeill, *Toynbee*, pp. 213–19.

77. Ibid., pp. 94, 161, 213; Toynbee, *Experiences*, pp. 233–39, 261–67.

78. Toynbee, *Study of History*, vol. 2, pp. 302–31; Toynbee, *Civilization on Trial*, p. 56. Pieter Geyl regarded the final volumes of *A Study of History* as "a blasphemy against Western Civilization" because Toynbee "will have it that Western Civilization is doomed, and indeed why should he care? Western Civilization means nothing to him." See Geyl, "Toynbee as Prophet," pp. 363–64, 377.

79. See, for example, P. Bagby, *Culture and History: Prolegomena to the Comparative Study of Civilizations* (London, 1958); C. Quigley, *The Evolution of Civilizations: An Introduction to Historical Analysis* (New York, 1961); M. Melko, *The Nature of Civilizations* (Boston, 1969); C. H. Brough, *The Cycle of Civilization: A Scientific, Determinist Analysis of Civilization, Its Social Basis, Patterns and Projected Future* (Detroit, 1965).

80. B. Mathews, *Young Islam on Trek: A Study in the Clash of Civilizations* (New York, 1926), pp. 41, 196, 216–18; R. W. Bulliet, *The Case for Islamo-Christian Civilization* (New York, 2004), pp. 1–4.

81. B. Lewis, "The Roots of Muslim Rage," *Atlantic Monthly*, September 1990, pp. 56, 60. Lewis had first used the phrase much earlier, in 1957; see R. Bonney, *False Prophets: The "Clash of Civilizations" and the Global War on Terror* (Oxford, 2008), p. 54.

82. S. Huntington, "The Clash of Civilizations?" *Foreign Affairs* 72 (1993): 22–49; Huntington, *The Clash of Civilizations and the Remaking of World Order* (London, 1997).

83. Huntington, *Clash of Civilizations*, pp. 12–13, 40.

84. Ibid., pp. 21, 26–27, 29, 44–47.

85. Ibid., pp. 55, 47.

86. Ibid., pp. 13, 321.

87. Ibid., pp. 71–72, 301–11.

88. Ibid., pp. 20–21, 34, 183.

89. Ibid., p. 312.

90. A. Sen, *The Argumentative Indian: Writings on Indian History, Culture and Identity* (London, 2005), pp. 136–37.

91. Huntington, *Clash of Civilizations*, p. 29.

92. Ibid., pp. 46–47, 56; Fernández-Armesto, *Civilizations*, p. 23.

93. Huntington, *Clash of Civilizations*, p. 135.

94. Ibid., pp. 137–38.

95. Sen, *Argumentative Indian*, pp. 54, 302, 308. Sen himself always takes (wholly justified) exception to being categorized as a "Hindu economist."

96. Sen, *Argumentative Indian*, pp. 76, 284–87.

97. F. Halliday, *Islam and the Myth of Confrontation: Religion and Politics in the Middle East* (London, 2003 ed.), p. xii.

98. Sen, *Argumentative Indian*, pp. 55–56. For a fuller discussion of these matters by the same author, see A. Sen, *Identity and Violence: The Illusion of Destiny* (New York, 2006), esp. pp. 1–17, 40–58.

99. Huntington, *Clash of Civilizations*, pp. 43, 66–67; D. W. Wengrow, *What Makes Civilization? The Ancient Near East and the Future of the West* (Oxford, 2010), pp. xvii–xviii, 12–13.

100. W. H. McNeill, "Decline of the West?" *New York Review of Books*, January 9, 1997, pp. 18–22; K. A. Appiah, *Cosmopolitanism: Ethics in a World of Strangers* (New York, 2006).

101. For useful surveys of the responses to Huntington, and subsequent writings, see J. O'Hagan, "Beyond the Clash of Civilizations?" *Australian Journal of International Affairs* 59 (2005): 383–400; B. Bhutto, *Reconciliation: Islam, Democracy and the West* (London, 2008), pp. 233–73; Bonney, *False Prophets*, pp. 48–51; Todorov, *Fear of Barbarians*, pp. 86–99.

102. R. E. Rubenstein and J. Crocker, "Challenging Huntington," *Foreign Policy*, no. 96 (1994): 113–28; S. M. Walt, "Building Up New Bogeymen," *Foreign Policy*, no. 106 (1997): 176–89.

103. J. Fox, "Two Civilizations and Ethnic Conflict: Islam and the West," *Journal of Peace Research* 38 (2001): 459–72; R. Inglehart and P. Norris, "The True Clash of Civilizations," *Foreign Policy*, no. 135 (2003).

104. B. Russett, J. Oneal, and M. Cox, "Clash of Civilizations or Realism and Liberalism Déjà Vu? Some Evidence," *Journal of Peace Research* 37 (2000): 583–608; E. A. Henderson and R. Tucker, "Clear and Present Strangers: The Clash of Civilizations and International Conflict," *International Studies Quarterly* 45 (2001): 317–38; N. Ferguson, *Civilization: The West and the Rest* (London, 2011), pp. 313–14.

105. Huntington, *Clash of Civilizations*, p. 30. The role of the neocon intellectuals in promoting (and in some ways misrepresenting) the Huntington thesis is fully discussed in Bonney, *False Prophets*, chs. 3, 4, 6.

106. E. Abrahamian, "The US Media, Huntington, and September 11," *Third World Quarterly* 24 (2003): 529–44; Bonney, *False Prophets*, p. 40.

107. Bonney, *False Prophets*, chs. 7, 8; D. Reynolds, *America, Empire of Liberty: A New History* (London, 2009), pp. 558–61.

108. Bonney, *False Prophets*, pp. x, 2–3; Todorov, *Fear of Barbarians*, pp. 90–92.

109. Bonney, *False Prophets*, pp. 5–9; C. Hitchens, "What I've Learnt," *Times Magazine* (London), July 25, 2010, p. 6.

110. Sen, *Identity and Violence*, p. 68.

111. S. Halper and J. Clarke, *America Alone: The Neo-Conservatives and the Global Order* (Cambridge, 2004), esp. pp. 331–32.

112. R. Sanders, "Iraq: The Blair Mission," *Prospect*, February 2010, p. 25; P. Toynbee, "Forgotten Lessons," *Guardian*, March 28, 2003; P. Riddell, "Forget the Money, It's the Political Costs That Will Hurt," *Times* (London), March 27, 2003.

113. Bonney, *False Prophets*, p. 47.

114. D. Milliband, " 'War on Terror' Was Wrong," *Guardian*, January 15, 2009.

115. Editorial, "End of the Clash of Civilizations," *New York Times*, April 12, 2009; http://www.whitehouse.gov/the_press_office/Remarks-by -President-Obama-to-the-Turkish-Parliament-4-06-09.

116. http://www.whitehouse.gov/the_press_office/Remarks-by-the -President-at-Cairo-University-6-04-09. For another approach, see J. Sacks, *The Dignity of Difference: How to Avoid the Clash of Civilizations* (London, 2002).

117. J. S. Mill, *Essays on Politics and Culture* (London, 1962 ed.), pp. 51–52; Ferguson, *Civilization*, p. xxvii.

118. Bulliet, *Case for Islamo-Christian Civilization*, pp. 1–9.

119. Fernández-Armesto, *Civilizations*, pp. 25–26.

120. Bonney, *False Prophets*, pp. 224–29.

121. Sen, *Identity and Violence*, pp. 16–21; Bonney, *False Prophets*, pp. 229–31.

122. K. Clark, *Civilisation: A Personal View* (London, 1969), pp. xvii, 1–7.

123. A. Kuper, "Culture and Identity Politics," *British Academy Review* 9 (2006): 6; D. Senghaas, "A Clash of Civilizations—An Idée Fixe?" *Journal of Peace Studies* 35 (1998): 127–32. For a recent example of the continued appeal of the Manichean view of the world, see N. Cliff, *Holy War: How Vasco da Gama's Epic Voyages Turned the Tide in a Centuries-Old Clash of Civilizations* (London, 2011).

CONCLUSION

1. J. Black, "Contesting the Past," *History* 93 (2008): 227.

2. E. S. Morgan, *Inventing the People: The Rise of Popular Sovereignty in England and America* (New York, 1988), pp. 13–15.

3. A. Sen, *Identity and Violence: The Illusion of Destiny* (New York, 2006), pp. xii–xiii.

4. Matthew Arnold, "Dover Beach" in M. Arnold, *The Poems of Matthew Arnold, 1840–1867* (London, 1913), pp. 401–02; M. MacMillan, *Dangerous Games: The Uses and Abuses of History* (New York, 2009), p. 43.

5. For two contrasting views of the "fall" of apartheid, see H. Giliomee, "Surrender Without Defeat: Afrikaners and the South African 'Miracle,' " *Daedalus*, no. 126 (Spring 1997): 113–46; G. M. Fredrickson, "The Strange Death of Segregation," *New York Review of Books*, May 6, 1999, pp. 36–38.

6. R. Kipling, "We and They," in *Debits and Credits* (London, 1926), pp. 263–64.

7. W. Cantwell Smith, "Christianity's Third Great Challenge," *Christian Century*, April 27, 1960, pp. 505–08.

8. V. S. Naipaul, *India: A Million Mutinies Now* (London, 1998), p. 395.

9. For some recent and honorable exceptions, see S. Pinker, *The Better Angels of Our Nature: Why Violence Has Declined* (New York, 2011); S. Bowles and H. Gintis, *A Cooperative Species: Human Reciprocity and Its Evolution* (Princeton, 2011); M. Pagel, *Wired for Culture: The Natural History of Human Co-operation* (London, 2012); R. Sennett, *Together: The Rituals, Pleasures and Politics of Co-operation* (London, 2012). Significantly, none of these authors is an historian: Pinker is a psychologist, Bowles and Gintis are behavioral scientists, Pagel is an evolutionary biologist, and Sennett a sociologist.

10. T. Bender, *A Nation Among Nations: America's Place in World History* (New York, 2006), p. 301.

11. J. H. Plumb, *The Death of the Past* (London, 1969), p. 141.

12. W. G. Runciman, "Altruists at War," *London Review of Books*, February 23, 2012, p. 19; J. H. Elliott, "Rats or Cheese?," *New York Review of Books*, June 26, 1980, p. 39.

13. W. H. McNeill, "Mythistory, or Truth, Myth, History, and Historians," *American Historical Review* 91 (1986): 7.

14. U. Frevert, "European Identifications: What European History Can and Cannot Contribute," *European Studies Forum* (Spring 2008): 12–21.

INDEX

Aborigines, 159, 190
accommodationism, 205–6, 209–10,
    214, 253
Adam, 137, 138, 177, 178
Affair, The (Snow), 258
Afghanistan, 252
African National Congress (ANC), 197
Age of Revolution, The (Hobsbawm), 130
Agincourt, Battle of, 61
Akbar, Emperor, 49
Albania, 67, 80, 114
Alexander the Great, 235
Alfonso VI, King of Castile, 31
Alfred the Great, 59, 70
All Children Together, 51
Alliance of Civilizations, The, 256
Al Qaeda, 252
Also Sprach Zarathustra (Nietzsche), 138
America as a Civilization (Lerner), 240
American Association of Physical
    Anthropologists, 205
American Dilemma, An (Myrdal),
    210–11
Amores, Francisco de, 47
Anderson, Benedict, 57, 87
Anderson, Perry, 124, 129
Angelou, Maya, 6
Anglican Church, 41, 47, 72
Anglo-Saxon Chronicle, 59–60
Anglo-Saxons, 174, 176, 186–9, 193,
    198, 200–1, 206–7, 208, 227
Annaliste school, 55, 123
anti-Semitism, 175, 179, 188, 189,
    193–6, 198, 199, 201–2, 203, 204,
    210, 212, 261
apartheid, 4, 196–203, 210, 213, 215,
    216
"Appeal Against Female Suffrage, An"
    (Ward), 161

Appeal of One-Half of the Human Race
    (Thompson), 133–4
Arabs, 27–9, 30, 31–2, 35, 42, 50, 80,
    199, 214, 225, 252, 253
Arbroath, Declaration of (1320), 61
Are Men Necessary? (Dowd), 136
aristocracy, 69, 74–5, 98, 99, 100, 101,
    102, 103, 104, 119–21, 122, 126–7,
    156
Aristophanes, 158
Aristotle, 33, 123, 137, 143, 149, 153,
    177
Arnold, Matthew, 260
Aryan, The: His Social Role (Lapouge),
    188
Aryans, 184–5, 188, 189, 194–6, 200,
    210, 261
Ash, Timothy Garton, 7
Ashraf Pahlavi, Princess, 164
Ash's Dictionary, 220
Atlantic Charter (1941), 211
Attila the Hun, 225
Augsburg, Peace of (1555), 38, 46
Augustine, Saint, 177–8
Australia, 68, 69, 73, 88, 158, 159, 161,
    187, 188, 190, 191, 193, 208, 212
Austria, 64–5, 68, 72, 75, 79, 188, 195,
    201
Austro-Hungarian Empire, 67, 68, 71,
    72, 73, 78, 159, 198, 201, 228, 229
Awolowo, Obafemi, 83
Azeglio, Massimo d', 71

Bagehot, Walter, 69
Baldwin, Stanley, 119
Balfour Declaration (1917), 80
Bancroft, George, 70
Bandaranaike, Sirimavo, 164–5

barbarians and barbarism
  see civilization
"Barbarism: A User's Guide"
  (Hobsbawm), 231
Barbarism and Civilization (Wasserstein),
  231
Barnabas, Saint, 23
Baron-Cohen, Simon, 139, 151
Baronio, Cesare, 40
Barrios de Chungara, Domitila, 168
Barzun, Jacques, 205, 217
Beard, Charles A., 240
Beard, Mary R., 240
Beauvoir, Simone de, 135, 149, 152, 162,
  164, 166, 170
Bede, Venerable, 59–60
Belgium, 64–5, 191
Bell, Clive, 229
Bell, David, 70–1
Bellini, Gentile, 35
Belloc, Hilaire, 40
Benedict, Ruth, 210
Benedict XVI, Pope, 136, 140, 172
Benjamin, Walter, 231
Berlin Wall, 84, 96, 110, 117, 242
Berman, Edgar F., 136
Bernstein, Eduard, 108
Best, Geoffrey, 131
Bethlen, Gábor, 43
Bharatiya Janata Party (BJP), 48–9
Bible, 11–12, 22, 23, 30–1, 32, 38–9, 42,
  45, 52, 58, 137–8, 143, 146, 149,
  154, 172, 176, 177–80, 197, 203,
  204, 253
bin Laden Osama, 6, 252
Birgham, Treaty of (1290), 61
Bismarck, Otto von, 69, 124
blacks, 4, 114, 146, 163, 167, 175, 177,
  178, 179–82, 185–6, 189–93,
  196–203, 209–15, 216, 248, 260,
  261
Blair, Tony, 252, 253–4
Bloch, Marc, vii, 55
Blumenbach, Johann Friedrich, 181,
  183–4
Boas, Franz, 204, 205, 210
Bodin, Jean, 42, 44
Bolsheviks, 110–12, 117, 119, 132, 230
Boswell, James, 219–20
Bouvines, Battle of, 61

Boyne, Battle of the, 50
brain capacity, 136, 138, 144–5, 151,
  182, 184–5
Braudel, Fernand, 33, 55–7, 66, 73, 123
Brenner, Robert, 123
Breuilly, John, 57
British Association for the Advancement
  of Science, 205
British Empire, 70, 73, 74, 75, 77, 80,
  82, 83, 186–91, 198, 199, 206, 208,
  212, 226, 227–8, 229, 230, 241
  see also Great Britain
Brunn, Geoffrey, 241
Bryce, James, 53, 187
Bucer, Martin, 41
Buckle, H. T., 226
Buddhism, 240, 247
Buffon, Georges-Louis Leclerc, Comte
  de, 181, 183
Bulgaria, 67, 84, 114
Burckhardt, Jacob, 226
Bush, George H. W., 242–3
Bush, George W., 3, 4, 5, 6, 7, 243, 252,
  253–4, 259
Byars, W. V., 53
Byzantine Empire, 20, 25–6, 27, 31,
  225

Calvin, John, 42
Calvinism, 40, 42, 46, 47, 197
Camper, Peter, 182
Canada, 68, 69, 73, 88, 187, 188, 190,
  191, 193, 199, 208, 212, 248
capitalism, 75, 97, 98, 99, 100–1, 102,
  104, 107, 108–9, 114–18, 119, 120,
  121, 124, 126, 148, 149–50, 157,
  195, 242–3, 260
Caribbean islands, 73, 82, 83, 176, 180,
  183, 209–10
"Cast Away Illusions" (Mao), 93
Castellio, Sebastian, 42, 44
Castillon, Battle of, 61
Castro, Fidel, 114
Catherine II, Empress of Russia, 63–4,
  225
Catholic Church, 5, 13, 15–16, 28, 31,
  32, 37–52, 64, 72, 76, 85–6, 130,
  140, 161, 167, 172, 199
Cavour, Camillo Benso, Count of, 69

Chamberlain, Houston Stewart, 188, 193
Chamberlain, Joseph, 73, 78, 199
"Changing History" (MacAleese), vii
Chanson de Roland, La, 60
Charlemagne, 64
Charles V, Holy Roman Emperor, 65–6, 221
Charles V, King of France, 61
Charles IX, King of France, 41
Chaucer, Geoffrey, 60
Chiang Kai-shek, 114
China, 73, 88, 114, 115, 116, 124, 128, 162, 190, 191, 193, 207, 208, 210, 226, 234, 245–6, 247, 250
Chinese Exclusion Act (1882), 193
Christianity, 4, 11–12, 13, 15–39, 40, 42–5, 47, 48, 50, 52, 58, 64, 84, 130–1, 137–8, 143, 144, 146, 149, 154, 158, 172, 176, 177–80, 193, 197, 202, 203, 204, 206, 209, 215, 221, 222–4, 228, 230, 237, 238–9, 240, 243–4, 248, 253, 255, 260, 262, 263, 276*n*
    see also Catholic Church; Protestantism
Churchill, R. S., 219
Churchill, Winston S., 114, 116–17, 211, 219, 230, 317*n*
"Civilisation" (Churchill), 219
civilization, 219–64
    barbarism vs., 15–16, 220–33, 236, 240, 254–5, 263–4, 316*n*–17*n*
    clash of, 242–54, 256
    definition of, 219–20, 246–7, 254–7
    development of, 226–8, 242, 254–5
    Eastern, 226, 234, 240, 245–8, 250
    hegemony and, 245–6
    historical analysis of, 4, 219–54, 255, 263–4, 316*n*–17*n*
    as human identity, vii, 3, 4, 221–2, 233, 235–6, 238, 242, 243, 244, 246, 249, 253, 254–7, 263–4
    imperialism and, 226–7, 238, 241, 246
    "Kultur" compared with, 220, 227–8, 229, 234–5
    Manicheanism in, 8–9, 228, 251–3, 255
    morality and, 227
    nationalism compared with, 227–8, 236–7 238, 244, 247–8, 249, 255

plurality of, 233–4, 242, 255–7
race compared with, 228, 244, 264
religion compared with, 221, 228, 237, 238–9, 240, 244–8, 251, 252–3, 255, 256
rise and fall of, 233–42, 251–3
warfare and, 228–9, 232, 251–3
Western, 5, 226–9, 233, 234–42, 244–5, 248, 250, 252–7
"Zivilisation" compared with, 220, 227–8, 234–5
Civilization and Its Discontents (Freud), 231
Civilization of the Renaissance in Italy, The (Burckhardt), 226
Civilizing Process, The (Elias), 227
Civil War, British, 38
Civil War, English, 121
Civil War, U.S., 68, 73, 124, 191–2
Clark, Kenneth, 256
Clash of Civilizations and the Remaking of the World Order, The (Huntington), 244–54
class, 93–132
    agricultural (peasantry), 103, 111, 115, 117, 118, 119–21, 123, 126, 200
    consciousness of, 4, 98–9, 120–1, 124, 126–32, 141, 149–50, 164, 166–7
    economic impact of, 75, 96–102, 104, 105, 107, 108–9, 114–18, 119, 120, 121, 123, 124, 126, 131, 148, 149–50, 155–6, 157, 195, 242–3, 260
    "for itself" vs. "in itself," 98–9, 135–6, 156
    formation of, 99–100, 101, 106, 119–29, 141, 149–50
    gender compared with, 128, 132, 133, 135–6, 140–2, 147–50, 152, 155–6, 157, 158, 161–3, 164, 166–9, 170, 171
    global application of, 112–13, 115, 116–18, 121, 128
    historical analysis of, 95, 98, 104, 108, 110, 114–15, 117, 118–32, 196
    as human identity, 3, 4, 92, 95–108, 110, 112, 114–15, 118, 119, 120, 123–32, 133, 155–6, 174, 255, 258, 263

class *(continued)*
  industrialization and, 94, 100–6,
    108–9, 110, 111, 112, 115, 117–18,
    120, 121, 122, 127–8, 131, 140–2,
    149–50, 155–6, 158, 161, 171
  labor and, 68, 77, 98, 101, 102–3,
    108–9, 121, 124, 128, 155, 193
  Manicheanism in, 8–9, 114–15,
    128–31
  Marxist analysis of, 93–132, 133, 135,
    141, 149–50, 168, 174
  means of production and, 98, 101,
    102, 103, 104, 105–6, 107, 118, 132,
    139, 155
  middle (bourgeoisie), 75, 93, 95, 97,
    100, 102, 103–4, 107, 110, 111, 112,
    113, 115, 117, 119–20, 121, 122,
    124, 126–7, 128, 141, 142, 148,
    149–50, 155–6, 157, 161–3, 166,
    168, 196, 200, 216
  nationalism and, 75, 96, 97–8, 105,
    108, 109–14, 118, 119, 123–4, 125,
    128, 131, 132
  political and social aspects of, 98,
    102–5, 106, 107–18, 119, 121, 123,
    126, 128
  private property and, 68, 98, 99, 100,
    102, 103, 104, 107, 123, 126, 150
  race compared with, 174, 175, 176,
    183, 189, 196, 200, 214–15, 216
  religion compared with, 96–7, 105,
    118, 119, 121, 123–4, 125, 130–1,
    132
  revolution and, 95, 100, 101, 102, 105,
    106, 108, 109–12, 115, 116, 117–19,
    121–2, 124, 126–8, 148, 163, 196
  struggle of, 69, 93, 99, 101, 106,
    110–12, 116, 118–21, 123
  urbanization and, 103–6, 108, 158
  working (proletariat), 94, 95–8, 99,
    100, 102–7 (118) (110–112), 115,
    117–28, 142, 148, 155–6, 157, 161,
    167, 168, 196, 238
Cleveland, Grover, 193
Clinton, Bill, 3, 7, 218, 251
Cobban, Alfred, 127
Cold War, 114–17, 240, 242–3, 244,
    245, 250, 251, 253
Commons Sense (Paine), 138
Commonwealth Franchise Act (1902),
    190

Communism, 75, 81, 82, 84–6, 88, 94,
    96, 107–18, 119, 120, 122, 124, 125,
    127–9, 130, 131, 195, 203, 216, 230,
    240, 241, 242–3, 246, 253
Communist International (Comintern),
    113
Communist League, 108
Communist Manifesto, The (Marx and
    Engels), 75, 94, 95, 97–8, 102, 106,
    107–18, 122, 123, 131, 132, 133,
    174
Communist Party Historians' Group,
    120
Concerning Heretics (Castellio), 42
*Condition of the Working Class in England,
    The* (Engels), 84, 107
Condorcet, Marie Jean Antoine Nicolas
    de Caritat, Marquis de, 145
Confederation of Warsaw (1573), 42–3
Constant, Baron d'Estournelles de, 209
Constantine I, Emperor of Rome, 15,
    17, 18, 20
Constantinople, 20, 25, 27, 31, 34, 224
Constitution, U.S., 186, 192–3
Contarini, Gasparo, 41
contraception, 164, 171
Cook, Thomas, 74
Coolidge, Calvin, 193
Cornish, Samuel, 186
Counter-Reformation, 37–48
Courcelle, Pierre, 231
craniometry, 182, 183
Crécy, Battle of (1346), 61
Crèvecoeur, J. Hector St. John de, 181
Crick, Francis, 217
Cromwell, Oliver, 50
Crusades, 14, 27, 28, 30, 31, 33, 35, 36,
    179, 252
Cuban Missile Crisis (1962), 117
cuius regio, cuius religio principle, 43–4
Curtis, William, 186
Curzon, George, 68
Czechoslovakia, 71, 72, 79, 84, 86, 114,
    116, 195, 201

Dalrymple, William, 33–4
Dangerous Games (MacMillan), vii
Darwin, Charles, 108, 137, 143, 183,
    185
Dawson, William, 77

Deakin, Alfred, 191
Dean, Jodi, 169
Declaration of Independence, 147
Declaration of the Rights of Women
(Gouges), 145
Decline and Fall of the Roman Empire, The
(Gibbon), 15–27, 37, 222–33, 235,
237, 238–9
Decline of the West, The (Spengler),
234–6, 237
de Gaulle, Charles, 53–5, 57, 73, 89, 90
de Klerk, F. W., 213
democracy, 78–9, 84–6, 118, 119, 124–5,
241, 242–3, 245, 247, 250, 252
Denmark, 59, 60, 77, 159, 201
Descartes, René, 145
Descent of Man, The (Darwin), 138, 185
Deutscher, Isaac, 131
de Wet Nel, Michel Daniel Christiaan,
197
Díaz, Porfirio, 124, 127
Dictionary of Races and Peoples, 187
Different Races of Mankind, The (Kant),
180
Dilke, Charles, 186–7
Disraeli, Benjamin, 175
Dobb, Maurice, 119, 120
Doll's House, A (Ibsen), 147
Dowd, Maureen, 136, 166
Dred Scott decision (1857), 182, 186
DuBois, W. E. B., 206–7, 209–10
Dühring, Eugen, 188
Duifhuis, Hubert, 46
Durkheim, Emile, 233
Dutch Reformed Church, 41, 197, 203,
204

Ecclesiastical History of the English People
(Bede), 59–60
Economist, 69
Eden, Garden of, 138, 149
Edict of Milan (313), 15, 19, 20, 21, 22
education, 47, 50–2, 69, 137, 140, 143,
144, 145–6, 147, 150, 153, 158–9,
163–4, 165, 166, 168, 187, 188–9
Education (Northern Ireland) Act
(1978), 51
Eisenhower, Dwight D., 114
El Cid, 31
Elias, Norbert, 227

Elizabeth I, Queen of England, 32, 34,
62–3
Elliott, Marianne, 51
Emancipation Proclamation (1863), 186,
191
Emerson, Ralph Waldo, 176
Emile (Rousseau), 138
Engels, Friedrich, 75, 93–118, 122, 123,
124, 126, 129–32, 133, 135, 139,
147–8, 156, 163, 164, 174, 175, 176,
231, 259
English Traits (Emerson), 176
Enlightenment, 26, 144–5, 178, 179–81,
220–2
Equal Rights Amendment (ERA), 164
Essay on Government (Mill), 134
Essay on the Inequality of Human Races
(Gobineau), 175–6
Essential Difference, The (Baron-Cohen),
139
Eusebius, 15, 23
Eve, 137, 138, 177
Expansion of England, The (Seeley), 186–7
Experiences (Toynbee), 258

Faisal I, King of Iraq, 80, 83
Fear of Barbarians, The (Todorov), 7
Febvre, Lucien, 55
Female Eunuch, The (Greer), 163, 166
Feminine Mystique, The (Friedan), 162–3
Feminism: A Very Short Introduction
(Walters), 133
Ferguson, Wallace K., 241
Fernández-Armesto, Felipe, 37, 247, 255
feudalism, 98, 100, 102, 104, 111,
119–21, 123, 124, 126
Feuerbach, Ludwig, 95, 96
Fichte, Johann Gottlieb, 97
Fifteenth Amendment, 186, 192–3
Final Solution, 195–6, 201–2
FitzRalph of Armagh, 61
Fletcher, Richard, 36
Fleurie, H. J., 205
Foner, Eric, 193
Foundations of the Nineteenth Century, The
(Chamberlain), 188
Fourteenth Amendment, 186, 192–3
France, 32, 38, 39, 43, 44, 46, 47, 53–7,
60, 61, 65, 67, 69, 70–1, 72, 73, 74,
75, 77, 79, 80, 82, 88, 89, 100, 104,

France *(continued)*
110, 113, 114, 119, 121, 122, 123,
125, 127, 133, 144–5, 158, 159 161,
162, 175, 180, 188, 191, 201, 204,
208, 211, 212, 220, 221, 226, 227–8,
229, 230–1, 235, 248, 260
Francis I, King of France, 34, 65
Franco, Francisco, 119
Franco-Prussian War, 89, 228
Frederick I Barbarossa, Holy Roman
Emperor, 64
Frederick II, King of Prussia, 59, 62,
63–4
Fredrickson, George M., 196–7
Freeman, E. A., 186, 187
French Revolution, 63, 67, 104, 121,
122, 127, 144, 158, 235
Freud, Sigmund, 37, 138, 143, 149, 231
Friedan, Betty, 157, 162–3, 164, 166,
167, 168, 261
"From Social History to the History of
Society" (Hobsbawm), 132

Gaimar, Geffrei, 60
Gandhi, Mohandas K., 191, 202, 206,
215
Garibaldi and the Making of Italy
(Trevelyan), 124–5
Garvey, Marcus, 207
Geertz, Clifford, 6, 89
Gellner, Ernst, 57
gender, 133–73
biology of, 136, 138, 141, 142, 143,
144–5, 147–8, 151–2, 156, 158, 165,
169
class compared with, 128, 132, 133,
135–6, 140–2, 147–50, 152, 155–6,
157, 158, 161–3, 164, 166–9, 170,
171
complications and contradictions in,
151–7
consciousness of, 4, 133, 135–6,
149–50, 156–70
difference vs. equality in, 156–7, 160
difference vs. inferiority in, 136–42,
145–6, 156–7
economic aspect of, 140–2, 149–50,
153, 155–6, 164, 168, 171
equality vs. sameness in, 142–50, 151,
156–7, 160, 167–8

feminist critique of, 133–42, 145–9,
150, 156–9, 161–73, 261
as global designation, 137, 140, 145,
146–7, 152, 157, 160, 161–9, 170
history of, 140–50, 155–6, 157, 165–6,
169–70
as human identity, 134–5, 140, 143–4,
146, 147, 148–9, 152–3, 172–3
legal status of, 140, 143–4, 147, 154,
161, 163–4
literature on, 134, 135, 137–9, 144–9
Manicheanism in, 8–9
men, 69, 134–6, 136–50
morality and, 146–7, 160, 162
nationality compared with, 133, 135,
152, 161–9, 170, 171
patriarchy and, 100, 157, 163, 165,
167, 170–1, 172
political aspect of, 133–4, 139, 140,
143, 144–8, 153
race and, 133, 146, 154, 163, 167, 168,
169, 176, 189, 214–15
religious views on, 135, 137–8, 139,
140, 144, 146–7, 149, 152, 154, 161,
162, 167, 170, 171, 172
separate sexes in, 134–5, 139–42,
148–57, 160, 167–8, 170–3
as social construct, 140–5, 147–8, 149,
151
trans-, 139–40
see also women
Genesis, Book of, 137, 143, 146,
177–8
Genghis Khan, 225
George III, King of England, 63, 226
German Ideology, The (Marx and Engels),
94, 98–9, 107
Germany, 40–1, 47, 59, 60, 61, 66, 67,
68, 69, 84, 88, 89, 97, 101, 221,
248, 260
East, 84, 114, 116
Imperial, 67, 68, 69, 70, 71, 72–3,
74, 75, 76–7, 78, 79, 110, 113, 124,
159, 175, 188, 191, 193–4, 198, 220,
222–3, 227–9, 231, 232, 234
Nazi, 81–2, 193–8, 200, 201–2, 203,
204–5, 212, 216, 230–1
West, 84
Gibbon, Edward, 4, 15–27, 30, 31, 37,
140–1, 222–33, 235, 237, 238–9,
243, 251, 255, 317*n*

Gilbert, W. S., 260
Giving (Clinton), 3
Gladstone, William, 16, 69
Gobineau, Joseph Arthur, Comte de, 175–6, 183, 184–5, 200
God, 11, 19, 30, 38–9, 53, 137, 146, 147, 174, 176, 177–8, 185–6, 197, 199, 204, 215
Goebbels, Joseph, 195, 198, 201
Goldman, Emma, 148
Gorbachev, Mikhail, 117
Göring, Hermann, 195–6
Goths, 175, 221, 222–3, 228, 232
Gouges, Olympe de, 145, 158
Gould, Stephen Jay, 218
Grant, Madison, 187
Gray, John, 138–9, 140, 142, 151, 154
Great Britain, 38, 41, 47, 50–2, 59–64, 65, 67, 69, 72, 75, 88, 89, 93, 94, 105, 106, 110, 119–29, 133–4, 139, 141–2, 150, 159, 160, 161, 162, 175, 180, 185, 186–9, 198, 207, 208, 241, 248
Great Depression, 81, 119, 240
Greater Britain (Dilke), 186–7
Great Exhibition (1851), 75
Greece, 23, 33, 34, 58, 67, 71, 75, 91, 123, 126, 137, 144–5, 146, 153, 158, 177, 179, 184, 221, 235, 236–9, 247
Green, J. R., 70
Greer, Germaine, 133, 152, 156, 157, 163, 164, 167–8, 171, 259
Gregory VII, Pope, 64
Grimké, Angelina, 146
Grimké, Sarah, 146
Grossman, Vasily, vii
Guevara, Che, 114, 116
Guise, Charles de, 41
Guizot François, 70, 96, 104, 122, 226, 254
Gustavus Adolphus, King of Sweden, 39–40

Habsburg dynasty, 32, 43, 47, 64, 68, 72, 73, 195, 201
Handbook of Oratory, The (Byars, ed.), 53
Hankins, Frank H., 205
Haraway, Donna, 170
Harper's Weekly, 186

Harrington, James, 123
Hartley, David, 219
Hegel, Georg Wilhelm Friedrich, 93, 94, 95, 96, 97
Henri IV, King of France, 43
Henry V, King of England, 61, 63
Henry V (Shakespeare), 63
Henry of Huntingdon, 60
Herder, Johann Gottfried von, 184, 188, 227
Heydrich, Reinhard, 195–6
Hill, Christopher, 119, 121, 123, 129
Hilton, Rodney, 119, 120–1, 123
Himmler, Heinrich, 195, 201, 202
Hinduism, 48–9, 50, 84, 206, 217, 240, 247–8
Hines, Melissa, 152
Hirschfeld, Magnus, 205
Histoire de la civilisation en France (Guizot), 226
Historian's Craft, The (Bloch), vii
History of the World in 100 Objects, A (MacGregor), 219
History of Western Civilization, A (Watts), 241
History Workshop Journal, 123
Hitchens, Christopher, 252
Hitler, Adolf, 82, 119, 188, 194–6, 198, 200, 201, 204–5, 210, 211, 230
Hobbes, Thomas, 38
Hobsbawm, Eric, 57, 88, 90, 109, 119, 120, 121–2, 123, 124, 125, 129, 130, 131, 231
Ho Chi Minh, 114, 116
Hodgkin, Thomas, 227
Holocaust, 193–6, 201–2, 212
Holy Roman Empire, 38, 43, 46, 47, 61, 64, 65–6, 221
Homer, 58
Homo Sapiens, 211–12
hooks, bell, 167
Horn, Alfred, 75
Howard, Michael, 90
Hugo, Victor, 226, 228
Human Genome Project, 217
human solidarity
  cosmopolitanism in, 66–7, 74, 75–6, 85, 86–8, 91, 92, 97, 125, 250
  diversity in, 8–10, 259–64
  as form of identity, 3–10, 13, 81, 131, 258–64

human solidarity *(continued)*
historical analysis of, vii, 3–10, 258, 259, 262, 263–4
monolithic identities vs., 20, 37, 115–16, 127–8, 154–5, 199–203, 206–7, 209–10, 225, 246, 248, 252–3, 259
political aspect of, 15–25, 131, 259, 262
stereotypes and, 35–6, 48, 59, 60–2, 63, 176, 178, 192, 210–11, 228, 254
see also civilization; class; gender; nationalism; race; religion; women
Humboldt, Wilhelm von, vii
Hume, David, 180
Humphrey, Hubert, 136
Hundred Years War, 61, 63, 65
Hungary, 43, 60, 64–5, 68, 71, 72, 79, 80, 84, 113, 116, 120, 187
Huns, 223, 225, 228, 264, 317n
Hunt, James, 184
Huntington, Samuel P., 4, 244–54, 255, 256
Hussein, Saddam, 243, 252

Ibsen, Henrik, 147
Identity of France, The (Braudel), 55–7
immigration, 73, 76, 86, 88, 187, 190–1, 193, 196, 199, 200–1, 202, 208, 212–13
Immigration Act (1924), 208
Immigration Commission, U.S., 187
Immigration Restriction Act (1913), 191
Immorality Act (1950), 196, 197, 202
India, 34, 48–9, 82, 83, 84, 184, 202, 212, 217, 234, 247–8
Indochina, 73, 114, 115, 212, 214
industrialization, 76–7, 94, 100–6, 108–9, 110, 111, 112, 115, 117–18, 120, 121, 122, 127–8, 131, 140–2, 149–50, 155–6, 158, 161, 171, 196, 203
Infidels (Wheatcroft), 11, 29
Innocent III, Pope, 64
International Congress of Women (1915), 162
International Council of Women, 159, 162

International Monetary Fund (IMF), 86
International Women's Suffrage Alliance, 159
International Women's Year (1975), 164–5, 168
Into Battle (R. S. Churchill, ed.), 219
Introduction to the History of Civilization in England (Buckle), 226
Iraq, 14, 79, 80, 83
Iraq War, 14, 243, 252, 253
Ireland, 50–2, 59, 61, 63, 72, 76, 79, 175, 199, 200–1
Isaac de Étoile, 30
Islam, 4, 5, 13, 25–37, 38, 40, 44, 47, 48–9, 50, 80, 84, 86, 88, 154, 172, 179, 237, 240, 243–4, 247–8, 255, 276n
Israel, 49, 58–9, 80
Italy, 27, 34, 62, 66, 67, 68, 69, 71, 75, 79, 81–2, 88, 124–5, 161, 162, 175, 187, 201, 220, 221, 223, 227, 229, 230
Italy and Her Invaders (Hodgkin), 227

James, Henry, 161
Jameson, Franklin, 78
Japan, 58, 81–2, 124, 207–8, 210, 211, 247
Jaurès, Jean, 122
Jebb, Eglantyne, 81
Jefferson, Thomas, 181–2, 183
Jenkins, Roy, 253
Jesus Christ, 11–12, 13, 14, 15, 19–20, 22, 30, 38, 46, 91, 146, 178
Jewish Question, The (Dühring), 188
Jewry's Victory over Teutonism (Marr), 188
Jews, 23, 24, 30, 32, 34, 42, 47, 49, 50, 58–9, 80, 91, 93, 97, 144, 146, 154, 175, 179, 187, 188, 189, 193–6, 198, 199, 201–2, 203, 204, 210, 212, 252, 261
Joan of Arc, 61, 70
John Chrysostom, 23
John of Gaunt, 63
John Paul II, Pope, 86, 130
Johnson, Lyndon B., 115
Johnson, Samuel, 219–20, 222, 257
Jones, Gareth Stedman, 106, 129

Julian the Apostate, Emperor of Rome, 22, 23
Justinian I, Emperor of Rome, 25, 224

Kagan, Robert, 252
Kames, Henry Home, Lord, 180
Kant, Immanuel, 180, 183
Kaplan, Benjamin J., 44
Karabell, Zachary, 50
Kautsky, John H., 116
Kautsky, Karl, 108, 112, 116
Kennedy, John F., 117
Kennedy, Randall, 216–17
Khrushchev, Nikita, 116, 117
Kiernan, Victor, 130
King, Martin Luther, Jr., 213, 215, 261
Kipling, Rudyard, 187, 190, 261–2
Kissinger, Henry, 251
Knox, Robert, 174–6, 177, 183, 184, 200, 211, 259
Koran, 25, 30–1, 32, 35
Kristol, William, 252
Ku Klux Klan, 192, 207
Kultur contra Zivilisation (Nietzsche), 228

labor movement, 68, 77, 108–9, 121, 124, 128, 155, 193
Lactantius, Lucius, 178
landowners, 68, 98, 99, 100, 102, 103, 104, 107, 123, 126, 150
Lansing, Robert, 79
Lapouge, Georges de, 188, 193
Lavater, Johann Kaspar, 182
League of Nations, 79, 80, 81, 208
Lebanon, 79, 80
Lecky, W. E. H., 40
Lefebvre, Georges, 122
Lenin, V. I., 81, 110–12, 113, 114, 115, 124, 196
Leo Africanus, Joannes, 35
Lerner, Max, 240
Letters on the Equality of the Sexes (Grimké), 146
Lewis, Bernard, 243–4
liberalism, 104, 123, 131, 160, 167, 172, 256
Life and Fate (Grossman), vii
Lincoln, Abraham, 69

Linnaeus, Carolus, 181, 183
Lippmann, Walter, 13
Livy, 158
Lloyd George, David, 79
Lodge, Henry Cabot, 187
Lorde, Audre, 168
Louis VI, King of France, 60, 61
Louis IX, King of France, 60
Louis XIV, King of France, 63
Louw, Eric, 198
Luce, Henry, 240, 241
Lueger, Karl, 202
Lukács, Georg, 99
Luschan, Felix von, 209
Luther, Martin, 38, 40, 51
Lutheranism, 40–1, 42, 47
Luxemburg, Rosa, 132
Lysistrata (Aristophanes), 158

MacAleese, Mary, vii
Macartney, George, 226
Macaulay, Thomas Babington, 40, 70
MacGregor, Neil, 7, 219
Machiavelli, Niccolò, 221
MacMillan, Margaret, vii
Maier, Charles, 68, 86, 87
"Making of a Ruling Class, The" (Thompson), 93
Making of the English Working Class, The (Thompson), 124–5, 132
Malan, D. F., 197
Malcolm X, 213
Mandela, Nelson, 213, 215, 261
Mani, 12
Manicheanism, 3–15, 19, 24–5, 27, 29, 38, 39, 41, 43, 48, 52, 114–15, 128–31, 188, 196, 209–10, 228, 251–3, 255, 259, 260
Manifesto Addressed to the Working People of Austria (Marx), 98
"Manifesto to the Proletariat of the Entire World" (Trotsky), 113
Mann, Thomas, 228
Man's Most Dangerous Myth (Montagu), vii, 210
Mao Zedong, 93, 114, 115
Marcus Aurelius, Emperor of Rome, 16
Marr, William, 188
Martel, Charles, 27

Marty, Martin E., 13
Marx, Karl, 75, 93–118, 120, 122, 123,
    124, 126, 129–32, 133, 135, 139,
    147, 163, 164, 174, 175, 176
Marxism, 75, 93–132, 133, 135, 139,
    141, 147, 149–50, 163, 164, 168,
    174, 175, 176
Mather, James, 11
Mathews, Basil, 243
Matthew, Gospel according to, 11–12,
    13, 38, 52, 253
Maud, John, 197–8, 203, 204
Mauss, Marcel, 233
Mazarin, Jules, 70–1
Mazzini, Giuseppe, 53, 97
McKnight, Reginald, 215
McNeill, William H., 6, 263–4
Medici, Catherine de', 41
*Mediterranean and the Mediterranean
    World in the Age of Philip II, The*
    (Braudel), 55–6, 66
Mehmed II, Sultan, 35
Mein Kampf (Hitler), 200
Melanchthon, Philipp, 41
Mellon, Andrew, 77
men, 69, 134–6, 136–50
*Men Are from Mars, Women Are from
    Venus* (Gray), 138–9, 140
Mexico, 47, 68, 86, 124, 127, 164–5, 168,
    201, 217
Michelet, Jules, 70
Middle Ages, 24, 35, 57, 59–60, 64, 66,
    70, 71, 101, 102, 126, 154, 178–9
Middle East, 9, 33, 35, 48, 78, 79, 80, 82,
    83, 88, 89, 210, 214, 234, 244, 248
Mill, James, 134, 147
Mill, John Stuart, 147, 254
Mixed Marriage Act (1949), 196–7
Mommsen, Theodor, 70
Montagu, Ashley, vii, 205, 210, 211
Montaigne, Michel Eyquem de, 222
Moreau de Saint-Méry, Médéric Louis
    Elie, 183
Morgan, Robin, 164, 165–6, 173
Morton, A. L., 119–20
Motley, John Lothrop, 40
Mugabe, Robert, 214, 216
Muhammad, 25, 30, 32
Muhammad and Charlemagne (Pirenne),
    28–9, 30

Mulcaster, Richard, 62
Mussolini, Benito, 82, 119, 230
Myrdal, Gunnar, 210–11

Naipaul, V. S., 262
Nantes, Edict of (1598), 43, 46
Napoleon I, Emperor of France, 67, 235
National American Woman Suffrage
    Association, 159
nationalism, 53–92
    allegiance to (patriotism), 4, 17–18,
        22, 68, 69–71, 78–9, 80, 85–6, 193
    borders for, 68–9, 75–8, 80, 81, 83–4,
        85, 89, 91, 96, 113–14, 189, 201–2,
        249
    civilization compared with, 227–8,
        236–7 238, 244, 247–8, 249, 255
    collapse of, 67–8, 72–3, 79, 84–6, 96,
        110, 117, 242–3
    colonialism and, 54, 79, 80, 82–4,
        88–9, 114, 115, 116, 198–200, 212,
        216
    cosmopolitanism and, 66–7, 74, 75–6,
        85, 87–8, 91, 97, 125, 250
    definition of, 53–5, 89–92
    democracy and, 78–9, 84–6, 118, 119,
        124–5, 241, 242–3, 245, 247, 250–2
    economic aspect of, 66, 75, 76–7, 81,
        86–7, 89, 116
    emergence of, 57–67, 78–9, 81, 88–92,
        124
    ethnic minorities in, 69, 76–7, 79–81,
        84, 87–8, 89
    gender compared with, 133, 135, 152,
        161–9, 170, 171
    geography and, 4, 57, 60–1, 64, 65–9,
        71, 73–8, 83–4, 86, 87, 89–90, 128,
        201–2, 212, 214–15
    historical analysis of, 55–67, 70–2, 87,
        89–92
    as human identity, 3, 56–7, 58, 60–1,
        64, 68–71, 73, 78–89, 255, 258, 263
    immigration and, 73, 76, 86, 88
    imperialism and, 15–25, 47, 54, 63–7,
        72–6, 78, 79, 80–4, 88–9, 91, 114,
        115, 116, 186–91, 198–200, 203,
        206–9, 211, 212, 213–14, 216, 261
    independence of, 54, 78–80, 81, 83–9,
        114, 115, 116, 213–14, 247

international treaties and, 34–5, 54,
    65–6, 201, 208, 258
language and, 60, 62, 65, 69, 71, 74,
    78, 79, 80–1, 83, 84, 88, 89
laws of, 58, 65, 68–70
Manicheanism in, 8–9
in modern period, 57, 67–79
monarchy and, 61–7, 69–70, 72–3,
    74, 124
myths and traditions of, 53–5, 60–2,
    65, 69–72, 89–92
of nation-states, 54–5, 56, 67–9, 78–9,
    88–9, 109, 189
origins of, 57–67
political aspect of, 5, 6, 53, 65, 68–70,
    86, 91–2
in postmodern period, 78–89
religion and, 54, 58–9, 64, 66, 69, 70,
    72, 80–1, 83, 84, 86, 88, 89, 90–1,
    92
secularism in, 54, 64, 70
stereotypes and, 59, 60–2, 63
territories of, 57, 58, 60–1, 65–9, 71,
    73–8, 87, 89–90, 201–2
totalitarianism and, 110, 112–13, 116,
    118, 119, 194–6, 242–3, 253
trading networks of, 32–5, 66, 75, 81,
    89, 116
treaties of, 34–5, 54, 65–6, 201, 208,
    258; *see also specific treaties*
unification in, 67, 68, 70–2, 79–80
voting franchise in, 69, 72, 73, 134,
    138, 146–7, 148, 158–62, 171, 190,
    200, 212
warfare and, 60–1, 65–8, 74, 84, 91,
    214
see also specific empires and nations
Nationalist Party, 196–7
National Life and Character (Pearson),
    206
National Organization for Women
    (NOW), 163, 167
National Union of Women's Suffrage
    Societies, 159
National Women's Political Caucus, 163
Native Americans, 186, 187, 198, 201
Native Land Act (1913), 190
Naturalization Act (1790), 182
Negro, The (DuBois), 207
neoconservatism, 4, 251–3, 256

Netherlands, 41, 46, 47, 64–5, 67, 82,
    186, 211, 212
Nettesheim, Heinrich Cornelius Agrippa
    von, 62
New Left Review, 120
Newman, John Henry, 16
New Testament, 11–12, 22, 23, 38–9, 42,
    52, 58, 137, 253
New York Times, 3, 136
New Zealand, 73, 77, 88, 158, 159, 161,
    187, 188, 190–1, 193, 212
Nietzsche, Friedrich, 138, 228, 229
Nkomo, Joshua, 214
North Atlantic Treaty Organization
    (NATO), 241
Nott, Josiah, 184

Obama, Barack, 216–17, 254
Observations on Man (Hartley), 219
Old Testament, 12, 58, 137, 143, 146,
    177–8
Old World in the New, The (Ross), 187
On the Natural Variety of Mankind
    (Blumenbach), 181
Origin of Species (Darwin), 185
Orléans, Battle of (1429), 61
Osiander, Lucas, the Elder, 40
Otto I, Holy Roman Emperor, 64
Ottoman Empire, 25, 27–8, 29, 31, 32,
    67, 73, 78, 80, 224, 229, 236–7

Pagden, Anthony, 29
Paine, Tom, 138, 145, 154
Pakistan, 82, 84, 217, 247
Pan-African Congress (1900), 206
pan-Africanism, 206–7, 209–10
Pappus, Johannes, 40
Parkman, Francis, 70
Pashas (Mather), 11
Passing of the Great Race, The (Grant),
    187
Past and Present, 120
Paul, Saint, 23, 91, 137, 146
Pearson, Charles, 206, 207
Peloponnesian War, 158
People's History of England, A (Morton),
    119–20
Perle, Richard, 252

Pevsner, Nikolaus, 201
Philip II, King of Spain, 64
Philippines, 193, 200
phrenology, 182, 183
Piagnol, André, 231
Pirenne, Henri, 28–9, 30, 32
Plato, 33, 144–5, 149, 153, 177
Plea for the Citizenship of Women, A
    (Condorcet), 145
Plumb, J. H., 263
Plutarch, 158
Poitiers, Battle of (732), 27, 35;
    (1356) 61
Poland, 38, 42–3, 44, 47, 49, 71, 76–7,
    79, 84, 85–6, 114, 116, 130, 195,
    201
Portugal, 67, 71, 121, 162, 178, 179
Poullain de La Barre, François, 144–5
Prince, The (Machiavelli), 221
Princes' War, 38
Processes of History, The (Teggart), 233–6
Protestantism, 5, 13, 15–16, 32, 37–52,
    64, 72, 97, 158, 161, 162, 187, 197,
    199, 203, 204
Prussia, 63–4, 72–3, 74, 93

Qianlong, Emperor of China, 226

race, 174–218
    African Americans and, 114, 146, 163,
        167, 181–2, 185–6, 190, 191–3, 200,
        203, 209–15, 216, 248, 261
    assimilation of, 201–2, 205–6
    biological basis of, 182, 183, 184–5,
        194, 195, 202, 204, 210–12
    "blood purity" in, 179, 189, 190–1,
        194–5, 201–2, 204
    categories of, 174–6, 178, 179, 181–4,
        187, 189, 194, 198–215, 217
    citizenship and, 181–2, 194, 248
    civilization compared with, 228, 244,
        264
    civil rights movement and, 114, 163,
        190, 212–13, 214, 216, 261
    class compared with, 174, 175, 176,
        183, 189, 196, 200, 214–15, 216
    color line in, 206–7, 209–10, 213–14
    consciousness of, 4, 206–7, 213–15

    contradictions in, 203–15
    discrimination and prejudice in
        (racism), 4, 167, 178–82, 184,
        185–215, 262
    economic aspect of, 179, 180, 195,
        203, 205–6
    education and, 187, 188–9
    equality and, 174–6, 179–82, 185–6,
        189–93, 196–218, 219
    ethnic divisions in, 69, 76–7, 79–81,
        84, 87–8, 89
    evolution of, 174–5
    gender compared with, 133, 146,
        154, 163, 167, 168, 169, 176, 189,
        214–15
    genetics and, 139–40, 205, 211–12,
        217
    hierarchies of, 174–6, 179–80, 185–6,
        189–93, 196–218, 219
    historical analysis of, 174, 176–89,
        194–6, 203–15, 216
    as human identity, 3, 4, 13–14, 174,
        175, 176, 177, 185–6, 188, 197,
        199–200, 203–18, 258, 260
    imperialism as related to, 186–91,
        198–200, 203, 206–9, 211, 213–14,
        216
    laws on, 182, 186, 189–203, 212–13
    literature on, 174–8, 180–9, 210–12
    Manicheanism in, 8–9, 188, 196,
        209–10
    mixing of (miscegenation), 175, 178,
        179, 183–5, 187, 190–1, 192, 194–5,
        197, 198–203, 212–13, 216, 217
    monogenic vs. polygenic theories of,
        180–1, 183, 185, 197, 217–18
    nationality and, 176, 178, 180,
        181–203, 206–9, 211, 212, 213–15,
        216
    political aspect of, 179, 181–2, 188,
        189, 190, 192, 196–7, 200, 205–6,
        211–12, 216–17
    in "postracial" societies, 216–18
    religion as related to, 176, 177–80,
        185–6, 189, 197–8, 199, 203, 204,
        206, 209, 212, 215, 217–18
    scientific research on, 182, 183, 205,
        210–12, 217
    segregation of, 4, 191–3, 196–203,
        209–15, 216

skin pigmentation and, 177, 178, 217
slavery and, 176, 177, 178, 179, 180–2,
  186, 191–2
stereotypes in, 176, 178, 192, 210–11
theories of, 174–6
"volk" concept of, 184, 188, 193–6,
  201–2, 203, 204–5, 210
white supremacy in, 4, 191–3,
  198–203, 204, 205–6, 209–15, 216,
  261
Race: A Study in Modern Superstition
  (Barzun), 205
Races and Racism (Benedict), 210
Races of Europe, The (Ripley), 187
Racism (Hirschfeld), 205
Radical History Review, 123
Ranke, Leopold von, 56, 70
Reagan, Ronald, 117
Reagon, Bernice, 152
Reddie, James, 184
Reeves, William Pember, 77
Reformation, 14, 37–48
Regino of Prüm, 59
religion, 11–52
  as belief system, 12–13, 16, 30–1,
    37–8
  Catholics vs. Protestants in, 5, 13,
    15–16, 32, 37–52, 64, 72
  in Christianity vs. Islam, 4, 13, 25–37,
    38, 40, 44, 47, 84, 179, 237, 240,
    243–4, 248, 255, 276*n*
  Christianity vs. paganism, 13, 15–27,
    28, 40, 50, 222–4, 260
  civilization compared with, 221, 228,
    237, 238–9, 240, 244–8, 251, 252–3,
    255, 256
  class compared with, 96–7, 105, 118,
    119, 121, 123–4, 125, 130–1, 132
  conversions in, 17, 18, 20, 30, 97, 179,
    193
  ecclesiastical hierarchy of, 15–16
  economic impact of, 32–5, 49–50
  in education, 47, 50–2
  freedom of, 40–8, 72
  gender as viewed in, 135, 137–8, 139,
    140, 144, 146–7, 149, 152, 154, 161,
    162, 167, 170, 171, 172
  geographical distribution of, 21, 23–4,
    27–9, 32–4, 38, 40–1
  heresies and sects in, 12, 14, 19–22,

    25, 28, 30–1, 37–49, 118, 130, 139,
      262
  Hindus vs. Muslims in, 48–9, 50
  historical analysis of, 15–25, 29–37,
    45–6, 48–52
  as human identity, 3, 12–14, 25–6,
    29–30, 31, 33, 37, 38–9, 40, 41–2,
    45–6, 48, 49–52, 58–9, 89, 90–1, 92,
    96, 255, 258, 262, 263
  Manicheanism in, 8–9, 11–15, 19,
    24–5, 27, 29, 38, 39, 41, 43, 48, 52,
    130–1
  monotheism in, 11, 19, 26–7, 30
  nationalism compared with, 54, 58–9,
    64, 66, 69, 70, 72, 80–1, 83, 84, 86,
    88, 89, 90–1, 92
  persecution in (martyrdom), 19–22,
    31, 40–4, 48–9, 130
  political influence of, 31–5, 42–4,
    48–52
  polytheism in, 16–17, 19
  reconciliation in, 39–41
  secularism vs., 4, 23, 48, 54, 64, 70, 92,
    138, 144, 146–7, 172, 241, 243–4,
    245
  segregation in, 50–2
  stereotypes in, 35–6, 48
  superstition in, 15–16
  theology in, 19–20, 26, 40–6
  tolerance in, 16–17, 19, 26, 28, 33–7,
    40–8, 49
  wars of, 14–15, 27–9, 31, 37–8, 43,
    48–52
  see also specific religions
"Religion: The Glue that Binds Society
  Together" (Marx), 97
Renan, Ernest, 89–90
Republic, The (Plato), 144
Revolutionary War, U.S., 124
revolutions of 1848, 94, 100, 101, 105,
  122, 184
Reynolds, David, 213
Rheinische Zeitung, 94
Rhodes, Cecil, 187, 188–9
Rhodes Scholarships, 187, 188–9, 198
Ricardo, David, 96, 98
Rice, Condoleezza, 214
Richard II (Shakespeare), 63
Richelieu, Armand Jean du Plessis,
  Cardinal, 43, 70–1

Ripley, William Z., 187
Rise of American Civilization, The (Beard and Beard), 240
Risorgimento, 68, 71, 124–5
Rodgers, Daniel T., 169–70
Roe v. Wade, 164
Rogerson, Barnaby, 32
Roman Empire, 4, 15–29, 31, 38, 58, 123, 126, 158, 177, 178, 179, 184, 221, 222–33, 235, 238–9, 255, 316n–17n
Romania, 67, 79, 84, 114
Rome, 22, 25, 27, 35, 62, 221, 223, 227, 230–1
Romulus Augustulus, Emperor of Rome, 223
Roosevelt, Franklin D., 210, 211
Roosevelt, Theodore, 187
"Roots of Muslim Rage, The" (Lewis), 243–4
Ross, E. A., 187, 205
Rostow, Walt, 114–15
Rousseau, Jean-Jacques, 138, 145
Rude, George, 119, 121
Rumsfeld, Donald, 252–3
Runciman, Steven, 102
Russian Empire, 5, 63–4, 65, 67, 69, 70, 71, 73, 74, 78, 80, 85, 88, 109–12, 119, 124, 159, 188, 207, 225–6
Russian Revolution, 95–6, 109–12, 124, 127–9, 132, 230

St. Bartholomew's Day massacre (1572), 39
Saint-Simon, Henri de, 95, 96, 133
Salmon, Lucy, 166
Sarkozy, Nicolas, 88
Sartre, Jean-Paul, 149
Save the Children Fund, 81
Schama, Simon, 127
Schmalkaldic War, 38
Scotland, 41, 59, 60–1, 63, 72, 199
Scott, Joan, 156
Second Sex, The (Beauvoir), 149, 162
Seeley, John, 186–7
Ségur, Comte de, 225
Sen, Amartya, 49, 219, 248, 260
Seneca Falls Convention (1848), 146–7, 159, 160

September 11th attacks (2001), 4, 14, 29, 36, 37, 251–2, 253
Servetus, Michael, 42
Sevenfold Colloquium, The (Bodin), 42
Seyssel, Claude, 62
Shakespeare, William, 63
Shepard, Alexandra, 154–5
Shiite Muslims, 32, 80, 253
Simar, Théophile, 204–5
Six Books of the Republic, The (Bodin), 42
Skarga, Peter, 45
slavery, 73, 123, 126, 137, 150, 153, 154, 169, 176, 177, 178, 179, 180–2, 186, 191–2, 203
Smith, Adam, 95, 96, 98
Smuts, J. C., 190, 197
Snow, C. P., 116, 258
Soboul, Albert, 122
social Darwinism, 185, 186, 191, 209
socialism, 77, 101, 108, 109, 110, 111, 112–13, 133, 157, 160, 163, 233
Socialist History of the French Revolution (Jaurès), 122
Soho, Tokutomi, 208
South Africa, 4, 73, 187, 188, 190, 191, 196–203, 206, 213, 215, 216
Soviet Union, 54, 55, 57, 81, 82, 84–6, 110–18, 120, 127–9, 230, 241, 242–3, 244
Spain, 27, 31, 32, 38, 43, 47, 59, 62–5, 67, 69, 72, 88, 89, 113, 119, 161, 175, 178, 179, 186, 223, 247
Spanish Civil War, 113
Spengler, Oswald, 234–6, 237, 238, 239, 242, 247
Stages of Economic Growth, The (Rostow), 114–15
Stalin, Joseph, 112–13, 116, 130, 230
Strydom, J. G., 197
Studies in the Development of Capitalism (Dobb), 120
Study of History, A (Toynbee), 237–42, 263
Subjection of Women, The (Mill), 147
Suffield, Lord, 18
Suffrage Alliance, 162
Suger of Saint-Denis, 61
Suleyman I, Sultan, 32, 34, 35
Summers, Larry, 136
Sunni Muslims, 32, 80, 253

Supreme Court, U.S., 164, 182, 192–3, 212–13
Survey of European Civilization, A (Ferguson and Brunn), 241

Tamerlane, 225
Tancred (Disraeli), 176
Taney, Roger B., 182
Taylor, A. J. P., 74
Teggart, Frederick J., 233–6, 242
Thatcher, Margaret, 117, 118, 129, 166, 262
Thierry, Jacques Nicolas Augustin, 96, 104, 122
Third World, 82–3, 115, 164–5, 168–9
Thirty Years War, 38, 39, 43–4, 66
Thomas, Keith, 39
Thompson, E. P., 93, 119, 121, 123, 124–5, 127, 128, 132, 142
Thompson, William, 133–4, 140–1, 151, 170
Time, 240
Tito (Josip Broz), 116
Todorov, Tzvetan, 7
Torda, Declaration of (1568), 42
Toynbee, Arnold J., 4, 236–42, 243, 246, 247, 251, 255, 258, 263–4
Treitschke, Heinrich von, 97, 188
Trent, Council of, 41
Trevelyan, G. M., 70, 124–5, 317n
Trotsky, Leon, 113, 117, 124
Truman, Harry S., 114
Tukhachevsky, Mikhail, 230
Turner, Frederick Jackson, 77–8
Tyrrell, Ian, 54, 91

Ulster Covenant (1912), 50
United Nations, 86, 142–3, 144, 147, 164–5, 168, 211–12, 255–6
    Convention on the Elimination of All Forms of Discrimination Against Women (1979), 143, 144
    Declaration on the Elimination of Discrimination Against Women (1967), 142–3, 144, 147
    Educational, Scientific and Cultural Organization (UNESCO), 211–12

Universal Race Congress (1911), 209
Urban II, Pope, 28
Urban VIII, Pope, 43

Versailles, Treaty of (1919), 54, 201, 208, 231
Verwoerd, Hendrik, 197–8
Victoria, Queen of England, 74, 161, 229
Vietnam War, 114, 115, 116, 241
Vindication of the Rights of Woman, A (Wollstonecraft), 145–6
Virchow, Rudolf, 201
Vogelweide, Walther von der, 60
Voltaire, 180

Wagner, Richard, 184, 188
Walker, Francis Amasa, 193
Wallace, George, 174
Walters, Margaret, 133
Ward, Mrs. Humphry, 161
Wars of Religion, 38, 43
Washington, Booker T., 205–6
Washington, George, 70
Wasserstein, Bernard, 231
Watson, James, 217
Watts, Arthur, 241
Wedgwood, Josiah, 185
Weld, Theodore Dwight, 185–6
West, Cornel, 215
Western Question in Greece and Turkey, The (Toynbee), 236–7
Westphalia, Peace of (1648), 38, 43–4, 54, 56, 63
Wharton, Edith, 161
Wheatcroft, Andrew, 11, 29
Wheeler, Anna, 133
When Faiths Collide (Marty), 13
Whole Woman, The (Greer), 133
Wied, Hermann von, 41
William III, King of England, 63
William of Malmesbury, 60
William of Newburgh, 60
Williams, Raymond, 220
Wilson, William Julius, 216
Wilson, Woodrow, 78–9, 80, 81, 148, 187, 228–9
Wolffe, John, 14
Wollstonecraft, Mary, 145–6, 149, 166

women, 133–73
    black, 146, 167, 214
    brain capacity of, 136, 138, 144–5, 151
    consciousness-raising for, 158–70,
        164, 170–3
    discrimination against, 142–50, 163–4,
        168–9
    domestic duties of, 137, 138, 141–2,
        149–50, 162–3
    education of, 137, 140, 143, 144,
        145–6, 147, 150, 153, 158–9, 163–4,
        165, 166, 168
    equality and equal rights of, 133–5,
        136, 141, 149, 158, 160, 162, 163,
        167–8, 172, 260
    femininity of, 148–9, 153–6, 170–3
    as feminists, 133–42, 145–9, 150,
        156–9, 161–73, 261
    in first-wave feminism, 158–9, 161–2,
        169, 171
    as human identity, 3, 4, 13–14, 92,
        133–63, 166–73, 255, 258, 260
    as "inferior" or "second" sex, 133–5,
        149, 162
    liberation of, 133–4, 170–3, 258, 261,
        262
    married, 134, 160, 161, 162–3
    as mothers, 136, 137, 138, 139, 162–3
    movement for, 157, 158–73, 258, 261
    nationality of, 161–9, 170, 171
    organizations for, 159, 162, 163–4,
        166, 167, 170–3
    political influence of, 134, 138, 146–7,
        148, 158–70

    as radicals vs. reformers, 158–9, 160,
        161–2, 163, 167–8, 170–1
    religious views on, 137–8, 161, 162,
        167, 170, 171, 172
    reproductive rights of, 139, 164, 167,
        168, 185–6
    as "second sex," 162, 165
    in second-wave feminism, 162–70, 171
    "separate sphere" for, 140–2, 149–50
    sexuality of, 136, 161, 165, 167–8
    voting by, 72, 134, 138, 146–7, 148,
        158–62, 171
    working, 140–1, 149–50, 161, 164,
        165, 168
    see also gender
Women's Equity Action League, 163–4
Wood, Julia T., 152
World Council of Churches, 204
Worlds at War (Pagden), 29
World War I, 28, 29, 54, 67–8, 70, 72,
    73, 74, 78, 82, 89, 109–10, 113, 148,
    159, 162, 189, 194, 196, 198, 200,
    201, 204, 205, 208, 210, 228, 229,
    230, 233–4, 240
World War II, 54, 81–2, 84, 113, 195,
    210, 211, 213, 229–30, 240, 316n,
    317n

Young Islam on Trek (Mathews), 243

Zapata, Emiliano, 124
Zoroaster, 12

A NOTE ABOUT THE AUTHOR

Sir David Cannadine was born in Birmingham, England, in 1950 and educated at Cambridge, Oxford, and Princeton Universities. He is the editor and author of many acclaimed books, including *The Decline and Fall of the British Aristocracy*, *G. M. Trevelyan*, *Class in Britain*, *Ornamentalism*, and *Mellon*. He has taught at Cambridge and Columbia Universities and has been director of the Institute of Historical Research at London University. He is now Dodge Professor of History at Princeton University.

A NOTE ON THE TYPE

This book was set in Janson, a typeface long thought to have
been made by the Dutchman Anton Janson, who was a practicing
typefounder in Leipzig during the years 1668–1687. However, it
has been conclusively demonstrated that these types are actually
the work of Nicholas Kis (1650–1702), a Hungarian, who most
probably learned his trade from the master Dutch typefounder
Dirk Voskens. The type is an excellent example of the influential
and sturdy Dutch types that prevailed in England up to the time
William Caslon (1692–1766) developed his own incomparable
designs from them.

Composed by North Market Street Graphics,
Lancaster, Pennsylvania

Printed and bound by RR Donnelley,
Harrisonburg North, Virginia

Book design by Robert C. Olsson